A Rational Faith

A Rational Faith

An Introduction to the Philosophy of Richard Swinburne

Joshua R. Sijuwade

James Clarke & Co.

James Clarke & Co.
P.O. Box 60
Cambridge
CB1 2NT
United Kingdom

www.jamesclarke.co
publishing@jamesclarke.co

Hardback ISBN: 978 0 227 17842 3
Paperback ISBN: 978 0 227 17840 9
PDF ISBN: 978 0 227 17841 6
ePub ISBN: 978 0 227 17843 0

British Library Cataloguing-in-Publication Data
A record is available from the British Library

First published by James Clarke & Co., 2025

Copyright © Joshua R. Sijuwade, 2025

All rights reserved. No part of this edition may be reproduced, stored electronically or in any retrieval system, or transmitted in any form or by any means, electronic, mechanical, photocopying, recording, or otherwise, without prior written permission from the Publisher.

Contents

Foreword	vii
Introduction: Life, Works and Philosophical Foundations	1

Part 1: Bare Theism

1.	The Coherence of Theism	55
2.	The Existence of God	103
3.	The Problem of Evil	141
4.	The Reality of the Soul	178

Part 2: Ramified Theism

5.	The Metaphysics of Christian Theism	215
6.	The Plausibility of the Atonement	245
7.	The Probability of the Resurrection	273
8.	The Authenticity of Revelation	306
9.	The Rationality of Faith	338

Bibliography	367
Index	382

Foreword

I am very grateful to Joshua Sijuwade for writing this introduction to my philosophical and theological writings; and I commend his very full treatment of the controversial views on the many philosophical issues, which I have developed during a long life. Joshua summarises some of my views on the major issues in his Introduction, and then goes on to describe them more fully in subsequent chapters. That will be useful for those unfamiliar with the issues, who may not always fully understand them when they are first introduced. He explains with respect to each of my views, the context in which I developed a view, and goes on to discuss several objections which have been made to it by other philosophers, and suggests how I might respond to these objections. It is very useful to have many different objections to a view critiqued in the same place.

As Joshua explains, my major motivation for writing most of the books and articles which I have written, is to show that belief in the Christian creed is rational. I hope that I have considered seriously the objections to this view, before finally rejecting them; and that if I had reached a different conclusion, I would have acknowledged that. This major motivation led to my "philosophy-first" approach to theological doctrines, to begin the examination of theological doctrines by first investigating the purely secular philosophical concepts and theories which are taken for granted by theological doctrines. Thus, the doctrine that God caused the existence of the universe, presupposes a particular philosophical theory of the nature of causation, known as "agent causation". And the doctrine that humans have a life after death requires in my view a particular theory of personal identity, a version of what is called "substance dualism", according to which humans on earth consist of two separate substances – body and soul, of which the soul is the one part essential for personal identity. That theory allows not merely the possibility of our souls, and so us, continuing to exist after death, but our souls being united again with a body, as affirmed by the Christian doctrine of the resurrection of the body of each of us. Investigating some of these philosophical theories, in turn inevitably involved investigating relevant contemporary scientific theories.

But while that has been my major motivation, I believe also that it is important for purely secular reasons to hold correct views about most of the major philosophical issues which I have discussed, including views about what constitutes personal identity, the nature and fundamental principles of morality, free will, and our moral responsibility for our actions. I hope that my discussion of these issues has made a small contribution to their resolution. Like, I think, most philosophers, I have much enjoyed trying to work out the answers to philosophical questions, and arguing with others about them. I have been very blessed to be able to do this with my life; and I hope that Joshua's book, will help many readers to understand my views about these all-important issues.

Richard Swinburne

Introduction: Life, Works and Philosophical Foundations

The central aim of this work is to provide an introductory guide to Richard Swinburne's philosophical thought – as expressed through his main philosophical writings – in a way that balances accessibility, depth and range. Thus, this work focusses on presenting Swinburne's arguments in a clear and engaging manner, making his complex ideas more accessible to a broader audience while maintaining the integrity and depth of his philosophical reasoning. By covering a wide range of Swinburne's works, from his early trilogy (*The Coherence of Theism*, *The Existence of God* and *Faith and Reason*) to his later contributions, this guide offers a comprehensive overview of his thought and its development over time. Therefore, ultimately, this work seeks to demonstrate how Swinburne establishes the rationality of theistic and Christian faith through rigorous philosophical argumentation. By exploring his defence of the coherence of theism, the existence of God and the philosophical basis for Christian doctrine, this work thus highlights the strength and persuasiveness of Swinburne's case for the reasonableness of religious belief. Moreover, by engaging with critical objections to Swinburne's work and presenting compelling responses, this guide showcases the resilience and adaptability of his philosophical framework in the face of scholarly critique. In presenting Swinburne's ideas in an accessible yet thorough manner, this work aims to equip readers with a solid understanding of his contributions to the philosophy of religion and philosophical theology. This understanding will enable readers to appreciate the significance of Swinburne's work in demonstrating the compatibility of faith and reason, and its potential to provide a rational foundation for theistic and Christian belief. Therefore, as such, this work serves as an invaluable resource for those seeking to explore the philosophical underpinnings of religious faith and to engage with one of the most influential and rigorous defenders of theism and the Christian faith in contemporary philosophy. We shall now explore Swinburne's life and works, focussing on his educational background, academic positions and major philosophical achievements.

The Life of Richard Swinburne

Early Life and Education[1]

Richard Granville Swinburne was born on 26 December 1934 in Smethwick, a town in the metropolitan borough of Sandwell (near Birmingham) located in the West Midlands, England. He was the only child of William Henry Swinburne and his wife Gladys Edith Swinburne, neé Parker. Richard's mother's family were from the Lowestoft area, with his maternal grandfather working as an optician and his paternal grandfather running an off licence in London during World War II. Richard's father worked as a schoolteacher for much of Richard's early childhood and, around 1946, he took a position as musical education advisor to Essex County Council – one of the first to hold such a role. Later in his career, William became head of the music department at a polytechnic college in Colchester. Before Richard's birth, his mother worked as a secretary and, after he went away to boarding school, she worked as a secretary again to help pay his school fees, sometimes staying in London during the week and only returning to the family home in Colchester on weekends. The Swinburne family moved from Smethwick to Colchester, where they lived until Richard was seventeen, except for two years from 1939 to 1941, when, fearing wartime bombing, the family relocated to the village of Tiptree, in the Essex countryside. Richard vividly remembers seeing the sky filled with German bombers on their way to attack London and wondering aloud to his mother whether God would allow the Germans to win the war. Though his parents were not religious, he cannot remember a time when he did not believe in God. From ages seven to ten, Richard attended a private preparatory

---

1. The detailed biographical information provided here is based on personal correspondence with Richard Swinburne and the written interviews and autobiographical information featured in the bibliography.

school affiliated to Colchester Royal Grammar School, where his father taught. His mother arranged for him to have special Greek and Latin tutoring. When he was ten, Richard spent a year confined to bed with suspected tuberculosis (as the prescribed cure for the illness at that time was extended periods of bed rest). His mother looked after him and hired tutors to help him keep up with his studies. Being an only child in a strained marriage, she focussed intensely on encouraging his academic achievement.

After his recovery, Richard boarded at a preparatory school in Felixstowe for one and a half years. In 1946, he won a scholarship to Charterhouse, a top English public school (in Britain 'private school'), which he attended until 1952. Richard's mother was very happy about him being awarded this place, given her belief about the importance of a public school education for progressing efficiently through life. At Charterhouse, Richard continued his study of Greek and Latin, but was unable to fully participate in sports due to his health. He was confirmed in the Church of England at age sixteen. However, he largely kept his religious devotion private, not participating in school Christian groups. The school holidays were a particularly lonely time for Richard, as he returned to an empty home, with his mother working (in her previously held role as a secretary) and his father busy with musical activities, and an unhappy marriage. To keep occupied, Richard read extensively, kept scrapbooks of current events and went on outings with his mother. However, he had few friends and little family social life during those periods. That is, Richard's transition to boarding school led to a disconnection from his earlier school friends and left him without close friendships during school holidays at home. Moreover, due to his suspected tuberculosis, he was unable to participate fully in the school's sporting activities, which caused some of his peers to regard him as a "weed".[2] Additionally, most of his contemporaries at Charterhouse came from relatively affluent families, whereas Richard's background was more modest. These factors contributed to his feeling somewhat isolated during his time at the school. After finishing at Charterhouse, Richard completed two years of National Service from 1952 to 1954. He was able to spend most of that time intensively studying Russian language rather than military training. This allowed him to engage in deep intellectual

---

2. For Richard's specific referencing of this comment, see Baker-Hytch M. An interview with Richard Swinburne. *Religious Studies*. 2024: p.1.

conversations about philosophy, religion and politics with the other academically inclined young men in the Russian course.

In 1954, Richard began his studies at Oxford University. He had won an open scholarship to study Classics at Exeter College, but decided to switch to Philosophy, Politics and Economics (PPE). Studying PPE with a focus on philosophy would provide a broad base of knowledge of the modern world before he began training for his chosen vocation as an Anglican priest. However, Richard was disappointed that his philosophy tutor was absent during his first year, requiring him to focus on politics and economics rather than philosophy. He was also dismayed to find that Oxford philosophy at that time was dominated by ordinary-language philosophy, which focussed on analysing the use of language rather than addressing substantive questions. That is, the prevailing ordinary-language philosophy dismissed topics such as metaphysics and religion as little more than an antique speech-act game. It also largely ignored science, an area that intrigued Richard. The notable exception was Friedrich Waismann, a former member of the Vienna Circle and Oxford's lecturer in the philosophy of science. Waismann's lectures, particularly on space, time, and their connection to relativity theory, were the most inspiring Richard attended. These topics not only captured his intellectual curiosity but also seemed relevant to his hope of connecting philosophy to religion. On his own, Richard became convinced that modern science posed challenges to Christian belief that needed serious philosophical engagement – although the Church itself seemed complacent. He was especially concerned with the apparent conflict between science and human free will. Nevertheless, Richard performed very well academically, earning a first-class degree in PPE in 1957 after vigorously defending his exam results in his viva voce. He was accepted for ordination training in the Church of England but decided to stay on at Oxford to pursue a graduate degree in philosophy before embarking on an ecclesiastical career. This is that, during this time, Richard had begun to feel a calling to become a priest and hoped that philosophy might prove useful in addressing questions of religion.

From 1957 to 1959, Richard undertook a Bachelor of Philosophy (BPhil) degree, a two-year graduate programme that served as the main preparation for an academic career in philosophy. Supervised by Professor H.H. Price, Richard wrote his thesis on the relationship between different branches of science, focussing on the hierarchy between physics, chemistry, biology and psychology. This choice of topic reflected his recognition that he needed to seriously study science in order to address its challenges to theology. He also undertook a philosophical study of the rationality of religious belief. During his BPhil, Richard lived in St Stephen's House, an Anglo-Catholic seminary, where he also did theological study and spiritual formation in preparation for ordination. However, he delayed taking holy orders in order to finish his philosophical studies properly. From 1959 to 1961, he held a prestigious junior research fellowship at St John's College, Oxford. In 1960, Richard married Monica Holmstrom, a fellow Oxford student and devout Anglican. That year he also completed the Oxford postgraduate diploma in theology and passed his General Ordination Examination, formally qualifying him for the priesthood. Nevertheless, he received permission to delay his ordination in order to continue his studies in the philosophy of science.

Early Career: Leeds, Hull and Keele

In 1961, Richard took up a research fellowship at the University of Leeds. This position finally gave him the opportunity systematically to study the natural sciences alongside the philosophy of science. With the historians of science, Jerry Ravetz and Donald Cardwell, Richard studied key developments in physics and biology, including hands-on laboratory work. He came to believe that the criteria used to judge scientific theories, such as a theory's simplicity and ability to make testable predictions, could also be used to evaluate the probability of theism as an explanatory hypothesis. However, Richard's academic progress put a strain on his young family. His wife Monica was isolated at home while he worked. She had given up her own teaching career to raise their two daughters, born in 1961 and 1962. The Swinburnes lived a long way away from the university in Leeds but had little money for furnishings or social activities. Though Richard's flexible schedule allowed him to help with childcare (as Richard and Monica had two children together: Caroline and Nicola), Monica felt lonely and distant from his intellectual world.

In 1963, Richard obtained a permanent position as lecturer in Philosophy at the University of Hull, where he taught until 1972. During his early years there, the Swinburnes continued to live modestly. At first, they lived in a small house and lacked a car and telephone – and, though the Church of England still expected him to be ordained and serve as a priest-scholar, he reluctantly concluded that his family situation and demanding academic research made that impossible. This is that, outside of practical considerations, Richard initially felt a calling to become a priest, but his focus gradually shifted toward academic scholarship. He realised, over an extended period of time, the importance of providing a rational defense of religion, especially in an era when the dominant theological perspective held that "religion is entirely a matter of faith; you enter into religion, and you mustn't expect arguments, because that is demeaning to God". Richard found this approach insufficient for engaging the educated world, which demanded a more rigorous response. Believing he could make a greater impact as an academic philosopher, he pursued this path to help offer the intellectual defense he saw as essential. So, at Hull, Richard was able to develop his ideas about the philosophy of religion in conversation with his colleague Christopher Williams, a Roman Catholic philosopher who had had to leave the Benedictine order when he developed polio, and was thereafter confined to a wheelchair. Richard also got to know well the atheist philosopher J.L. Mackie, who was of great help to him by reading the manuscript of his two main first books on philosophy of science. The first of these was *Space and Time* (1968). In it, he used methods drawn from the analysis of scientific concepts to examine the philosophical foundations of space-time physics and cosmology. Though still a technical work, the book's publication established Richard as a young philosopher of science unusually open to religious questions. (Richard's personal relationship with Mackie deepened during this period, as Mackie, who had been appointed as the first Professor of Philosophy at the nearby University of York, frequently visited Hull with his colleague to attend fortnightly seminars and guest lectures. Their intellectual exchange was particularly fruitful in the areas of space, time, and confirmation theory, with Mackie providing valuable feedback on Richard's draft manuscripts. Their first public debate on the existence of God took place at Hull, marking the beginning of a long-standing philosophical dialogue. Even after both had moved on – Richard to Keele and Mackie to Oxford – their intellectual engagement continued. When Richard delivered his Wilde Lectures on the existence of God at Oxford in 1976, Mackie attended all eight lectures of the first series. Later, Mackie's *The Miracle of Theism* would serve as a response to Richard's *The Existence of God*. Despite their opposing views,[3] Mackie particularly valued Richard's rational approach to religious philosophy, which stood in contrast to the contemporary theological tendency to treat religion as an isolated language game).

In 1969-70, Richard was able to take a sabbatical as Visiting Associate Professor at the University of Maryland near Washington DC, which gave him the chance to visit other American universities. On returning to Hull, Richard published his second book, *An Introduction to Confirmation Theory* (1973), which developed a probabilistic model of scientific reasoning and which allowed him subsequently to apply this to the question of the probability of theism. Based on the strength of this work, he was promoted to a senior lectureship in philosophy at Hull.

Mid-Career: Professorship at Keele

In 1972, Richard was appointed Professor of Philosophy at the University of Keele, a position he held until 1984. Founded in 1949 as a pioneering experiment in interdisciplinary education, Keele required all undergraduates to take a common foundation year and live on its residential campus. Richard shared Keele's vision of integrating the sciences and humanities. In keeping with Keele's ethos, he and his family initially lived on campus, though they later bought their own house nearby.

As head of department, Richard had to devote more time to teaching and administration than at Hull. Nevertheless, he took advantage of the freedom offered by his chair to write three major works developing a systematic philosophy of religion. In *The Existence of God* (1979), Richard built on the logical analysis of theism he had begun in *The Coherence of Theism* (1977) by arguing that the theistic hypothesis had greater probability than its alternatives as an ultimate explanation for the existence and nature of the universe. While drawing some criticism from more positivistic philosophers, the work established Richard alongside Alvin Plantinga as a leading exponent of the rationality of religious belief. While Plantinga argued that religious belief could be a 'basic belief' which did not need any further justification - termed the thesis of 'Reformed Epistemology', Richard argued that such justification is available as the most probable explanation of the most general features of the universe.

---

3. Mackie, J.L. *The Miracle of Theism*. Oxford: Clarendon Press, 1982.

(Richard's personal relationship with Plantinga began during the latter's stay at Oxford in 1985-86, when Richard was delivering his first series of Wilde lectures. Despite their different approaches to religious epistemology, they developed a strong mutual respect and friendship. While Plantinga had argued in *God and Other Minds* that no probabilistic argument for God's existence was cogent, he came to appreciate Richard's work in providing such arguments that could potentially lead non-believers to faith. Plantinga's appreciation was evident in his review of the second edition of *The Existence of God* in the *Times Literary Supplement*, and his *Stanford Encyclopedia of Philosophy* entry on Religion and Science where he writes that Richard's work 'over the last 30 years or so has resulted in the most powerful, complete and sophisticated development of natural theology the world has so far seen'.[4] Their professional relationship was further cemented when Plantinga (after declining the Oxford Professorship himself) served as one of Richard's referees for the position. Overall, their close relationship continued to flourish both personally and professionally throughout the rest of their illustrious careers). In *Faith and Reason* (1981), Richard analysed the ethics of religious belief. Going beyond the usual debates about evidentialism and fideism, he argued that it could be rational to believe in God in the sense of trusting him and committing to a relationship with him, even if one was less than certain of his existence. This argument provided a distinctive reconciliation of the traditional divide between Catholic and Protestant views of justification by faith. While based at Keele, Richard also regularly returned to Oxford, holding a visiting position as Wilde Lecturer in Natural and Comparative Religion from 1975 to 1978. The lectures he delivered on the existence of God provided the basis for his 1979 book. Richard developed friendships with other Oxford philosophers of religion, such as Basil Mitchell (Nolloth Professor of the Philosophy of the Christian Religion at the University of Oxford, 1968–85); and his life changed considerably in 1985 when he was appointed as Mitchell's successor. He saw the position, which came with a fellowship at Oriel College, as an opportunity to reach a much wider audience. However, the transition was overshadowed by the end of his marriage. Richard's wife chose to separate from him

---

4. Plantinga, Alvin. "Religion and Science." In *Stanford Encyclopedia of Philosophy*, edited by Edward N. Zalta. Spring 2010 Edition. Stanford University, 2010, §2.

and remain in the Keele area, rather than move to Oxford. During this time, Caroline, Richard's eldest daughter, had finished reading Music at the University of Nottingham (later going on to work as a BBC radio presenter), and Nicola, Richard's second daughter, had also completed her degree in Geology at the University of Cambridge (later going on to study for a doctorate at the Open University, and subsequently holding a research fellowship at the University of California, Berkley). Though not legally divorced, Richard and Monica have continued to live separately, while keeping in contact with each other and occasionally meeting up. The estrangement was a source of considerable pain for Richard, who took up permanent residence in his college until his retirement in 2002 when he moved to live in an apartment in Oxford very close to the university.

Later Career: Nolloth Professorship at Oxford

At Oxford, now largely freed from undergraduate teaching and other administrative responsibilities, Richard was able to take his philosophical defence of Christian doctrine to a new level. In 1983 and 1984, he delivered the Gifford Lectures at the University of Aberdeen on topics related to the philosophy of mind, which later was to be published, in revised form in 1986, in the monograph *The Evolution of the Soul*. In these lectures, Richard used methods drawn from the philosophy of mind to argue for a dualistic account of human nature. Drawing in part on his earlier work on personal identity, he maintained that humans are composed of a physical body and a non-physical soul that can potentially survive the death of the body. He went on to argue that the Christian doctrines of the incarnation and resurrection of Christ are coherent, given a dualist anthropology. Richard further developed his Christian philosophical theology during his time as Nolloth Professor. In *The Christian God* (1994), he offered detailed philosophical analyses of the doctrines of the Trinity and Incarnation, the two most distinctive claims of Christian theism. Richard argued that a metaphysical model of the Trinity, as three distinct divine individuals (the Father, Son and Holy Spirit) united by a common divinity, best captures the apparently paradoxical statements about God's nature found in Scripture and the creeds. With respect to the Incarnation, he used the notion of divided consciousness to explain how one person (God the Son) could become incarnate as the man Jesus Christ while retaining his divine attributes and identity.

Richard's most notable work from this period was *Providence and the Problem of Evil* (1998). In this book, he presented a greater good theodicy, suggesting that the existence of evil is compatible with the existence of an all-powerful and all-good God because God would have good reasons for allowing evil and suffering to occur. Specifically, Richard proposed that God allows humans to experience suffering to provide them with opportunities to exercise free will and responsibility, develop moral character and be of great use. In developing this theodicy, Richard's main intention was to defend God's justice, sparking significant discussion and debate within theological and philosophical circles. Throughout his time at Oxford, Richard remained an active participant in scholarly debates about science, religion and the rationality of theistic belief. Richard generally argued that the findings of modern science were more compatible with theism than with naturalistic atheism. He was also a regular participant in interdisciplinary projects on science and religion sponsored by the John Templeton Foundation. In 1996, Richard published a popular abridgement of his work titled *Is There a God?* This short book presented Richard's core arguments for theism to a non-academic audience and has been widely used in schools and universities. Later in his career, Richard had the opportunity to engage in philosophical partnerships and deliver lectures in Eastern Europe and Russia. His proficiency in Russian, acquired during his national service, enabled him to lecture in Russian and foster connections with Russian philosophers and theologians. He chaired the 'Outreach to Russia' committee for the Society of Christian Philosophers, which was set up in 2000, and awarded a grant from the John Templeton Foundation to organise summer schools, conferences, and translation projects to promote the development of analytic philosophy of religion in Russia.

Post-Retirement: Publications and Media

Richard retired from his Oxford chair in 2002, but has remained active in research, writing and public engagement in his seventies and eighties. In 2003, Richard published *The Resurrection of God Incarnate*, a major study of the evidence for the divinity of Jesus Christ and especially for his resurrection from the dead. Using a probabilistic form of Bayesian reasoning, Richard argued that the historical evidence for the Resurrection confirms the hypothesis of

Jesus' divinity when combined with the prior probability that an incarnate God would live the sort of life that the Gospels attribute to Jesus. Although a work of Christian apologetics, the book is notable for its rigorous philosophical methodology and scrupulous treatment of biblical scholarship and ancient history. In his later years, Richard focussed a lot of his time on publishing 'second editions' of a number of his earlier books – with these second editions involving not merely a few corrections and additions, but the rewriting of a number of whole books, which included significant changes to certain positions. (Before and during his retirement Richard also published 'revised editions' of some of his works, which included only minor corrections and additions, as distinct from the published second editions of his works.) These second editions include *The Existence of God* in 2004, *Faith and Reason* in 2005, *Revelation* in 2007 and *The Coherence of Theism* in 2016.[5]

More recently, in 2024, Richard again focussed on tackling one of the most enduring questions in the philosophy of religion: the problem of evil. In his book, *Could a Good God Permit So Much Suffering? A Debate*, co-authored with James Sterba, Richard argued for the compatibility of God's existence with the presence of moral and natural evil in the world. This work not only provided a robust defence of theodicy but also fostered critical engagement by juxtaposing opposing viewpoints. The rigorous exchange between Richard and Sterba offered readers a comprehensive understanding of the philosophical issues at stake, making the book, in combination with that of *Providence and the Problem of Evil*, a significant contribution to contemporary debates on the problem of evil. Richard's philosophical interests extended well beyond the philosophy of religion. Of particular note is his *Epistemic Justification* (2001), a major work of epistemology that defends an internalist theory of epistemic justification, which he subsequently applies to the rationality of religious belief in his trilogy. In 2013, Richard published *Mind, Brain, and Free Will*, a wide-ranging study of the philosophy of mind that further develops his arguments against reductive materialism and in favour of substance dualism and libertarian free will, which featured earlier in *The Evolution of the*

---

5. Richard has thoughts to work on a second edition of the Christian God (which will incorporate his most recent insights concerning the Trinity, and other related ideas), and is also hoping to work on a separate book focused on Christian Ethics.

Soul. In this book, Richard engages extensively with recent work in neuroscience and cognitive psychology, arguing that the empirical evidence is more compatible with dualist anthropology than with the monistic theories favoured by many scientists.

In addition to his scholarly research, Richard devoted much of his retirement to communicating his ideas to popular audiences. In 2010, he published a revised edition of his earlier work, *Is There a God?* He published two more short introductory books, *Was Jesus God?* (2008), a summarised defence of the central Christian doctrines that featured in his tetralogy - consisting of his four books about Christian doctrine (*Responsibility and Atonement, Revelation: From Metaphor to Analogy, The Christian God* and *Providence and the Problem of Evil*) as well as *The Resurrection of God Incarnate*, - and *Are We Bodies or Souls?* (2019), which is an exploration and defence of substance dualism. He gave frequent public lectures and took part in numerous debates with leading atheists and critics of Christianity. While generally avoiding polemics, Richard robustly defended the intellectual credibility of the Christian worldview in the face of the New Atheist movement. His work has often been contrasted with that of Richard Dawkins. Dawkins had reviewed Richard's *Is There a God?* and discussed his arguments for theism in *The God Delusion* (2006);[6] Richard himself found Dawkins' objections philosophically unsophisticated, as he especially believed (as explained in more detail in his *British Library National Life Stories* interview) that he did not consider the work to have accurately represented the arguments of himself, nor those of the arguments that other religious people have produced in these contexts.[7] Media work also became an increasing focus during Richard's retirement. He recorded a number of video interviews for websites such as the *Closer To Truth* television series, which aims to present the views of leading thinkers on religion and science in an accessible format. He appeared in various live debates involving atheistic thinkers, such as Herman Philipse, and other leading philosophers of religion, such as Graham Oppy. He gave interviews to print and broadcast media around the world, especially

---

6. Dawkins, Richard. *The God Delusion*. Bantam Press, 2006.
7. For Richard's comments on Dawkins' work, see 'Science and Religion: Exploring the Spectrum', Richard Swinburne interviewed by Paul Merchant, 27 October 2015 to 3 March 2016. Transcript, British Library, National Life Stories Collection, C1672/15, 88-90.

Introduction: Life, Works and Philosophical Foundations 13

in the United States, Canada and Australia, where the public debate over the rationality of religious belief has been particularly active. In these appearances, Richard sought to present a philosophical case for the truth of Christian theism to a broad audience without engaging in religious proselytising.

Concerning the specific influences during Richard's academic career, he notably developed his philosophical approach independently of the 1950s Oxford philosophical establishment, including Ian Ramsey, the then Professor of Philosophy of Religion. Indeed, at that time, Philosophy of Religion was not even offered as an optional subject for undergraduate philosophy degrees. Instead, his intellectual framework was shaped by broader philosophical traditions: Carl G. Hempel and Paul Oppenheim's theory of scientific explanation, featured in their paper 'Studies in the Logic of Explanation,[8] which postulated hypotheses that entailed evidence, and Rudolf Carnap's work, in *Logical Foundations of Probability*,[9] on what he termed 'probability$_1$' (now generally known as 'epistemic probability') and its distinction from 'probability$_2$' (now generally known as 'statistical probability'). Richard also found inspiration in Saint Thomas Aquinas' rational approach to theology. These diverse influences converged in Richard's mind, leading him to develop his distinctive approach of constructing cogent probabilistic arguments for the existence of God.

In his personal life, Richard experienced a significant religious transition in his early sixties. In 1995, after several decades as a member of the Church of England, he was received into the Eastern Orthodox Church. This change had occurred because he had become disillusioned by what he saw as the Anglican Church's increasing tolerance of doctrinal deviation and unorthodox teaching, especially on core issues such as the Incarnation. He was attracted to Orthodoxy's combination of traditional liturgy and theology with a more conciliar and less centralised model of church authority. Nevertheless, Richard continued to see himself as an analytic philosopher of religion rather than a confessor of any particular denomination, and he remained on good terms with his Anglican colleagues. His experience within the Orthodox Church has been largely positive, particularly in his

---

8. Hempel, Carl G. & Oppenheim, Paul. "Studies in the Logic of Explanation." Philosophy of Science, 15(2), pp. 135-175, 1948.
9. Carnap, Rudolf. *Logical Foundations of Probability*. Chicago: University of Chicago Press, 1950.

local Greek parish in Oxford, which Richard described as active and friendly, served by dedicated priests, including the late Metropolitan Kallistos Ware, who founded the parish. However, Richard acknowledges the complex political landscape of Orthodox Christianity, which comprises fourteen independent jurisdictions that, while united in doctrine, often disagree over jurisdictional boundaries. Despite these internal conflicts, Richard particularly values the Orthodox emphasis on worship. And while the Orthodox church has traditionally been perceived as anti-intellectual, Richard has observed a growing openness to philosophical argumentation, a development he hopes to encourage through his work, including the volume *Natural Theology in the Eastern Orthodox Tradition*[10], which he co-edited with David Bradshaw.

Now 90 years old, Richard continues to write and speak on issues in Christian philosophy. He is widely regarded as one of the most important philosophical defenders of theism in the late twentieth and early twenty-first centuries. Through his rigorous and wide-ranging work over more than five decades, Richard has played a pivotal role in establishing the rationality of religious belief as a legitimate subject for philosophical inquiry. He has sought to demonstrate that traditional Christian doctrines can be expressed in a logically coherent way and justified by evidence and argument. While his specific theological positions remain controversial, his influence on the field is widely acknowledged by both supporters and critics. As Richard looks towards his tenth decade, he remains committed to engaging in serious philosophical dialogue about the truth of the Christian worldview.

The Works of Richard Swinburne

Swinburne's intellectual journey is marked by his efforts to reconcile traditional Christian beliefs with the prevailing materialistic worldview of modern intellectualism. Throughout his career, Swinburne has been deeply committed to fulfilling the vocation of a 'natural theologian' by demonstrating the intellectual credibility of the Christian faith, especially in the face of modern scientific and philosophical challenges. This part of the biography will explore Swinburne's engagement with the conflict between materialism and

---

10. Bradshaw, David and Swinburne, Richard (Eds.). *Natural Theology in the Eastern Orthodox Tradition*. IOTA Publications, 2023.

Christianity, his interaction with the legacy of logical positivism, and his development of a robust natural theology that defends theism and specific Christian doctrines through rigorous philosophical argumentation.

Intellectual Context: (i) The Conflict between Materialism and Christianity

Swinburne found himself confronted with a materialistic worldview that appeared to be in direct conflict with traditional Christian beliefs. Many modern intellectuals regarded core Christian doctrines, such as the incarnation of Christ, as utterly absurd. They subscribed to a notion of progress that seemed to leave Christianity behind. However, Swinburne was deeply drawn to traditional Christianity, and he was troubled by the Church's apparent indifference to the tension between modern knowledge and faith. Preachers would deliver pious sermons while failing to address the scientific and philosophical questions that weighed heavily on Swinburne's mind. He came to realise that underlying this indifference was a theological attitude that essentially dismissed the role of reason in establishing the foundations of Christianity. As Swinburne delved deeper into his academic pursuits, the importance of reconciling faith and reason became increasingly apparent. This theme would come to dominate his entire career – defending the core tenets of Christianity against philosophical criticisms. Swinburne worked tirelessly to establish the intellectual credibility of Christian theology and to challenge the prevailing secular assumptions of his time. A significant aspect of his approach involved thoroughly examining contemporary scientific theories and philosophical arguments to demonstrate how they could be harmonised with religious belief, rather than being in opposition to it.

Intellectual Context: (ii) The Legacy of Logical Positivism and Ordinary Language Philosophy

During Swinburne's time at Oxford as an undergraduate and graduate student and research fellow, he faced the challenge posed by 'ordinary language philosophy', an influential movement at Oxford. Proponents of ordinary language philosophy, such as J.L. Austin, in his work *How to Do Things With Words*,[11] and Gilbert Ryle, in his work *The Concept of Mind*,[12] argued that many philosophical problems arise from misunderstandings of the everyday use of language. They believed that by carefully analysing ordinary language, one could dissolve most (if not all) philosophical problems. The other influential philosophy in the Anglo-American world was that of 'logical positivism', which, as advocated by individuals such as Rudolf Carnap, in his essay 'The Elimination of Metaphysics Through Logical Analysis of Language',[13] Moritz Schlick, in his paper 'Positivism and Realism', and A.J. Ayer, in his work *Language, Truth and Logic*,[14] held that all propositions which could not be 'verified' (and it had a very demanding understanding of 'verified') were to be rejected as meaningless. Both of these philosophies had led to a sceptical stance towards metaphysical and theological claims in the early to mid part of the 20th century. Nevertheless, Swinburne appreciated the emphasis on clarity and rigour in Oxford philosophy and recognised the potential for employing philosophical tools to make Christian theology intellectually credible. This led him to pursue a career as a professional philosopher rather than an Anglican priest. He immersed himself in the study of modern science and the philosophy of science in order better to understand and challenge the materialistic worldview.

Swinburne found the scepticism of both ordinary language philosophy and logical positivism towards metaphysics limiting. He believed that philosophical inquiry should go beyond merely analysing language and should also address substantive metaphysical and theological questions, and that metaphysical and theological views were meaningful and capable of being 'verified'. Swinburne's engagement with both logical positivism and ordinary language philosophy and his subsequent rejection of their restrictive empiricism and linguistic scepticism, laid the groundwork for his ground-breaking work in analytic philosophy of religion. In this field, he rigorously defended religious language and the cogency of metaphysical claims, demonstrating their meaningfulness and intellectual credibility.

---

11. Austin, J.L. *How to Do Things with Words*. Oxford: Clarendon Press, 1962.
12. Ryle, Gilbert. *The Concept of Mind*. London: Hutchinson, 1949.
13. Carnap, Rudolf. "The Elimination of Metaphysics Through Logical Analysis of Language." *Erkenntnis*, vol. 2, no. 1, pp. 219-241, 1932.
14. Ayer, A.J. *Language, Truth and Logic*. London: Victor Gollancz, 1936.

Swinburne's rejection of these dominant philosophical trends was not merely an academic exercise but, rather, it was a foundational step in his broader project of using analytic philosophy to vindicate religious belief. Swinburne's major works often include detailed arguments against the central tenets of logical positivism and ordinary language philosophy, showing how theological discourse can be both meaningful and intellectually rigorous. He also explored the way in which the emphasis on empirical verification in logical positivism could be integrated into a more comprehensive epistemological framework that included rational belief in God. Through this synthesis, Swinburne aimed to show that religious beliefs could withstand the scrutiny of contemporary philosophical analysis and the findings of contemporary science.

Natural Theology: (i) Bare Theism

In beginning to establish the framework of 'Bare Theism' (or 'Bare Natural Theology'), which is a type of natural theological argumentation that focusses on analysing and defending the central tenets of theism, Swinburne's exploration of science and the philosophy of science revealed that scientific theories often describe entities and phenomena that are not directly observable. He argued that the justification for these theories lies in their simplicity and their ability to predict phenomena – with Swinburne specifically emphasising the crucial role of simplicity in selecting between competing theories. He then applied these principles to metaphysical theories, including theism and the Christian theological system, viewing them as 'superscientific' theories that explain the existence and nature of the universe. This approach allowed him to establish a robust 'natural theology' – a theological approach that assesses theism (and more specific forms of theism such as that of Christian theism) based on certain evidence or phenomena from the natural world – and thus construct a cumulative case for theism, employing the same criteria that underpin scientific reasoning to argue for the probable truth of religious claims. Swinburne's methodology involved the use of inductive probability to support the rationality of belief in God, a concept he meticulously developed and defended throughout his works. He identified five criteria for evaluating the probability of a hypothesis: its explanatory power, probability relative to background evidence (or knowledge), probability of the data relative to background evidence, scope, and simplicity. In his analysis, Swinburne highlighted that the success of scientific theories in explaining and predicting phenomena lent credence to a similar approach in theology, thereby supporting the rationality of theistic belief through a coherent and unified epistemological framework. Hence, within this context, and drawing inspiration from Saint Thomas Aquinas, Swinburne adopted a natural theological approach that employed the criteria of modern science and philosophy to argue for the existence of God. He believed that theistic belief could be demonstrated to be meaningful and probably true through rigorous argumentation and evidence. His programme aimed to establish the intellectual credibility of theism by addressing the challenges posed by modern science and philosophy. By combining Aquinas' medieval scholasticism with contemporary analytic philosophy, Swinburne developed a unique methodology that bridged classical and modern approaches to theology. He distinguished between bare natural theology, which argues for the existence of God, and ramified natural theology, which defends more specific Christian doctrines.

Now, in focussing on the former, one can see that Swinburne drew a distinction between scientific and personal explanations. Scientific explanations describe phenomena in terms of prior states and natural laws, while personal explanations involve the purposes and actions of agents. He argued that the existence of the universe and its fundamental laws could not be fully explained by science alone but required a personal explanation in terms of God's power and purposes. This distinction was crucial in his defence of theism, as it provided a coherent framework for understanding divine action and intention in a scientifically explainable world. Swinburne maintained that personal explanations, grounded in the intentions and purposes of agents, are indispensable for a comprehensive understanding of the universe. He elaborated on how personal explanations could not be reduced to inanimate explanations, emphasising the unique explanatory scope of personal causation in understanding the actions of a divine being. Swinburne's work in this area underscored the importance of recognising different types of explanations and their respective roles in a comprehensive understanding of reality, bridging the gap between empirical science and theological inquiry. This is that, within this context, Swinburne employed the cosmological argument to explain the existence of the universe. He argued that the complexity and orderliness of the universe required an explanation beyond scientific explanation. The existence of God, as an omnipotent, omniscient and perfectly free being, provided a simple and probable explanation for the universe's existence and the operation of natural laws. His detailed exploration of this argument highlighted the necessity of a first cause, which he identified as God, thereby providing a robust philosophical foundation for theism. Swinburne's version of the cosmological argument emphasised the explanatory power and simplicity of theism over competing naturalistic explanations. He argued that the intrinsic probability of theism is higher than that of rival hypotheses, owing to its simplicity and explanatory power, and developed a cumulative case that considered various aspects of the universe's existence and nature. His approach integrated traditional metaphysical insights with contemporary scientific knowledge, offering a modernised and rigorous defence of the cosmological argument that continues to influence both philosophical and theological discussions.

In addition to this, Swinburne also employed the teleological argument, or argument from design, focussing on the temporal and spatial order of the universe; he argued that the orderliness and fine-tuning of the universe, which allows for the existence of life, pointed to a purposeful creator. The improbability of such fine-tuning occurring by chance supported the hypothesis of a divine designer. By addressing modern scientific discoveries, such as the fine-tuning of physical constants, Swinburne strengthened the argument from design, making it relevant and persuasive in contemporary discourse. He meticulously argued that the fine-tuning of the universe for life is best explained by the existence of an intelligent designer. He maintained that the fine-tuning of the universe significantly raises the probability of theism compared to naturalistic accounts, presenting a detailed case for why a divine creator is the most probable explanation. Swinburne's work on this argument thus included sophisticated probabilistic analyses and an engagement with cutting-edge scientific theories, enhancing the argument's credibility and appeal to both theists and sceptics.

Swinburne's work extended beyond theism specifically to defend substance dualism, free will and central Christian doctrines. He argued for the existence of the soul as essential for life after death and for the existence of libertarian free will as a foundation for moral responsibility. Swinburne's defence of substance dualism was rooted in the belief that human beings are composed of both a physical body and a non-physical soul. He posited that the soul is necessary for personal identity and continuity beyond physical death, providing a basis for belief in an afterlife. This perspective was critical in his broader theological framework, which required a non-material aspect of human existence to make sense of life after death. In defending free will, Swinburne argued against determinism, emphasising that true moral responsibility requires that individuals have the genuine ability to make free choices. He maintained that without 'libertarian' free will, moral judgements and responsibility would be undermined, thus challenging materialistic and deterministic accounts of human behaviour. This defence of free will was integral to his arguments about the moral nature of human beings and their capacity to engage in meaningful relationships with God.

Natural Theology: (ii) Ramified Theism

In further establishing the framework of 'Ramified Theism' (or 'Ramified Natural Theology'), which is a type of natural theological argumentation that focusses on analysing and defending the central tenets of a particular theistic extension (such as Christianity, Islam or Judaism etc.), Swinburne's focus was on providing a tetralogy on Christian doctrine that explores the concept of God as a Trinity, the Incarnation, the atonement, the necessity of revelation and the problem of evil. In his examination of the Trinity, Swinburne argued for the coherence and necessity of understanding God as three persons of one essence, emphasising a 'social trinitarian' conception of the Trinity, where each of the individuals within the Trinity are persons and the one 'God' is identified as the collective of the divine individuals. He explored the Incarnation, positing that God becoming human in the person of Jesus Christ was a logical and coherent expression of divine love and a necessary step for human salvation. In discussing the atonement, Swinburne offered a detailed account of how Christ's sacrificial death reconciles humanity with God, addressing both the justice and love of God. He argued that the necessity of revelation is grounded in the limitations of human reason to fully comprehend divine truths without divine assistance. Swinburne tackled the problem of evil by proposing that the existence of evil is compatible with a perfectly good God, arguing that the presence of evil can be understood in the context of a greater divine plan that includes free will and responsibility. Swinburne argued that these doctrines were consistent with a perfectly good God and were supported by historical evidence, including the resurrection of Jesus Christ. Following the publication of his tetralogy, Swinburne focussed on providing a comprehensive defence of the Resurrection, arguing that it is a historically credible event and a cornerstone of the Christian faith. He meticulously analysed historical documents and testimonies, presenting a case that the resurrection of Jesus is the most probable explanation for the historical evidence available.

Swinburne's systematic approach to Christian doctrine not only reinforced the intellectual viability of these beliefs but also provided a comprehensive framework that addressed key theological concerns with philosophical rigour. Swinburne's exploration of Christian doctrines was deeply integrated with his broader philosophical work, reflecting his commitment to a coherent and comprehensive defence of the faith. He presented arguments for the internal coherence and moral acceptability of key Christian doctrines, arguing for their probability relative to the background of theism and historical evidence. Through his detailed and methodical approach, Swinburne aimed to show that Christian doctrines are not only logically consistent but also fully grounded upon the available historical and empirical evidence, thereby offering a robust intellectual foundation for Christian belief. His work remains a significant contribution to contemporary philosophy, providing a rigorous defence of faith that engages both philosophical inquiry and theological tradition.

More fully, with regards to Swinburne's overall influence within philosophy during his career (and post-career), one can take it to be the case that his work, in combination with that of Plantinga's, brought about the establishment and significant development of the field of 'analytic' philosophy of religion within contemporary philosophy. At its core, analytic philosophy of religion focusses on investigating the meaning and justification of central religious claims, using the best tools and techniques of analytic philosophy. In doing this, it thus covers a vast array of topics, spanning metaphysical, epistemological, ethical, and interpretive dimensions of religious belief and practice. That is, it is an area of philosophy that explores questions regarding religion, including the nature and existence of God, the examination of religious experiences, the analysis of religious language and texts, and the relationship between religion and science. Now, philosophy of religion is indeed an ancient discipline - being part of the earliest philosophical efforts - and its primary topics and problems emerge in reflections found in the ancient civilisations of Egypt, Mesopotamia, India, and China. The early Christian thinkers such as Saint Augustine (354–430 CE), Saint Anselm (1033–1109 CE), and, most importantly, Saint Thomas Aquinas (1225–1274 CE), all made significant contributions to the development of the field of philosophy of religion within the medieval period. During the 20th century, however - which we can term the era of ordinary language philosophy and logical positivism - philosophy of religion (alongside that of metaphysics) was generally deemed an unworthy area of philosophical inquiry, and thus was thrown to the side lines. However, the tide began to turn in the mid to latter part of the 20th century through the work of Plantinga in the 1960s and Swinburne in the 1970s. More specifically, in North America, through Plantinga's publication of *God and Other Minds* in 1967 - which argued for the epistemic rationality of religious belief (through demonstrating the parity of religious belief with belief in other minds),[15] and the *Nature of Necessity* in 1974 - which re-vitalised research on the ontological argument and introduced the highly influential 'Free-Will Defence' against the 'Logical Problem of Evil'.[16] And, in Europe, through Swinburne's publication of *The Coherence of Theism* in 1977, which sought, as noted previously, to meticulously demonstrate the coherence of the theistic concept of God - and the highly influential publication of *The Existence of God* in 1979, which argued, as also noted previously, for the probable existence of God, based on Bayesian epistemology - there was, as one could say poetically, a re-igniting of the intellectual flames for philosophy of religion in the hearts and minds of various philosophers, and a particular re-kindling of interest in rigorous philosophical analysis of religious claims and belief within the general field of analytic philosophy. Thus, through the pioneering work of Swinburne and Plantinga (amongst others), this field, one could say, was re-born in the form of analytic philosophy of religion. Hence, through the career of Swinburne, and his intellectual collaborators, the ancient field of philosophy of religion has been brought off the philosophical shelf and is now seen as a worthy area of philosophical research, dialogue, and debate within the 21st century.

---

15. Plantinga, Alvin. *God and Other Minds: A Study of the Rational Justification of Belief in God*. Ithaca, NY: Cornell University Press, 1967.
16. Plantinga, Alvin. *The Nature of Necessity*. Oxford: Clarendon Press, 1974.

Theoretical Approach: Philosophy First

Swinburne, as noted above, defines the field of philosophy of religion as one that investigates the meaning and justification of core religious claims using the most effective tools and methods of analytic philosophy. This thus involves closely examining the logical structure of religious beliefs, analysing key concepts and arguments, and thoroughly evaluating their coherence and probability. In line with this definition, one can understand that Swinburne's approach to religion and theology is one that takes a 'philosophy-first' approach. More fully, Swinburne's 'philosophy-first' methodology entails a systematic engagement with the most compelling philosophical arguments and theories available before applying them to the central religious and theological positions under analysis. Thus, unlike many philosophers of the past, such as Saint Thomas Aquinas, who began with established theological doctrines and employed philosophical reasoning to explicate and support these positions, Swinburne commences his investigations of various theological topics with an independent analysis of various general philosophical concepts. He begins by rigorously evaluating arguments in a number of domains, including metaphysics, epistemology, ethics and the philosophy of mind, without initially considering their theological ramifications. Moreover, Swinburne performs a critical engagement with a wide range of opposing philosophical viewpoints, by considering and addressing various counterarguments, which thus strengthens the coherence and persuasiveness of his own position. By doing all of this, Swinburne constructs a robust foundation of philosophical argumentation that is not contingent upon prior theological commitments. Thus, once this philosophical framework has been established, Swinburne then applies these concepts and carefully reasoned principles to the central religious and theological claims under focus. This approach ensures that his conclusions regarding, for example, the rationality of belief in God, the nature of the divine attributes and the problem of evil, are firmly grounded in rigorous philosophical analysis rather than predetermined theological assumptions. Hence, by eschewing theological presuppositions, Swinburne allows the philosophical arguments to guide his inquiry, potentially leading to conclusions that can subsequently inform and shape his theological views. Ultimately, Swinburne's approach aims to provide a clear, rational and philosophically robust method for understanding complex varied religious and theological positions, thus demonstrating that theological conclusions can be derived from well-supported philosophical reasoning rather than serving as the starting point for philosophical inquiry.

Major Works of Richard Swinburne

Swinburne's works in the philosophy of religion can be divided into two main series: a trilogy focussing on the philosophical foundations of theism; and a tetralogy exploring specific Christian doctrines. As noted previously, during his retirement, Swinburne has dedicated considerable effort to revising and expanding some of his earlier works, resulting in second editions that reflect both ongoing philosophical discussions and his deepening insights. These second editions serve to update and enhance his arguments in light of scholarly feedback and advancements in the field, ensuring that his substantial contributions continue to engage both current and future scholars in the fields of philosophy and theology. The trilogy, which forms the basis for his philosophical defence of theism, includes:

1. *The Coherence of Theism* (1977; revised 1993): This work argues for the logical consistency of theistic belief, addressing objections to the coherence of the concept of God.
Second Edition (2016): This second edition underwent extensive revision to reflect current discussions in philosophy relevant to theism, particularly those around omnipotence and the reconciliation of God's foreknowledge with human freedom. In this edition the structure of a number of chapters was altered for clarity and focus, notably with less of a focus on the issue of logical positivism (given its waning influence since the publication of the previous edition) and the introduction of a distinct chapter on metaphysical possibility to better distinguish it from logical possibility, and ultimately clarify and expand upon these complex philosophical issues. Furthermore, Swinburne introduced terminological updates to the content of various chapters to align the discussion with contemporary philosophical language and his own subsequent works, thus refining the

works' arguments to better handle modern critiques and inquiries concerning the coherence of theistic belief.
2. *The Existence of God* (1979; revised 1991): This work presents a cumulative case for the existence of God, employing various principles from the philosophy of science.
Second Edition (2004): This second edition incorporates substantial changes, particularly in refining and expanding the probabilistic arguments for the existence of God. Swinburne engages more directly with new objections and developments in the philosophy of religion, updating his treatment of classic arguments such as the cosmological and teleological arguments, and introducing lesser-known arguments such as those arising from divine providence and miracles. He also improved the clarity of the work's argumentation to make the complex philosophical discussions more accessible to readers. Moreover, Swinburne revises his approach to the problem of evil, acknowledging it as a more significant challenge than in the previous edition, and adjusts his arguments regarding the implications of an afterlife on the probability of God's existence.
3. *Faith and Reason* (1981): This work explores the relationship between faith and reason, arguing that religious faith is rational and can be supported by evidence.
Second Edition (2005): This second edition features several significant revisions that clarify and deepen the exploration of the rationality of religious faith. In this edition, Swinburne addresses new philosophical insights and criticisms that have emerged since the original publication. He elaborates on the rational foundations of religious faith, discussing in greater detail how faith and reason interact within a probabilistic and internalist framework. Swinburne also takes this opportunity to respond to contemporary views such as Alvin Plantinga's theory of warrant and John Hick's pluralistic hypothesis about the validity of all religions, ultimately reinforcing his argument that religious commitment should be based on the most probable truths offered by a religion's creed.

The tetralogy, which builds upon the philosophical foundation established in the trilogy, focuses on specific Christian doctrines, which include:

1. *Responsibility and Atonement* (1989): This work examines the moral aspects of Christian theology, particularly focussing on the concepts of sin, atonement and redemption.
2. *Revelation: From Metaphor to Analogy* (1992): This work investigates the nature of divine revelation and its role in religious belief, emphasising the importance of metaphor and analogy in understanding religious language.
Second Edition (2007): This second edition introduces substantial changes, focussing on a deeper exploration of how religious language, especially metaphors and analogies, aids in understanding divine revelation. For this edition, Swinburne extensively rewrote the text to include a new chapter that addresses whether traditional Christian moral teachings on topics such as divorce, homosexuality and abortion can be considered as revealed truths. Additionally, this edition features an appendix that employs probability calculus to structure the evidence supporting the Christian revelation, thus allowing Swinburne to address and counter criticisms against the use of probabilistic arguments in theological discourse, and thus ultimately offering a more rigorous foundation for arguing for veracity of revealed truth.
3. *The Christian God* (1994): This work explores the nature of the Christian God, discussing the attributes of God, the doctrine of the Trinity and the doctrine of the Incarnation.[17]
4. *Providence and the Problem of Evil* (1998): This work addresses the problem of evil, arguing that the existence of evil is compatible with the existence of an omnipotent, omniscient and perfectly good God.

In addition to these series, Swinburne has written other notable philosophical works that are outside of his trilogy/tetralogy that,

---

17. Again, as noted previously, Swinburne has thoughts to produce a second edition of this work.

nevertheless, contribute to his overall defence of theism and Christian doctrine:

> *Is There a God?* (1996; revised 2010): This work investigates the question of God's existence and serves as an accessible introduction to the central arguments featured in the trilogy.
>
> *The Resurrection of God Incarnate* (2003): This work provides a detailed defence of the resurrection of Jesus Christ, arguing for its historical credibility and theological significance.
>
> *The Evolution of the Soul* (1986; revised 1997): This work defends substance dualism, positing that human beings consist of both a physical body and a non-physical soul, and that there is no scientific explanation for the evolution of the soul.
>
> *Was Jesus God?* (2008): This work examines the veracity of the central Christian doctrines and serves as an accessible introduction to the central arguments featured in the tetralogy and the *Resurrection of God Incarnate*.
>
> *Mind, Brain, and Free Will* (2013): This work further analyses the concept of substance dualism, addressing contemporary debates about the mind-brain relationship and the nature of free will and moral responsibility.
>
> *Are We Bodies or Souls?* (2019): This work focusses on further defending substance dualism and serves as an accessible introduction to the central arguments featured in *The Evolution of the Soul* and *Mind, Brain, and Free Will* (with a focus on developing the arguments featured in these earlier works).
>
> *Could a Good God Permit So Much Suffering? A Debate* (2024): This collaborative work, co-authored with James Sterba, argues for the compatibility of God's existence with the presence of evil in the world.

Together, these works form a comprehensive and rigorous defence of theism and Christian doctrine, showcasing Swinburne's commitment to providing a robust defence of the veracity and rationality of theism and, more specifically, the Christian faith.

Final Reflections

Throughout his illustrious career, Swinburne remained committed to systematising and justifying his Christian beliefs with philosophical rigour and intellectual tenacity. He acknowledged the possibility of doubt but believed that rational arguments and evidence supported the truth of Christianity. His work aimed to establish the intellectual respectability of Christianity and to bridge the gap between rigorous philosophy and religious faith. Swinburne's influence extended beyond academic circles, as he sought to make his conclusions accessible to a broader audience through popular books and lectures. Despite the challenges and doubts, Swinburne's lifelong dedication to his vocation as a natural theologian remained unwavering. Swinburne's works remain a testament to the enduring relevance of natural theology and the philosophical defence of the Christian faith, influencing generations of scholars and believers alike. He argued that rational religious enquiry is, in fact, a moral obligation and based upon certain criteria for comparing the probabilities of different religious creeds, ultimately favouring Christianity based on these assessments. His legacy is characterised by a profound integration of faith and reason, inspiring ongoing dialogue and exploration in the fields of philosophy and theology.

The Philosophical Foundations of Richard Swinburne

In contemporary philosophy, the main fields of inquiry are metaphysics, epistemology and ethics. These domains explore fundamental questions about reality, knowledge and moral values. As explained previously, Swinburne has made significant contributions across these areas, as his work provides a detailed and structured framework that addresses essential philosophical questions through a rigorous analytical lens. By understanding Swinburne's views within metaphysics, epistemology and ethics, one can gain deeper insights into his contributions to the philosophy of religion. This foundational understanding will be unpacked in the following sections, allowing one to appreciate his philosophy-first approach to theological theorising, which will be explored further in subsequent chapters.

Metaphysics

Swinburne's metaphysical system is centred on a 'four-category' ontology, encompassing substances, properties, times and causation—where, at a general level, an 'n-category system' is one which holds that n different categories are necessary and sufficient for describing all phenomena. These categories are 'fundamental' within Swinburne's metaphysical system in the sense that they are not reducible to one another – unlike that of other metaphysical notions such as 'modality', which is 'reducible' within Swinburne's system (in the sense that modal notions concerning possibility and necessity are simply 'generalisations' of language used by substances, possessing certain properties, at particular times – and so the category of modality is reducible to the other fundamental categories). Now, in detailing the nature of these categories further, the first category, substances, refers to independently existing concrete objects, like desks, persons and particles, which can possess essential and accidental properties. Properties, the second category, are characteristics or features of substances, with a focus on their non-reductive nature and the concept of 'thisness', distinguishing individual substances even if they share all other properties. The third category, times, involves specific moments or periods where properties are instantiated in substances, integrating causality and temporal progression. The fourth category is that of causation, which focuses on the causal powers of substances, and their various liabilities to exercises these powers. This structured approach to metaphysics provides a detailed understanding of the world's constituents and their interrelationships, offering a robust foundation for exploring various complex philosophical questions about the nature of reality. It will now be important to further unpack this metaphysical framework.

Substances

The first ontological category of Swinburne's metaphysical framework is that of substances, which are defined as particular concrete objects that exist independently, are property bearers and can have other substances as parts. Everyday objects such as desks, persons and particles (such as photons) are to be identified as substances. Crucially, substances exist wholly at any given time – a desk existing on a Tuesday exists entirely on that day, not partially then and partially on another day – and are characterised by their ability to exist independently of other substances, except for their parts, which are also substances. One can distinguish between pure substances, which do not have other substances as parts, such as fundamental particles or human souls, and impure substances, which are composed of other substances, like desks or organisms. This distinction is critical for understanding the composition and continuity of substances over time. Furthermore, a differentiation can be made between essential and accidental properties of substances, where essential properties define the kind of substance it is, and accidental properties can vary without altering the substance's identity. Though, it is important to note that essential properties can also define (or help to define) what makes an individual substance the substance it is – when a substance of that kind does not have 'thisness' (the property of being a particular individual), as, according to Swinburne, not all substance have thisness.

Properties
The second ontological category of Swinburne's metaphysical framework is that of properties, which are characteristics or features of substances. Properties can be monadic, involving a single substance, or relational, involving multiple substances. For example, the colour of a rose is a monadic property, as it pertains to the rose itself. In contrast, the distance between two buildings is a relational property, as it depends on both buildings and their spatial relationship to each other. Moreover, properties are crucial in defining the identity and behaviour of substances. For instance, being red or reflecting light at a certain wavelength are properties of a surface. Against the reduction of all properties to mere powers to produce effects, a view held by some philosophers, one can understand that, while powers to produce effects are indeed properties, not all properties can be reduced to such powers. There must be more to some properties than just their ability to produce further events (where an 'event' is the instantiation of a property in a substance at a time, such as a ball becoming red at 3:00 PM); otherwise, an infinite regress would ensue, rendering the whole system of properties indistinguishable from any other similar system.

Within this conceptualisation of properties one can also introduce the notion of 'thisness' or haecceity, the property, as noted previously, of being a particular individual substance. Thisness distinguishes one substance from another, even if they share all other properties. This concept addresses scenarios where two qualitatively identical substances are distinct merely by being made of different matter. Thisness is crucial for understanding the identity of non-physical substances as well, where the individuality of a substance does not rely on its material composition but rather on its unique existence. This aspect of Swinburne's metaphysics ensures that each substance's identity is grounded in its particularity, not just its general properties. In conceptualising the nature of thisness, one can understand that it goes beyond the mere possession of certain characteristics – as it is what makes a substance the particular individual it is, even if all its other properties were to change. To illustrate, consider Max Black's scenario, introduced in his article 'The Identity of Indiscernibles',[18] where two identical spheres exist in an otherwise empty universe; even if the properties of these spheres were to change, each would retain its individual thisness, thus distinguishing it from the other despite their identical appearances. Thisness is not a property that can be described by universal or general terms but is unique to each individual substance. This notion thus helps one tackle philosophical problems such as the identity of indiscernibles, where two entities sharing all properties could still be distinct due to their thisness.

Times
The third ontological category of Swinburne's metaphysical framework is that of times, which are specific moments or periods at which properties are instantiated in substances. The world's history is a succession of these times, with each time involving the instantiation, transformation and cessation of properties in substances. This perspective integrates causality and temporal progression, where times are fundamental units of the world's history, driven by causal relationships. For instance, the time at which a desk is painted brown and later moved involves changes in the desk's properties at different times due to causal interactions – this is called an 'event'. Events, therefore, consist of properties possessed or not possessed by substances at specific times, or substances existing or not existing at certain times. However, since events are analysable in terms of substances, properties and times – and since none of these three can be reduced to any other – substances, properties and times (and causation) are thus the basic ontological categories in Swinburne's metaphysics.

---

18. Black, Max. "The Identity of Indiscernibles." *Mind*, vol. 61, no. 242, 1952, pp. 153-164.

With regard to the nature of time itself, this metaphysical framework considers time as a continuum, where any period consists of smaller, infinitely divisible periods. Time is not composed of discrete instants; instead, instants are boundaries of periods and do not constitute periods themselves. Instants mark the endpoints of periods, have no duration and cannot be aggregated to form periods. In addition to this, this framework differentiates between the topological and metric aspects of time: the ordering of events (topology) is independent of laws of nature, while the measurement of intervals (metric) requires consistent periodic processes governed by these laws. The causal theory of time, which is assumed within this framework, defines the future as periods that can be influenced by present actions, while the past consists of periods that could have influenced the present. This causal relationship delineates the flow of time and emphasises the impossibility of backward or simultaneous causation. Moreover, time cannot begin or end, as it would be logically impossible for there to be a period of time in which there is no time. Time is therefore eternal, with no beginning or end, and any understanding of the universe must account for this infinite divisibility and continuous nature of time.

Causation

The fourth ontological category of Swinburne's metaphysical framework is that of causation, where substances cause other substances to gain or lose properties or to begin, continue or cease to exist. This causal relationship is grounded in the causal powers of substances. Substances cause events by virtue of their inherent properties, which include causal powers and liabilities to exercise these powers under specific conditions. For example, a stone has the power to break fragile objects, and this power is exercised when the stone is dropped from a certain height. A distinction can be made between full causes, which are sufficient on their own to produce an effect, and partial causes, which are necessary parts of a collective that is sufficient for the effect. There is also a differentiation between active causes, which directly bring about effects, and permissive causes, which allow effects to occur by not preventing them. This nuanced view addresses complex causal interactions, such as the combined roles of a match and hydrogen in causing an explosion. A further key aspect of this causal theory is the account of mental causation and libertarian free will. Human souls are taken to possess causal powers that are not wholly determined by physical states or prior events, allowing for genuine free choice. This libertarian view contrasts with deterministic accounts of human action, thus underscoring the unique causal role of human agents. Intentional actions are fundamental exercises of causal power. When agents act intentionally, they exert causal influence directly, not merely as a result of being in a certain state. Additionally, this framework rejects the empiricist tradition that seeks to reduce causality to patterns of regular succession between events. Causation is seen as an irreducible relation between substances and events; and attempts to analyse it in terms of more basic categories are considered misguided. The notion of causation by substances is foundational and, while events can be causes, they do so in virtue of the substances involved. Causation is thus a fundamental category as it cannot be reduced to the three other categories of substance, properties and times. This view is thus to be contrasted with that of David Hume. Hume's view, grounded in his empiricism, posits that causation is not something we directly observe but rather a mental habit formed from consistently observing events together. For Hume, in his work *An Enquiry Concerning Human Understanding*,[19] when we say 'A causes B', we are simply noting that A and B have regularly appeared in sequence. He famously argued that we cannot perceive any necessary connection between cause and effect – only a sequence of events. For instance, when one billiard ball strikes another, we see the second ball move afterwards, but we do not directly perceive any 'causal power' driving this motion. Therefore, in Hume's view, causation is a product of mental association rather than an objective feature of the world.[20] In contrast, Swinburne advocates for a realist view of causation, where causality is seen as an inherent relationship between substances and their powers and liabilities. That is, for Swinburne, causation involves the actual exercise of the causal powers that substances possess under specific conditions, referred to as liabilities. For example, when a stone shatters a window upon being thrown, this is not merely a case of one event following another. Instead, it reflects the stone's intrinsic power to break fragile objects

---

19. Hume, David. *An Enquiry Concerning Human Understanding*. Edited by Tom L. Beauchamp. Oxford: Oxford University Press, 1999. (Original work published 1748), Section VII, Part II.
20. Hume, *An Enquiry*, Section VII, Part I.

and the liability that is triggered when it strikes them with sufficient force. This power is a fundamental property of the stone, and its exercise, under the right liability, leads to a real causal relationship. Thus, Swinburne views causation as a fundamental and irreducible aspect of reality, where substances have inherent powers and liabilities that determine their causal roles. In contrast, Hume sees causation as a construct of the human mind, based on observed patterns of succession between events, and denies the perception of any necessary connection or intrinsic causal powers within substances. This contrast underscores Swinburne's belief that causal relationships exist independently of our perceptions, grounded in the very nature of substances and their inherent properties. Now, outside Swinburne's four-category ontology (and their cognate notions) is a further concept that plays an important role within his metaphysical system: modality – which is, however, to be conceived of as a reducible notion within Swinburne's system.

Modality

Modality is another important (though, as noted previously, a non-fundamental, and thus reducible) aspect of Swinburne's metaphysical framework. At a general level, modality is concerned with the 'absolute' necessity, impossibility, or possibility of propositions, often in relation to different possible worlds or conditions (e.g., 'It is necessarily true that $2 + 2 = 4$ in all possible worlds' or 'It is possible that it will rain tomorrow, depending on the weather conditions'). However, within Swinburne's metaphysical system, the focus within modality is not on that of the traditional notions of 'possible worlds' – where a possible world is a hypothetical way in which the world could have been (for example a world where the Roman Empire never fell, or Hitler won WWII, or Abraham Lincoln was not assassinated etc.) – but an anti-realist view of modality is assumed termed 'logical nominalism'. Within this view, modal truths (i.e. truths concerning what is necessary and possible) belong primarily to sentences and depend solely on the conventions of human language. In other words, modality is to be understood to be simple generalisations of conventions of language. That is, modality only concerns relationships between public sentences to each other in such a way that there is a codification of certain rules for which sentences commit their utterer to. Thus, the realm of modality is ultimately concerned with human behaviour, a matter of psychology, rather than any deep form of metaphysics. Nonetheless, within this view of modality, further important distinctions can be drawn between logical and metaphysical modalities. This is that, for the former, logical possibility pertains to what can be conceived without contradiction (for example, 'It is possible that there is a world where unicorns exist'), while logical necessity involves propositions whose negation is self-contradictory or entails (i.e., leads to) a contradiction (for example, 'It is necessary that a bachelor is unmarried', as the concept of a 'married bachelor' entails a contradiction because if a bachelor were married, then this would entail that he would be both 'married and unmarried'). And whether or not a sentence entails a contradiction depends only on the rules of the language and can be determined *a priori* – that is, determined by a competent speaker of the language, even if that speakers does not know to what the referring expressions in the sentence are actually referring to. However, metaphysical possibility, impossibility and necessity go beyond mere logical coherence and entailment to include what is possible given the actual world's contingent facts. Thus, some propositions are metaphysically necessary because their truth depends on the actual world's contingent facts, yet they are discoverable only through empirical investigation, not *a priori* reflection (which is reflection that is independent of experience, like deducing mathematical truths such as '2+2=4' without needing to observe any physical objects). For instance, as noted by Saul Kripke, in his work *Naming and Necessity* (1980),[21] and Hilary Putnam, in his paper 'The Meaning of Meaning',[22] water being H_2O is a metaphysical necessity that is discovered *a posteriori* (which is a discovery made on the basis of experience, such as learning that water boils at 100°C by observing it in a laboratory). Or, so one thinks, as, in adapting another one of Kripke's famous examples of *a posteriori* necessities, one can, in fact, understand that metaphysical modalities (possibilities, impossibilities and necessities) *are* logical modalities (possibilities, impossibilities and necessities) – that is, the former are identical to (and thus, as a

---

21. Kripke, Saul. *Naming and Necessity*. Cambridge, MA: Harvard University Press, 1980.
22. Putnam, Hilary. "The Meaning of 'Meaning'." *Minnesota Studies in the Philosophy of Science* 7 (1975): pp. 131-193.

category, collapse into) those of the latter – and hence there are no *a posteriori* necessities, but all modality is simply *a priori*.

In further illustrating this position, we can focus on an example provided by Kripke: consider a time before the solar system was fully understood. Astronomers named a celestial body visible in the evening sky 'Hesperus' and a celestial body visible in the morning sky 'Phosphorus', using these names as 'rigid designators' – which are terms that always refer to the same object (substance, property, or event), whatever non-essential properties that object may gain or lose, or even always have (for example, 'Rishi Sunak' refers to that individual whatever might happen to him, for example whatever his occupation or age; whereas 'The Prime Minister of the United Kingdom' referred to that individual only when he held that position, and so is not a rigid designator). Thus, the celestial bodies are actually the same (the planet Venus) but the astronomers, unaware of this, thought the names referred to different celestial bodies. Similarly, Putnam uses the example of the term 'water'. In the eighteenth century, this word described the clear liquid found in rivers but people did not know that chemically it was H_2O. This lack of knowledge about water's chemical composition may have led to uncertainty about the term's application in certain contexts. For instance, could there be a transparent, drinkable liquid that looks and tastes like water but is not water? These terms are called 'uninformative designators', indicating that there are situations where we do not know the correct application of the term. Even a knowledgeable person in the eighteenth century might not always be certain when to use the term 'water' correctly. For a rigid designator to be an 'informative designator', anyone who understands the word's meaning must also understand the conditions for its proper application – assuming their cognitive faculties are functioning properly, they are in a good position to make judgements and they are not experiencing illusions. For example, the term 'blue' is informative because if you understand its meaning and your vision is normal, you cannot mistakenly apply it. Swinburne argues that while 'water' in the eighteenth century was an uninformative designator, the term 'H_2O' used today is an informative designator for the same substance. Kripke and Putnam both argued that while 'water is not H_2O' is not logically impossible, it is metaphysically impossible: one could deny that water is H_2O without a logical contradiction but, once we know that water is H_2O, it cannot be otherwise (anything that is not H_2O is not water, and anything that is H_2O is water). One, however, can contend that considering 'water is not H_2O' as logically possible only happens if we misunderstand what 'water' refers to. By replacing uninformative designators with informative ones, if we know a sentence is logically necessary, we also know it is metaphysically necessary. For instance, if we replace both terms in the sentence 'Hesperus is Phosphorus' with an informative designator 'X' that refers to the rocky matter of the planet, the sentence becomes logically necessary because it asserts that X is X; this also makes the identity of the celestial bodies metaphysically necessary in all circumstances. Thus, using informative designators to determine logical necessity allows us to recognise metaphysical necessity, which is a principle that is applicable to possibilities and impossibilities as well. Given these notions of informative and uninformative designators, metaphysical possibility collapses into logical possibility. The distinctions between metaphysical and logical possibilities, impossibilities and necessities are ultimately *a priori* rather than *a posteriori* as Kripke and Putnam argued. This implies that our understanding of these concepts can be achieved through reason and analysis alone, independent of empirical investigation.

In all, Swinburne's metaphysics provides a detailed and structured approach to understanding the fundamental nature of reality. By categorising the world's constituents into substances, properties, times and causation, and exploring their interrelationships, Swinburne offers a comprehensive framework for discussing various other important metaphysical notions. That is, his emphasis on the independence of substances, the non-reductive nature of properties and the importance of times and causal relationships ensures a robust metaphysics capable of addressing complex philosophical questions about the nature of reality.

Epistemology

Swinburne's epistemology presents a sophisticated and multi-layered approach that addresses the nature of justified belief through principles of internalist justification, probabilistic reasoning and the distinction between different types of probabilities. Central to his framework is the concept of epistemic justification, emphasising the internalist standpoint where beliefs are justified based on accessible reasons and evidence. This approach incorporates logical and epistemic probabilities to explain how evidence can increase or decrease the probability of a belief's truth, utilising probabilistic reasoning and Bayesian updating. Furthermore, Swinburne's principles of credulity and testimony highlight the foundational role of sensory experiences and social knowledge in justifying beliefs. The framework also addresses the problem of defeaters and knowledge, including solutions to Gettier problems by ensuring that justified true beliefs are not contingent on false premises. Overall, Swinburne's epistemology provides a comprehensive and systematic structure for understanding justified belief and knowledge formation. It will now be important to further unpack this epistemological framework.

Epistemic Justification
A central aspect of Swinburne's epistemology is the concept of epistemic justification, particularly from an internalist standpoint. At the centre of many modern theories of epistemic justification is the definition that a belief is justified if and only if it is based on adequate grounds. In grasping this position further, one can draw a distinction between externally and internally justified beliefs. Externally justified beliefs are those justified by external factors, such as the reliability of the sources or the evidence supporting the belief, without the believer necessarily being aware of these justifying factors. More formally, an externalist epistemology thus defines a belief being justified as it being caused in the right way, independently of whether the believer believes that it is so caused. For example, a person believes that the weather will be rainy tomorrow because they checked a reliable weather forecast. Even if they do not understand how weather models work or why the forecast is reliable, their belief is justified because it was caused in the right way – by consulting a trustworthy source. Hence, the justification does not depend on their understanding, only on the fact that the belief was formed through a reliable process. Internally justified beliefs, on the other hand, are those that the believer has a conscious understanding of and can articulate the reasons for holding. This is that internalist justification requires that the believer has access to the reasons or evidence supporting his belief upon reflection. This includes logical relations and coherence with other beliefs held by the individual. Thus, again, more formally, an internalist epistemology thus defines a belief being justified as it being self-justified or held on the basis of other beliefs accessible to the believer. For example, a person believes that water boils at 100°C because they have observed it happen, understand the principles of temperature and boiling, and can explain how heat energy causes

water molecules to move faster until they change state from liquid to gas. Their belief would thus be internally justified because they can articulate the reasons and evidence for it, and it coherently fits with their other beliefs about science and physics. Now, internally justified beliefs are considered to have greater epistemic value because they involve a deeper level of cognitive engagement and responsibility. When a belief is internally justified, the believer has access to the justifying reasons and can critically evaluate and reflect upon them. This process of internal reflection and understanding not only strengthens the belief but also aligns with a more robust conception of rationality. That is, the epistemic grounds and the transparency of reasons behind a belief are crucial for its epistemic worth. In addition to this, within this framework there is a further distinction that can be drawn between synchronic and diachronic justification. Synchronic justification refers to the justification of a belief at a specific moment, based on the evidence available at that time. In contrast, diachronic justification involves a temporal dimension, where a belief is justified over time through the continuous accumulation and assessment of evidence. For example, a scientific hypothesis might initially be weakly synchronically justified but can become strongly diachronically justified as more experimental evidence supports it over time.

Now, in returning to the general definition of a justified belief, three key aspects of this definition are the grounds, their adequacy and the basing relation. The grounds for belief encompass all the evidence a person can privately access, forming what are known as 'rightly basic beliefs'. A belief is rightly basic if it doesn't rely on other beliefs and is not perceived by the individual to do so. These beliefs may originate from experiences like sensory perceptions or memories, or from testimony. Additionally, grounds are deemed adequate if they render the belief or the proposition it conveys logically probable. The logical probability of a proposition p is defined as a specific type of probability where the connection between p making q probable is a logical truth. Once all evidence supporting p is considered, no further evidence can impact the hypothesis' probability. Such a form of probability, however, requires logical omniscience and is beyond the typical individual's capacity. Therefore, people should aim for epistemic probability, which evaluates how well evidence supports a proposition based on the evaluator's limited logical capacity but proper application of inductive criteria. A belief is justified if it is epistemically probable based on the subject's rightly basic beliefs, as long as this probability aligns with logical probability, meaning the individual correctly using objective criteria from beliefs that are indeed rightly basic and is caused by them in a straightforward manner with the belief that they provide evidential and causal support. However, it is important to note that grounds that justify a belief under normal conditions might not suffice under abnormal conditions. In such cases, the justification of a belief is overridden if the new circumstances introduce evidence that, along with existing evidence, insufficiently supports the original belief, thereby rendering it unjustified. Thus, an overriding defeater occurs when the original belief is falsified by the emergence of new, conflicting evidence. Now, that we have briefly outlined some of the central tenets of Swinburne's epistemology it will be helpful to further unpack these elements in more detail.

Probabilistic Reasoning

Probabilistic reasoning plays a significant role in epistemic justification, and there is an important distinction that can be drawn between logical and epistemic probabilities to explain how evidence can increase or decrease the probability that a given belief is true. Logical probability pertains to the formal relations between propositions and is often associated with deductive logic. It involves the degree of entailment between propositions. For example, if proposition A logically entails proposition B, then the logical probability of B given A is 1 (certainty). Epistemic probability involves evaluating how likely a proposition is to be true based on the available evidence. It assesses the strength of the evidence in supporting a given proposition. Propositions can have varying degrees of probability based on the quality and quantity of evidence backing them. For instance, if a weather forecast predicts rain, the probability that it will rain tomorrow is higher than if there were no such forecast or if the forecast predicted sunshine. This probabilistic approach helps in understanding how evidence can make a belief more or less justified. In addition to this, the use of the probability calculus helps to quantify the degree of justification and provides a framework for understanding how different pieces of evidence contribute to the overall justification of a belief. Bayes' theorem can thus be used to illustrate how prior probabilities are updated in light of new evidence. More precisely, Bayes' theorem is a theorem in probability theory that describes how to update the probability of a hypothesis based on new evidence (it is named after

Introduction: Life, Works and Philosophical Foundations

Thomas Bayes, who first proposed a special case of the theorem in the 18th century, in his essay 'An Essay Towards Solving a Problem in the Doctrine of Chances';[23] however, the theorem was later generalised and extensively developed by Pierre-Simon Laplace, who, in his own essay 'Mémoire sur la probabilité des causes par les évènemens',[24] independently rediscovered and extended Bayes' original ideas). It is expressed mathematically as follows:

$$P(h/e.k) = \frac{P(e/h.k)P(h.k)}{P(e.k)}$$

In this formula, P(*h*/*e.k*) represents the posterior probability, or the probability of the hypothesis *h* given the evidence *e* and the background knowledge *k* (where background knowledge (or background evidence) is what we take for granted when examining the detailed evidence for a hypothesis). P(*e*/*h.k*) is the likelihood, or the probability of observing *e*, assuming *h* is true. P(*h.k*) is the prior probability of the hypothesis, or the probability of the hypothesis on the background knowledge alone (which reflects the probability of *h* before considering the new evidence) – and the extreme case of this is the 'intrinsic probability' of the hypothesis, which is the prior probability of the hypothesis on *no* contingent evidence (this is what sometimes is called the probability on a mere tautology). Last, P(*e.k*) is the probability of the evidence, given only the background knowledge alone (and thus the probability of the evidence under all other possible hypotheses). It will be helpful to illustrate the inner workings of this formula through an everyday example: let's say someone is trying to determine if a friend is likely to have come to their party. They receive evidence by noticing their friend's favourite car parked outside the party venue. And their background knowledge includes the fact that this friend is known to drive this particular car. In this scenario, P(*h*/*e.k*) represents the probability that the friend came to the party, given that their car is seen outside and knowing that they own this

---

23. Bayes, Thomas. "An Essay Towards Solving a Problem in the Doctrine of Chances." *Philosophical Transactions of the Royal Society of London*, vol. 53, 1763, pp. 370-418.
24. Laplace, Pierre-Simon. "Mémoire sur la probabilité des causes par les évènemens." *Mémoires de l'Académie Royale des Sciences de Paris*, vol. 6, 1774, pp. 621-656.

car. This reflects how confident the person is that their friend is at the party after considering all the evidence. $P(e/h.k)$ is the probability that they would see the car outside if the friend is indeed at the party and typically drives this car. This captures how likely it is that the evidence would appear as it does, assuming the hypothesis is true. $P(h.k)$ represents the prior probability of the friend attending the party, based solely on the background knowledge the person has about them, such as how likely they are to attend parties in general. This prior reflects the initial estimation of the probability before considering the specific evidence of the car. Lastly, $P(e.k)$ is the probability that the car would be seen outside based on the background knowledge alone, considering all other possible explanations, such as someone else driving a similar car. This reflects how probable the evidence is under different hypotheses, not just the one being considered. Bayes' theorem mathematically updates the probability of a hypothesis based on new evidence – through the process of conditionalisation – thus formalising the process of hypothesis confirmation. Thus, in the previous example, seeing the friend's car outside the party venue updates the belief about whether they attended the party. Initially, it might have seemed unlikely that they would come, but the evidence of their car increases the probability that they did. Bayes' theorem thus allows for the formalisation of this shift in confidence, updating the belief from the prior probability based on the new evidence. Through this process of conditionalisation, the theorem, therefore, helps to mathematically confirm or adjust the likelihood of the hypothesis regarding the friend's attendance. Now, within this probabilistic context, certain criteria can be used for determining the probability of a hypothesis, which is grounded on four fundamental tenets:

> 1. *the criterion of yielding the data* (i.e. the criterion that assesses whether the hypothesis yields the data, when otherwise it would not be expected);

> 2. *the criterion of fitting with background knowledge* (i.e. the criterion of assessing whether the hypothesis meshes with other hypotheses that are rendered probable by these criterion);

3. *the criterion of scope* (i.e. the criterion assessing how much the hypothesis seeks to explain); and

4. *the criterion of simplicity* (i.e. the criterion that assesses whether the hypothesis posits the existence and operation of few substances, few kinds of substance, with few simple properties behaving in mathematically simple kinds of way).

Thus, by utilising this criteria, which can be fed into the framework of Bayes' theorem, one can then calculate the logical (epistemic) probability of a given hypothesis, conditioned on the evidence.

Principles of Credulity and Testimony

Two epistemic principles are of great importance within Swinburne's epistemology: the principle of credulity and the principle of testimony. The principle of credulity posits that every basic belief a person holds inherently carries a probability that reflects the intensity of the belief within his or her cognitive structure. In simpler terms, what appears to be true to a person, based on his/her experiences and perceptions, is probably true – unless there is counterevidence against it. Our perceptual beliefs and experiences should be trusted *prima facie*. For instance, if it seems to a person that he sees a tree, then there is probably a tree unless there is evidence suggesting he is mistaken (e.g. a hallucination or illusion). This principle underpins much of the epistemological framework proposed here by suggesting that sensory experiences provide a basic form of justification for beliefs. Now, closely related to the principle of credulity is the principle of testimony, where the trust in perceptual beliefs extends to the testimony of others. That is, if a person tells us something he has experienced or knows, it is probably true unless there is substantial evidence to the contrary. This principle is crucial because it acknowledges the social aspect of knowledge acquisition, where much of what we know comes from what others report. The reliance on testimony is thus justified by its general reliability, as people typically tell the truth because it benefits them socially and practically to do so. These principles underpin much of the epistemological framework proposed here by suggesting that sensory experiences and testimony provide a basic form of justification for beliefs. Hence, a belief's grounds consist of rightly basic beliefs regulated by these principles.

Problem of Defeaters and Knowledge
The notion of defeaters also plays an important role in Swinburne's epistemology, where a defeater is evidence that undermines or counters the justification of a belief. There are two types of defeaters: undermining and overriding defeaters. An undermining defeater challenges the connection between the evidence and the belief, while an overriding defeater presents new evidence that directly contradicts the belief. For example, if someone believes a suspect's fingerprints prove their guilt but learns that fingerprint analysis has a high error rate in dusty conditions, and the fingerprint evidence that they posses is of this kind, this undermines the connection between the evidence and the belief. In contrast, if someone believes they saw a friend in a crowded place but then learns that friend was out of town, this new evidence serves as an overriding defeater by directly contradicting the original belief.

On the basis of this conceptualisation of defeaters, one can also understand that nature of knowledge and the challenges posed by Gettier problems. A Gettier problem arises when someone has a justified true belief, but the belief's justification is flawed because it depends on a false premise. For example, a person might believe there is a sheep in the field because he sees a shape that looks like a sheep. Unbeknownst to him, what he sees is a cleverly disguised dog but there is, by coincidence, a real sheep hidden from view. Swinburne's approach to solving Gettier problems involves adding a clause to the definition of knowledge that excludes beliefs formed on the basis of false propositions. This ensures that for a belief to count as knowledge, it must not only be true and justified, but also that its justification must not rest on any falsehoods. Hence, knowledge, according to Swinburne, is thus (internally) justified true belief that is not contingently based on any epistemically defeasible premises.

In all, Swinburne's epistemology is a robust framework that emphasises the principles of credulity and testimony, the probabilistic nature of epistemic justification, the importance of internalist perspectives and the need to account for defeaters. His approach provides a comprehensive structure for understanding how we form justified beliefs and how these beliefs can lead to knowledge. By integrating these elements, Swinburne offers a nuanced epistemological view that incorporates the immediacy of direct experiences into a coherent and systematic belief network.

Ethics

Swinburne's ethical framework, much like his metaphysics and epistemology, is systematically comprehensive, encompassing moral realism, moral supervenience, a distinct moral epistemology and an integrative normative theory. Central to his ethics is the concept of moral realism, asserting the objective truth of moral propositions and the existence of moral facts independent of individual or cultural beliefs. This is further elaborated through the notion of moral supervenience, where moral properties are systematically tied to non-moral properties. Swinburne's moral epistemology emphasises discovering moral principles through intuition and rational reflection, achieving coherence via reflective equilibrium. Additionally, his normative theory integrates deontological ethics and virtue ethics, emphasising both adherence to moral duties and the cultivation of virtuous character traits. This multifaceted approach provides a robust structure for understanding the nature of morality, balancing objective moral principles with the development of moral virtues. It will now be important to further unpack this ethical framework.

Moral Realism and Supervenience

Central to Swinburne's ethical framework is the concept of moral realism, which holds that some moral propositions attributing moral properties to actions are true. Moral realism asserts that moral facts exist independently of our beliefs or perceptions, meaning that certain actions can be objectively right or wrong regardless of individual or cultural opinions. This perspective grounds moral judgements in an external reality, thus suggesting that ethical truths are not simply matters of personal preference or societal convention but are discoverable features of the world. This philosophical stance allows for the possibility of objective moral knowledge, where moral statements can be true or false in the same way as factual statements about the natural world. At a general level, there is great diversity and complexity of goodness within reality, as there is the goodness of natural beauty and human attributes, such as the beauty of galaxies, rivers and paintings, the litheness and power of birds and tigers, and the various admirable aspects of human beings, including their physical and mental capabilities, sense of humour and sense of colour. However, moral goodness is a distinct species, possessed by agents and their actions. The primary variety of this species is objective moral goodness, which is inherent in acts like paying one's debts or visiting the lonely, regardless of an agent's personal beliefs about the moral value of these actions. Thus, within this moral realist framework, one can distinguish between various kinds of moral goodness, where actions may be objectively good (good actions based on facts independent of personal feelings or opinions), or subjectively good (good actions based on personal feelings, tastes or opinions), supererogatory (good actions that are beyond the call of duty – commendable but not required) or obligatory (good actions that are required by duty). Also, conversely, they may be objectively bad (bad actions based on facts independent of personal feelings or opinions) or subjectively bad (bad actions based on personal feelings, tastes or opinions), and wrong (actions that are morally unacceptable or unjustifiable) or merely – Swinburne's word – 'infravetatory' (slightly blameworthy actions but not necessarily wrong).

A further important concept within the ontological structure of this moral framework is the notion of moral supervenience, where a property of one kind (e.g. moral properties) supervenes on a property of another kind (e.g. non-moral properties) if it is metaphysically necessary that for any object that has a supervening property, there is some base property such that anything with that base property also has the supervening property *because* it has the base property. This concept ensures that moral properties are not random but are systematically tied to non-moral properties. Hence, moral properties strongly supervene on non-moral properties, meaning that an action's moral status depends on its non-moral characteristics. For example, Florence Nightingale's actions are morally good because they involve caring for the sick, a non-moral property; and the moral wrongness of Hitler's invasion of Poland is due to its non-moral properties, such as being an act of aggression against a peaceful nation. Given this, there is a distinction between contingent and necessary moral truths. Contingent moral truths depend on specific non-moral facts about the world, while necessary moral truths hold across all possible worlds. For instance, it is a contingent moral truth that helping someone in a specific situation is good, but it might be a necessary moral truth that actions involving kindness are good in general. Moreover, the role of moral principles in guiding action is also an important element of this framework. This is that, moral principles

Introduction: Life, Works and Philosophical Foundations 47

are not merely hypothetical imperatives but categorical ones. Hence, moral obligations hold regardless of an individual's desires or interests, providing a firm foundation for moral duties. For instance, the principle that it is wrong to cause unnecessary suffering holds irrespective of whether someone wants to avoid causing suffering.

Epistemological Method for Morality
Another important aspect of Swinburne's ethical framework is a particular moral epistemology that focusses on the moral principles, that were noted before, and that are discovered through a combination of intuition and rational reflection – thus revealing the underlying moral truths that govern our judgements. Moreover, just as logical principles are recognised through their intrinsic nature and necessity, moral principles are recognised through reflective equilibrium and *a priori* reasoning. Reflective equilibrium, as a form of moral epistemology, involves adjusting our beliefs about specific cases and general principles until they are coherent, providing a method for discovering the logically necessary moral truths. Reflective equilibrium is thus effective as a moral epistemology because it systematically harmonises our moral intuitions with our rational reflections, leading to a more consistent and comprehensive moral framework. Moreover, within this view of the discovery of moral truths, moral disagreement and the possibility of moral progress are able to be addressed. This is that reflective equilibrium can help individuals and groups move towards agreement on moral principles by highlighting commonalities in their moral intuitions and the principles underlying their judgements. This process can lead to convergence on true moral principles over time, even among those with initially divergent views. For example, two individuals might initially disagree on the morality of capital punishment, but through reflective equilibrium, they might find common ground in the shared value of human dignity, leading to a more refined and agreed-upon principle. Similarly, societies have historically held conflicting views on the permissibility of slavery. Through reflective equilibrium, reflecting on intuitions about human equality and freedom, these views evolved, leading to a broad consensus that slavery is morally impermissible. Most children, although brought up in very different cultures, quickly acquire a concept of morally significant actions – those it is important to do or not do – and these concepts are seen as objectively true. Reflective equilibrium helps refine these moral

concepts and principles by ensuring they are coherent with our considered moral judgements. This process involves moving back and forth between specific judgements and general principles, adjusting each until a stable equilibrium is reached. For example, a child might learn that honesty is important but, through reflective equilibrium, it also comes to understand that honesty must sometimes be balanced with kindness, leading to a more nuanced understanding of when and how to tell the truth. Reflective equilibrium is not only useful for understanding moral principles but also plays a crucial role in refining our ethical frameworks. By continually reassessing and reconciling our moral intuitions with broader ethical theories, we can improve our moral understanding and address inconsistencies in our beliefs. Consider the evolving views on environmental ethics; as our understanding of ecological interdependence grows, reflective equilibrium helps integrate these insights into our moral framework, promoting more sustainable and ethical behaviour. This iterative process of reflection and adjustment helps in developing a more comprehensive and coherent ethical system that better aligns with our considered judgements and experiences.

Integrative Normative Theory

A further important part of Swinburne's ethical framework is a normative theory that serves as an integration of deontological ethics and virtue ethics. At its core, deontological ethics emphasises the importance of moral rules and duties. This aspect is evident in the focus on obligations and the moral significance of actions performed out of duty. Agents are morally responsible for their intentional actions, particularly those that fulfil obligations. Moreover, there is a distinction between obligatory acts, which are actions that one is duty-bound to perform, and supererogatory acts, which are actions that go beyond what duty requires. This clear delineation of duties is a hallmark of deontological ethics, where the rightness or wrongness of actions is determined by adherence to moral rules rather than by their consequences. Furthermore, within this ethical framework, the deontological stance is further exemplified with regard to the concept of moral responsibility, where agents are worthy of praise or blame based on their fulfilment or neglect of their duties. This includes performing actions despite significant contrary desires, which highlights the role of willpower and commitment to duty in this ethical framework. The moral worth of an action is not solely determined by its outcome but by the agent's intention and adherence to moral duties. In addition to deontological elements, the present normative framework also incorporates significant aspects of virtue ethics. Virtue ethics, rooted in Aristotelian philosophy, emphasises the development of good character and the importance of virtues in achieving moral excellence. The intrinsic goodness of certain dispositions and the importance of cultivating virtues such as courage, generosity and integrity are central. A morally good character is characterised by these virtues, and the habitual performance of virtuous actions is important for moral development. Within this normative framework, three kinds of moral goodness can be identified: objective goodness, spontaneous goodness and subjective goodness. Objective goodness, as noted previously, refers to actions that are inherently good, such as helping others or keeping promises. Spontaneous goodness pertains to the natural, unforced inclination to perform good actions, reflecting a well-developed moral character. And subjective goodness, as also noted previously, involves performing actions based on one's belief in their moral worth, even if those beliefs are mistaken. This tripartite classification underscores the importance placed on both the actions and the character of the moral agent. Thus, by integrating deontological and virtue ethics, this approach offers a comprehensive understanding of moral responsibility. It does not solely focus on the adherence to moral rules but also considers the development and expression of virtuous character traits. This dual emphasis allows for addressing a broader range of moral phenomena, from the fulfilment of specific duties to the cultivation of a virtuous life.

In all, Swinburne's ethical framework offers a comprehensive perspective that emphasises the metaphysical necessity of moral principles, the role of reflective equilibrium in discovering these principles and the categorical nature of moral obligations, which all provide a robust and coherent approach to understanding morality and guiding moral action.

One can thus see that Swinburne's philosophical framework presents a robust and nuanced approach to understanding the complexities of reality, knowledge and morality. His metaphysics delineates a clear structure of substances, properties, times and causation providing a coherent ontology that addresses the fundamental nature of reality. In epistemology, Swinburne emphasises probabilistic reasoning and the principles of credulity and testimony to explore the nature of justified belief and knowledge.

And his ethical framework integrates moral realism, the supervenience of moral properties and an integration of various elements of deontological ethics and virtue ethics. Understanding these components of Swinburne's philosophy, as unpacked in the preceding sections, is crucial for appreciating his contributions to the philosophy of religion, with this comprehension thus facilitating a deeper exploration of his philosophy-first approach to theological theorising introduced above.

Structure and Plan of Action

The structure of the chapters of this work does not follow the chronological publication scheme of Swinburne's major works as listed above but is instead organised in a manner that aligns with the structure of Swinburne's philosophical aim – moving from his defence of bare theism to that of his defence of ramified theism. More specifically, the first part of this work focusses on bare theism, exploring the coherence of theism, the existence of God, the reality of the soul, and the problem of evil. The second part delves into ramified theism, examining the Christian concept of God, atonement, the resurrection of Jesus, the Christian revelation and the rationality of believing the Christian creed. Thus, the plan of action is as follows:

> Chapter 1 focusses on Swinburne's work *The Coherence of Theism*, in which he aims to establish that the central claims of theism are logically consistent and coherent.

> Chapter 2 examines the existence of God, delving into Swinburne's *The Existence of God*, in which he evaluates the truth of theistic claims by weighing empirical evidence and rational arguments both for and against the probability of the existence of God.

> Chapter 3 addresses the problem of evil, exploring Swinburne's *Providence and the Problem of Evil*, in which he grapples with the challenge posed by the existence of evil to belief in the existence of God.

Chapter 4 looks at the existence of the soul, analysing Swinburne's *Mind, Brain, and Free Will*, in which he argues that humans are not just physical beings but also possess non-physical souls, and that this dualism allows for genuine free will and moral responsibility.

Chapter 5 investigates the Christian concept of God, examining Swinburne's *The Christian God*, which delves into the metaphysics and philosophical defensibility of the Christian doctrines of the Trinity and the Incarnation.

Chapter 6 focusses on Swinburne's *Responsibility and Atonement*, in which he defends the philosophical implications and plausibility of the Christian doctrine of atonement.

Chapter 7 examines the Resurrection, analysing Swinburne's *The Resurrection of God Incarnate*, in which he presents an argument for the probability of the resurrection of Jesus.

Chapter 8 investigates Swinburne's *Revelation: From Metaphor to Analogy*, in which he examines the nature of divine revelation and its authenticity.

Chapter 9 addresses the rationality of believing the Christian creed, delving into Swinburne's *Faith and Reason*, in which he defends the compatibility of faith and reason and the rationality of the Christian faith.

By navigating this work we shall be able to see that Swinburne's philosophical thought, grounded in analytic rigour and meticulous argumentation, provides a compelling case for the rationality of the Christian faith. By systematically addressing the coherence, evidential support and philosophical defensibility of key religious beliefs, Swinburne offers a robust foundation for the compatibility of faith and reason – thereby showing that one can indeed have a rational faith. Thus, this work will demonstrate the enduring significance of Swinburne's contributions to the fields of philosophy and theology, ultimately inviting further exploration and discussion of his ideas.

Part 1

Bare Theism

Chapter One

The Coherence of Theism

This chapter serves as an introduction to Swinburne's *The Coherence of Theism* (hereafter, *CT*), which is a comprehensive examination of the logical consistency of the central claim of theism – which is the claim that there exists a God with attributes such as omnipotence, omniscience and perfect goodness. Swinburne aims to demonstrate that these attributes are logically coherent and can coexist within a single being. The chapter introduces readers to the central aim and structure of Swinburne's arguments, situating them within the broader context of the philosophy of language. It outlines the major sections of the work, including an analysis of the logical coherence of the divine attributes, the philosophical and theological foundations of religious language, and a defence of theism against various logical challenges. By providing this overview, the chapter prepares readers to engage deeply with Swinburne's systematic and rigorous examination of the logical consistency of the central claims of theism.

The Coherence of Theism: Background

Central Aim

The central aim of *CT* is to investigate and demonstrate the coherence of theism. Swinburne seeks to establish that theism – the claim that there exists a God possessing certain defined attributes such as omnipotence, omniscience, perfect freedom, perfect goodness and others – is logically (metaphysically) possible and thus coherent. He argues that these divine properties can consistently coexist within a being that satisfies the theistic concept of God. *CT* is structured to address various philosophical challenges and objections to the coherence of theistic claims – with it involving a detailed examination of religious language, and the attributes that compose a 'contingent' and 'necessary' God. Through rigorous analysis and argumentation, Swinburne aims to show that theism is a rational and philosophically defensible position by countering claims that it is inherently contradictory or incoherent.

Historical Significance

CT was published in 1977 as the first work in Swinburne's trilogy on theism. The immediate historical context of *CT* involves debates about the logical consistency of theistic claims within the emerging field of analytic philosophy of religion, which had been reinvigorated a decade earlier through the work of Alvin Plantinga (specifically through his work *God and Other Minds*). Philosophers such as those in the logical positivist tradition famously challenged the meaningfulness of theological statements about God, arguing that such statements are not empirically verifiable and therefore lack cognitive significance. Antony Flew, on the other hand, in his essay, 'Theology and Falsification',[1] formulated the falsifiability challenge to religious claims, arguing that for a claim to be meaningful, there must be some way to falsify it, which he believed was often not possible with religious assertions. *CT* can, therefore, be seen as a response to these challenges, as it aims to show that theistic beliefs can be formulated in a meaningful, and thus logically coherent, manner. *CT* thus provided a comprehensive philosophical framework for addressing the meaning and coherence of theism.

The influence of *CT* over the decades thus led to significant scholarly engagement and debate, necessitating a revised edition in 1993. However, by 2016, Swinburne had the opportunity, through the publication of a second edition of *CT*, to refine his arguments in light of further ongoing discussions in the field of metaphysics and religious

---

1. Flew, Antony. "Theology and Falsification." In *New Essays in Philosophical Theology*, edited by Antony Flew and Alasdair MacIntyre, pp. 96-99. London: SCM Press, 1955.

language (which included advancements in the understanding of modality provided by the work of Saul Kripke and Hilary Putnam).

Literary Structure

The literary structure of *CT* is divided into three main parts: 'Religious Language', 'A Contingent God' and 'A Necessary God'. However, in following the 'philosophy-first approach' detailed in the previous chapter, it will be helpful to follow, in our exploration of *CT*, a dual structure of 'philosophical framework' and 'theological application', which we now state more fully as follows:

1. *Philosophical Framework – Modality and Language*: The first part of *CT* focusses on an analysis of modality, the nature of language and the conditions that must be satisfied for a sentence to express a coherent proposition. This part thus involves a rigorous examination of the modal notions of logical and metaphysical possibility/impossibility and necessity/contingency, the nature of religious language, and the definitions and uses of words in both mundane and theological contexts – where Swinburne analyses different accounts of how words used to describe God mean what they do, arguing that, while some theological propositions can be expressed using words in their ordinary senses, others require words to be used in analogical senses to maintain their coherence.
2. *Theological Application – The Concept of God*: The second part of *CT* focusses on applying the established philosophical framework to specific theological claims concerning the nature of God. Swinburne investigates the coherence of various divine properties such as omnipotence, omniscience, perfect freedom, perfect goodness, creative action, eternity and necessity. In performing this investigation, Swinburne examines whether it is coherent to claim that a non-embodied spirit with these properties exists and maintains that, while traditional theism's claims are complex, they can be shown to be coherent through careful philosophical analysis and, ultimately, inductive reasoning (which is introduced by Swinburne in the follow up to *CT*, *The Existence of God*).

We shall now unpack in greater detail the various areas covered in both parts of *CT*.

Themes

Philosophical Framework: Modality and Language

In this section, Swinburne introduces the philosophical framework underpinning his examination of the concept of theism. Swinburne begins with an exploration of the nature of modality and establishes criteria for assessing coherent propositions. He then extends this analysis to metaphysical possibility, discussing the roles of necessity and possibility as discovered through empirical investigation. Swinburne also analyses the nature of religious language by examining how words used in religious contexts can express coherent propositions about divine attributes. Furthermore, he also explores medieval and modern accounts of religious language, highlighting their approaches to religious language. Finally, Swinburne addresses attitude theories, critiquing the view that credal sentences merely express intentions or attitudes rather than factual propositions.

Logical Possibility

A sentence is a string of words that have meaning when put together according to grammatical rules, and words and sentences derive their meaning from the usage of a large group of speakers. A proposition is determined by the meaning of the type sentence that expresses it and the truth conditions of the token sentence that expresses it. Moreover, understanding the truth conditions of a sentence involves knowing the criteria that determine under what conditions the sentence would be true, including the commitments (or 'mini-entailments') to which a speaker is committed by asserting the sentence. This leads us to the way the meanings of words and sentences are learned through syntactic and semantic rules, i.e. we form an understanding of a word's or a sentence's meaning by learning rules for their use, which are divided into 'syntactic' and 'semantic' rules. These rules reflect the shared beliefs of the language community and define the criteria for meaning. Such rules can be explicitly taught or learned through exposure to language use. Syntactic rules state the 'mini-entailments' of a word, while semantic rules describe paradigm examples of the substances or properties to which a word correctly applies. Thus, different people might derive different beliefs about the sense of a word based on different sets of rules or paradigm examples. Nonetheless, understanding the meanings of words and the conditions under which sentences are true involves learning which sentences imply others and when sentences are true or false. If one sentence implies another, the speaker is committed to the implied sentence even if they do not fully understand it.

Now, in understanding the modal status of a proposition, one can understand that a proposition is metaphysically impossible if it involves a contradiction and metaphysically possible if it does not involve a contradiction and could be true if the world were different in some conceivable way. A metaphysically necessary proposition is one that is true regardless of how different the world could be. The primary type of metaphysically possible/impossible/necessary proposition is a logically possible/impossible/necessary proposition, which is expressed by a logically possible/impossible/necessary sentence. A logically impossible sentence must be false by virtue of purely *a priori* considerations, meaning it entails a contradiction based on the rules of the language in which it is expressed. Conversely, a logically possible sentence does not entail such a contradiction. In addition to this distinction, a proposition could be metaphysically impossible without being logically impossible if it could only be true if some other logically impossible proposition were true. Similarly, a proposition could be metaphysically necessary without being logically necessary if its negation could only be true if some different logically impossible proposition were true. Thus, a metaphysically contingent proposition is one that is neither necessary nor impossible, and a logically contingent proposition is one that is logically possible but not logically necessary.

To further refine our understanding of the nature of modality, the logical modality of sentences can be examined through the method of reflective equilibrium, a process, as noted in the previous chapter, that involves one finding a balance between different beliefs and principles. The method of reflective equilibrium involves discovering broader criteria for the application of a sentence type by considering numerous examples of its correct use. This method thus helps in determining the logical modality (possibility, necessity or impossibility) of sentences by reflecting on more and more examples of their correct application and understanding how these sentences would be used under different circumstances. More specifically, reflective equilibrium assumes that the simplest account of the use of sentences in various narrowly described sets of circumstances is the account that most likely describes how such sentences would be used under all circumstances. This approach allows us to refine our understanding of the meaning of sentences and the conditions under which they are true or false. Hence, by systematically considering paradigm examples and counterexamples, we can develop a coherent set of beliefs about the logical status of sentences, as we encounter new examples and counterexamples. This process involves an iterative examination of our initial beliefs and the logical entailments of sentences, where we adjust our understanding to achieve a balance between different beliefs and principles. Hence, by reflecting on the use of sentences in various contexts, we can better grasp their logical modality and ensure that our beliefs are coherent and justified. However, if *a priori* arguments do not lead to agreement about a sentence's logical modality, it may be possible to use an 'indirect', inductive method – based on empirical evidence and probabilistic reasoning – to show that the sentence is probably logically necessary, possible or otherwise. This approach, as with the more 'direct' approaches detailed above, assumes that logical modality can be discovered through 'armchair' reasoning, even if it requires superior cognitive abilities to survey all possible entailments and scenarios.

Metaphysical Possibility
As noted previously, the logical modality of a sentence – that is, whether it is logically impossible, necessary or possible – is constituted by whether it or its negation entails a contradiction, and is something discoverable *a priori*, at least by a superior being if not by ordinary humans. Traditionally, it was taken to be the case that there is no stronger form of impossibility than logical impossibility, and there is no stronger form of necessity than logical necessity. However, in the 1970s, the philosophers Saul Kripke, in his work *Naming and Necessity* (1980),[2] and Hilary Putnam, in his paper 'The Meaning of Meaning',[3] highlighted the existence of many sentences and their negations which did not seem to entail any contradiction but appeared to be necessarily true or necessarily false with a strength equivalent to logical necessity or impossibility. These sentences are referred to as '*a posteriori*'

---

2. Kripke, *Naming*, pp. 96-105.
3. Putnam, " Meaning.", pp. 140-143.

metaphysically necessary or impossible because their necessary truth or falsity is dependent on logically contingent facts. These facts are discoverable only through empirical investigation, such as scientific or historical research, rather than through mere reflection on the meanings of the sentences used to describe the world. Thus, these sentences' metaphysical necessity or impossibility is determined by their dependence on logically contingent facts, making their modal status discoverable only *a posteriori*. Putnam demonstrated the idea that some sentences are metaphysically necessary but not logically necessary with the example 'water is H_2O'. In the early nineteenth century, 'water' was used to refer to the clear, drinkable liquid found in rivers and seas, but people did not know its chemical composition. They used 'water' as a term for the substance, not knowing it was H_2O. Once it was discovered that water is H_2O, this fact was now taken to be a metaphysically necessary truth because the substance in our rivers and seas is essentially H_2O. That is, this fact does not entail a contradiction if negated, making it logically contingent but metaphysically necessary. Before this discovery, the necessity of 'water is H_2O' was not known *a priori* but only subsequently through scientific investigation. Moreover, according to Kripke, the same could also be said for identities such as 'Hesperus is Phosphorus' (where, as noted previously, Hesperus and Phosphorus both refer to the planet Venus), which are metaphysically necessary but logically contingent because their necessity is based on the contingent fact that Hesperus and Phosphorus are the same object. That is, this fact is discoverable only through empirical observation and not through *a priori* reasoning.

To shed further light on the notion of identity across possible worlds, Kripke and Putnam introduced the concepts of rigid and non-rigid designators. Rigid designators, as noted previously, are terms that refer to the same object in every possible world where that object exists. For example, proper names such as 'Aristotle' or 'Hesperus' are considered rigid designators because they refer to the same individual or celestial body in all possible worlds where they exist. On the other hand, non-rigid designators, such as 'the teacher of Alexander the Great' or 'the evening star', may refer to different objects in different possible worlds, depending on the circumstances. These distinctions help to clarify the nature of identity statements and their modal status, as the necessity or contingency of such statements can be determined by the rigidity of the designators involved. Despite the apparent clarity of the distinction between *a priori* and *a posteriori* necessities, one can challenge the notion of *a posteriori* necessities altogether through the introduction of 'informative' and 'uninformative' designators – where for an informative designator to be provided, it is necessary that anyone who understands the term also understands the conditions under which it applies (or the defining words used). Conversely, uninformative designators refer to terms where there may exist situations where we are uncertain about its appropriate application. For instance, 'red' is an informative designator because we can recognise something as red if it looks like a known red object under normal conditions. Similarly, properties such as 'fragile' or '10 metres long' are informative because we can determine their truth through observation or experience without needing to know their underlying essence. In contrast, 'jade' is uninformative because it can refer to a wide range of things such a colour, the minerals nephrite or jadeite, a flirtatious girl or a disreputable woman etc., requiring further analysis to determine its exact nature. So, given this distinction in designation, the appearance of *a posteriori* necessity arises from the use of uninformative designators in identity statements. Consider Kripke's example of 'Everest' and 'Gaurisanker': these two names refer to the same mountain, but this fact is discoverable only through empirical investigation. In earlier times, explorers named a mountain seen from Tibet 'Everest' and a different-looking mountain seen from Nepal 'Gaurisanker'. These names referred to the same mountain, but this was only learnt through exploration. Hence, the statement 'Everest is Gaurisanker' is necessarily true because it refers to the same mountain, although this necessity was discovered empirically and not through *a priori* reasoning. Thus, Kripke argues that the statement 'Everest is Gaurisanker' is an example of an *a posteriori* necessary truth.[4] However, it can be understood that the apparent necessity of this statement is due to the uninformative nature of the designators 'Everest' and 'Gaurisanker' – that is, these names do not convey any information about the essential (intrinsic) properties of the mountain they refer to. In contrast, if we replace these uninformative designators with informative ones, such as 'the tallest mountain in the world' for 'Everest' and 'the mountain located at such-and-such coordinates' for 'Gaurisanker', the necessity of the identity statement becomes accessible *a priori*. Hence, by using 'informative designators'

---

4. Kripke, *Naming*, p.100.

that capture the essential properties of the objects they refer to, the necessity of the identity statement can be determined through logical reasoning alone, without the need for empirical investigation. This can then be extended to other examples of *a posteriori* necessities, such as 'water is H_2O', for, by replacing the uninformative designator 'water' with the informative designator 'H_2O', the necessity of the identity statement becomes a matter of logical necessity rather than *a posteriori* necessity. Thus, given all of this, one can understand that the apparent distinction that has been drawn between metaphysical and logical modalities is, in fact, a false distinction – as metaphysical necessity (possibility and impossibility) is reducible to logical necessity (possibility and impossibility), and thus the apparent *a posteriori* status of some necessary truths is merely a result of the use of uninformative designators in our language. Therefore, these truths, and other forms of modal truths, are, in fact, discoverable *a priori*.

The Words of Theology

Theology uses words of ordinary language in their normal senses, and also gives new senses to these words. Many theological terms such as 'wise', 'good' and 'powerful' are used in their mundane senses when referring to non-theological matters. Moreover, even technical theological terms such as 'omnipotent' and 'omniscient' can be defined using ordinary words, implying that theology often relies on the ordinary senses of words. In exploring the implications of theology using ordinary words in their mundane senses, one can understand that theology can describe an unfamiliar world by attributing ordinary properties to unusual degrees or combinations. For example, God is described as a very powerful person, more so than any known human, and his power is combined with perfect goodness. Conceiving a very different world by extending familiar properties to extraordinary levels is indeed plausible, as science often uses ordinary words to describe phenomena beyond normal human experience, such as atoms and molecules, which indicates that theology can similarly use mundane words to convey extraordinary theological concepts. The proponent of the atomic theory of chemistry, for example, describes solids, liquids and gases consisting of millions of molecules, using ordinary words like 'particle' and 'group' in their common senses, but applied to much smaller scales. Similarly, theologians describe God's attributes using ordinary language, suggesting these attributes exist in extraordinary degrees or combinations.

Now, in considering the possibility that theology assigns new senses to ordinary words, such words are to be used analogically (in a 'stretched sense'), meaning that they retain some but not all of their previous meanings. For instance, 'wisdom' attributed to God shares some characteristics with 'wisdom' in humans but also differs significantly. Analogical senses allow words to apply to God in ways that extend their mundane uses. For example, the word 'person' can be used analogically to describe God, even though God is not a person in the mundane sense. Hence, understanding these new analogical senses involves learning new syntactic or semantic rules. To further illustrate how new senses can be introduced to describe unfamiliar phenomena, one can imagine a community of humans born blind, isolated from sighted humans. They are intelligent and have developed their other senses well, distinguishing objects of touch, hearing, smell and taste. Moreover, they describe touch objects as 'hard' or 'soft', 'sharp' or 'blunt' and so on. However, they have no words for colours. Now, a genius in this community proposes that humans might have a fifth sense to detect properties undetectable by the other four senses. He suggests using 'loud' and 'sharp' in new analogical senses to describe these properties. To do this, he amends the syntactic and semantic rules: an object can be 'loud' or 'sharp' if it resembles paradigm examples of loud or sharp objects more than it resembles quiet or blunt objects. Additionally, he suggests that 'loud' or 'quiet' could also describe properties of surfaces, not just noises. The genius gives the community models for 'loud' or 'quiet' in the wider sense, postulating properties common to sounds and surfaces. This scenario illustrates how new senses can be introduced to describe unfamiliar phenomena. In reality we can also see that quantum theory parallels this, where light behaves both as particles and waves, leading to the use of analogical senses for these terms to describe light's dual nature. This is that light exhibits wave-like behaviour in phenomena such as interference and diffraction, and particle-like behaviour in phenomena such as the photoelectric effect. This requires extending the definitions of 'wave' and 'particle' so that they are no longer mutually exclusive but instead describe different aspects of the same entity, photons. In theology, similar extensions occur, as words such as 'powerful' and 'wise' are stretched analogically to describe God's attributes, in a way that exceeds human experience. Hence, just as quantum theory uses 'wave' and 'particle' in new, broader senses, theology uses familiar terms in new ways to articulate the nature of God.

It is important to note that, with regard to the nature of metaphor, a word used analogically has a newly established sense and can be consistently used in that sense across different contexts. In contrast, a metaphor's meaning varies with its context, and the proposition expressed by a metaphorical sentence depends on surrounding sentences and cultural background. While metaphor is common in biblical texts, creeds usually aim for expression of clear doctrine and thus use words in mundane or analogical senses. However, some metaphors do appear in creeds, such as describing Christ as 'light from light' in the Nicene Creed (the authoritative declaration of belief of mainstream Christianity produced by the Council of Nicaea [325 CE]), which requires understanding the cultural and religious context to grasp its full meaning. The use of analogical senses in theology is thus akin to how metaphors in scientific theories help describe phenomena that do not fit neatly into existing categories, thus enhancing our understanding through extended meanings.

Medieval Accounts of Religious Language
The use of ordinary words in special ways to describe God is a common theme in theological discourse. Theologians, such as Saint Basil of Caesarea, believed that, while humans could understand some aspects of God on Earth, a fuller understanding would only come in the afterlife. Basil argued, in his work *Against Eunomius*[5], that humans could know God's properties or 'energies', such as his greatness, power, wisdom and goodness, without implying that these terms were used in unusual senses. This distinction emphasised the Eastern Church's perspective on the knowability of God's energies versus his essence. However, this perspective shifted in the next century when Pseudo-Dionysius introduced, in his work *The Divine Names and The Mystical Theology*,[6] the notion of the *via negativa*, claiming that God's essence is incomprehensible and that we can only understand what God is not, rather than what he is. This led to the assertion that positive statements about God, such as 'God is good',

---

5. Basil of Caesarea. *Against Eunomius*. Translated by Mark DelCogliano and Andrew Radde-Gallwitz. The Fathers of the Church: A New Translation, vol. 122. Washington, D.C.: The Catholic University of America Press, 2011.
6. Pseudo-Dionysius the Areopagite. *The Divine Names and The Mystical Theology*. Translated by C.E. Rolt. Mineola, NY: Dover Publications, 2004.

should be interpreted negatively or causally, which is insufficient to capture the essence of theistic claims.

Saint Thomas Aquinas responded, in his *Summa Theologica* I, Q. 12,[7] to the *via negativa* by asserting that positive statements about God do convey some understanding of his nature. Aquinas proposed that these statements are used analogically, meaning the properties signified are the same, but the way they are present in God differs from their presence in creatures. For instance, Aquinas argued that knowledge, whether in humans or God, shares the same fundamental characteristics but manifests differently. Human knowledge involves potentiality and fallibility, whereas God's knowledge is infallible and ever-present. Thus, predicates such as 'wise' and 'good' are used analogically when applied to God, reflecting a difference in the mode of signification rather than the property itself. Moreover, Aquinas argued that names would be meaningless if they did not help us understand something about the being they describe. That is, if the names used for God and creatures were entirely different in meaning (purely equivocal), we should gain no understanding of God through those names, as their meanings are derived from their use for creatures. Thus, it would be pointless to describe God as a being, as good, or similar terms. Therefore, when we use the same words for both humans and God, we do so analogically, meaning the terms reflect a similarity in meaning but differ in application between humans and God. However, in saying this, Aquinas recognised that the property signified (*res significata*) in statements like 'God knows that p' and 'Socrates knows that p' is the same. For Aquinas, 'univocally' means 'in the same sense' (*significatio*) and the modern sense of 'univocal' is that of a word being used to signify the same property. Therefore, according to Aquinas, words such as 'good' and 'powerful' are actually used univocally when applied to both God and humans. Subsequent to Aquinas, Duns Scotus argued, in his *Ordinatio*,[8] more explicitly, for a univocal application of terms such as 'existence', 'wisdom' and

---

7. Thomas Aquinas. *Summa Theologica*. Translated by Fathers of the English Dominican Province. New York: Benziger Bros., 1947. First Part, Question 12.

8. Duns Scotus, John. *Ordinatio*. In Duns Scotus on the Will and Morality, edited and translated by Allan B. Wolter, pp. 20-457. Washington, D.C.: Catholic University of America Press, 1986.

'goodness' to both God and creatures. This is because he believed these terms retain the same meaning across different contexts but vary in the degree or manner of their application. For Scotus, this univocal application was crucial for theological inquiry, as it provided a consistent and accessible conceptual framework to discuss divine and human attributes.

In the twentieth century, theological discussions evolved further as modern theologians and philosophers continued to explore how ordinary words can describe the divine attributes. Ian Ramsey introduced the concept of 'models' and 'qualifiers' in religious language, through his work *Religious Language: An Empirical Placing of Theological Phrases,* [9] suggesting that terms like 'God is good' use human models of goodness but are qualified to reflect divine attributes. Hence, Ramsey emphasised the distinctive logical behaviour of religious language and the use of multiple models to capture complex theological concepts. Building on Ramsey's ideas, I.M. Crombie, in his work *An Examination of Plato's Doctrines,* offered a more detailed account,[10] suggesting that predicates in theology are used analogically and that terms like 'God loves us' require a deliberate departure from normal language practice. Crombie argued that these terms affirm a parable and express a resemblance between human and divine properties, even if the exact nature of this resemblance remains beyond full human comprehension.

Adding another layer to the discussion, William Alston provided, his book *Divine Nature and Human Language: Essays in Philosophical Theology*[11], a functionalist account, that paralleled Immanuel Kant's earlier ideas, featured in his work *the Critique of Pure Reason*[12]. Alston claimed that psychological properties such as belief and intention are defined by their functional roles within a network of states that influence behaviour. Functionalism, in this context, thus aims to

---

9. Ramsey, Ian T. *Religious Language: An Empirical Placing of Theological Phrases.* Eugene, OR: Wipf and Stock, 2011.
10. Crombie, I. M. *An Examination of Plato's Doctrines.* 2 vols. London: Routledge and Kegan Paul, 1962-1963.
11. Alston, William P. *Divine Nature and Human Language: Essays in Philosophical Theology.* Ithaca, NY: Cornell University Press, 1989.
12. Kant, Immanuel. *Critique of Pure Reason.* Translated by Paul Guyer and Allen W. Wood. Cambridge: Cambridge University Press, 1998.

understand the divine attributes based on their roles and effects rather than their intrinsic nature. This approach allows human concepts to be applied to divine properties in a coherent manner. Alston thus argued that this framework could be applied to the divine properties, allowing terms like 'God's beliefs' to be understood through their effects on the world, even if the underlying nature of these beliefs differs radically from human beliefs. Alston's functionalist approach thus aligns with Kant's view that religious language uses analogies to describe the relationship between God and the world, similar to the relationship between humans and their actions.

Attitude Theories
Credal sentences are meaningful and usually express propositions that make claims about realities beyond sensory experience. However, contrasting views emerged in the twentieth century, when some writers denied that religious utterances, particularly credal sentences, express propositions. They argued that these utterances express intentions to live in certain ways, attitudes of approval for certain behaviour, or something else entirely. One prominent advocate of this anti-realist view was R.B. Braithwaite, who claimed, in his work *An Empiricist's View of the Nature of Religious Belief*,[13] that religious assertions express an intention to follow a moral behaviour policy, accompanied by implicit or explicit statements of certain stories. For instance, stories about Jesus Christ or the creation of the world serve to illustrate examples of desirable behaviour. Thus, according to Braithwaite, these stories provide a behavioural framework, rather than serving as factual assertions about historical or supernatural events. Religious language, in his view, is similar to a moral guide rather than a declaration of metaphysical truths. Braithwaite argued that religious believers are essentially committing to a behaviour, rather than asserting beliefs in the ordinary sense. He suggested that credal sentences function similarly to moral sentences, guiding conduct without necessarily being verifiable or expressing factual propositions. Despite Braithwaite's compelling argument, one can point out that, even if religious utterances commit individuals to certain behaviour, this does not capture the full meaning of credal

---

13. Braithwaite, R.B. *An Empiricist's View of the Nature of Religious Belief.* Cambridge University Press, 1955.

sentences, as credal sentences do appear to express propositions about reality. Furthermore, non-Christians might adopt similar behaviour inspired by Christian stories without using credal sentences or being considered Christian believers. When people lose their faith, they typically cease to assert credal sentences because they no longer believe the metaphysical claims, not because they abandon certain behaviour. Moreover, Braithwaite's account is influenced by verificationism, which was a philosophical theory dominant in the mid-twentieth century that held that statements must be empirically verifiable to be meaningful. However, propositions do not need to be verifiable to express meaningful claims; more so, credal propositions can be 'weakly verifiable' in a way similar to scientific hypotheses. Weakly verifiable statements are those that cannot be directly confirmed or falsified through empirical observation but that can be indirectly supported by their consistency with other established facts, theoretical coherence and their explanatory power within a given framework. Hence, credal propositions are weakly verifiable in that they gain support through their coherence with the broader religious worldview and their explanatory role within that context.

Now, opposing the anti-realist view were proponents of Wittgensteinian fideism, such as D.Z. Phillips. Wittgenstein's concept of language games, which studies the usage and context of sentences within different forms of discourse, influenced Phillips' view. Phillips argued, in his work *Faith and Philosophical Enquiry*,[14] that religious language constitutes its own language game, independent of other language games like science or history. Moreover, Phillips claimed that religious utterances should be understood within their own context and criteria, rather than being judged by the standards of other disciplines. Phillips suggested that understanding religious language involves studying when and where religious sentences are used and their purpose. Phillips emphasised that religious concepts have meaning within the context of religious practice, not in comparison to other forms of language. For Phillips, religious language expresses the right moral or emotional attitude towards the world and proper behaviour, rather than making factual claims about history or a suprasensible reality. This approach aligns with Wittgenstein's notion that the meaning of

---

14. Phillips, D.Z. *Faith and Philosophical Enquiry*. Routledge & Kegan Paul, 1970.

a word is its use in the language, underscoring that religious language has its own logic and grammar distinct from scientific discourse. However, Phillips' account faces criticism for misrepresenting the intentions of the vast majority of religious language users. That is, most believers who pray for something genuinely hope their prayers will influence events, similar to petitioning an earthly ruler. Moreover, phrases such as 'the Resurrection of the Dead' have traditionally been understood as affirming beliefs in survival after death, not just expressing moral attitudes. These criticisms highlight that religious language historically aims to convey specific theological truths and existential claims about the nature of reality, God and human destiny, rather than merely functioning as moral or emotive expressions. In other words, religious language has historically been used to make factual claims about God's nature, actions and the afterlife.

In conclusion, Swinburne's philosophical framework offers a foundational understanding of how logical and metaphysical modality informs theological discourse. By distinguishing between logical and metaphysical necessity, he clarifies the nature of propositions and their truth conditions. Moreover, Swinburne's examination of theological language reveals the complexities of using ordinary words to convey extraordinary religious concepts, balancing the use of mundane and analogical senses. Furthermore, the survey of medieval and modern perspectives on religious language underscores the ongoing effort to articulate the divine attributes coherently. Finally, Swinburne's critique of attitude theories reaffirms the significance of credal sentences as expressions of factual propositions about a suprasensible reality, thus setting the stage for a deeper exploration of the CT's central tenets.

Theological Application: The Concept of God

In this section, Swinburne extends his philosophical framework to explore the nature of theism within the context of his broader argument. He begins by defining the nature and characteristics of persons, particularly focussing on the concept of a non-embodied, omnipresent spirit, which is central to understanding God in various theistic traditions. Swinburne then addresses the attributes of God as the creator of the universe and examines the logical coherence of God's omnipotence, omniscience, perfect freedom, perfect goodness, eternal (everlasting) existence and necessity. Through a meticulous analysis of these divine properties, Swinburne aims to demonstrate their logical possibility and coherence, ultimately arguing for the coherence of the theistic conception of God.

An Omnipresent Spirit

A spirit is a person without a body, and thus the fundamental theistic claim is that God, who is identified as an omnipresent spirit, is a non-embodied person. A person is defined as a mental substance, characterised by having mental properties essentially. A mental substance necessitates the presence of mental properties, and a 'pure mental substance' requires only pure mental properties (i.e., properties that do not require the instantiation of physical properties) for its existence, whilst a physical substance requires only physical properties. Mental properties include perceiving objects and intentionally performing actions, which entail 'privileged access' by the subject experiencing them. However, mental properties can also include physical components, such as seeing a door and involving the physical existence of a door. There are also such things as neutral properties, which are neither mental nor physical, like formal or disjunctive properties. These properties indicate that some attributes are accessible through experience, yet do not fit neatly into mental or physical categories.

Now, mental events, to which a person has privileged access, are crucial in further conceptualising a mental substance. There are five kinds of pure mental events: sensations, thoughts, intentions, beliefs and desires. Sensations, thoughts and intentions are conscious events, while beliefs and desires, though not always conscious, can become so. The capacity to have conscious events is itself a pure mental event, which highlights the intrinsic mental nature of human beings. Humans are thus defined as mental substances with sophisticated propositional events, capable of beliefs, thoughts, intentions and moral judgements.

Intentional actions are also important for identifying persons, where an intentional action is an action that is guided by an intention, usually involving bodily movements. That is, intentional actions are understood as those driven by an intention that an agent actively tries to realise, often through bodily movements. Whereas, instrumentally basic actions, such as moving an arm, are done without needing a belief about how to do them, unlike more complex actions requiring such beliefs. This distinction underscores the innate capability to perform certain actions without deliberation, contrasting with actions that necessitate deliberation. In addition to this, there is a distinction between instrumentally and causally basic actions, with the latter being actions initiated by trying, which inevitably succeed if attempted. Causally basic actions, which are primarily intentions, thus highlight the fundamental nature of 'trying' as an immediate, successful action. Thus, most bodily actions involve non-intentionally causing internal bodily events, whereas causally basic actions are primarily intentions.

To explore what it means for a person to have a body, one can further investigate the possible relationships had by physical objects, with five aspects being identified: bodily disturbances causing sensations, awareness of bodily states, the ability to move body parts directly, perception from the body's location, and non-rational effects of bodily states on thoughts and feelings. These aspects delineate the physical interdependencies of bodily experience, contrasting with the divine omnipresence that transcends these limitations; God, as an omnipresent spirit, is not limited by these aspects. God can move any part of the universe directly, knows what happens everywhere without causal chains and is not confined to a particular location or dependent on the universe to act or know. This description aligns with the classical theological view that God, by virtue of his omnipotence and omniscience, operates beyond the constraints of physical embodiment. Thus, God is not embodied in the traditional sense, but as an omnipresent spirit, he can cause effects and acquire knowledge directly.

Now, arguments against the logical possibility of a spirit often focus on the necessity of a body for expressing pure mental properties. In addressing these arguments, it is important to note that pure mental properties do not inherently require a body for their expression. A person can have unexpressed wants or fears, and a spirit can express these through actions affecting the physical world. For instance, an omnipresent spirit could influence weather patterns to express concern or manifest messages in natural formations to communicate desires. Thus, against Terence Penelhum's claim, in his encyclopaedia entry 'Personal Identity',[15] that identifying criteria are necessary

---

15. Penelhum, Terence. "Personal Identity." In *The Encyclopedia of Philosophy*, edited by Paul Edwards, pp. 95-107. New York: Macmillan, 1967.

for non-embodied persons, one can say that personal identity is an ultimate (basic) fact, not reducible to physical or mental properties, and thus it is indeed logically possible for there to be a person without a body.

Consider a thought experiment to illustrate this further: imagine a person gradually losing the ability to be affected by physical substances like alcohol or drugs, while his rational thinking remains unaffected. Suppose this person no longer feels physical pains, aches or thrills, yet becomes aware of events in other bodies and objects. He is able to perform actions like moving objects or communicating across distances without any physical intermediaries. Despite these changes, the person retains his capacity for thinking, reasoning and feeling. This scenario, although extraordinary, is conceivable and demonstrates that personal identity can exist independently of physical continuity. Hence, it is logically possible for an omnipresent spirit to exist, as the essence of personal identity does not rely on physical or mental continuity alone.

Hence, in delving into the nature of personal identity, complex theories, which analyse identity through bodily and mental continuity, are to be contrasted with the 'simple theory' that sees personal identity as an ultimate, unanalysable fact. Complex theories often falter under scenarios where bodily or mental continuity is ambiguous, whereas simple theories assert identity as an inherent, indivisible reality. While bodily and mental continuity provide evidence of identity, they do not constitute it. Moreover, as thought experiments, such as the previously adduced one, demonstrate that personal identity can persist without any physical or mental continuity, ultimately, there is indeed support for the logical possibility of the existence of a (non-embodied) omnipresent spirit.

Free and Creator of the World

The theist claims God is the creator of the world or the universe, understood in both narrow and wide senses. In the narrow sense, it includes all physical and mental substances spatially related to the Earth, while the wide sense encompasses all substances, including those not spatially related to us or any purely mental substances. God is asserted to be the creator of all things, visible and invisible, as stated in the Nicene Creed. To clarify this claim, it must be qualified to exclude God himself and any abstract objects, such as numbers or logical relations, which exist necessarily and independently. Theists typically believe that God's action is needed not only for the beginning of existence but also for its continuation, thus making God both the creator and sustainer of all things. While natural reason alone cannot prove whether the universe had a beginning or has always existed, it can prove the existence of a creator. Therefore, God sustains the universe in existence at each moment, making him the creator of the universe in a continuous sense.

Now, in exploring the relationship between causation and laws of nature, David Hume's regularity theory, introduced in his works *A Treatise of Human Nature* and *An Enquiry Concerning Human Understanding*,[16] defines laws as universal regularities in event patterns – with some modern philosophers having expanded this to include statistical laws and the distinction between fundamental and non-fundamental laws[17]. Nonetheless, according to Hume, causation is determined by laws of nature, and an event causes another if it belongs to kinds related by these laws. However, an alternative theory, the relations-between-universals (RBU) account, suggests that laws are contingent relations between properties, such as the law of gravity being a relation of physical necessity. Moreover, the substances-powers-and-liabilities (SPL) theory posits that causation is an unanalysable relation between substances and their effects, defined by the causal powers and liabilities of substances. The RBU theory aligns with the SPL account, as both involve substances exercising causal influence, although the SPL theory emphasises personal agency and intention, and thus the latter account is the best way to understand divine and human action.

To further understand God's actions, theism claims God's actions are free, meaning they are not causally influenced by anything external to him. That is, God acts because he chooses to, driven by reason alone, and not by non-rational causes. This contrasts with human actions, which are influenced by various causal factors. A perfectly free person, therefore, is not influenced by non-rational factors and acts solely based on reason. As noted previously, an intentional action

---

16. Hume, David. *A Treatise of Human Nature*. Edited by L. A. Selby-Bigge. 2nd ed. Oxford: Clarendon Press, 1978. (Original work published 1739-1740); Hume, *An Enquiry*.
17. Such as the theory provided in Lewis, David. *Philosophical Papers*, Volume II. Oxford: Oxford University Press, 1987.

involves doing something with a purpose or reason, which must be regarded as a good thing. Now, a person cannot act without a reason, and thus, a perfectly free agent will always choose the action he believes to be the best. However, when faced with multiple equally good actions, a perfectly free person will choose one without being governed by reason. That is, there are scenarios where God might have to choose between an infinite number of actions, each better than the last – and thus, there might not always be the best possible action – and hence there being no unique best action available to God. In such cases, reason does not dictate which action to take, allowing God to choose freely.

Omnipotent

Traditionally, within patristic and medieval thought, omnipotence has typically been conceptualised as the ability to cause any event or perform any intentional action. Nevertheless, it is quite clear that issues arise, particularly regarding logically impossible events, which cannot be caused by any being due to their inherent contradictions. Recognising these issues, Aquinas instead asserted, in his work *Summa Theologica* I, Q. 25, Art.3,[18] that God's omnipotence does not extend to logically impossible events, as these do not fall within the realm of the feasible. This viewpoint can be considered an initial step towards a coherent account of omnipotence, which can be made more precise through examining additional concepts such as instants of time, the direction of causation, the relationship between omnipotence and free will, and certain paradoxes that have been raised against the cogency of omnipotence. In understanding the relationship between events occurring at instants of time and over periods of time one can propose two theories: the I-theory, which posits that events can occur at instants independently of periods, and the P-theory, which asserts that events at instants are fundamentally linked to periods of time. In this context, one can affirm the veracity of the P-theory as instants are zero-dimensional boundaries of one-dimensional periods. Consequently, an event happening at an instant is fundamentally to be analysed in terms of what happens over periods of time. This implication suggests that an omnipotent being must be able to cause events over periods of time rather than at isolated instances.

---

18. Aquinas, *Summa*. First Part, Question 25, Article 3.

Accordingly, when addressing the direction of causation, one needs to analyse the logical possibility of backward or simultaneous causation. That is, as causation is asserted to be a relation between a substance and an event – understood as the exercise of causal influence – in applying the P-theory, one can take simultaneous direct causation to be impossible because a cause must act over a period that encompasses both the time before the event and the time during the event. Similarly, backward causation can also be taken to be logically impossible, as no event at a later time can cause an earlier event. The impossibility of backward and simultaneous causation thus allows one to refine the definition of omnipotence by elucidating the temporal constraints on causation.

Furthermore, in examining the relationship between omnipotence and free will, we must consider the logical possibility of an omnipotent being who is also perfectly free and omniscient. This exploration reveals that an omnipotent being, to be truly omnipotent, must act without any non-rational influences, as true freedom entails making choices based solely on rationality – and thus goodness. This means an omnipotent being cannot perform an action believed to be bad or less good than the best (or equally best) possible action. Consequently, an omnipotent being must have complete knowledge of the past and the present in order to discern the best possible actions, ensuring that every action taken is the best or equally good. Thus, an omnipotent being inherently possesses other divine properties, such as omniscience and perfect freedom – that is, the latter properties are entailed by the possession of the former property. Such a being will be a person with the capability to intentionally cause events and possess knowledge of all places and events without dependence on external sources. Moreover, this being will also be the creator and sustainer of the universe, causing or permitting all logically contingent events. Therefore, an omnipotent being will be perfectly free, only performing actions that are rationally justified as the best or good, possess knowledge of all past and present events and be the creator and sustainer of all reality.

Now, on the basis of all of these considerations, one can understand that for a being to be considered omnipotent during some period T, it must satisfy several criteria. First and foremost, in each sub-period within T, the being must know all logically necessary propositions and all logically contingent true propositions about every time earlier than the beginning of that sub-period, as well as all the propositions entailed by those propositions. Second, the being must not be influenced by non-rational influences, ensuring that its actions are perfectly rational and free from external or internal compulsion. Third, the being must be able to cause by an act beginning at any instant t and ending at any instant t_2, both during that period, any logically contingent event M beginning at any instant t_1 later than t and ending at t_2, which does not require the being to be influenced by non-rational influences in order to perform that act.

This refined definition allows one to also address the well-known paradox of the stone, which questions whether an omnipotent being can create a stone too heavy for itself to lift. The paradox presents a challenge to the concept of omnipotence by suggesting a potential contradiction: if an omnipotent being can create such a stone, then it is not omnipotent because it cannot lift it; if it cannot create the stone, then it is not omnipotent because there is something it cannot create. In response, one can argue that an omnipotent being can avoid this contradiction by simply not being able to create such a stone. The reasoning here is that if an omnipotent being is essentially everlasting and omnipotent (as will be argued later), then creating a stone it cannot lift would imply its own non-existence, as it would contradict its essential properties. An omnipotent being, by definition, cannot cause an event at t that would negate its own omnipotence or existence. Therefore, the paradox does not successfully undermine the possibility of an omnipotent being, as the scenario it proposes is logically inconsistent with the nature of omnipotence. Moreover, even if it is posited that an omnipotent being could lose its omnipotence by performing certain actions, it would not perform such actions. As noted previously, the nature of omnipotence includes omniscience and perfect freedom to avoid actions of a non-rational nature – and performing an action that would result in self-contradiction or loss of omnipotence is exactly an action of this type. Therefore, the possibility of losing omnipotence through certain actions does not undermine this concept, as an omnipotent being would inherently possess the discretion to avoid such scenarios, maintaining its omnipotence indefinitely. Similarly, the McEar objection, introduced into the literature by Plantinga, in his work *God, and Other Minds*, and which posits a being that can only perform one action (e.g. scratching its left ear) and is therefore considered omnipotent in that very limited sense, can also be addressed by this refined definition.[19] The McEar objection aims to trivialise omnipotence by suggesting that a being with an extremely narrow capability could still be deemed omnipotent if that capability is the only one it has and it can perform it without limit. However, the refined definition ensures that an omnipotent being must have the capacity to cause any logically possible event within its power. This broader scope of causal capabilities inherently excludes beings with such narrowly defined abilities. A being limited to a single trivial action, such as scratching its left ear, does not meet the criteria for omnipotence under this definition because it lacks the comprehensive ability to cause any possible event. Thus, the refined definition of omnipotence inherently excludes the McEar objection by requiring a broader and more substantial range of capabilities, ensuring that true omnipotence cannot be trivialised by such narrowly defined and limited examples.

Omniscience

A person is omniscient at a particular time if he knows of all true propositions that they are true at that time. Initially, this seems logically possible since people can know a lot, so why not everything? However, an objection based on arguments from A.N. Prior, in his article 'The Formalities of Omniscience',[20] and Norman Kretzmann, in his paper 'Omniscience and Immutability',[21] raises a challenge. They claim that a person could be omniscient in this sense only if he were the only person and it was the only moment of time. This challenges the understanding of God's omniscience above, as it includes knowledge of the actions of many people over many moments. In addition to this, according to Kretzmann, some propositions, such as 'it is now t_1', can only be known at t_1. Similarly, personal knowledge such as Jones knowing 'I am in hospital' is exclusive to Jones at that time. Thus, God's omniscience must address these indexical propositions that are tied to specific times, places or people, which complicates the coherent account of omniscience. This

---

19. Plantinga, *Minds*, pp. 168-173.
20. Prior, A.N. "The Formalities of Omniscience." *Philosophy* 37, no. 140 (1962): pp. 114-129.
21. Kretzmann, Norman. "Omniscience and Immutability." *The Journal of Philosophy* 63, no. 14 (1966): pp. 409-421.

suggests that omniscience should be understood not only as knowing of all true propositions that they are true but also as a comprehension of the meaning and references of these propositions, which is a more nuanced understanding than simply knowing everything. Therefore, defining omniscience as knowing of all true propositions that they are true, including understanding the specific context and reference of each proposition, presents a more accurate and coherent account of what it means to be omniscient.

Within the various theistic religions (Judaism, Christianity and Islam), humans are taken to have the freedom to choose between good and evil, and God, according to individuals such as Saint Augustine of Hippo and Aquinas (and other luminaries), is taken to have complete foreknowledge of these choices – omniscience in the 'strong sense'. However, despite the weight of tradition in support of this position, one can understand that if God foreknows human actions, those actions clearly cannot be free – that is, knowing these actions would contradict the nature of ('libertarian') free will, which is the ability to do otherwise without causal influence. This issue can be further seen by taking into account Nelson Pike's argument, which asserts that a belief held at a specific time about a future event is a 'hard fact' – a fixed event determined by past and present circumstances that cannot be altered by future actions. Thus, if, for instance, God knows in 1974 that Jones will mow the lawn in 1976, this belief in 1974 is a hard fact and cannot be altered by future events. Therefore, if Jones has libertarian free will in 1976, his action cannot be predetermined by God's prior knowledge. This also creates a problem concerning God's foreknowledge of his own future actions, as knowledge of these actions would also negate his freedom to choose otherwise. Hence, in order to preserve free will, one must assert that even an omnipotent being cannot have foreknowledge of future free choices.

Moreover, divine foreknowledge presents problems concerning the cogency of moral responsibility because, if all actions are foreknown by God, it implies a form of determinism that undercuts the libertarian notion of free will, which is essential for genuine moral responsibility. As noted previously, libertarian free will requires that individuals have the ability to choose otherwise in any given situation, making them the ultimate source of their actions. If God possesses complete foreknowledge of human actions, it implies that these actions are predetermined and fixed, negating the possibility of individuals being true originators of their actions. This thus undermines the basis for moral culpability, as individuals cannot be held morally responsible for actions that they were predetermined to perform. For example, consider the biblical story of Jonah and the city of Nineveh. God tells Jonah to warn Nineveh of its impending destruction due to its wickedness. However, the people of Nineveh repent, and God spares the city, changing his initial plan based on their actions. This story illustrates a scenario where human free will (the people of Nineveh choosing to repent) affects divine action. If God had absolute foreknowledge of all actions, the notion of genuine repentance and God's response to it becomes problematic, as it would imply that the repentance and subsequent divine response were predetermined. Ultimately, the perspective that moral responsibility requires libertarian free will underscores the incompatibility of God's omniscience in the 'strong sense' with human free will. If individuals are to be morally culpable, they must be the ultimate source of their actions, a condition that is not met if all actions are foreknown and thus predetermined.

Now, one might seek to pursue another path to reconcile divine omniscience with human free will, such as that of Plantinga in his work *God, Freedom and Evil*,[22] who assumes an Ockhamist view that suggests that God's beliefs about future actions are soft facts, whose truth value depends on future events. However, this position is clearly problematic, as a belief at a given time constitutes a hard fact. In the sense of 'belief' relevant to this discussion, someone's having a belief at a time t is a hard event at that time. Given that knowledge entails belief, Plantinga's account would require redefining omniscience so that God's beliefs about future events are soft facts. This redefinition implies that God's belief at t about an event in the future could be altered by that future event, contradicting the nature of a hard fact. This approach fundamentally changes the traditional understanding of divine omniscience, leading one to need to reject Plantinga's suggestion as it renders the concept of omniscience significantly different from its established meaning.

Another proposal is that propositions about future free actions are neither true nor false until the actions occur. This allows a being to be omniscient without knowing these propositions. However, this use of 'true' differs from the ordinary use, where propositions

---

22. Plantinga, Alvin. *God, Freedom, and Evil.* Grand Rapids, MI: Eerdmans, 1977, pp. 66-73.

about the future can be true or false. This approach does not align with traditional theological claims about God's knowledge. The traditional view holds that God has comprehensive foreknowledge, but redefining truth in this context undermines the long-held doctrine of divine omniscience. Additionally, if future propositions are not yet true or false, it implies a significant shift in how divine knowledge is perceived, which challenges centuries of theological understanding concerning this concept.

A further proposal to be examined is that of Molinism, which, was introduced by Luis De Molina in his work *Concordia* (*Concordia liberi arbitrii cum gratiae donis, divina praescientia, providentia, praedestinatione, et reprobation*),[23] posits that God has (middle) knowledge of what free creatures would do in any circumstance. Molinism thus suggests that God knows all true counterfactuals of freedom – hypothetical statements about what free creatures would choose to do in any given situation – before these creatures are even created, and thus God possesses middle knowledge 'pre-volitionally'. This allows God to have complete foreknowledge of all events while preserving human free will. However, one can critique this position by asserting that true counterfactuals of freedom cannot be known before the events occur, as there is no grounding state of affairs that makes them true or false. For a proposition to be true, there must be a corresponding state of affairs that grounds its truth. In the case of counterfactuals of freedom, no such grounding exists because the hypothetical situations they describe have not yet occurred and may never occur. This makes the truth of these counterfactuals baseless and contingent upon future free actions, which undermines the basis for middle knowledge. Without a basis in reality, these counterfactuals remain groundless and thus cannot provide a firm foundation for divine middle knowledge. Therefore, Molinism fails to offer a satisfactory solution to the tension between divine omniscience and human free will, as the reliance on these ungrounded counterfactuals makes Molinism implausible and thus Molinism cannot reconcile the concept of divine foreknowledge with libertarian free will.

---

23. The relevant part of this work concerning the notion of middle knowledge has been translated into English in: Molina, Luis de. *On Divine Foreknowledge: Part IV of the Concordia*. Translated by Alfred J. Freddoso. Ithaca, NY: Cornell University Press, 1988.

Therefore, in taking into account these issues, God's omniscience should be understood in a *weaker sense*, where God knows of all true propositions, that they are true, up to the present and their necessary implications but does not have foreknowledge of future free actions. That is, God's omniscience must include knowledge of the past and present, and exclude knowledge of all future free actions, which allows us to maintain human and divine freedom, and ultimately moral responsibility.

Perfect Goodness and a Source of Moral Obligation
Morally good actions are ones that, all reasons considered, are better to do than not to do. With these actions being either obligatory, supererogatory or creative acts – while morally bad actions can be either wrong or infravetatory (bad but not wrong). Obligatory actions are duties owed to others, while wrong actions are those obligatory not to do. For example, feeding and educating children, keeping promises and telling the truth are morally obligatory actions, whereas murder, rape and theft are wrong actions. Moral goodness is thus understood as actions that there is an overriding reason to do; and thus, in application to God's actions, one can understand that, as God is omniscient, and thus will know all necessary moral truths and all relevant contingent facts, and is perfectly free, and thus has no non-rational influences determining his choices (and so is solely guided by reason), God will always perform the best action, or the best kind of action or, in the absence of a best action/kind of action, an equally good action/kind of action[24]. Hence, an omnipotent, omniscient and perfectly free being will thus be perfectly good, acting always in accordance with reason. Moreover, God's moral goodness will also include actions that might be considered bad if performed by humans but are justified by God's unique status as creator and sustainer of life. For instance, God has the right to take away life, as it is a gift from God. However, God also has obligations, such as keeping promises and ensuring that the lives of sentient beings are worth living.

---

24. This position assumes 'motivational internalism' (the view that moral judgments are intrinsically motivating); for more on the nature of this concept, see Björnsson, Gunnar, Caj Strandberg, Ragnar Francén Olinder, John Eriksson, and Fredrik Björklund (Eds.) *Motivational Internalism*. Oxford: Oxford University Press, 2015.

With regard to moral obligations, a theist typically holds that God is the ultimate source of moral obligation, implying that God's commands create moral duties for humans. According to this view, our obligation to obey God's commands stems from God's status as our creator and supreme benefactor. God's creation of humans and the universe, along with the provision of life and its sustaining conditions, grounds the moral duty of gratitude and obedience. This gratitude is expressed through fulfilling the obligations set by God's commands, thus recognising his authority and benevolence. For example, the command to keep the Sabbath holy becomes a moral obligation for believers, not because resting on a specific day is intrinsically good, but because God has commanded it. Similarly, acts of worship and other religious duties are seen as obligatory due to divine command. This framework implies that God's commands are not arbitrary but are grounded in his omniscience and perfect goodness. Conversely, the view that morality supervenes on the non-moral suggests that moral truths exist regardless of whether God commands them. That is, certain actions are inherently good or bad based on their nature and the reasons that exist for doing or refraining from them. For instance, the wrongness of acts like murder and theft is seen as intrinsic, grounded in the harm and injustice they cause, rather than merely because they are prohibited by divine command. Hence, there are necessary moral truths that even God recognises and abides by. Also, for instance, Aquinas and Scotus argued in their works the *Summa Theologica* and *Ordinatio*, that fundamental moral principles, such as the duty to love and reverence God, are self-evident and not contingent upon divine will[25]. These principles are thus seen as logical necessities, much like mathematical truths, which God himself acknowledges. Thus, there are fundamental moral principles that are independent of God's will, and many specific moral obligations arise from God's commands. For example, while it might be a necessary moral truth that we should show gratitude to benefactors, it is God's command that specifies how we should express this gratitude through particular actions. Therefore, while some moral obligations are contingent on divine command, the

---

25. For Aquinas, see: Aquinas, Thomas. *Summa Theologiae*, I-II, q. 94, a. 2. For Scotus, see: Duns Scotus, John. *Ordinatio*, III, suppl., dist. 37; *Ordinatio*, IV, dist. 17.

foundation of these obligations lies in necessary moral truths about the nature of goodness, justice and beneficence.

Eternity and Immutability

The theistic belief that God is an eternal being posits that God exists now, has always existed, and will always continue to exist. This implies that God is eternal both backwards and forwards. If it is logically possible for an omnipotent being to exist now, it is also logically possible for that being to exist at every other period of time, thereby being everlasting. Some argue that endless life would be tedious or pointless, but one can counter this by suggesting that an omnipotent being could ensure that life is neither tedious nor boring, and there would always be meaningful actions to perform, thus giving life purpose. In understanding this, the distinction between the topology of time (the succession of periods) and the metric of time (the measurement of these periods' lengths) is important. That is, time must have a topology to exist, but it need not have a metric. Moreover, in further defining this conception of the nature of time, one can distinguish between two states concerning the beginning of time: (i) existing after a period in which it did not exist; and (ii) existing for only a finite number of periods of equal finite length. The first state is more appropriate for discussing the existence of the universe and time itself. The universe, under this state of affairs, began to exist if there was a time before it existed, aligning with the idea of the universe having a specific starting point, such as the Big Bang. The second state of affairs, which involves existing for a finite number of periods of equal finite length, is less practical and relies on the assumption of a consistent time metric. This assumption is problematic, especially when considering the chaotic state before the universe's formation or under varying laws of nature.

Moreover, time itself cannot logically begin or end because it is intrinsically linked to the succession of periods and change. Therefore, time is infinite and continuous, without a start or end point. An everlasting God would exist for every period of time without a beginning or an end. This allows for a coherent understanding of God's eternal nature and his relationship with the temporal universe.

Now, Christian theology, since the third and fourth centuries, has held the view that God is timeless, a view that is influenced by Neoplatonism and which suggests that God exists outside time and perceives all events – past, present and future – simultaneously.

Boethius, in his work *The Consolation of Philosophy* (*De Consolatione Philosophiae*),[26] described this timelessness as God having 'the complete possession all at once of illimitable life', implying that God's knowledge and actions occur in an 'eternal present'. However, a more nuanced view of God's relationship with time, as noted above, suggests that God's eternity might be better understood through the concept of 'everlastingness' rather than timelessness. This perspective posits that God exists through all periods of time without beginning or end but is still involved in a temporal sequence. An everlasting God can engage with temporal events and maintain personal relationships with humans, experiencing real change in response to human actions without compromising divine perfection. However, if God were timeless, this would render him incapable of genuine interaction with the temporal world. That is, a timeless God would be similar to a predetermined script rather than a responsive and relational being. The dynamic and interactive nature of God depicted in the Hebrew Bible and the Christian New Testament, in which God reacts to human actions with anger, forgiveness and intervention, is incompatible with a strictly timeless existence. Moreover, if God is timeless, and thus perceives all events in a single, eternal present, God's awareness of all events happens simultaneously, without temporal succession. However, this reveals that simultaneity implies a temporal relationship, which conflicts with the idea of timelessness. Moreover, for God to know events as they happen implies that all events are occurring at the same time from God's perspective. This leads to logical contradictions, such as God being aware of two historically distinct events – like the destruction of Jerusalem by the Babylonians in 587 BCE and by the Romans in 70 CE – as if they were happening simultaneously. This notion is logically impossible because it would require distinct temporal events to occur at the same time, which defies the ordinary understanding of temporal order and succession. Philosophers such as Eleonore Stump and Norman Kretzmann, in their essay 'Eternity',[27] have tried to address this by proposing a special kind of simultaneity, termed 'eternal-temporal (or E-T) simultaneity', where events in human history

---

26. Boethius. *The Consolation of Philosophy*. Translated by V.E. Watts. London: Penguin Books, 1969, p. 164.
27. Stump, Eleonore, and Norman Kretzmann. "Eternity." *The Journal of Philosophy* 78, no. 8 (1981): pp. 429-458.

are simultaneous with God's eternal knowledge without being simultaneous with each other. This concept draws an analogy to the theory of relativity, where simultaneity is relative to different frames of reference. However, this analogy is insufficient to explain fully how two non-simultaneous events can be perceived as simultaneous by an eternal being. Therefore, it is almost impossible to coherently maintain that God is timeless while also interacting with the temporal universe, as such interaction necessitates some form of temporal framework, which is incompatible with timelessness. Ultimately, the concept of a timeless God is fraught with logical difficulties and theological inconsistencies. Instead, understanding God as everlasting allows for a coherent and meaningful interaction with the temporal universe, aligning better with the scriptural portrayal of a living, responsive and relational God.

Now, similar conclusions can be reached for God's immutability – as one can distinguish between a 'strong' form, in which God cannot change in any respect, and a 'weak' form, in which God cannot change in respect to his essential, intrinsic properties – which are properties that God must have in order to exist. Given God's everlasting nature, he cannot change with respect to essential properties such as omnipotence, omniscience and perfect goodness. However, real change, as opposed to a Cambridge change (a change in an object's properties or relations without an intrinsic alteration to the object itself, for example, when a person becomes shorter than their friend simply because their friend grew taller), involves intrinsic properties, and God's knowledge of unalterable and future events must change as the universe changes. This is that, God must have distinct conscious experiences because an omniscient God must have changing knowledge as the universe changes, knowing the entire history up to each moment and what future states he can cause. Even before the universe existed, God might have had different experiences or a single continuous thought; and, by creating a universe governed by laws of nature, God established metric time, giving his intentions, knowledge and thoughts a temporal framework. Thus, the stronger form of immutability is incompatible with God being everlasting. This specific desire for a completely immutable God stems from Neoplatonic philosophy, which held that unchanging things are superior. However, perfection might consist in response to change, rather than in a static condition, and thus a weakly immutable God seems to capture this view of perfection best.

God's Necessary Properties

According to the argument of the previous sections, it is thus logically possible for there to be an eternal, omnipotent person, provided that eternal is understood as everlasting and omnipotent, as was also described in the previous sections. This person, referred to as a 'deity', possesses omnipresence, perfect freedom, omniscience and perfect goodness and is a source of moral obligation, as these properties are entailed from the property of omnipotence. For example, focusing on the derivability of the property of omniscience from the property of omnipotence, for God to be omnipotent, that is him being able to cause any event that it is logically possible that he could cause, then he must, at the minimum, possess knowledge of what occurred in the past (and what is occurring now in the present) in order for him to know of (and believe no false propositions about) what events are logically possible for him to bring about at any given point in time. Thus, to be omnipotent, God must also be omniscient, with this requirement holding for all of the other divine properties.

Now the concept of theism does not rely on words being used analogically; rather, the terms are used in their ordinary senses or are defined by such words. However, it is to be acknowledged that not all reasonable people may accept the direct proof of logical possibility, focussed on conceivability, that has been offered thus far due to differing interpretations of logical entailment. Nevertheless, in exploring whether it is logically possible for a being to be essentially a deity, one can consider if such a being could exist without possessing all the properties of a deity – with these properties including being everlasting, and thus implying having always existed and always continuing to exist. A being could remain omnipotent indefinitely unless perfect goodness required abandoning omnipotence. That is, an omnipotent being could always ensure its continued existence unless it chose otherwise, thus emphasising that such a being would only cease to exist or be omnipotent if it allowed it. Turning our attention to the nature of personal identity, if God is essentially backwards and forwards everlasting, he can only be considered a person in an analogical sense. That is, personal identity is ultimate and cannot be analysed in terms of continuity of body or mental properties. Hence, for God to be a person, what makes him that person must also be ultimate. If God is essentially omnipotent and backwards everlasting, he would not be the same person if he had less power at any earlier time. This leads to the conclusion that God's identity is not based on individual thisness but rather on being a 'supreme form'. To support this view, one can take into account Plato's concept of forms, which provides conceptual grounds for conceiving God as a supreme form, determining everything without having underlying thisness. This view aligns with the idea that God is not merely an unchanging impersonal principle but the ultimate determining factor for everything. This can also be seen as being analogous to modern theories of laws of nature, where fundamental laws are seen as changeless entities that govern the behaviour of substances.

To reconcile the idea that God is both a person and a supreme form, one would need to modify the semantic and syntactic rules for person and form to include God's unique nature. This involves retaining the same examples of persons and forms while allowing for the possibility of a being, whose identity is constituted solely by essential properties, lacking individual thisness. One thus needs to show how it is indeed logically possible for there to be a person in this new sense who is also a form. There are three main approaches to addressing this issue: direct, semi-direct and indirect (inductive) approaches. The direct approach involves attempting to show *a priori* that it is logically possible for God to be both a person and a form. However, this method is inadequate as it is difficult to convince those who doubt the logical possibility of the concept due to differing understandings of the terms used in defining this concept and the overall complexity of the concept. The semi-direct approach, similarly, seeks to demonstrate logical possibility but incorporates some empirical data to support the arguments. Yet, it also tends to fall short for similar reasons as the direct approach, as it may not sufficiently address the inherent complexities and abstract qualities involved in the concept of God as both a person and a form. The indirect (inductive) approach, on the other hand, emphasises deriving the logical possibility from observed phenomena. This approach involves presenting evidence that an essentially everlasting and omnipotent person best accounts for the order and existence of the universe: that is, the evidence from the physical universe and the conformity of everything within it to laws leading to the evolution of conscious beings is well explained by positing a God who is a person and supreme form and, thus, it is more probable than not that such a hypothesis is logically possible and thus coherent.

Now, one can ask the important question whether there could be more than one divine being? According to Scotus, no, which he states in his *Ordinatio*,[28] as each would negate the other's power. However, one can counter this position by suggesting that an agreement could be established between the divine beings concerning how they would exercise their power, and this would not diminish their omnipotence since they would act within agreed limits. The challenge here is that this would require prior agreement, which might not be possible. Nonetheless, multiple divine beings could exist if one being caused the existence of another, creating a dependent relationship in which each being respects the other's sphere of influence (more on this in Chapter 5).

A Necessary Being
The theistic claim that God is a necessary being – which means, most simply, that it is not a mere fortunate chance that a divine being exists – includes two accounts: the 'weak' account, which understands God as uncaused, and the 'strong' account, which sees God as metaphysically necessary. More specifically, concerning the weak account, Aquinas held, as expressed in his work *On the Power of God* (*Quaestiones Disputatae de Potentia Dei*),[29] that God is a necessary being in the sense that he is not subject to corruption and will continue to exist forever – given that his essence is to exist. Hence, God is distinguished from other necessary beings like angels and human souls by asserting that God's necessity does not come from elsewhere. While this view explains why there is always a God if he exists, it makes God's existence seem like a brute fact, implying that God's existence might be at the mercy of chance. Thus, though an affirmation of this position was previously made (in the first edition of *The Coherence of Theism*), it can be now found problematic because it suggests that God's existence is contingent on pure chance. The strong account posits that God is a metaphysically necessary being, meaning it is metaphysically necessary that a divine being exists. This view implies that God's existence is a logically necessary truth. Saint Anselm's

---

28. Scots, 'Ordinatio', pp. 180-181.
29. Aquinas, Thomas. *On the Power of God* (Quaestiones Disputatae de Potentia Dei). Translated by the English Dominican Fathers. Westminster, Maryland: The Newman Press, 1952. Question 5, Article 3.

ontological argument, featured in his work *Proslogion* 2,[30] is an example of this account, defining God as 'that, than which nothing greater can be conceived' and claiming that such a being must exist in reality to be the greatest conceivable being. However, most philosophers have rejected ontological arguments as unsound. One reason why that it is not logically possible for any substance, including God, to exist necessarily, is that no positive existential sentence can be logically necessary. This position stems from Hume's claim that the mere non-existence of any being cannot entail a contradiction. Consequently, no positive existential sentence, which asserts the existence of a being with certain properties, can be logically necessary. Therefore, the existence of God, understood as a logically necessary being, is not feasible. This conclusion challenges the strong account of divine necessity. Hence, one needs an 'intermediate' account, which suggests that, if a divine being exists, there is a kind of necessity stronger than the weak account but weaker than the strong account. This view holds that God has aseity, deriving his necessity from himself. On the basis of a modified principle of sufficient reason (MPSR), which states that every event has a substance as its total or partial cause, the existence of God, or the universe if there is no God, must be explained by a kind of causal necessity intrinsic to the substance itself. This intrinsic causal necessity, or 'ontological necessity', makes it inevitable that God exists – that is, in an analogical ('stretched') sense of cause, God everlastingly 'causes' himself to exist and thus would always exist, no matter how different the world was.

Now, the properties that most theists attribute to God are logically possible for a being to have, including being essentially everlasting and ontologically necessary. At times, understanding these properties requires, as noted previously, using predicates in analogical senses. This is that God's essence – the conjunction of his necessary and sufficient properties – is what makes him God and causes his existence. However, humans cannot fully comprehend God's essence due to limited sensory experiences and reasoning capabilities and, according to Aquinas, even the Blessed in Heaven can only see God's essence but not fully understand it. Moreover, the Eastern patristic

---

30. Anselm of Canterbury. *Proslogion*. In Saint Anselm: Basic Writings, translated by S.N. Deane, pp. 47-80. Chicago: Open Court, 1962. See especially Chapter 2.

tradition claims that humans can know God's attributes but not his essence (οὐσία). This tradition emphasises that God's essence is unknowable, while his attributes or energies are manifestations of his nature. This aligns with Aquinas' view, by suggesting that humans can know some essential properties of God but not the full extent of his essence. Hence, while it is logically possible for there to be a divine being who is essentially ontologically necessary, humans cannot fully understand what it would be like for such a being to exist. Thus, such necessity might be plausible but is not provable by direct or semi-direct means; rather, one can take it to be probably logically possible, and thus coherent, as the hypothesis that there is a God provides a probable explanation for the existence of the universe and its order, even though the full nature of God's necessity remains a profound mystery.

Holy and Worthy of Worship

It has been argued that it is (probably) logically possible for there to be an eternal, omnipotent person (understood as everlasting and omnipotent in a specific sense), which includes being an omnipresent spirit, perfectly free, the creator of any universe, omniscient in a weak sense, perfectly good and a source of moral obligation. This conception relies on understanding various words in analogical senses. While the coherence or incoherence of these claims cannot be directly proven, there could be an inductive proof of their coherence based on evidence for their truth. Now, if there is an omnipotent person who has given life and all the good things it contains, subject to using it as he commands, there is a duty to express great gratitude and fulfil his commands. Major theistic religions believe gratitude is owed not only for life but also for God's interventions in human history. For Christians, this includes God acquiring a human nature – living as Jesus Christ – revealing deep truths, dying on the Cross, and rising from the dead, all of which deserve enormous gratitude. To worship a being with the kind of worship theists offer to God involves showing the greatest possible explicit respect. In drawing from Immanuel Kant's idea of treating rational beings as ends in themselves, featured in his work *Groundwork of the Metaphysics of Morals*,[31] there is a

---

31. Kant, Immanuel. *Groundwork of the Metaphysics of Morals*. Translated by Mary Gregor. Cambridge: Cambridge University Press, 1998, pp. 36-37.

moral obligation to show explicit respect to benefactors. This respect extends to those who have done much for us, such as parents, rulers and significant others, and is especially strong for those on whom we depend for our existence, growth and flourishing. Moreover, respecting benefactors includes recognising their contributions through titles, honours or other forms of acknowledgement. This respect should be proportionate to the benefit received and the cost to the benefactor. For God, who is the supreme benefactor, this respect translates into worship, which involves recognising God's greatness, omnipotence and ultimate role as creator and sustainer of everything.

Turning our attention to the concept of holiness, Rudolf Otto distinguishes, in his work *The Idea of the Holy*,[32] the personal properties of God from his non-personal, 'numinous' aspects, which evoke feelings of awe, wonder and creaturely consciousness. Recognising God's greatness should involve such feelings, with one, for example, acknowledging God's intrinsic causal necessity as something wholly other and mysterious. This recognition includes feelings of awe and respect towards God's personal properties, as well as his eternal, omnipotent and perfectly good nature. Otto's analysis includes God's overabounding nature, which involves a dynamic, active and compelling presence. These characteristics align with the personal properties of the God described, who acts in time and responds to human conditions with anger, mercy and love. This temporal being, as opposed to a timeless entity, can engage with humans in a meaningful and personal way. Thus, the God described, with attributes of essential omnipotence, perfect goodness and ontological necessity, would not only be worthy of worship but also embody holiness in its fullest sense. This is that this being, if he exists, would deserve the highest degree of respect and worship, beyond that due to any human or other being.

In conclusion, Swinburne's application of his philosophical framework provides grounds for affirming the coherence of the central theistic claims. By defining a person as a mental substance with essential mental properties, Swinburne lays the groundwork for understanding God as an omnipresent, non-embodied spirit. His detailed examination of the divine attributes – omnipotence, omniscience, creative actions, perfect

---

32. Otto, Rudolf. *The Idea of the Holy*. Translated by John W. Harvey. Oxford: Oxford University Press, 1923.

freedom, perfect goodness and eternal existence – demonstrates that these characteristics are logically possible and compatible with the theistic worldview. Swinburne effectively counters objections to the coherence of these attributes, arguing that a being with such properties is not only (probably) logically possible but also provides a robust explanation for the existence and order of the universe. Through this rigorous analysis, Swinburne reinforces the rational foundation of theism, paving the way for a deeper exploration of the veracity of theism in subsequent work.

Critical Engagements

The Coherence of Theism has garnered significant attention and sparked various critical engagements from scholars, as Swinburne's work endeavours to demonstrate that the concept of God, as understood across the various world religions, is logically coherent. However, several critics have challenged different aspects of Swinburne's arguments featured in this work. Scholars such as Peter van Inwagen, Ronald Hepburn, Adel Daher, Herman Philipse and Terence Penelhum have raised objections that question the coherence and methodology of Swinburne's theistic claims. This section explores these critical engagements and presents responses that align with Swinburne's philosophical perspective.

Peter van Inwagen

Critical Engagement. Peter van Inwagen, in his review article of the *Coherence of Theism*,[33] criticises the reliance on the imaginative capacity needed to comprehend some of Swinburne's arguments. He criticises Swinburne's reliance on the storytelling method to demonstrate the coherence of theism and argues that questions of possibility cannot be resolved merely by imagining scenarios. This is that, van Inwagen contends that Swinburne's approach, which asks the reader to imagine themselves as an omnipresent spirit, does not adequately prove coherence. He points out that, while one can attempt to imagine these scenarios, it does not guarantee their coherence

---

33. Van Inwagen, Peter. 'The Coherence of Theism'. *The Philosophical Review* 88, no. 4. (Oct., 1979), pp. 668-672.

because conceivability (imagination) alone is not a reliable measure of logical possibility.

Critical Response. An adherent of Swinburne's position can offer several responses to van Inwagen's criticisms: first, Swinburne's use of imagination is not merely storytelling, but a sophisticated philosophical tool for exploring logical possibility. That is, the scenarios he asks readers to imagine are carefully constructed to probe the boundaries of the coherence of given theistic concept. This approach aligns with a long tradition in philosophy, from Descartes' evil demon to contemporary thought experiments in philosophy of mind. Second, Swinburne's method does not rely solely on naïve imagination but involves rigorous conceptual analysis. When asking readers to imagine themselves as an omnipresent spirit, Swinburne is not appealing to sensory imagination, but to a more abstract form of conceptual imagination that engages with the logical structure of the concept itself. This process involves carefully examining the attributes of omnipresence and their logical implications, rather than simply picturing a ghostly figure. Third, Swinburne's approach can be understood as an exercise in what philosophers call 'modal epistemology' – the study of how we can know what is possible or necessary. By carefully constructing these imaginative scenarios, Swinburne is providing a method for accessing modal knowledge, which is crucial for understanding the nature of God and other metaphysical concepts. Furthermore, Swinburne's use of imagination can be seen as a form of 'conceivability argument', which has a respected place in philosophy. While conceivability does not guarantee possibility, it provides strong *prima facie* evidence for it. Swinburne's scenarios are not merely conceivable in a superficial sense, but in a deeper, more rigorous sense that approaches what David Chalmers, in his essay 'Does Conceivability Entail Possibility?',[34] calls 'ideal conceivability'. Last, Swinburne's method aligns with recent work in the philosophy of modality, such as that of Timothy Williamson, who argues in his work *The Philosophy of Philosophy*,[35]

---

34. Chalmers, David J. "Does Conceivability Entail Possibility?" In *Conceivability and Possibility*, edited by Tamar S. Gendler and John Hawthorne, Oxford: Oxford University Press, 2002, pp. 145-200.
35. Williamson, Timothy. *The Philosophy of Philosophy: Second Edition*. Malden, MA: Wiley-Blackwell, 2021.

that our capacity for counterfactual reasoning is fundamental to our understanding of metaphysical modality. Swinburne's thought experiments can thus be seen as exercises in counterfactual reasoning about the nature of God and theism.

In sum, Swinburne's use of imagination in exploring the logical possibilities of theism is a philosophically rigorous method, grounded in a long tradition of thought experiments and modal epistemology. While van Inwagen's critique highlights potential pitfalls, a closer examination reveals that Swinburne's approach is far more than mere storytelling. By carefully constructing imaginative scenarios, Swinburne illuminates the conceptual space of theism and provides a compelling case for its coherence.

Ronald Hepburn

Critical Engagement. Ronald Hepburn, in his review article of the *Coherence of Theism*,[36] raises concerns about Swinburne's use of analogical language. Hepburn acknowledges that Swinburne attempts to show the coherence of central theistic claims by using extended or analogical meanings of terms. However, he argues that this method – that is, the inductive method – fails to provide a clear 'proof' of coherence. By stretching the meanings of words, Swinburne makes it harder to ensure that the statements remain meaningful and logically consistent. Hepburn suggests that Swinburne's arguments leave some theistic claims still open to challenge on grounds of incoherence.

Critical Response. An adherent of Swinburne's position can offer several responses to Hepburn's criticisms: first, Swinburne's use of analogical language is not a mere linguistic trick, but a sophisticated philosophical approach rooted in the long tradition of negative theology and the *via negativa*. This tradition, stretching back to thinkers like Pseudo-Dionysius and Maimonides, recognises the inherent limitations of human language when discussing the divine. Hence, Swinburne's approach can be seen as a modern refinement of this venerable tradition, using analogical reasoning to bridge the gap

---

36. Hepburn, Ronald W., 'The Coherence of Theism by Richard Swinburne', *Philosophy* 54, no. 207 (1979), pp. 125-7.

between finite human concepts and infinite divine attributes. Second, the use of extended or analogical meanings is not a weakness but a strength of Swinburne's method. This is because it allows for a more nuanced and flexible exploration of theistic concepts that, by their very nature, transcend ordinary human experience. This approach is particularly crucial when dealing with concepts such as eternity and necessity, which cannot be adequately captured by literal, univocal language. Third, Swinburne's inductive method should not be judged by the standards of deductive proof, as Hepburn seems to suggest. The strength of inductive reasoning lies in its ability to accumulate evidence and increase probability, even in the absence of absolute certainty. In the realm of theological and metaphysical inquiry, where deductive proofs are rare, this approach is not only valid but often the most appropriate method available. Furthermore, Swinburne's use of analogical language can be understood as an application of the principle of charity in interpretation. By extending the meanings of terms, Swinburne is attempting to find the most coherent and meaningful interpretation of theistic claims, rather than settling for a simplistic or literal reading that might lead to apparent contradictions. Last, it is important to note that Swinburne's approach aligns with contemporary developments in philosophy of language, particularly theories of semantic holism and conceptual role semantics. These theories suggest that the meaning of terms is not fixed but depends on their role within a broader conceptual framework. Thus, Swinburne's extended use of language can be seen as an attempt to construct a coherent semantic framework for theistic discourse.

Ultimately, Hepburn's concerns about Swinburne's use of analogical language, whilst understandable, do not undermine the philosophical validity of his approach. By situating his method within the rich traditions of negative theology and semantic holism, Swinburne demonstrates the flexibility and explanatory power of theistic language. His inductive and analogical approach, far from being a weakness, allows for a nuanced exploration of divine attributes that respects the inherent limitations of human understanding.

Adel Daher

Critical Engagement. Adel Daher, in his review article of the *Coherence of Theism*,[37] highlights the difficulties that arise when Swinburne tries to expand the initial definition of God to include necessary existence. Daher points out that using terms like 'person' in analogical senses introduces uncertainty and makes it challenging to maintain that 'God exists' is coherent in this expanded sense. Daher asserts that Swinburne's method of proving coherence indirectly, by showing good grounds for accepting the belief, fails to address the core issue of logical coherence directly.

Critical Response. An adherent of Swinburne's position can offer several responses to Daher's criticisms: first, Swinburne's expansion of the definition of God to include necessary existence is not an arbitrary addition, but a logically necessary step in developing a coherent concept of a 'deity'. This aligns with the long-standing tradition in philosophical theology, from Anselm to Plantinga, which argues that necessary existence (of a weak, intermediate or strong sense) is a perfection and thus an essential attribute of God. Second, the use of analogical language for terms like 'person' when applied to God is not, as noted previously, a weakness but a strength of Swinburne's approach. It acknowledges the *sui generis* nature of God while still maintaining meaningful discourse about God. This approach, as detailed previously, is rooted in the classical theistic tradition, which recognises that human concepts, when applied to God, must be understood in a more 'stretched' sense. Third, Swinburne's method of demonstrating coherence indirectly through inductive reasoning is not a failure to address logical coherence, but rather a sophisticated approach to metaphysical inquiry. In dealing with ultimate questions about the nature of reality, direct logical proofs are often impossible. Swinburne's method thus recognises this limitation and provides a cumulative case for the coherence of theism based on multiple lines of evidence and argument. Moreover, Swinburne's approach can be seen as an application of inference to the best explanation (IBE), a widely accepted form of reasoning in philosophy and science. By showing that theism provides the best explanation for a wide range of phenomena,

---

37. Daher, Adel, 'Richard Swinburne, The Coherence of Theism', *International Journal for Philosophy of Religion* 12, no. 4 (1981), pp. 245-8.

Swinburne is indirectly demonstrating its coherence and plausibility. Additionally, as noted previously, Swinburne's method aligns with recent developments in modal epistemology, particularly the idea of abductive inference to possibility. This approach suggests that we can reasonably infer the possibility of a concept based on its explanatory power and coherence with our best theories about the world. Last, it is important to note that Swinburne's arguments for the coherence of theism are part of a broader cumulative case. While each individual argument (that will be featured in the *Existence of God*) might not provide absolute certainty, together they form a robust framework that significantly increases the probability of theism's coherence. Daher's critique underestimates the philosophical sophistication and methodological rigour of Swinburne's approach.

Despite Daher's reservations, Swinburne's expansion of the definition of God and his indirect method of demonstrating coherence are philosophically sound. By recognising the necessity of divine attributes like necessary existence and employing sophisticated forms of reasoning like inference to the best explanation, Swinburne constructs a robust cumulative case for theism's coherence. Whilst no single argument may be decisive, together they form a compelling philosophical case that addresses the complexities of metaphysical inquiry.

Herman Philipse

Critical Engagement. Herman Philipse, in his work *God in the Age of Science*,[38] criticises the concept of God as a person by emphasising that our understanding of personhood is fundamentally tied to physical embodiment. He argues that all paradigm examples of persons, such as humans and animals, are bodily beings whose personhood is inextricably linked to their physical presence and interactions within the physical world. Given that personhood involves attributes like physical sensations, spatial location and temporal existence, applying this concept to God, who is traditionally conceived as a non-physical, spiritual entity, becomes incoherent. Thus, Philipse concludes that God cannot be literally considered a person, as the essential characteristics defining personhood are inherently tied to bodily existence, which God lacks.

---

38. Philipse, Herman, *God in the Age of Science? A Critique of Religious Reason* (Oxford: Oxford University Press, 2012).

Critical Response. An adherent of Swinburne's position can offer several responses to Philipse's criticisms: first, Philipse's argument commits the fallacy of hasty generalisation by assuming that all persons must be physical beings simply because our paradigm examples are. This ignores the possibility of non-physical persons, a concept that has been seriously entertained in the philosophy of mind and philosophical theology for centuries. Descartes' 'cogito' argument, for instance, suggests that personhood is fundamentally tied to thought rather than physicality. Second, Swinburne's conception of God as a person is grounded in a more sophisticated understanding of personhood that focusses on essential attributes like consciousness, intentionality and agency. These attributes are not necessarily dependent on physical embodiment. Moreover, recent developments in philosophy of mind, such as Chalmers' arguments for dualism, in his work *The Character of Consciousness*,[39] support the coherence of non-physical persons. Third, Philipse's critique fails to account for the flexibility and extensibility of our concepts. Our understanding of personhood has evolved over time to include entities that were once considered non-persons (e.g. women, slaves, certain racial groups). This historical precedent suggests that our concept of personhood is not fixed but can be expanded based on philosophical and theological insights. Furthermore, Swinburne's approach can be seen as an application of perfect being theology, a method that defines God's attributes by considering the simplest type of personal being. From this perspective, God's personhood would be the supreme instantiation of personal attributes, transcending the limitations of human personhood while retaining its essential features. Moreover, Swinburne's concept of divine personhood aligns with recent work in the cognitive science of religion, which suggests that humans have a natural tendency to conceptualise supernatural agents in personal terms – and thus this cognitive predisposition supports the coherence and comprehensibility of the concept of a divine person.

In the final analysis, Philipse's critique of divine personhood relies on an overly narrow conception of what constitutes a person. And by focussing on essential attributes like consciousness and agency rather than mere physical embodiment, Swinburne's understanding of God as a person is both philosophically defensible and resonant with

---

39. Chalmers, David J. *The Character of Consciousness*. New York: Oxford University Press, 2010.

human cognitive predispositions. Far from being incoherent, the notion of a divine person emerges as a sophisticated and compelling way of understanding the nature of God.

Terence Penelhum

Critical Engagement. Terence Penelhum, in his review article of the *Coherence of Theism*,[40] points out that Swinburne's extensive engagement with various philosophical issues may detract from his main argument. He argues that Swinburne's defence of theism is intertwined with positions in the philosophy of mind, logic and morality, which not all theists may accept. This complexity could dilute the apologetic value of Swinburne's work, making it seem that theism depends on contentious philosophical doctrines.

Critical Response. An adherent of Swinburne's position can offer several responses to Penelhum's criticisms: first, Swinburne's approach reflects the inherently interdisciplinary nature of the philosophy of religion – the concept of God touches upon fundamental questions in metaphysics, epistemology, ethics and the philosophy of mind. Thus, by engaging with these diverse philosophical areas, Swinburne is not diluting his argument but rather demonstrating the far-reaching implications and the coherence of theism across multiple domains of inquiry. Second, Swinburne's method aligns with the principle of reflective equilibrium, which, as noted above, seeks to achieve coherence between our considered judgements across various domains. Thus, by showing how theism integrates with and illuminates issues in the philosophy of mind, logic and morality, Swinburne is strengthening the overall case for theism's explanatory power and rational acceptability. Third, Swinburne's comprehensive approach can be seen as a response to the increasing specialisation and fragmentation in philosophy. That is, by synthesising insights from various philosophical subdisciplines, he is offering a unified worldview that can compete with naturalistic alternatives on multiple fronts simultaneously. In addition to this, Swinburne's engagement with diverse philosophical issues serves to pre-emptively address potential objections to theism. By establishing connections between

---

40. Penelhum, Terence. 'Review of The Coherence of Theism'. *The Journal of Philosophy* Vol. 77, No. 8 (Aug., 1980), pp. 502-508.

theism and well-regarded positions in other areas of philosophy, he is fortifying theism against critiques that might arise from these domains. Last, it is important to note that, while Swinburne's arguments may involve contentious philosophical doctrines, this is not unique to theism. Any comprehensive worldview, whether theistic or naturalistic, will inevitably engage with controversial philosophical positions. Swinburne's approach actually strengthens theism by showing its compatibility with a range of sophisticated philosophical frameworks.

Contrary to Penelhum's concerns, Swinburne's engagement with diverse philosophical issues is a strength, not a weakness, of his approach. By demonstrating the coherence and explanatory power of theism across multiple domains, Swinburne offers a unified worldview that can stand toe-to-toe with competing naturalistic frameworks. His interdisciplinary method, far from diluting his apologetic, elevates the discourse surrounding theism to a new level of philosophical depth and sophistication. In an era of increasing specialisation, Swinburne's comprehensive vision stands as a beacon of intellectual unity and rigour.

* * *

In all, *CT* offers a rigorous philosophical defence of the coherence of theism, which has provoked thoughtful critiques from various scholars. The objections raised by Peter van Inwagen, Ronald Hepburn, Adel Daher, Herman Philipse and Terence Penelhum address fundamental aspects of Swinburne's methodology and arguments. In response, one can defend Swinburne's position expressed in *CT* by highlighting the importance of philosophical imagination (conceivability), the role of inductive reasoning, the use of analogical language and the necessity of addressing interconnected philosophical issues. These responses collectively reinforce the coherence of theistic belief and demonstrate Swinburne's commitment to a robust and intellectually rigorous defence of the coherence of theism.

Conclusion

In conclusion, this chapter has provided a comprehensive guide to Swinburne's *Coherence of Theism*, outlining the central aim, structure and themes of the work. Swinburne's detailed examination of the attributes of God – such as omnipotence, omniscience and perfect goodness – demonstrates that theistic claims are metaphysically possible and thus logically coherent. By addressing certain philosophical and theological challenges, Swinburne underscores the compatibility of theism with rigorous logical and metaphysical analysis, emphasising the importance of careful philosophical inquiry in forming justified religious beliefs. His exploration of religious language, personal identity and the coherence of divine properties highlights the depth and rationality of the theistic worldview. As readers explore *The Coherence of Theism* for themselves, they will be better equipped to appreciate Swinburne's rigorous defence of the coherence of theism and its significance in contemporary philosophy.

Chapter Two

The Existence of God

This chapter serves as an introduction to Swinburne's *The Existence of God* (hereafter, *EG*), which is a comprehensive investigation of the truth of theism by weighing empirical evidence both for and against the probability of the existence of God. Swinburne aims to demonstrate whether it is more probable than not that God exists, using a Bayesian analysis of this important issue. The chapter introduces readers to the central aim and structure of Swinburne's arguments, situating them within the broader historical and intellectual context. It outlines the major sections of the work, including the nature and justification of explanation, and the application of these principles to various arguments for the existence of God. By providing this overview, the chapter prepares readers to engage deeply with Swinburne's systematic and rigorous examination of the evidence that underpin his probabilistic argument for the existence of God.

The Existence of God: Background

Central Aim

The central aim of *EG* is to evaluate the veracity of theism by assessing arguments from experience for and against the existence of God. Building on the groundwork laid in *CT*, which focussed on the internal coherence of theism, *EG* seeks to determine the probability of God's existence based on empirical evidence and a robust Bayesian analysis. *EG* thus rigorously examines various arguments related to the existence of God, assessing their strengths and weaknesses to establish whether theism is indeed more probable than not and thus is a defensible philosophical position.

Historical Significance

EG was published in 1979 as the second work within Swinburne's trilogy of theism. The immediate historical context of *EG* involves debates about the cogency of natural theology and the rationality of theistic belief within the philosophy of religion. Medieval thinkers such as Saint Thomas Aquinas and Saint Anselm of Canterbury made significant contributions to natural theology, with Aquinas' *Summa Theologica* and Anselm's *Proslogion* forming the foundation of much subsequent thought. However, during the Enlightenment, philosophers such as David Hume, in *Dialogues Concerning Natural Religion*,[1] and Immanuel Kant, in *Critique of Pure Reason*, critically examined these traditional arguments, questioning their validity and the limits of human understanding in arguing for God's existence from a natural theological basis.

EG is thus to be seen as a work that engages deeply with these historical debates, aiming to demonstrate that theistic beliefs can withstand rigorous scrutiny and remain philosophically viable. The influence of *EG* over the decades thus led to considerable scholarly engagement, necessitating a second edition in 2004. However, by this time, Swinburne had had the opportunity to refine his arguments in response to ongoing discussions in the field. Specifically, Swinburne addressed various critiques and incorporated recent philosophical developments, thus enhancing the depth and robustness of the original arguments featured in the first edition.

Literary Structure

The literary structure of *EG* is not explicitly divided into parts. However, for continuity with the previous chapter, we shall retain our terminology and dual structure as follows:

---

1. Hume, David. *Dialogues Concerning Natural Religion.* Edited by Norman Kemp Smith. Indianapolis: Bobbs-Merrill, 1947.

1. *Philosophical Framework – Nature and Justification of Explanation*: The first part of *EG* focusses on the nature of inductive arguments and the principles underlying the justification of explanation. It discusses the conditions that must be satisfied for a hypothesis to be considered a good explanation, specifically emphasising simplicity and explanatory power. This thus involves a rigorous examination of different types of explanations, such as scientific explanation, personal explanation and their relation to probability theory.
2. *Theological Application – Arguments for the Existence of God*: The second part of *EG* applies the established philosophical framework to specific arguments for the existence of God. It examines various classical arguments from natural theology, such as the cosmological and teleological arguments, as well as more contemporary arguments from consciousness, providence, history, miracles, religious experience and the problem of evil and divine hiddenness. It thus evaluates the explanatory power of theism, relative to the evidence provided by these arguments, in comparison to rival hypotheses, ultimately arguing that theism offers a more simple, and thus probable, explanation of the evidence, and, therefore, the existence of God should be taken to be more probable than not, given the various arguments of natural theology.

We shall now unpack in greater detail the various areas covered in both parts of *EG*.

Themes

Philosophical Framework: Nature and Justification of Explanation

In this section, Swinburne introduces the philosophical framework underpinning his examination of the existence of God. Swinburne's analysis of inductive arguments begins by distinguishing between deductive and inductive reasoning – deductive arguments aiming to provide certainty and inductive arguments aiming to establish the probability of a conclusion. Swinburne categorises inductive arguments further into P-inductive and C-inductive types. Moreover, using confirmation theory, Swinburne assesses the probability of hypotheses based on cumulative evidence. He differentiates between personal and scientific explanations, arguing that theism provides a personal explanation for the universe's existence and order, thereby providing grounds for assessing the probability of theism through detailed inductive reasoning.

Inductive Arguments

In distinguishing between deductive and inductive arguments, a valid deductive argument is one where the premises make the conclusion certain. For example, if no material bodies travel faster than light and a car is a material body, then it follows that the car does not travel faster than light. In contrast, inductive arguments do not guarantee the conclusion but make it probable. For instance, if 70 per cent of the inhabitants of the Bogside are Catholic and Doherty is an inhabitant of the Bogside, it is probable, but not certain, that Doherty is Catholic. Another type of inductive argument involves generalising from specific observations, such as observing 100 black ravens and concluding that all ravens are black. This conclusion goes beyond the evidence and is less certain, yet the observed evidence increases its probability.

Building upon these foundations of inductive reasoning, most scientific arguments are inductive. For example, observations and experiments by scientists such as Tycho Brahe, in his work *Astronomiae Instauratae Mechanica*,[2] Johannes Kepler,[3] in his work *Astronomia Nova*,[4] and Galileo Galilei, in his work *Sidereus Nuncius*, made Isaac Newton's theory of motion, featured in his work *Philosophiae Naturalis Principia Mathematica*,[5] more probable. Similarly, Charles Darwin's data on evolution by natural selection, featured in his work *On the Origin of Species by Means of Natural Selection, or the*

---

2. Tycho Brahe: Brahe, Tycho. *Astronomiae Instauratae Mechanica*. Wandsbek: Levinus Hulsius, 1598.
3. Johannes Kepler: Kepler, Johannes. *Astronomia Nova*. Heidelberg: Vögelin, 1609.
4. Galileo Galilei: Galilei, Galileo. *Sidereus Nuncius*. Venice: Thomas Baglioni, 1610.
5. Isaac Newton: Newton, Isaac. *Philosophiae Naturalis Principia Mathematica*. London: Joseph Streater, 1687.

Preservation of Favoured Races in the Struggle for Life,[6] also added to the probability of his theory. Hence, while these data often do not make their conclusions certain, they do indeed increase their probability. An inductive argument is thus one where the premises either confirm or support the conclusion, but do not guarantee its truth, making the argument not deductively valid. Such arguments are often used in various fields to investigate whether observed data supports the likelihood of a specific explanatory hypothesis. There are two forms of inductive argumentation: a correct P-inductive argument and a correct C-inductive argument. A correct (and thus 'good'/'strong') P-inductive argument makes the hypothesis overall probable based on the premises. A correct (and thus 'good'/'strong') C-inductive argument increases the overall probability of the hypothesis based on the premises – this is that, it makes the conclusion more likely or probable than it would be otherwise. An argument from evidence to the truth of the hypothesis is correct if the evidence is more likely to be found if the hypothesis is true than if it is false. Given these criteria for persuasive arguments, a good argument for or against the existence of God must be either a good deductive argument or a good P-inductive or C-inductive argument. However, it is important to note that in reinforcing the validity of these arguments, arguments for God's existence should not be treated in isolation. While individual arguments might not be conclusive, they can collectively support the conclusion. For example, the cumulative effect of different pieces of evidence, like Smith having blood on his hands, standing to gain from a murder and being near the crime scene, can make it probable that Smith committed the crime. Similarly, combining various arguments for God's existence can collectively increase the probability of theism. This approach involves evaluating each argument individually and then considering their cumulative effect. While no single argument provides a valid deductive proof of God's existence – as one can indeed deny the conclusion of any deductive argument for God's existence, whilst still affirming the truth of each of its premises – many arguments together can form a strong P-inductive case for theism. So, in moving from individual to collective evidence assessment, one can understand that to assess the probability of

---

6. Charles Darwin: Darwin, Charles. *On the Origin of Species by Means of Natural Selection, or the Preservation of Favoured Races in the Struggle for Life*. London: John Murray, 1859.

hypotheses based on evidence, one should employ the methodology of 'confirmation theory'. Confirmation theory is a framework that evaluates how evidence supports – and thus confirms – a hypothesis, or refutes – and thus disconfirms – a hypothesis. In assessing data through confirmation theory, probabilistic methods such as Bayes' theorem (noted previously) will often be used.

Now, within this framework, a differentiation can be made between statistical probability, physical probability and inductive probability – with the last being most relevant to the investigation at hand. Statistical probability, also known as frequency probability, refers to the long-run frequency of events occurring in a given set of trials. It is often used in contexts where repeated trials and relative frequencies are considered. Physical probability, or objective probability, deals with the inherent tendencies or propensities of physical systems. This type of probability is often invoked in physics and other natural sciences to describe the likelihood of physical events based on natural laws. Inductive probability thus concerns how evidence supports a hypothesis, regardless of who is assessing it; and it is this type of probability that is crucial in philosophical and scientific reasoning, as it allows for the evaluation of hypotheses based on the strength of supporting evidence.

The Nature of Explanation

When theists argue from phenomena such as the existence of the universe or some feature of it to the existence of God, they are arguing for a causal explanation in terms of the intentional action of a person. This is a type of 'personal' explanation, where events are explained by the actions of rational agents with specific intentions. In contrast, scientific explanations, which are common in everyday life and science, explain phenomena through events, processes, states, objects and their properties at certain times. Scientific explanations often involve natural laws and initial conditions to account for why something happens. To provide a true explanation of an event E, one must state what brought E about and why it was effective. For example, explaining a high tide involves detailing the positions of the moon, the sea and Earth, and citing the inverse square law of attraction. Thus, explanations have two components: the 'what' (independent actual factors) and the 'why' (reasons for efficacy). A full cause is thus a set of factors sufficient for E's occurrence and explaining the 'why' might involve citing natural laws that ensure the cause's effectiveness.

In further determining the nature of scientific explanation, primarily for those who follow Hempel's model of deductive-nomological (DN) explanation, one can understand that these involve explaining an event E by deducing it from initial conditions and universal laws. For example, the ignition of gunpowder in certain conditions, combined with the law that ignited gunpowder explodes, explains a particular explosion. However, scientific explanations can also be probabilistic, explaining events through statistical laws that increase the likelihood of their occurrence. One can also draw a distinction between laws of nature and accidental generalisations – as posited by Humean accounts – as laws of nature involve physical necessity or probability and can generate counterfactuals, whereas accidental generalisations do not. Thus, in addition to its inadequacy concerning laws of nature, Humean accounts also fail because they make the existence of a causal relationship dependent on the entirety of the universe's future history. This implies that whether A causes B now depends on events that will happen in the distant future, which is counter-intuitive as causation should be determined by present circumstances. Additionally, Humean accounts do not adequately support counterfactuals, such as asserting what would happen if a particular event occurred under different conditions, since they lack a deeper necessity beyond mere regularities. Thus, causation cannot be properly explained by merely observing patterns of events; instead, it requires an understanding of the inherent powers and liabilities that substances possess, which dictate their causal interactions, and thus the substances-powers-and-liabilities account, detailed previously, is to be favoured, where laws of nature are regularities in the causal powers and liabilities of substances.

Now, in further understanding personal explanation, one can see that it involves explaining an event E as brought about by a rational agent P with an intention J. For example, a person's movement might be explained by his intention to move and his basic power to move his limbs. Personal explanation can be either basic, where the agent's action directly causes E, or mediated, where E is the result of a basic action A that causes E through intermediate steps. Moreover, personal explanation cannot be reduced to scientific explanation, as intentions are not passive states but actions in themselves. However, it is possible for there to be both personal and scientific explanations for the same event, as two explanations can coexist if one helps explain the causes and reasons of the other. For instance, the motion of a hand can be explained both by physiological processes and by the person's intention to move it. However, overdetermination, where two full explanations are completely independent yet both sufficient for the occurrence of E, is rare and typically involves coincidence.

In the context of theism, God's actions are best explained in the form of a personal explanation, which cannot be further explained scientifically, as God's actions are not contingent on physical states or natural laws; God, being perfectly free, acts independently of the physical world. Hence, God's actions can only be understood through personal explanation, where God's intentions alone explain his actions. However, this type of explanation is distinct from most mundane personal explanations because it involves a person without a body – a spirit – who acts directly on the universe. Thus, personal and scientific explanations can coexist and complement each other, but in the case of divine action, personal explanation stands alone as the only plausible account.

Justification of Explanation

In understanding the grounds for believing that a proposed explanation of a phenomenon is a true explanation, one again has to make a distinction between the two types of explanation introduced previously: a scientific explanation and a personal explanation. For scientific explanations, the amended Hempelian account, as noted previously, states that the occurrence of a phenomenon E is explained if laws of nature L and initial conditions C necessitate or make E more probable. Hence, a proposed scientific explanation is considered true if the laws and initial conditions it cites are actual laws of nature and occurred as stated. That is, the explanation's probability is high if the law L has high prior probability and great explanatory power. The prior probability of a theory depends on its fit with background knowledge and its intrinsic features, such as simplicity and scope. A theory fits well with background knowledge if it postulates entities and laws similar to those already known to exist. The theory's intrinsic probability increases with simplicity, meaning it postulates fewer entities and properties, uses simpler mathematical formulations, and covers more phenomena without unnecessary complications. That is, a simpler theory is one with fewer and more observable properties, fewer kinds of entities, fewer kinds of properties and mathematically simpler laws. Simplicity also includes the preference for hypotheses attributing infinite values over large finite ones, as seen in science concerning the preference for postulating light that had infinite velocity until disproven by data. While a theory with great scope might be less probable due to its extensive claims, the loss in simplicity often outweighs the gains. Newton's theory of motion, for instance, was considered highly probable because of its simplicity and explanatory power, despite its vast scope. Thus, scope falls out of the analysis of large-scale theories, and one is only to retain simplicity as the determiner of the prior probability of a given theory. The same criteria of prior probability and explanatory power can also be applied to personal explanations, where an event E is attributed to the actions of a rational agent P with certain beliefs, intentions and powers. Effects are attributed to other humans based on the assumption that they have powers, intentions and ways of acquiring beliefs similar to our own (which expresses the 'principle of charity') and as simple as possible (which expresses the 'principle of simplicity', detailed previously). This method also extends to animals and hypothetical rational agents such as aliens or poltergeists, where intentions and powers that lead to expected behaviour are postulated. Thus, when postulating non-embodied agents, such as poltergeists, the explanatory power of such hypotheses depends on their ability to predict phenomena otherwise inexplicable. That is, if a poltergeist's actions make certain events highly probable, and no better scientific or personal explanation exists, the hypothesis is confirmed by the evidence. Personal explanations are thus justified using the same criteria as scientific explanations: simplicity, fitting with background knowledge and explanatory power.

As noted earlier in this chapter, and more fully in the introductory chapter, one can utilise Bayes' theorem to formalise the relationship between hypothesis h, evidence e, and background knowledge k. Where, as previously stated in this chapter, the theorem states that the posterior probability of P($h/e.k$) depends on the prior probability of P(h/k), the explanatory power of the hypothesis with respect to e P($e/h.k$), and the prior probability of P(e/k) This framework thus helps assess the probability of a hypothesis by considering how well it predicts evidence and fits with prior knowledge. For h to be confirmed by evidence e, e must be more likely to occur if h is true than if h is false. This principle, known as the 'relevance criterion', is thus crucial for evaluating inductive arguments and determining the overall probability of hypotheses.

Complete Explanation

As noted previously, the justification for postulating a personal explanation of phenomena is based on the prior probability and explanatory power of that explanation. The explanatory power of the hypothesis depends significantly on the prior probability of the phenomena, which is how likely the phenomena would occur regardless of whether the proposed explanation is correct. Thus, a key factor in assessing the strength of an argument from phenomena to God's existence is whether those phenomena would likely occur without divine agency. Phenomena could exist apart from God if they have a scientific explanation, another personal explanation, or if they could exist uncaused. However, there are certain phenomena that cannot be explained scientifically, which fall into two categories: those 'too odd' to fit into established scientific patterns and those 'too big' to fit into any scientific pattern. For phenomena that are too odd, it must be shown that they do not follow from the best scientific theories and that any attempt to include them would make these theories excessively complex and improbable. Alleged miracles, such as levitations or sudden healings, are examples of such odd phenomena. Additionally, the existence of living organisms or conscious beings is scientifically inexplicable – as will be further explained later. Phenomena too big for scientific explanation include the existence of states of affairs and the operation of the most fundamental laws of nature. Science can explain why certain events follow others, but it cannot explain why there are any states of affairs at all or why the most fundamental laws hold. These big and odd phenomena often serve as starting points for arguments for the existence of God, suggesting that their explanation lies beyond science and possibly in the existence of a divine being.

Now, with regard to different levels of explanation, a 'full' explanation accounts for a phenomenon entirely based on cause and reason, while a 'complete' explanation includes factors that have no further explanation at the time of their existence or operation. A complete explanation, therefore, is one where the factors involved do not themselves require further elucidation within the current context of understanding. An 'ultimate' explanation extends to all

The Existence of God

factors leading up to the phenomenon, with no further explanation of these factors. Finally, an 'absolute' explanation involves factors that are self-explanatory or logically necessary, though logically contingent phenomena cannot have absolute explanations. Within a theistic context, a complete explanation involving God would cite his intentions and existence as ultimate factors, whereas the universe, its states and laws do not inherently provide such a terminus, as God's existence and intentions are better suited to be the terminus of an explanatory chain. Now, the criteria for judging an explanation as complete are its prior probability (simplicity and fit with background knowledge) and explanatory power (the extent to which it necessitates or renders phenomena probable). For scientific laws, an explanation reaches a terminus when further attempts to explain it would decrease simplicity without significant gains in explanatory power. The same criteria apply to personal explanations, in which case the agency, intentions and beliefs of persons must be considered. In both scientific and personal explanations, explanations justify each other based on these criteria. A scientific explanation could theoretically explain a personal one and vice versa if it results in gains of prior probability and explanatory power. Reaching a complete explanation within either domain depends on the inability to improve explanatory power or prior probability by postulating new factors. A personal explanation for phenomena, such as the existence of God, is justified by its prior probability and explanatory power. Thus, phenomena that cannot be explained scientifically due to their oddity or vastness might indeed point to the existence of this type of being. Therefore, by distinguishing between full, complete, ultimate and absolute explanation for arguing for God's existence provides a more satisfactory terminus for explanation than the universe itself. As an explanation should be considered complete when adding more factors decreases simplicity without improving explanatory power. So, affirming the veracity of a theistic explanation, especially when scientific ones are inadequate, is indeed strongly justified.

In conclusion, Swinburne's philosophical framework provides a means of assessing the probability of theism based on a rigorous examination of the nature inductive arguments, cumulative evidence, and scientific and personal explanations. Swinburne asserts that, while individual arguments for God's existence may not be conclusive, their collective force can form a strong C-inductive case for theism – and thus, together, a strong P-inductive case as well. Swinburne's approach thus involves evaluating each argument individually and then considering their cumulative effect, contending that the combination of various pieces of evidence can significantly increase the probability of theism. This cumulative approach, supported by confirmation theory, ultimately aims to show that the total evidence makes theism more probable than not.

Theological Application: Arguments for the Existence of God

In this section, Swinburne applies his philosophical framework to assess the probability of theism, focussing on both its prior probability and explanatory power. He begins by discussing the prior (intrinsic) probability of theism, defining God as an omnipotent, omniscient and perfectly free being whose existence provides a natural terminus for explanations. Swinburne argues that the intrinsic features of theism – similar to scientific preferences for hypotheses that include entities with infinite values – provides this hypothesis with a significant prior probability. Swinburne then examines the explanatory power of theism using Bayes' theorem, emphasising that theism offers a coherent and comprehensive explanation for the world's observed order and complexity. Given this, this section thus explores specific arguments such as the cosmological and teleological arguments, the argument from consciousness and morality, and the argument from providence, each illustrating how theism provides a probable account for various phenomena. Swinburne concludes by addressing the problem of evil and discussing the role of miracles and religious experiences in supporting the theistic hypothesis, ultimately reaching the conclusion that, on the basis of the evidence adduced, the existence of God is more probable than not.

The Intrinsic Probability of Theism
The theist's claim is that various phenomena require explanation and that theism provides a natural stopping point for these explanations. The correctness of this claim depends on the prior probability of theism and its explanatory power. The focus is on the prior probability of theism, examining how simple the hypothesis is. More specifically, the intrinsic probability of theism, $P(h/k)$, which is the probability

of the hypothesis independent of all propositional data, is influenced solely by its simplicity. Theism, which posits a God of infinite power, knowledge and freedom (in the manner defined in the previous chapter), forms a natural terminus point for explanation. It is also clear that theism provides a simpler explanation for the existence and operations of the world compared to other hypotheses, making it a natural candidate for the explanatory stopping point that explains other things without requiring an explanation itself. While the intrinsic probability of theism may be low, it is significantly greater than that of many alternative hypotheses.

Now, in further developing this position, as a starting point, one can define God, in a similar way to the previous chapter, as a spirit, a non-embodied person who is omnipresent, omnipotent, omniscient, perfectly free and perfectly good. God is also the creator of all things, responsible for the existence and operation of all logically contingent things. Moreover, God is not dependent on anything for knowledge or power and can control all states of affairs directly. God's omnipotence means that he can do whatever is logically possible, while his omniscience means he knows all that it is logically possible to know at any time (in the weak sense defined in the previous chapter). God's perfect goodness entails that he always does the morally best action and no morally bad action. Additionally, God necessarily possesses these properties, meaning that he cannot cease to be omnipotent or omniscient while remaining God. Given this understanding of God, one can thus take the hypothesis of theism to be very simple because it postulates a single omnipotent, omniscient and perfectly free being. This simplicity is comparable to the scientific preference for hypotheses with zero or infinite values over those with specific finite limits. For example, scientists prefer hypotheses of infinite velocity to large finite velocities due to the neatness and simplicity of infinity. Similarly, postulating an omnipotent being is simpler than a being with specific limited power. God's beliefs, being omniscient, are also infinitely simple. Human beliefs are finite, and often false or unjustified, but God's beliefs, as part of his essential properties, cannot be false. Therefore, God has all the knowledge it is logically possible to have. God's perfect freedom is also simple by it lacking specific tendencies or influences, thus making God's intentions uncaused and based on reason alone.

On the basis of this, God is a terminus of complete explanation – in that, if a state of affairs is explained by God's actions, no further explanation is needed. That is, as God's powers come from his omnipotence, his beliefs from his omniscience and his intentions are chosen freely, God's existence is an ultimate explanation, as he is self-sufficient and does not depend on any other factor – with all of God's properties, as noted in the previous chapter, being entailed (that is, following from) his omnipotence, omniscience and perfect freedom. As an omnipotent being, God can control all states of affairs. As an omniscient being, God knows everything without relying on physical senses, which thus makes him an omnipresent spirit. God's role as creator means that everything happens either because he makes it happen or permits it. Moreover, if moral judgements are true or false propositions, then an omniscient God would know the truth of all moral judgements. Furthermore, a perfectly free agent, such as God, would always do what he believes to be the morally best action and avoid morally bad actions. Therefore, God's perfect goodness is a logical consequence of his omniscience and perfect freedom.

Theism thus postulates one very simple person who is essentially omnipotent, omniscient and perfectly free. This being is also omnipresent, the creator of all things and perfectly good. The simplicity of theism makes it a highly probable hypothesis compared to other hypotheses about the existence of the universe: the intrinsic probability of theism is high due to its simplicity, making it a strong candidate for explaining the existence and features of the universe. In other words, theism provides the simplest and most natural terminus for explanation.

The Explanatory Power of Theism
The occurrence of certain phenomena will confirm the existence of God if it is more probable that these phenomena will occur if there is a God than if there is not. The force of arguments from evidence e to hypothesis h depends on the explanatory power of theism regarding those phenomena. Theism is more likely to be true if it makes the occurrence of evidence (or phenomena) e more probable than if theism were false. The intrinsic probability of e is the sum of the probabilities of e given different hypotheses, including theism. Thus the likelihood of e occurring uncaused or caused by a lesser being is very low, making theism a more probable explanation for e. Now, God, being omnipotent, can bring about any logically possible state of affairs – with God's actions being solely guided by perfect goodness, meaning that he will do any action that is the best or an action of

the best kind. God would thus create a world that reflects his moral values, including keeping promises, telling the truth and promoting good. However, there is no unique best of all possible worlds that God could create, as there could always be a better world with more conscious beings enjoying it. This leads to the conclusion that God's perfect goodness requires him to create a variety of good states of affairs, including worlds with humanly free agents capable of moral awareness and significant free choice – as this good is something that God himself does not possess. However, humanly free agents, who are beings with moral awareness and limited freedom, need bodies and thus a physical universe to exercise their freedom and responsibility. These agents must have the power to make significant differences to themselves, others and the physical world through their choices. This thus requires a public space where their actions and perceptions can be realised, making a physical universe something that is required for their existence. Hence, the existence of humanly free agents and a beautiful physical universe is highly probable if there is a God. That is, God would create such agents with free will to interact with and love, and they would need a physical environment to fulfil their potential. Moreover, God has reason to create animals and a beautiful inanimate world, although these do not possess the same kind of goodness as humanly free agents. However, the universe and its features, as will be shown below, are 'too odd and big' for scientific explanation alone to handle comprehensively. That is, scientific theories often struggle with the complexity and enormity of certain phenomena, leading to the possibility that these aspects are better explained by positing the existence of God. Theism thus has significant explanatory power regarding the existence of a physical universe and humanly free agents. Therefore, the simplicity of the theistic hypothesis and its ability to account for the observed phenomena make it a highly probable explanation. The probabilistic arguments for theism, that are now to be unpacked, thus focus on showing that it is more likely to be true than alternative hypotheses, and thus provides a strong case for the existence of God based on the evidence and the intrinsic probability of the hypothesis of theism.

The Cosmological Argument
Cosmological arguments typically start from the existence of the physical universe, a complex object consisting of all physical objects spatially related to each other and to no other physical object.

This definition allows for the logical possibility of other physical universes, but for the argument's purpose, the focus remains on our universe. In the history of religious thought, Aquinas' arguments are often critiqued as some of his least successful philosophical efforts. Conversely, Leibniz's and Samuel Clarke's arguments are generally considered more persuasive and insightful. Yet, while these arguments' starting points are evident facets of experience, no deductive argument from the universe's existence to God's existence is valid. Instead, the cosmological argument should be assessed as a C-inductive or P-inductive argument.

In formulating this argument, one can understand that scientific explanations of the universe's existence account for its state at any given time by referencing previous states and the laws of nature. However, this chain of explanations extends only so far. If the universe had a beginning, its initial state must have been caused by something outside the chain of physical events. Whether the universe is finite or infinite in age, scientific explanations alone cannot account for its existence, rendering the universe's existence an inexplicable brute fact if only scientific causality is considered. However, if God, as a person, brings about states of affairs by intention, then God could be the universe's cause. This idea aligns with Leibniz's assertion that an infinite series of states does not provide a sufficient reason for the universe's existence. The existence of the universe over time is something too big for science to explain and requires a personal explanation. This is that God's continuous intention and action provide not merely a partial explanation but a full and ultimate reason for the universe's existence over time.

Moreover, theism is simpler than alternative explanations involving multiple gods or finite gods, as it proposes a single omnipotent, omniscient and perfectly good being, which is a simpler and more probable hypothesis. Moreover, Hume's suggestion that polytheism is as good an explanation as theism can be countered by the principle that multiplying causes without necessity is contrary to true philosophy. Theism thus provides a simpler explanation for the universe's existence. The choice is thus between the universe as a brute fact and God as the ultimate explanation. The universe's existence is indeed less simple and thus less expected *a priori* than God's existence. And as the probability that God would create a physical universe is quite high – given his desire to bring about the existence of humans with free will – the argument from the universe's existence to God's existence is thus a strong C-inductive argument. The cosmological argument compellingly supports theism by demonstrating the necessity of a personal explanation for the complex physical universe's existence. And objections from philosophers such as Hume, featured in his work *Dialogues Concerning Natural Religion*,[7] against the conclusion reached here can indeed be countered. Hume asserts that the universe as a whole does not require a separate explanation beyond the explanation for each of its parts. That is, Hume argued that, if each individual component within the universe can be explained by its preceding causes, then the entire collection of these components, the universe itself, does not need an additional overarching explanation. However, one can challenge this position by pointing out that explaining each part does not account for the existence of the whole – something outside the chain needs to be posited to explain the existence of the chain itself. Even if there is a scientific explanation for each part of the universe, this does not explain why the universe as a whole exists rather than not existing at all. There is thus a fundamental gap in Hume's argument, suggesting that the existence of the universe still requires an ultimate cause that cannot be explained solely by the sum of its parts. One thus needs to posit the existence of God as a personal cause who is not part of the universe but acts from outside it, and thus can provide a complete and ultimate explanation for the existence of the universe.

Teleological Arguments
The universe exhibits both spatial and temporal order. Spatial order refers to the regularities of co-presence, such as the arrangement of roads in a town or books in a library. Temporal order, on the other hand, is about the regular succession of events, as seen in the laws of nature described in physics, chemistry and biology. This temporal order is evident in the universe's conformity to simple, formulable scientific laws, which could have naturally been chaotic but are instead orderly. Within the Christian Scriptures, we see the prophet Jeremiah arguing from the order of the world to the reliability and power of a single God – hence, this reaction to the world's comprehensibility as evidence of a comprehending creator is deeply embedded in human consciousness. Also, historically, Aquinas' fifth way, featured in his

---

7. Hume, *Dialogues,* Parts II and IX.

work *Summa Theologica* I, Q. 2, Art. 3.[8] has been taken to argue that the regular behaviour of inanimate things suggests they are directed by an intelligent being. While this argument may provide good evidence for a designer, it is not a valid deductive argument as it does not necessarily follow that all order must be brought about by a person. The argument from temporal order should thus, again, be considered as an inductive argument rather than a deductive one.

In further conceptualising this evidence, one can understand that not all initial conditions or laws of nature would allow the existence of human bodies – with the universe being described as 'tuned' for human evolution if its laws and initial conditions permit this to occur. The universe is thus 'fine-tuned' for human evolution because the constants of its laws and variables of its initial conditions need to lie within very narrow ranges for human bodies to exist. For instance, carbon-based life, which forms the basis for human bodies, requires stable yet metastable compounds that can store and process information. Given the standard theory of quantum mechanics and relativity, with their constants and initial conditions, the fine-tuning required for human life is very precise. This level of fine-tuning is highly improbable without some form of intentional design. Theism thus posits that God would create a world with humanly free agents who need to learn about the effects of their actions. For this learning to occur, the world must exhibit simple and reliable regularities. Hence, theism predicts that God would bring about an initial singularity or an arrangement of substances with powers and liabilities conducive to these regularities. A God-created universe would likely be governed by simple laws, making the regularities observed in nature more probable under theism than in a Godless universe. The complex arrangement of parts in human bodies, much like a machine, thus suggests a purposeful design. More precisely, this spatial order, characterised by the intricate and systematic arrangement of parts in human and animal bodies, highlights the precise organisation needed to enable functionality and adaptation to the environment. The evolution of these complex structures from simple inorganic matter to highly specialised organs and systems underscores the improbability of such occurrences without deliberate design. The finely tuned laws and initial conditions necessary for such evolution further reinforce the argument for intentionality in

---

8. Aquinas, *Summa*. First Part, Question 2, Article 3.

the creation of the universe. Moreover, the regularities of temporal succession, such as seeds growing into plants and the alternation of day and night, illustrate how natural phenomena consistently follow certain patterns. These phenomenal regularities, observable in everyday life, are underpinned by more fundamental regularities governed by the laws of physics and chemistry, indicating an inherent order in the universe that facilitates the existence and sustainability of life. Thus, the spatial order, coupled with the regularities of temporal order, found within our universe forms the basis of the teleological argument. This is that, without a fundamental explanatory cause, it is highly improbable that objects would consistently conform to simple laws, as the SPL (substances-powers-and-liabilities) account of laws suggests that the regularities in the behaviour of objects are due to their inherent powers and liabilities. Hence, the existence of such regularities is more probable under theism than in a Godless universe, making it a significant piece of evidence for the existence of God. Thus, the fine-tuning, and the probability of temporal and spatial order presents a compelling case for theism. The order and regularities observed in the universe are more plausibly explained by the existence of a divine creator than by chance – and thus the argument from temporal and spatial order to God's existence is a strong C-inductive argument.

Argument from Consciousness and Morality
Mental properties are those to whose instantiation the subject has privileged access, such as sensations and thoughts. Physical properties are those without such privileged access. Mental substances, as noted previously, are defined as those with at least one essential mental property, contrasting with physical substances that only have physical properties. Humans are to be identified as mental substances with souls, which are pure mental substances that exist independently of the body. Yet, given the laws of nature, there is no reason to expect conscious life to evolve. The integration of physical laws does not suggest that brain states would produce sensations or thoughts; and the idea that detailed psycho-physical connections – specific brain events causing specific mental events – are able to constitute a scientific explanation is incorrect. As such, connections are too complex and varied to be explained by a simple scientific theory. While brain events cause mental events and vice versa, this does not imply that scientific laws govern these connections. The connections

between mental events and brain events are detailed and specific, which thus suggests that they are not random but designed. Hence, the improbability of these connections occurring naturally implies the need for an explanation beyond science. Thus, it is posited here that God, being omnipotent, can join souls to bodies, causing specific brain event/mental event connections. Moreover, God has good reason to create humanly free agents who need bodies to experience sensations, form beliefs and execute purposes. Yet, these connections, such as brain events causing sensations or thoughts, are improbable without a divine cause – that is, they are 'too odd' for science to account for them. The existence of these connections is thus a strong C-inductive argument for the existence of God.

Now, focussing on the existence of morality, one can understand that moral truths must be logically contingent in order to provide an argument for God's existence. These types of truths depend on natural properties and contingent moral truths, such as the wrongness of specific actions, require explanation. Actions such as promise-keeping and truth-telling, which lack easy utilitarian justification, may be better explained by the existence of God. However, convincing those who deny either the obligatoriness of such actions or the probability that they lead to the *summum bonum* (the highest good) is challenging. This is that, for an argument for the existence of God to be compelling, it must show that certain moral truths are more likely under theism than any alternative theory. Again, promise-keeping, for instance, may be considered obligatory if it leads to the *summum bonum*, which is more plausible if there is a God. Without God, the alignment of promise-keeping with the *summum bonum* becomes less probable. This argument is valid, but its first and third premises are highly questionable. Some will deny that promise-keeping is always obligatory, while others will deny that promise-keeping is more likely to lead to the *summum bonum* if there is a God. As such, the argument faces substantial scepticism and must address these foundational disagreements if it is to advance effectively. Thus, it is actually the phenomena of moral awareness, which is necessary for significant human choices, that is, in fact, improbable in a Godless universe. If God exists, he will ensure humans develop moral awareness to make free choices between good and evil. However, without God, there is no particular reason why genetic mutations would produce creatures with moral beliefs. While altruistic behaviour might have Darwinian explanations, moral awareness goes beyond mere altruism; and God has significant reason to give humans moral awareness, as it enables them to make meaningful moral choices. This probability adds to the cumulative case for theism – it is a strong C-inductive argument for the existence of God – as the likelihood of all these phenomena occurring in a Godless universe is very low. That is, the improbability of conscious life and moral awareness arising naturally, coupled with the detailed and specific connections between mental and physical events, suggest a divine creator. These arguments, along with the cosmological and teleological arguments, thus form a cumulative case for theism, making it more probable than any alternative theory.

The Argument from Providence

It is a great good for humans to affect their lives, acquire knowledge and form their own characters, which is called a choice of 'destiny'. Humans are responsible for their bodies, including their maintenance and improvement through actions like eating, exercising and sleeping. Moreover, the environment extends these choices, presenting dangers such as rivers, cliffs and predators, which require humans to learn survival skills. This challenging environment thus allows humans to develop the skills and knowledge necessary for their flourishing. Now, to make significant choices in a dangerous environment, humans must begin in ignorance and be guided by natural desires and aversions. Natural desires for food, sleep and sexual intercourse ensure survival until knowledge is acquired; and painful sensations from touching hot or sharp objects teach avoidance behaviour. As humans learn about the world, they can choose to take risks or avoid dangers, thereby shaping their experiences and understanding.

The regularities in nature and the human ability to discover and use them are crucial for survival and flourishing. These regularities make scientific inquiry possible, allowing humans to propose and test theories. Human intelligence would be unable to discover fundamental laws without the ability to construct instruments like microscopes and telescopes. The choice to engage in science and apply its discoveries is a significant one for individuals and societies. Moreover, doing good actions makes it easier to do good in the future, while bad actions lead to more natural bad behaviour. This process of character formation gives humans the opportunity to become morally better or worse over time. A God who wants to give humans significant choices would ensure that character formation occurs gradually through consistent effort. Furthermore, humans are interdependent and benefit from cooperation and, thus, society's organisation into specialised labour enhances living standards and enables complex projects like building aeroplanes and sending rockets to the moon. Cooperation in a worthwhile task is a good thing, and a God would create a world where such cooperation is necessary and rewarding. Also, required assistance, where one person helps another without expecting anything in return, allows humans to participate in God's creative work on similar terms – and this can be seen in the parent-child relationship, where parents provide for their children without immediate reward.

Now, significant responsibility requires the ability to harm as well as benefit others. A world where humans can only help each other would limit their responsibility. God, like a good parent, would delegate responsibility to humans, allowing them to make their own judgements and choices. However, this delegation includes the potential to harm, which gives humans profound responsibility for each other. Moreover, death is also to be expected in a providential world. This is due to the fact that death introduces the possibility of supreme self-sacrifice and irreversible actions, making human choices more significant. A world without death would lack the ultimate seriousness and finality of decisions. Thus, natural death provides a limit to suffering and allows for significant moral choices and responsibilities. Within this type of world, God would also create beings, animals, who are unburdened by moral awareness and free will. Animals lack the power to do significant harm and do not engage in complex moral decisions. However, they still contribute to the world by seeking their own good and avoiding harm, providing opportunities for humans to exercise responsibility and care.

The opportunities and responsibilities humans have in a providential world thus provide strong evidence for the existence of God – that is, a good C-inductive argument for the existence of God. The significant choices humans can make, the challenges they face and the responsibilities they bear align with the idea of a good God who seeks to give humans meaningful lives. The argument from providence thus supports theism by showing that a world with such opportunities and responsibilities is more probable if God exists than if he does not.

The Problem of Evil

Evil, which is defined as a 'bad states of affairs', can be divided into two different types: moral and natural evils. Moral evils arise from human intentional choices or negligence, leading to bad actions or outcomes. Natural evils, on the other hand, encompass all other types of suffering, such as diseases, accidents and natural disasters. If there is a God, he permits moral evils and seemingly causes natural evils through the natural processes he created. In a world where humans are free agents, evils are inevitable. These include biologically useful unpleasant sensations, such as pain signalling danger, and emotions like fear in hazardous situations. Moral evils are also inevitable as humans have significant power to harm each other and are not causally determined always to do good. Thus, there will be suffering inflicted on each other by humans, alongside the moral evil of choosing to do wrong. Now, the concept of 'higher-order' defence posits that natural evil provides opportunities for valuable emotional responses and free choices. Compassion, for instance, can only be felt if others suffer. Hence, this involvement with others' suffering is good as it deepens emotional connections. A world with some pain, allowing for compassion, is as good as one without pain and thus without compassion; and a good God can be justified in permitting moral evils for the sake of the goods that their existence makes possible. Moreover, good people sometimes allow evils for greater goods, such as parents permitting a child's suffering during dental surgery for healthier teeth. God, unlike parents, could produce the good without the suffering, but doing so would prevent greater goods, like free choice and significant moral actions. God, who creates a world where suffering helps others, benefits from this specific arrangement. Being of use to the perfectly good source of all being is indeed fortunate. However, if some lives are on balance bad, God is obliged to provide a compensatory period of good life after death. Moreover, there are limits to the suffering a good God would allow. The suffering must not be excessive in intensity or duration and, thus, natural death provides a limit to suffering, removing agents from a world where they can suffer at the hands of others. This limit is necessary for a good God to maintain moral order. The sheer quantity of evil in the world does challenge the belief in a good God. However, each instance of suffering allows for greater goods, such as opportunities for courage and compassion. While the extent of suffering seems excessive, the overall good achieved justifies the amount of evil. More specifically, a world with free agents inevitably involves significant evils, both moral and natural. However, these evils are necessary for the greater goods they enable, such as free choice, moral responsibility and deep emotional connections. God's allowance of evil is justified by the greater goods that result and God's provision of compensation – namely, that of life after death – for those who suffer excessively.

In addition to compensating for suffering through life after death, the concept of the Incarnation is also significant because, if God allows humans and animals to suffer as much as they do, it is consistent with his perfect goodness that he would share in that suffering. Just as good parents share in the challenges they impose on their children, a perfectly good God would share in human suffering through the Incarnation. This sharing of suffering serves not only as a means of solidarity but also as a way to exemplify ultimate compassion and empathy. By becoming incarnate, God provides a profound demonstration of his commitment to humanity, reinforcing the belief that he is not a distant or indifferent deity but one who is intimately involved in the human experience and deeply understands the human condition. This 'theodicy' thus provides a way to reconcile the existence of a good God with the presence of evil in the world.

Alongside the challenge to belief in God brought about by the problem of evil is that of the problem of divine hiddenness. This problem suggests that God's hiddenness serves a purpose similar to the presence of evil. This is that the state of agnosticism, including honest doubt about God's existence, can provide significant benefits. It allows individuals to make a serious and free choice between good and evil without overwhelming evidence of God's presence that would compel their actions out of fear or desire for reward rather than genuine moral decision making. This 'epistemic distance' is necessary for true moral freedom and the development of virtues such as faith and trust. Additionally, the hiddenness of God provides believers with the opportunity to demonstrate their faith and help others come to belief through genuine acts of kindness and example, rather than through coercion or overwhelming evidence.

From this perspective, the presence of evil and divine hiddenness together can be seen as components of a broader framework that allows for significant moral development. On the one hand, one can indeed affirm the fact that the occurrence of evil provides a good C-inductive argument against the existence of God, as it complicates the theistic hypothesis – by one needing to affirm the possibility of a compensatory afterlife and the Incarnation. However, on the other hand, this argument is not strong enough to refute theism entirely (it is not a strong P-inductive argument against theism), particularly when considering the possibility of life after death and the Incarnation, which are integral to Christian theism – these additional hypotheses thus reduce the force of the C-inductive argument against (Christian) theism specifically. Importantly, the argument from hiddenness does not constitute a good C-inductive argument against the existence of God. The goodness of the states that agnosticism makes possible depends on their being temporary, and the conditions for a perfectly good God to permit or bring about the evil of agnosticism are satisfied. This makes it possible for agnostics to have the great good of a serious free choice between good and evil, while also allowing religious believers to help agnostics reach true religious belief, thus demonstrating their own faith and compassion in the process.

Argument from Miracles and History

Many people see the hand of God in the sudden emergence of wise men, prophets and great leaders who bring significant moral, political or religious insights. Figures such as Muhammad, Jesus Christ and Abraham are central to their respective religious traditions. The rapid spread of Christianity, despite severe persecution, is often cited by Christians as evidence of divine intervention. Similarly, the fulfilment of prayers, particularly those concerning recovery from serious illnesses, is seen by some as compelling evidence of God's existence. The occurrence of these types of events is often disputed because they seem to violate natural laws. These include the resurrection of Jesus, levitations and medical miracles. The occurrence of such events would suggest intervention by a power outside nature, such as God.

Now, a miracle is defined as an event that violates natural laws, as conceptualised through the SPL account – where the laws of nature are summaries of the powers and liabilities of substances. A violation occurs when an event that could not occur under the normal operation of these laws happens. For example, if Mars were to deviate from its elliptical orbit without a repeatable cause, this would be a violation of natural laws. Some events might seem like violations but could be exceptions permitted by more fundamental laws or entirely new natural laws not yet understood. Nonetheless, true violations indicate intervention by an external agent, such as God. Events such as the Resurrection, if they occurred, would be beyond the explanatory power of natural laws, making them candidates for divine action. Moreover, importantly, strong testimony from reliable witnesses can sometimes outweigh the background evidence against the occurrence of miracles. However, Hume argued that, even if numerous witnesses report a miracle, their testimony is less reliable than the consistent and vast evidence supporting the regularity of natural laws. Hume posited that the improbability of miracles is so great that it would be more reasonable to assume that the testimony is mistaken or deceptive than to believe that a natural law has been violated. His principle is that a wise person proportions his belief to the evidence, and the uniform experience supporting natural laws overwhelmingly outweighs the evidence for any purported miracle. However, one is able to respond to Hume's critique by re-evaluating the weight of testimony and the prior probability of miracles. If the testimony comes from multiple independent and credible witnesses, the combined evidence, *contra* Hume, can indeed become compelling.

Additionally, if these witnesses have nothing to gain and potentially much to lose by their testimony (such as facing persecution), their accounts gain further credibility. Moreover, the prior probability of miracles changes significantly if one considers the existence of a divine being. If God exists and has the attributes of omnipotence, omniscience and perfect goodness, the occurrence of miracles becomes more likely because a God with these attributes could and would have reason to intervene in the natural order for specific purposes, such as answering prayers or authenticating a prophet's message. Evaluating the evidence for miracles thus requires considering not just the improbability of the event given natural laws, but also the probability of the event given the existence of God. If independent arguments and evidence (such as cosmological and teleological arguments etc.) make the existence of God probable, then the occurrence of miracles becomes correspondingly more probable. This shifts the balance of evidence and suggests that the testimony of miracles should be taken more seriously. Thus, while there is some evidence for the occurrence of miracles – and they cannot be dismissed *a priori à la* Hume – a more detailed examination of historical evidence is required to strengthen these arguments. Hence, this all provides a weak C-inductive argument from particular historical events to the existence of God. Thus, one is indeed invited to consider additional historical evidence to determine whether a stronger argument can be made (as will be provided in later chapters).

The Argument from Religious Experience

If there is a God, one might expect him to reveal himself individually to some people. However, God would likely avoid too evident and public manifestations, as this would curtail human freedom to choose between good and evil. Hence, God's private and occasional manifestations to certain individuals are to be expected. The argument from religious experience claims that many have experienced God, or something connected with God, and hence know and can testify to his existence. At a more specific level, religious experiences can be understood as conscious mental events. In relation to this, there is a distinction between external descriptions, which entail the existence of an external thing, and internal descriptions, which do not. For example, saying 'I talked to God last night' is an external description that implies God's existence, whereas saying 'I had an auditory sensation that seemed to come from God' is an internal description that does not. Useful arguments from religious experience should be phrased as internal descriptions. Religious experiences are thus those that seem (epistemically) to the subject to be experiences of God or some supernatural entity. This definition captures the most important experiences for the purpose of the argument, as they appear to wear their religious origin on their face. Thus, a subject experiences God if the experience of seeming to perceive God is caused by God's presence. Now, religious experiences can be classified into five types: (i) experiences of ordinary objects seen as divine, such as someone looking at the night sky and suddenly seeing it as God's handiwork; (ii) experiences of unusual public objects, such as witnessing events like the resurrection appearances of Jesus or the appearance of Mary at Fatima, where the subject perceives a public event as religious; (iii) private sensations describable by normal vocabulary, such as Joseph's dream of an angel in Matthew 1:20-21, which is considered a religious experience because Joseph perceived the angel as real, not just a dream figure; (iv) private sensations not describable by normal vocabulary, where sensations are analogous to normal ones but are so unusual they lack proper descriptive vocabulary; and (v) non-sensory experiences involving situations where it strongly seems to the subject that he is aware of God or a timeless reality without any sensory input. Mystics claiming to experience God through nothingness fall into this category. It is a principle of rationality to trust how things seem to be, in the absence of special considerations. Thus, if it seems to a person that he has experienced God, then he probably has. This principle, the principle of credulity, as noted previously, states that how things seem (epistemically) to a subject is good grounds for belief about how things are – with special considerations being able to challenge the principle of credulity. First, if the subject or the conditions under which the experience was had are generally unreliable, the claim can be doubted. Second, if similar claims have proven false in the past, the new claim can be questioned. Third, if it is very improbable on background evidence that the object of the experience was present, the claim is less credible. Fourth, if there is a plausible alternative explanation for why it seemed to the subject that he experienced God, the claim can be doubted. Moreover, conflicting religious experiences are also an issue: different religious traditions report experiences of different deities or supernatural entities. However, this does not necessarily discredit all religious experiences, as conflicting descriptions may not always entail true contradictions. For example, God might be known under different names in different cultures.

Nonetheless, religious experiences, when taken at face value and in the absence of special considerations that challenge their validity, are able to provide *prima facie* evidence for the existence of God. The cumulative testimony of many individuals reporting religious experiences strengthens the argument for theism, making it a significant part of the overall case for God's existence. That is, according to the principle of credulity, someone who has had a religious experience that seems to be of God has valid grounds for believing in God's existence, assuming there are no overriding objections – with this being especially true if the experience is particularly compelling. The only way to counter this belief is to demonstrate that it is significantly more probable that God does not exist. However, if the probability of God's existence, based on the evidence adduced in the previous sections, is considerably less than half, then individual religious experiences need corroboration from others with similar experiences – and such corroboration is indeed available. Therefore, unless the prior probability of God's existence is extremely low, the collective testimony of religious experiences should be enough to support the belief in God – and thus the argument from religious experience being a (moderately) strong C-inductive argument for the existence of God.

The Balance of Probability

In previous sections, it has been argued that various phenomena are more probable if there is a God than if there is not. The existence of the universe, its conformity to order, the existence of conscious animals and humans with moral awareness, humans having great opportunities for cooperation in acquiring knowledge and moulding the universe, the pattern of history, some evidence of miracles and religious experiences, are all phenomena that one has reason to expect if there is a God and less reason to expect otherwise. For each of these phenomena, the probability that they occur given theism is greater than the probability that they occur without it, making each argument a good C-inductive argument for the existence of God. Now, in using principles of probability, the probability of theism can be calculated by considering the prior probability of theism, the probability of the evidence given theism and the probability of the evidence without theism. In utilising the methodology of Bayes' theorem (where h is the hypothesis [of theism], e is the evidence [of natural theology], and k is the background knowledge [including the previously adduced evidence of natural theology]), a probabilistic argument for theism can be formulated that takes into account this data:

$$P(h/e.k) > \tfrac{1}{2}$$

As has been affirmed previously, the prior probability of theism $P(h/k)$ is significantly high due to its simplicity compared to other hypotheses. Furthermore, the explanatory power of theism $P(e/h.k)$ is high because the existence of God makes the observed phenomena more likely (with the evidence provided from evil and hiddenness also being taken into account). On the other hand, the probability of the evidence occurring without theism $P(e/\neg h.k)$ is low, given the complexity required for alternative explanations to account for the same phenomena. Therefore, it is to be concluded that the posterior probability of theism $P(h/e.k)$ is more than 0.5. Thus, theism is more probable than its negation, and the argument from all the phenomena forms a strong P-inductive argument for the existence of God.

In conclusion, Swinburne's application of his philosophical framework provides grounds for assessing the probability of theism.

Swinburne establishes that theism, characterised by the simplicity of a single omnipotent, omniscient and perfectly free being, provides a natural and probable explanation for the existence and order of the universe. Using Bayes' theorem, Swinburne demonstrates that the cumulative evidence from cosmological and teleological arguments, consciousness and morality, providence and religious experiences significantly bolsters the case for theism. While acknowledging the challenge posed by the problem of evil, he argues that the overall evidence, including the occurrence of miracles and historical phenomena, supports theism as a more probable hypothesis than its alternatives. Ultimately, Swinburne concludes that theism offers a robust and rational explanation for the world's existence and features, making it a compelling framework for understanding the universe and our place within it.

Critical Engagements

The Existence of God has received significant attention and sparked various critical engagements from scholars, as Swinburne's work seeks to demonstrate that the existence of God is more probable than not and, thus, God can be taken to (probably) exist. However, several critics have challenged different aspects of Swinburne's arguments featured in this work. Scholars such as Paul Draper, Joshua Golding, Richard L. Sturch, Herman Philipse and Adolf Grünbaum have raised objections that question the cogency and methodology of Swinburne's theistic claims. This section explores these critical engagements and presents responses that align with Swinburne's philosophical perspective.

Paul Draper

Critical Engagement. Paul Draper, in his festschrift essay 'Simplicity and Natural Theology'[9], provides a detailed critique of Swinburne's reliance on simplicity as a central criterion for assessing the probability of theism. Draper proposes that coherence – the internal mutual support among a hypothesis's components – may be more

---

9. Draper, Paul. "Simplicity and Natural Theology." In *Reason and Faith: Themes From Swinburne*, edited by Michael Bergmann and Jeffrey E. Brower, pp.48-63. Oxford: Oxford University Press UK, 2016.

fundamental than simplicity, thus challenging one of the key pillars of Swinburne's natural theology. He contends that many of Swinburne's examples of simplicity (such as having fewer laws or more elegant mathematical descriptions) can be reinterpreted as instances of greater coherence, where a theory attributes real uniformity to the world rather than one dictated by ad hoc definitions. Draper further suggests that replacing simplicity with coherence has profound implications for Swinburne's argument. First, if coherence is more central than simplicity, then the a priori assessment of theism's intrinsic probability changes: theism may not necessarily outperform its competitors if those competitors are comparably coherent, even if they appear more 'complex'. Second, Draper questions whether the uniformity of natural laws, which Swinburne cites as strong evidence for a single divine source, is truly unlikely under alternative, non-theistic explanations if one emphasises coherence instead of simplicity. Thus, according to Draper, Swinburne's case for theism as the best explanation, built significantly on the putative simplicity of theism, risks being weakened when coherence becomes the primary evaluative standard.

Critical Response. An adherent of Swinburne's position can offer several responses to Draper's criticisms: first, while Draper proposes coherence as fundamental, this does not necessarily negate the importance of simplicity in theory choice. In Swinburne's framework, simplicity functions alongside other theoretical virtues – such as explanatory power, scope and fit with background knowledge – to capture the notion that fewer distinct or ad hoc assumptions often yield a more unified theory. Thus, simplicity and coherence need not be in competition; instead, simplicity may help generate the coherence Draper prefers. Second, the historical and philosophical success of simpler explanations – both in the sciences and in metaphysics – lends credence to Swinburne's emphasis on simplicity as an a priori indicator of truth. By positing fewer fundamental entities and principles, theism can be seen as offering a high degree of unification and elegance, attributes that closely align with the broader epistemological practice of inference to the best explanation. Third, the claim that nature's uniformity is "not unlikely" under non-theistic accounts presumes those accounts can rival the explanatory breadth of theism. An advocate of Swinburne may contend that only theism provides a truly coherent explanation of why such uniformity should obtain at a fundamental level – especially given the existence of embodied moral agents – which cannot be so readily accounted for by purely naturalistic or piecemeal hypotheses. Lastly, even if one adopts Draper's coherence criterion, the single-person God of theism might remain a uniquely coherent hypothesis, as polytheistic or 'quasi-theistic' alternatives entail a multiplicity of divine agents with potentially divergent powers and motivations – undermining their own internal coherence.

Hence, while Draper's analysis highlights the subtleties of simplicity in Swinburne's arguments, it does not decisively refute the position that theism, grounded in a unified and parsimonious principle, retains significant plausibility within the broader landscape of philosophical explanations for the nature and existence of reality.

Joshua Golding

Critical Engagement. Joshua Golding, in his review article of the *Existence of God*,[10] questions the effectiveness of Swinburne's inductive arguments, particularly in their ability to cumulatively establish the probability of God's existence. Golding points out that, while Swinburne's arguments individually increase the probability of theism, they may not be sufficient to overcome a low prior probability of God's existence. That is, Golding notes that Swinburne's strategy relies on a series of inductive arguments, each contributing to a cumulative case for theism. However, the overall probability remains a contentious issue, especially given the challenges in assigning precise numerical values to probabilities in philosophical arguments. He criticises the reliance on a cumulative approach that, while logically sound, may not practically convince sceptics due to the subjective nature of probability assessments and the inherent difficulties in measuring the prior probability of God's existence.

Critical Response. An adherent of Swinburne's position can offer several responses to Golding's criticisms: first, Swinburne's cumulative case approach should not be viewed merely as a series of independent arguments, but as a sophisticated Bayesian network in which each piece of evidence informs and reinforces the other pieces.

---

10. Golding, Joshua, 'Richard Swinburne, The Existence of God, 2nd ed.', *Notre Dame Philosophical Reviews*, University of Notre Dame Press, 4 April 2005.

This holistic approach aligns with contemporary developments in epistemology, particularly coherentist theories of justification, which emphasise the importance of mutual support among beliefs. Second, Golding's critique underestimates the power of Bayesian reasoning to overcome low prior probabilities. Even with a very low prior, sufficiently strong evidence can dramatically increase the posterior probability. Swinburne's approach leverages this mathematical fact, demonstrating how multiple lines of evidence can collectively overcome initial scepticism. Third, the subjective nature of probability assessments in philosophical arguments is not unique to theism but is a feature of all metaphysical reasoning. Swinburne's methodology, far from being a weakness, offers a rigorous framework for making such assessments explicit and open to critical scrutiny, thus advancing the dialogue in a productive manner. Furthermore, Swinburne's approach aligns with recent work in formal epistemology, particularly the principle of maximum entropy. This principle provides a rational basis for assigning prior probabilities in the absence of specific information, thus ultimately addressing Golding's concerns about the arbitrariness of prior probability assignments. Last, it is important to note that Swinburne's strategy is not merely about convincing sceptics, but about providing a rational framework for belief. That is, by offering a comprehensive and integrated case for theism, Swinburne demonstrates that belief in the existence of God can be rationally justified, even if it does not compel universal assent.

Despite Golding's reservations, Swinburne's cumulative case approach demonstrates remarkable philosophical rigour. By leveraging the power of Bayesian reasoning and coherentist epistemology, Swinburne is able to construct a formidable probabilistic framework capable of mounting a persuasive case for theism. Whilst the subjective nature of probability assignments remains a challenge, Swinburne's approach represents a significant advancement in the rational justification of religious belief.

Richard L. Sturch

Critical Engagement. Richard L. Sturch, in his review article of the *Existence of God*,[11] critiques Swinburne's use of Bayesian probability, arguing that the lack of precise numerical values undermines the

---

11. Sturch, Richard L., '*The Existence of God*, Second Edition, by Richard Swinburne', *The Journal of Theological Studies* 57, no. 1 (2006), pp. 401-5.

effectiveness of the cumulative case strategy. Sturch suggests that, without clear probabilistic measures, Swinburne's arguments may fail to convincingly establish theism as more probable than not. Sturch highlights the difficulty in applying Bayesian principles to philosophical arguments about God's existence, given the inherent challenges in quantifying subjective probabilities. He notes, as with Golding, that Swinburne's application of Bayesian reasoning relies heavily on the subjective assessment of prior probabilities, which can vary widely among individuals and thus reduce the objectivity and persuasive power of the arguments.

Critical Response. An adherent of Swinburne's position can offer several responses to Sturch's criticisms: first, Swinburne's use of Bayesian probability should be understood not as an attempt to provide precise numerical values, but as a rigorous framework for understanding the logical structure of evidential reasoning. This approach aligns with the forms of Bayesianism developed by philosophers such Richard Jeffrey, which focusses on comparative rather than absolute probabilities. Second, Sturch's critique overlooks the heuristic value of Bayesian reasoning in theological arguments. Even without exact numerical values, the Bayesian framework provides a powerful tool for analysing the relative strength of different lines of evidence and their cumulative impact. This approach mirrors scientific practice, where Bayesian methods are often employed qualitatively to assess competing hypotheses. Third, Swinburne's application of Bayesian principles to theistic arguments represents a significant advancement in natural theology, bringing rigour and clarity to debates that have often been characterised by imprecision. By formalising intuitive notions of evidential support, Swinburne's approach allows for more precise critiques and refinements of theistic arguments. Last, it is important to note that Swinburne's use of Bayesian reasoning is part of a broader philosophical project that includes careful conceptual analysis and rigorous argumentation. The probabilistic framework complements, rather than replaces, these traditional philosophical methods.

Whilst Sturch's concerns about the quantification of probabilities in Swinburne's arguments are valid, they do not undermine the overall value of his Bayesian approach. By employing probabilistic reasoning as a tool for analysing the structure of evidential support, Swinburne brings much-needed clarity to the field of natural theology. His integration of Bayesian principles with traditional philosophical methods represents a significant contribution to the ongoing dialogue between faith and reason.

Herman Philipse

Critical Engagement. Herman Philipse, in his work *God in the Age of Science*,[12] offers a comprehensive critique of Swinburne's arguments, first, by questioning the principle of credulity, suggesting that religious experiences are subjective and culturally influenced. Thus, their credibility as evidence for theism is dubious. Philipse also challenges Swinburne's reliance on simplicity, noting it can lead to the rejection of more complex but potentially accurate explanations. Additionally, Philipse criticises the predictive power of theism, arguing that it lacks the ability to generate empirically testable and falsifiable predictions, which limits its explanatory power and usefulness as a scientific theory.

Critical Response. An adherent of Swinburne's position can offer several responses to Philipse's criticisms: first, Philipse's critique of the principle of credulity overlooks its fundamental role in epistemology. Far from being a mere tool for validating religious experiences, this principle underpins our basic trust in sensory perception and memory. Second, Philipse's challenge to Swinburne's use of simplicity mischaracterises its role in Swinburne's arguments. Simplicity is not employed as a blunt instrument to reject complexity, but as part of a sophisticated framework for theory evaluation that includes explanatory power, scope and fit with background knowledge. This approach mirrors the use of theoretical virtues in scientific reasoning, as elucidated by philosophers of science such as Thomas Kuhn and Ernan McMullin, with the latter defending the use of theoretical virtues in his work *The Inference that Makes Science*.[13] Third, the criticism regarding predictive power fails to appreciate the nature of theism as a metaphysical hypothesis rather than a scientific theory. Swinburne's approach can be understood within the framework of inference to the best explanation (IBE), in which explanatory power is not limited to generating novel predictions but includes the ability to

---

12. Philipse, *God*.
13. McMullin, Ernan. *The Inference That Makes Science*. Milwaukee, WI: Marquette University Press, 1992.

provide virtuous explanation of existing phenomena. This aligns with the work of philosophers such as Peter Lipton on IBE and its role in both scientific and philosophical reasoning, which was defended by him in his work *Inference to the Best Explanation*.[14] Last, it is important to note that Swinburne's arguments are not intended to provide a mathematical-style proof, but rather to demonstrate, in a similar way to science and history of the various phenomena that they investigate, the rational acceptability of theism. By offering a comprehensive and integrated case that addresses multiple aspects of reality, Swinburne provides a sophisticated philosophical framework for understanding the world that goes beyond narrow empiricism.

Although Philipse's comprehensive critique poses significant challenges to Swinburne's arguments, a closer examination reveals the resilience of Swinburne's approach. By grounding his use of the principle of credulity and simplicity in a broader epistemological framework, Swinburne demonstrates the coherence of his methodology. Moreover, by situating his arguments within the context of inference to the best explanation, Swinburne offers a compelling case for the explanatory power of theism that goes beyond narrow empirical considerations.

Adolf Grünbaum

Critical Engagement. Adolf Grünbaum, in his article 'The Poverty of Theistic Cosmology',[15] provides a detailed critique of Swinburne's cosmological arguments, particularly focussing on the notion of the Primordial Existential Question (PEQ) – the question of why there is something rather than nothing (or why the universe exists at all). Grünbaum argues that Swinburne's appeal to the PEQ is fundamentally flawed, as it rests on ill-founded assumptions. Grünbaum contends that the very existence of the universe and its laws does not require external causal explanation, contrary to Swinburne's claims. He argues that the demand for such an explanation is based on dubious presuppositions, such as the principle that there must be a reason for the existence of anything at all. Grünbaum also criticises

---

14. Lipton, Peter. *Inference to the Best Explanation*. London: Routledge, 1991.
15. Grünbaum, Adolf, 'The Poverty of Theistic Cosmology', *British Journal for the Philosophy of Science* 55, no. 4 (2004), pp. 561-614.

Swinburne's reliance on the simplicity of theism as an explanatory hypothesis, arguing that simplicity does not necessarily translate to greater likelihood or truth. Additionally, he questions the coherence of Swinburne's claim that theism can explain the existence of the universe *ex nihilo*, pointing out that this does not transform scientific brute facts into results that are, in fact, explained.

Critical Response. An adherent of Swinburne's position can offer several responses to Grünbaum's criticisms: first, Grünbaum's dismissal of the PEQ overlooks its profound philosophical significance. As the PEQ aligns with fundamental principles in metaphysics and modal logic, particularly the principle of sufficient reason as developed by philosophers such as Leibniz and contemporary advocates such as Alexander Pruss. Hence, Swinburne's engagement with the PEQ can be seen as part of a rich philosophical tradition that seeks to understand the ultimate nature of reality. Second, Grünbaum's contention that the universe's existence does not require external causal explanation fails to appreciate the distinction between scientific and metaphysical explanations. Swinburne's arguments operate at a metaphysical level, addressing questions of ultimate origins that lie beyond the scope of scientific inquiry. This approach aligns with recent work in 'metametaphysics', which explores the nature and limits of metaphysical explanation. Third, as with Philipse, Grünbaum's critique of Swinburne's use of simplicity mischaracterises its role in Swinburne's arguments – as, again, simplicity is not employed as a guarantee of truth, but as part of a sophisticated framework for theory evaluation that includes explanatory power, scope and fit with background knowledge. Last, it is important to note that Swinburne's arguments are not intended to replace scientific explanations but to complement them by addressing questions of ultimate origins and meaning. This approach aligns with the concept of 'non-overlapping magisteria' proposed by Stephen Jay Gould,[16] which recognises the distinct but complementary roles of science and metaphysics.

Grünbaum's critique, whilst incisive, does not fully appreciate the depth and nuance of Swinburne's engagement with the Primordial Existential Question. By situating his arguments within the rich tradition of analytic metaphysical inquiry and by distinguishing

---

16. Gould, Stephen. J. 'Nonoverlapping Magisteria'. *Natural History* 106 (March 1997): pp. 16–22.

between scientific and philosophical explanations, Swinburne offers a robust defence of theism's ability to address ultimate questions of existence and meaning. Whilst Grünbaum's objections raise important points, they do not decisively undermine the philosophical foundations of Swinburne's project.

In all, *EG* offers a rigorous philosophical defence of theism, which has provoked thoughtful critiques from various scholars. The objections raised by Paul Draper, Joshua Golding, Richard L. Sturch, Herman Philipse and Adolf Grünbaum address fundamental aspects of Swinburne's methodology and arguments. In response, one can defend Swinburne's position expressed in *EG* by highlighting the integration of diverse lines of evidence, the systematic application of Bayesian reasoning, the value of simplicity and the philosophical legitimacy of addressing questions like the Primordial Existential Question. These responses collectively reinforce the probability and veracity of theistic belief and demonstrate Swinburne's commitment to a robust and intellectually rigorous defence of theism.

Conclusion

In conclusion, this chapter has provided a comprehensive guide for readers of *The Existence of God*, highlighting the central aim, structure and themes of the work. Swinburne's detailed analysis of inductive arguments, the nature and justification of explanation, and various classical and contemporary arguments for the existence of God demonstrate the rational defensibility of theism. By addressing both historical and modern challenges to theistic claims, Swinburne reinforces the evidential support for, and thus probability of, God's existence. This guide emphasises the significance of Swinburne's philosophical methodology and the importance of cumulative evidence in supporting theistic belief. As readers explore *The Existence of God* for themselves, they will be better equipped to appreciate Swinburne's rigorous defence of the veracity of theism and its significance in contemporary philosophy.

Chapter Three

The Problem of Evil

This chapter serves as an introduction to Swinburne's *Providence and the Problem of Evil* (hereafter, *PPE*), which is a comprehensive examination of the challenge posed by the existence of evil to belief in an omnipotent, omniscient and perfectly good God. Swinburne aims to demonstrate that the existence of evil is not logically incompatible with theism. He argues that God permits certain evils because they are necessary for achieving greater goods, such as free will, moral growth and the development of virtues. The chapter introduces readers to the central aim and structure of Swinburne's arguments, situating them within the broader context of contemporary debates in the philosophy of religion. It outlines the major sections of the work, including an analysis of the necessity of theodicy, the philosophical and theological underpinnings of evil, and the construction of a coherent theodicy that reconciles the existence of evil with divine providence. By providing this overview, the chapter prepares readers to engage deeply with Swinburne's systematic and rigorous examination of the problem of evil, demonstrating that its existence is not logically incompatible with theism.

Providence and the Problem of Evil: Background

Central Aim

The central aim of *PPE* is to address the challenge posed by the existence of evil to the belief in an omnipotent, omniscient and perfectly good God. Swinburne seeks to demonstrate that the existence of evil is not logically incompatible with theism. He argues that God permits certain evils because they are necessary for achieving greater goods, such as free will, moral growth and the development of virtues. *PPE* is structured to tackle both philosophical and theological issues related to the problem of evil. It involves a detailed analysis of the nature of evil and the reasons why a benevolent God might allow it to exist.

Historical Significance

PPE was published in 1998 as the fourth book in Swinburne's tetralogy on Christian doctrine. It is important to note that, even though *PPE* is part of the tetralogy on Christian doctrine (and thus includes certain teachings found within Christianity), the overall focus of the work is on rebutting the problem of evil, which is traditionally an issue against a general theistic conception of God, and thus this work fits better with the project of bare theism, rather than that of ramified theism. The immediate historical context of *PPE* involves broader debates about the nature of evil and its relation to the existence of God. Philosophers such as J.L. Mackie, in *The Miracle of Theism*, William Rowe, in 'The Problem of Evil and Some Varieties of Atheism',[1] and Paul Draper, in 'Pain and Pleasure: An Evidential Problem for Theists',[2] had famously challenged the compatibility of the existence of evil with the belief in a benevolent God. Moreover, Alvin Plantinga had also famously responded to these challenges (specifically that of Mackie in his paper 'Evil and Omnipotence'),[3] in the form of the free will defence, most notably in his work *God, Freedom, and Evil*.[4] *PPE* thus seeks directly to address the challenges raised by these philosophers and to provide an alternative to Plantinga's approach, by proposing a structured framework for understanding how a good God could justifiably permit evil. This robust approach to this perennial issue has thus significantly influenced subsequent philosophical discussions about the problem of evil and the existence of God.

---

1. Rowe, William L. "The Problem of Evil and Some Varieties of Atheism." *American Philosophical Quarterly* 16, no. 4 (1979): pp. 335-341.
2. Draper, Paul. "Pain and Pleasure: An Evidential Problem for Theists." *Noûs* 23, no. 3 (1989): pp. 331-350.
3. Mackie, J.L. (1955). "Evil and Omnipotence." *Mind*, 64(254), pp. 200-212.
4. Plantinga, 'Freedom'.

Literary Structure

PPE is divided into four main parts: 'The Problem of Evil', 'The Good Goals of Creation', 'The Necessary Evils' and 'Completing the Theodicy'. However, for continuity with the previous chapters in this book, we shall retain the terminology and dual structure as follows::

1. *Philosophical Framework – The Need for Theodicy*: The first part of *PPE* focusses on establishing the philosophical framework for theodicy. Swinburne discusses the necessity of theodicy, defining it as an account of reasons why God might allow evil to occur. Without a theodicy, the existence of evil counts as evidence against the existence of God. Swinburne explores various strands of theodicy within the Christian tradition, emphasising that an adequate theodicy must demonstrate that the existence of evil is compatible with the greater good that God aims to bring about. Swinburne identifies key criteria for a successful theodicy such that God is justified in permitting the existence of evil if: (i) it serves a greater good and the evil is a necessary condition for the realisation of this greater good; (ii) God has the right to allow the evil to occur; (iii) God does everything possible to bring about the good without the evil; and (iv) the expected value of allowing the evil is positive. These criteria form the backbone of Swinburne's philosophical framework, guiding his analysis throughout. In further elucidating this framework, Swinburne also investigates the goods that God aims to achieve, such as beauty, moral and intellectual development, and the capacity for worship, arguing that many of these goods cannot be realised without the existence of certain evils.
2. *Theological Application – Construction of Theodicy*: The second part of *PPE* applies the established philosophical framework to specific theological claims about the nature of God's providence and the necessity of evil. Swinburne argues that many theological claims about God's providence can be better understood when viewed through the lens of

the goods that God aims to achieve and the necessity of certain evils in realising those goods and, thus, provides reasons within this perspective for why God would bring about certain evils within the world. Swinburne thus focusses on addressing the role of free will in God's plan for creation. He contends that significant moral freedom, which allows humans to choose between good and evil, is a necessary condition for genuine love and moral growth. This freedom, however, inevitably leads to the possibility of moral evil. Swinburne argues that the potential for such evil is a necessary cost over a wide range of greater goods that justify God's permittance of evil – and even if they do not, there will be adequate compensation provided in the afterlife.

We shall now unpack in greater detail the various areas covered in both parts of *PPE*.

Themes

Philosophical Framework: The Need for Theodicy

In this section, Swinburne introduces the philosophical framework that is necessary to address the problem of evil, which centres on the need for one to provide a theodicy – a justification of God's existence in the face of evil. Swinburne explains the complexities of moral and natural evil, setting the stage for a deeper exploration of why a perfectly good and omnipotent God might allow bad states to occur. He critiques and refines traditional arguments against God's existence based on the presence of evil and presents a sophisticated defence that considers greater goods and the limitations of divine action. Swinburne then contextualises his theodicy within the Christian tradition, exploring historical and theological perspectives on evil and suffering, and extends his analysis to the intrinsic goodness of creation, mental states, actions and worship.

Problem of Evil

There is a necessity for one to formulate a theodicy – a justification for God permitting the existence of evil. This arises from the challenges posed by the existence of morally bad states, which seem incompatible with the concept of an omnipotent and perfectly good God. The existence of such states necessitates a defence that can reconcile the reality of suffering and evil with the traditional attributes ascribed to God. Hence, a theodicy aims to provide possible reasons why God, despite his omnipotence and perfect goodness, might permit the existence of evil. These reasons must show that allowing certain bad states to occur could lead to a greater good that outweighs the bad. Additionally, there is a distinction between a theodicy and a defence. While a theodicy attempts to provide possible reasons for God allowing evil, showing that it is logically compatible with his goodness and omnipotence, a defence only needs to show that the existence of evil does not contradict the existence of God. A defence aims to demonstrate that the atheist's argument fails conclusively to prove God's non-existence by highlighting that the premises used may not necessarily lead to the conclusion that God does not exist. A successful defence refutes the atheistic argument by showing that the coexistence of God and evil is possible, even if we do not know the specific reasons God might have for permitting evil. The term 'theodicy' and 'defence' are thus interchangeable and can thus encompass any justification that addresses the problem of evil, whether it provides specific reasons or merely shows compatibility between God and the existence of evil. Thus, in formulating a theodicy, it is crucial to distinguish between 'good' and 'bad' rather than 'evil' when discussing actions and states of affairs. 'States of affairs' includes both the events that happen to people and their intentional actions. Pain and suffering are bad states of affairs but are not necessarily evil unless caused or allowed by an agent with malevolent intent. Thus, again, the real issue at hand is the existence of bad states of affairs that seem inconsistent with the actions of a perfectly good and omnipotent being.

Now, it is important to distinguish between moral and natural evil. Moral evil encompasses all bad states deliberately caused by humans doing what they believe to be wrong or by negligently failing to do what they believe to be good. This includes direct actions like inflicting pain or failing to prevent harm, as well as actions such as lying or breaking promises where no suffering results. Natural evil, on the other hand, includes bad states not directly caused by humans, such as diseases and natural disasters, as well as bad desires and temptations that lead to actions like greed and deceit. In addition, in a broader sense, 'moral' is understood as including the sense of 'overall' or 'overriding', where morally good acts are those that are good overall. Obligations, such as keeping promises or not harming others, fall under morally good acts but, as noted previously, there are also supererogatory acts that go beyond obligation, such as giving to charity at one's own expense. Morally bad acts, conversely, are those that are bad overall and include wrong acts that wrong God, termed as sins. Given this, the argument against the existence of God based on the presence of morally bad states can then be presented as follows:

1. If God exists, he is omnipotent and perfectly good.
2. A perfectly good being would not allow any morally bad state to occur if he could prevent it.
3. An omnipotent being can prevent all morally bad states.
4. There exists at least one morally bad state.
5. Therefore, there is no God.

This argument is a valid deductive argument, meaning that if the premises are true, the conclusion follows logically. However, premise two can be challenged, as a perfectly good being might allow bad states to occur for the sake of greater goods. As it is not always wrong to bring about or allow a bad state if it leads to a greater good. For example, a parent might allow a child to suffer the temporary pain of a visit to the dentist for the greater good of dental health. Similarly, God might allow suffering to achieve greater goods that humans cannot fully comprehend.

Hence, to further refine the argument, premise two can be developed into a more sophisticated version that takes into account the possibility of greater goods resulting from bad states. The revised premise two thus states:

2. A perfectly good being will never allow a morally bad state to occur if (i) he can prevent it – unless it is the only way to achieve a greater good (i.e. it is the necessary condition for the realisation of the greater good), (ii) he has the right to allow it, (iii) he does everything else possible to achieve the good, and (iv) the expected value of allowing the bad state is positive.

Now, the theist's defence is that God allows bad states to occur only if they meet the four-fold criteria featured in the above premise. Thus, this defence requires it to be shown that each bad state allowed by God meets the conditions of having a morally justifiable reason. Moreover, while this defence may not always be evident to humans, it is reasonable to believe that God has justifiable reasons for allowing bad states to occur. Thus, addressing the problem of evil requires a theodicy that explains how bad states of affairs can coexist with the existence of a perfectly good and omnipotent God. This involves recognising the potential for greater goods that might justify the presence of bad states and understanding the limitations and self-imposed constraints on God's actions.

Theodicy in Christian Tradition
The problem of evil is particularly pressing within theistic thought due to the dual commitments to God's omnipotence and perfect goodness. Denying either attribute, as some such as the Manichaeans did, can bypass the problem of evil. Manichaeism posited that God was not strong enough to prevent evil because Good (God) and Evil were two equally powerful forces. In a similar vein, modern process theologians such as Charles Hartshorne and John Cobb have claimed that God is not omnipotent and that evil exists because God cannot eliminate it. However, traditional Christian theodicy maintains that God is omnipotent and perfectly good, and the existence of evil must be reconciled within this framework.

Now, within traditional Christian thinking concerning the problem of evil, evil has been conceived of as *privation boni*, or the absence of good. This idea, which was influenced by Neoplatonism, suggests that evil is not a real, positive entity but rather a lack of some good that ought to be present. Pseudo-Dionysius described evil as 'purposeless, ugly, lifeless, mindless, unreasonable, imperfect'; and Aquinas, in his work *Summa Theologica* I, Q. 4, Art.1,[5] also supported this view, stating that nothing is called bad in so far as it is an entity, but rather in so far as it lacks some being, such as a man being called bad if he lacks virtue. Despite the appeal of this view, it is indeed implausible, as pain and suffering, bad desires and wicked acts are more than mere absences of good; they are positive states that cannot be fully explained by *privatio boni*. Most Christian thinkers have argued that God allows evil to occur for the sake of greater goods that

---

5. Aquinas, *Summa*. First Part, Question 4, Article 1.

could not be achieved otherwise. Augustine, in his work *Enchiridion*,[6] likened the universe to a beautiful picture that is enhanced by well-managed shadows, suggesting that the presence of sinners can, in a broader view, contribute to the overall beauty of creation. Thus, this greater good defence posits that some evils make possible greater goods, although specifying these goods in every instance remains challenging.

However, what is central to many theodicies is the free will defence, which asserts that moral evil results from the misuse of human free will, and free will, of the libertarian kind, is a great good because it allows humans to make meaningful choices and develop moral virtues. Additionally, the concept of the Fall is another crucial element in many theodicies. Augustine, in his work *The City of God*,[7] and later theologians saw Adam's sin as causing not only human mortality and suffering but also a proneness to sin transmitted through generations. This view, while prominent in Western Christianity, is not universally accepted. For example, Eastern Orthodox theology tends to emphasise the immature nature of humanity at creation and sees the Fall more as a stage in human development rather than a catastrophic event. Moreover, Augustine's idea of original guilt, which makes all humans guilty for Adam's sin, has been rejected by many modern theologians as morally untenable. Other strands of theodicy have also emerged within the Christian tradition. The Book of Job, for example, grapples with the question of suffering without providing a systematic explanation, instead highlighting the inscrutability of God's ways; and the New Testament, while not offering a comprehensive theodicy, suggests that suffering can serve a purpose, such as revealing God's works or testing faith. Additionally, the value of suffering in moral and spiritual development is also a theme that is especially prominent in Eastern Orthodox thought. Thus, a comprehensive theodicy integrates various elements from the Christian tradition to show that God has good reasons for allowing both moral and natural evil; and, despite various reasons that have been put forward in Church history, this will include emphasising

---

6. Augustine of Hippo. *Enchiridion on Faith, Hope and Love*. Edited by Henry Paolucci. Washington, D.C.: Regnery Gateway, 1961.
7. Augustine. *The City of God Against the Pagans*. Edited and translated by R. W. Dyson. Cambridge University Press, 1998, Book XIII, Chapter 14, pp. 569-570.

the importance of human free will and the potential for suffering to contribute to greater goods. The question to be faced is what exactly these greater goods are.

Beauty

On the basis of Genesis 1:1-19, which emphasises the inherent goodness of God's creation, a perfectly good God will seek to perform many good actions and avoid bad ones, with good actions deriving their goodness from bringing about states of affairs that are intrinsically good. The goodness or badness of states arises from their impact on someone or something, thus it is important to understand who or what benefits or suffers from these states. Moreover, there is no general formula for identifying good and bad states of affairs due to their diverse nature. G.E. Moore's *Principia Ethica* (1903) argues that intrinsic goods and evils are highly complex wholes composed of parts that have little or no value independently. However, in diverging from Moore's suggestion that many ordinary things lack intrinsic value, one can posit that every concrete thing, such as a stick or stone, has value simply by existing and that this intrinsic goodness does not arise solely from their benefit to someone or something else. Additionally, the existence of all concrete things – stones, icebergs, wind, fire, mountains and valleys – is inherently good. The more of them, the better, especially when arranged beautifully. This beauty can be likened to sculpture and dance, thus suggesting that a moving sculpture of trillions of trillions of concrete things emerging from simple beginnings is even more admirable. The beauty of the non-conscious world, both inorganic and organic, is evident and needs a poet to bring it to life. This beauty is expressed well in popular science books with their prose poetry that explains the simplicity of natural laws and the magnificence of cosmic and biological evolution. In connecting this beauty of the universe with the affirmation in the Bible concerning the goodness of the inanimate world, one can understand that this theme has been a constant in Christian theology, with medieval theologians agreeing that everything that exists is good by virtue of its existence. That is, these theologians debated whether this goodness was intrinsic or derived from participation in a good God. However, in siding with Augustine, one can take the position that the goodness of stones is intrinsic and not dependent on their creator.

Concerning the goodness of works of art, one can ask the question whether a work of art is only good if someone admires it. Admiration stems from the belief that the artwork possesses inherent beauty, which exists independently of recognition. However, even if recognition were necessary, God would admire the universe he created, and it is good for the beautiful universe to be admired by conscious beings. Thus, humans, with their advanced telescopes, are in a privileged position to admire the universe's beauty both in its present state and as it emerged from the Big Bang. Now, while the existence of any concrete thing is good, its non-existence is not intrinsically bad but merely the absence of a good state. If non-existence were bad, any world would be a bad place due to the countless things it lacked. Moreover, ugliness, as a negative quality, is not prevalent in the pre-human world but arises with human actions that render something potentially beautiful ugly.

It is thus clear that there is goodness and beauty within the inanimate world, which underscores God's interest in creating it. Moreover, Jesus' words about the lilies of the field illustrate the inherent beauty and goodness of creation. The intrinsic value of existence and the beauty inherent in the natural world thus suggest that a good God would naturally seek to bring about and sustain such beauty.

Thought and Feeling

The existence of the inanimate world is clearly a good state of affairs; however, the animate world of animals and humans is better due to their mental lives filled with beliefs, thoughts, desires, sensations and purposes. First, beliefs are views about how the world is, which are not readily changed at will, and true beliefs (i.e., views of the world that correspond to facts or reality) are intrinsically good, and thus provide a basic good for both the believer and the objects of belief. Moreover, true beliefs, especially those concerning rational agents and sentient beings, have instrumental value, such as a true belief about which road leads home fulfilling the desire to be home. Beyond instrumental value, true beliefs are also intrinsically good because they acknowledge reality and give a metaphorical life after death to past individuals. Also, remembering the past accurately honours those who lived it and preserves their deeds and experiences, making it a significant good. It is also of great importance to have true beliefs about moral matters, as they guide actions and enhance one's moral character. Individuals are intrinsically better for having the correct outlook on moral issues, such as believing it is good to help the needy and wrong to harm others; and strong true beliefs are particularly valuable as they provide clarity on how the world is and influence actions more firmly. Moreover, true beliefs, especially those justified by proper criteria, are better and contribute significantly to human rationality.

Second, desires are involuntary inclinations to perform actions or have things happen and the satisfaction of desires is inherently good for the desirer, as it aligns the world with his or her longings. Moreover, enjoyment or pleasure arises from the believed satisfaction of present desires, adding to the good of actual satisfaction. Sensory pleasure, for instance, is a primitive form of enjoyment that is good when the desire is for something not intrinsically bad. Having desires indicates a state of engagement with the world. Desires focussed on the well-being of others or shared desires enhance mutual concern and involvement, creating a triple good when such desires are fulfilled. There is also an importance for having persisting desires, which have special value when they are eventually satisfied, and desires that contribute to biological or long-term utility.

Third, emotions are mixed states involving combinations of beliefs, desires and sensations. Emotions are valuable when they are rightly focussed on good states of affairs. For example, righteous anger involves a true belief that wrong has been done and a good desire to address it, urged on by appropriate sensations. Respect is another valuable emotion, involving the belief in someone's greatness and the desire to acknowledge it. Aesthetic contemplation of beauty combines true beliefs and right desires focussed on what is genuinely beautiful, constituting a considerable good. Also, love, in its various senses, involves a complex mix of beliefs, desires and sensations. Loving others means believing in their good qualities, desiring their well-being, and wanting to share experiences and desires with them. Love is intrinsically good, especially when it persists despite inadequate satisfaction. Grieving the loss of a loved one, for instance, is a proper tribute to his or her importance and indicates the depth of the love that existed.

So, true beliefs, good desires and rightly focussed emotions are good for both the individual who has them and the individuals they concern. These mental states should be interdependent and fulfilled, reflecting a good creation by a good God. The higher animals possess simpler kinds of beliefs and desires, while humans exhibit more sophisticated ones, which expresses the diverse goodness of animate beings. A good God would create beings with such mental lives, and the existence of animals provides humans with opportunities for generous love and care, thus further enriching the creation.

Action
A distinction can be made between spontaneous causes, such as plants producing seeds, and intentional actions, which are performed with specific goals in mind. A cause is inherently good because it involves an agent contributing to a state of affairs, making intentional actions particularly valuable. The intrinsic goodness of an action is determined by its objective and subjective goodness. An action is objectively good, as noted previously, if its nature or consequences are good, regardless of the agent's beliefs. Conversely, an action is subjectively good if the agent believes it to be good and performs it for that reason. Actions are better when they are both objectively and subjectively good, thus establishing the importance of aligning the agent's beliefs and intentions with the actual outcomes of his actions.

Now, even if an agent unintentionally brings about a good state of affairs, it can still count as a good action. For example, if someone buys a house and unintentionally saves the seller from bankruptcy, the goodness of the action is derived from its beneficial consequences, regardless of the agent's intention. Even unsuccessful attempts to do good have value, as the effort and intention behind the action contribute to the overall goodness. For instance, if someone tries to save a life but fails, and his efforts lead to the development of a life-saving technique in the future, his action is still considered good. As the value of such actions lies in the agent's intention and the eventual positive outcomes – thus demonstrating the inherent goodness of striving to achieve good ends. Additionally, actions resulting from free will, particularly when chosen between good and bad options, are of greater value. Specifically, actions of 'serious free will' – where an agent chooses between good and bad actions – and 'very serious (or significant) free will' – where the choices involve moral implications – are of greater value. Why this is the case is because the exercise of free will, especially in difficult circumstances, enhances the value of an action. The ability to make free choices, particularly between morally significant alternatives, is a great good for the agent, as this capacity makes the agent an ultimate source of influence in the world, contributing to the overall goodness of his actions. Moreover, the more serious the free will and the stronger the temptation to do wrong, the greater the value of choosing to do good. In short, there is thus an importance to be had by moral struggle and the triumph of good over temptation.

Again, there is indeed a broad scope of responsibility that comes with free will, as one has the opportunity to influence the world positively or negatively. It is good for agents to have the power to make significant differences in the world, whether by benefiting themselves and others or by seeking knowledge and power. It is also good for agents to have the choice of whether or not to seek and acquire knowledge, as this pursuit contributes to their overall goodness because knowledge, both theoretical and practical, enhances an agent's ability to make informed decisions and act responsibly. Also, the pursuit of knowledge involves cooperative study and discussion, which reflects the value of intellectual and moral inquiry. Furthermore, the intrinsic goodness of helping others and being of use is also of vital importance. That is, helping others, whether through intentional actions or involuntarily, is a significant good for the helper. This perspective thus challenges the common view that well-being is solely derived from personal possessions or experiences. Being of use to others enhances one's sense of purpose and contributes to overall well-being. Moreover, while intentional actions aimed at good outcomes are particularly valuable, the value of actions that inadvertently result in good consequences is also important. This broader understanding of the goodness of actions underscores the importance of contributing to the welfare of others, whether intentionally or unintentionally.

There is thus a great importance in having opportunities to do good actions and in the inherent value of exercising free will. A good God would create agents with the capacity for significant moral choices and the ability to influence the world positively. Human free will, supported by true moral beliefs and knowledge, allows for meaningful and responsible actions and the presence of bad states of affairs provides opportunities for agents to demonstrate moral virtue and contribute to the greater good.

Worship

The states discussed so far – knowledge, good desires and actions – are inherently good whether or not God exists. However, certain states are intrinsically good only if God exists, primarily those related to a right relationship with God. A good God, for his sake and for the sake of his creatures, would thus desire that beings capable of knowing, interacting with and loving him should do so. Certain propositional knowledge about deep truths of the universe, the source of our being and moral truths leads to an understanding of our duties, including expressing gratitude to God and seeking to do his will. Because God is the supreme benefactor – sustaining our existence, powers, pleasures, knowledge and desires – we owe him gratitude and service. And this obligation extends to supererogatory acts, which go beyond mere duty.

Now, all human wrongdoing to other creatures is also a wrong against God, as misusing a gift from a benefactor wrongs the benefactor, and God, as the giver of life and all our abilities, is wronged when we harm others. Additionally, harming another creature wrongs God, who is the creator and sustainer of all beings. Thus, all wrongdoing is sin, which thus enhances the moral weight of our actions. In reflecting on the nature of God, God's omnipotence and perfect goodness make him holy and deserving of awesome reverence. This reverence is not merely for God's benefit but is also for our well-being, aligning us properly with our ultimate source and sustainer. Knowing God exists is part of fulfilling our duty to express gratitude and do his will, and God would naturally want us to have this knowledge. The ways God might reveal himself, so that we can have this knowledge, would either be through arguments from the natural world that suggest his existence or through powerful, direct experiences of his presence. Despite the inadequacies of human concepts to describe God fully, these concepts give us some understanding, which God would seek to deepen by making his presence known. As our creator, God seeks to interact with us, and this interaction includes feeling his presence, communicating with him and cooperating in producing further good. Thus, like a loving parent, God desires us to share our thoughts and requests with him, even though he already knows them, and asking God for good things makes the resultant good better because of our involvement in its creation. Moreover, as there is intrinsic value to be had by friendship – particularly with benefactors and good individuals – friendship with

God would be the highest form of such a relationship. Now, within present reality, God interacts with humans in limited but significant ways, with the promise of a fuller interaction in the afterlife. Present interactions might include helping us see arguments for his existence, experiencing his presence and understanding our vocations. One can ask, however, why God's interaction with humans is currently limited? Well, it is because such limitations serve greater goods, because the desire for a deeper experience of God and the duty to worship him unfulfilled in the present state are seen as bad states. However, these limitations might serve to develop human character and free will, preparing us for a fuller interaction with God in the afterlife. This afterlife, known as the 'beatific vision' or 'deification', is where the blessed share in the divine life. the question of who will enjoy this afterlife varies within Christian tradition, but it generally includes those who have lived good lives and accepted God's truth. Moreover, concerning the interaction between God and humans from the latter's perspective pre-mortem, which is expressed through prayer, one can understand that petitionary prayer, asking God to bring about good states or remove bad ones, is a duty and God answers some prayers, not all, as answering every prayer might not always be expedient. Nevertheless, the involvement of human responsibility in prayer aligns with the value of free will and active participation in God's plan. In all, worship can be understood to be not only a duty but also a profound good that aligns us with our Creator and sustainer, enriching our lives and fulfilling our deepest desires.

In conclusion, Swinburne's philosophical framework provides a means to address the profound challenge posed by the problem of evil. By differentiating between moral and natural evil, he sets a clear framework for understanding the complexities of bad states of affairs. Moreover, by integrating historical and theological insights, Swinburne highlights the importance of human free will, the intrinsic goodness of creation, and the value of intentional actions. Finally, Swinburne emphasises the significance of a wide range of good states of affairs, arguing that the limitations on divine interaction serve greater goods and prepare humans for a fuller divine experience in the afterlife. Swinburne's nuanced approach thus provides a robust framework for reconciling the existence of evil with belief in God.

Theological Application: Construction of Theodicy

In this section, Swinburne applies his philosophical framework to the problem of evil to construct a theodicy that enables one to address the challenge of reconciling the existence of evil with belief in an omnipotent, omniscient and perfectly good God. Swinburne explores the necessity of acknowledging moral evil and human free will, discussing how logical constraints and the inherent value of free will justify the presence of moral evil. Swinburne also extends this examination to the range of moral evil and responsibility, highlighting the significance of meaningful human choices and the development of moral virtues. He also addresses natural evil, emphasising its role in providing opportunities for moral and spiritual growth, and the necessity of knowledge acquisition for making informed moral choices. Additionally, Swinburne discusses the evils of sin and agnosticism, the rights of God and the complex task of weighing good against bad to construct a coherent and comprehensive theodicy.

The Fact of Moral Evil and Free Will

God's ability to provide all the good things and avoid all bad things, as detailed in the previous section, is limited by logical constraints because some good states are logically incompatible with each other. For instance, it is good for John to be married monogamously to Mary and also good for him to be married monogamously to Ann, but it is not logically possible for him to be married to both at the same time. Similarly, it is good for Bill and Bob to be President of the United States in the same year, but they cannot both hold the position simultaneously. Furthermore, some good states entail the presence of bad states, such as the happiness of a winning football team necessitating the unhappiness of the losing team. Thus, even God cannot bring about logically impossible states or actions that defy logical coherence.

Building on this, one can thus understand that it is logically impossible for God to grant humans 'very serious free will' – the ability to choose between good and wrong with serious moral implications – without allowing the possibility of them making wrong choices; and the more agents with this freedom and the greater the temptations they face, the more likely it is that wrong choices will be made. This defence, known as the free will defence, posits that the possibility of moral evil is a necessary condition for the existence of meaningful free will. Plantinga has been a major proponent of the free will defence. However, issues can be identified with his account, as Plantinga argues that God has middle knowledge – a concept that was explored in Chapter 1 and is best construed as the ability to know (pre-volitionally) how every possible being would freely choose in any possible circumstance. The problem with this is that it seems God could create only those beings who would always choose the good – and thus, there should not be evil within the world. In addition to this Plantinga puts forward the notion of 'universal transworld depravity', which posits that it is logically possible that every possible being would choose wrong in some circumstances. So, again, the problem with this is that if God truly had middle knowledge, he could create beings who always choose the good – and thus, again, *contra* universal transworld depravity, there should be no evil within the world. Thus, in taking a more general approach to the free will defence than that which has been provided by Plantinga, one can understand that God cannot prevent moral evil without eliminating free will, which is a greater good. Free will allows humans to make meaningful moral choices, contributing to their moral development and the overall goodness of the world. However, the occurrence of wrong choices is an inevitable by-product of this freedom. Moreover, in order for humans to have very serious free will, they must have desires ('temptations') that can lead to wrong actions. That is, in order to have a meaningful choice between good and evil, humans must experience desires that are out of proportion to the goodness of the actions desired. These bad desires are a necessary condition for the exercise of serious free will. Bad desires, such as the temptation to deceive, harm or act selfishly, are inherent to human nature. The presence of these desires allows individuals to make significant moral choices, enhancing the value of their actions. While bad desires are themselves a form of natural evil, they are essential for the possibility of moral growth and the exercise of free will.

The existence of moral evil is thus a necessary condition for the greater good of free will. That is, God cannot grant humans the capacity for meaningful moral choices without allowing the possibility of wrong actions, and the presence of bad desires and the logical constraints on God's actions are integral to the exercise of this type of free will.

The Range of Moral Evil and Responsibility
The principle of honesty (i.e., an epistemic principle introduced here by Swinburne, that states that individuals are to seek to express beliefs truthfully based on their genuine convictions) emphasises that God has an obligation not to systematically deceive humanity. This principle means that God must create a world where people can discover the truth about how it works and what is morally good or bad. It would thus be morally wrong for God to create a world where humans are led to have false views on important matters without the possibility of discovering the truth. This is likened to a teacher who must not deceive students in a way that they cannot uncover the truth. This principle is crucial because it ensures that human choices are significant and informed by an understanding of their consequences, both factual and moral. Moreover, for human choices to be meaningful, they must have real consequences for the individuals making them. That is, humans must have the power to influence their own well-being, for better or worse. Hence, God allows people to make choices that can harm or benefit themselves, such as maintaining their health through proper diet and exercise or damaging it through neglect or harmful behaviour like smoking. Moreover, there is an importance concerning the possession of factual and moral knowledge in making these choices – in that, ignorance, while generally a lack of a good state, can also be a necessary condition for making significant choices, as this initial state of ignorance allows individuals to choose whether or not to seek knowledge and understanding. Nevertheless, individuals must start with a basic understanding of right and wrong, such as the principles of justice and, over time, through discussion, experience and reflection, people can develop a deeper understanding of morality, including the importance of mercy and generosity beyond strict justice. Starting with simpler moral teachings and gradually progressing to more complex ones allows for a meaningful choice in moral development. This process can be seen in reality through the progression from the morality of the Old Testament to the more developed teachings of the New Testament, particularly the Sermon on the Mount.

Now, having significant responsibility for oneself inevitably involves the risk of making bad choices. However, this risk is necessary for the good of having true freedom and responsibility. This includes the ability to develop one's character, make long-term commitments and influence one's own future for better or worse. The possibility of becoming morally corrupted by continually making bad choices is a real danger, but it is also part of the significant responsibility that comes with free will. A good God would thus allow this level of responsibility while providing opportunities for individuals to turn back and make better choices over time. Moreover, it is good for humans to have the power to benefit or harm others, as this provides significant opportunities for moral action. This includes responsibilities such as parenting, caring for animals and contributing to society. This responsibility inevitably leads to instances of moral evil, as some individuals will choose to harm others. However, the greater the responsibility, the more significant the moral choices available to individuals. Limiting this responsibility would thus diminish the moral significance of human actions. The existence of moral evil is an inevitable consequence of the significant freedom and responsibility that God grants to humans. The more freedom and responsibility individuals have, the more opportunities they have to make significant moral choices, both good and bad. This freedom allows for the development of moral virtues and the potential for great good, but it also means that moral evil is a likely and unavoidable outcome. This trade-off is thus necessary for the greater good of meaningful moral agency and the development of a morally significant character. Thus, meaningful freedom and responsibility require the possibility of making bad choices, and this possibility is essential for the development of moral virtues and significant moral agency.

Natural Evil and the Scope for Response
Natural evil, such as diseases, natural disasters and congenital disabilities, provides a broader range of responses than moral evil. Natural evil is not directly caused by human actions, making it a distinct category that allows for a variety of good responses and opportunities for moral development. It plays a crucial role in allowing humans to develop good desires and perform good actions. The existence of pain and suffering enables individuals to cultivate virtues such as compassion, patience and courage. For example, the pain experienced by others provides an opportunity for individuals to feel and express compassion, even if this compassion does not lead to immediate action. This ability to respond emotionally to the suffering of others, whether they are close or distant, is an important aspect

of moral development. Moreover, while it would be better if there were no pain at all, a world with some pain and some compassion is considered better than a world without either. The presence of pain allows for deep concern for others, which can only exist if there is something bad to worry about. The range of compassion should also extend widely, encompassing not only those nearby but also those in distant lands and times, for the ability to care for people far removed from oneself, facilitated by modern technology such as television and the internet, enhances the moral quality of individuals and society as a whole. Furthermore, the 'higher-order-goods defence' argues that natural evil provides opportunities for good actions that would not otherwise exist. For instance, physical pain gives the sufferer a choice to endure it with patience or to bemoan his lot. This pain also gives friends and others a chance to show sympathy or callousness, thus creating a context for moral decisions and growth, and the choices made in response to pain and suffering allow individuals, as noted above, to develop virtues such as patience, sympathy and courage. Alongside this defence, one can also understand that certain goods can only arise in the presence of evil. For example, the courage shown in the face of great suffering is more significant than courage shown under less trying circumstances. The involvement with sufferers at their lowest points allows for the demonstration of deep empathy and support, making the acts of helping and caring more meaningful. In addition to these points, experiencing and responding to suffering allows individuals to develop moral beliefs and desires, thus shaping their character over time. The persistence in doing good despite difficulties is crucial for forming a genuinely good character.

One objection to the necessity of natural evil is that the appearance of suffering, rather than real suffering, could provide the same opportunities for moral growth. However, against this, one can understand that creating a world where humans seem to suffer without actually suffering would be deceptive and violate the principle of honesty. Hence, true moral growth requires real challenges and genuine responses to actual suffering. Furthermore, another objection is that the existence of moral evil alone could provide sufficient opportunities for the development of virtues such as courage and sympathy. However, relying solely on moral evil, caused by human actions, would require an increase in human malevolence and inbuilt depravity. Hence, it would require a more horrible world for humans, who were naturally inclined to cause suffering to each other rather than responding to natural challenges.

Now, concerning animal suffering, one can understand that this form of suffering provides similar opportunities for good actions as human suffering. Animals display courage, affection and resilience in the face of natural threats, contributing to the richness of life. Animal suffering is not inherently evil unless it involves significant pain and the actions of animals, such as seeking food or rescuing their young, are valuable and meaningful. Additionally, it is also to be noted that the extent of animal suffering is uncertain, but it is likely less intense and complex than human suffering. This is that, even though it is quite clear that animals probably do not possess libertarian free will, their capacity for suffering seems to be less than that of humans. For example, in chimpanzees – our closest relatives – the part of the brain responsible for processing pain is roughly three times smaller than in humans. This indicates that, while animals do experience suffering, it is likely to a much lesser extent than humans. On the whole, it can be concluded that only certain animals suffer, and those that do probably experience less suffering than humans. Nonetheless, animal suffering still offers opportunities for humans to show compassion and care, and for animals to engage in actions that enhance their lives. Moreover, for all forms of suffering, one can take into account the intrinsic goodness of helping others and being of use: both the helper and the one being helped benefit from these interactions. The helper gains the opportunity to perform good actions, while the one in need provides this opportunity and receives care and support. This dynamic thus creates a mutual benefit and deepens the moral and emotional connections between individuals.

Ultimately, natural evil, while inherently bad, is necessary for the development of significant goods. It provides opportunities for humans to grow morally, to form meaningful relationships and to perform actions that enhance their own lives and the lives of others. The existence of natural evil allows for the demonstration of virtues and the formation of character, making it an essential aspect of a world created by a good God.

Natural Evil and the Possibility of Knowledge
There is necessity for humans to possess true beliefs about the effects of their actions in order for them to make meaningful choices between good and evil. The goodness or badness of an action often depends

on its effects, such as the harm caused by kicking someone or the life-sustaining benefit of feeding the starving. Thus, for God to grant humans this choice, he must ensure that people have justified true beliefs about the consequences of their actions. This justification is crucial because without it, humans could not trust their beliefs, leading to systematic deception, which, again, would violate the principle of honesty. Additionally, these justified true beliefs cannot generally depend on false beliefs, as this would create a deceptive system. For instance, if erroneous reports about heroin always leading to death were the basis for believing that heroin is lethal, then the system would be inherently deceptive. Therefore, God must provide a mechanism for humans to acquire knowledge of the effects of their actions in a reliable way, typically through observation and learning from natural processes. More specifically, God must establish a system of natural processes that produce predictable outcomes to allow humans to acquire knowledge. These processes enable humans to learn from their observations and understand the causal relationships in the world. For example, observing that certain actions lead to pain or pleasure helps humans make informed decisions about their behaviour. Thus, without natural processes, humans would lack the necessary knowledge to make meaningful choices. This knowledge is not just about immediate effects but also about long-term consequences, such as understanding the environmental impact of certain actions or the genetic effects of certain behaviour. The regularity and predictability of natural processes provide a stable foundation for acquiring this knowledge.

One can thus see that natural evil is this specific mechanism and process for enabling humans to acquire this knowledge and thus learn the effects of their actions. Now, God might implant true beliefs about the consequences of actions; however, such knowledge would not be as well-justified as knowledge acquired through experience. For instance, believing that setting hydrogen on fire causes an explosion is better justified if it results from observing such events rather than from an implanted belief. Consequently, the presence of natural evil allows humans to observe the regularities of the natural world and understand the causal relationships between actions and their consequences. This understanding is vital for making informed moral choices, and thus this ability to learn from experience and seek new knowledge is integral to the exercise of free will. Knowledge of the consequences of actions allows for significant moral choices and the development of virtues. Without such knowledge, free will would be empty, as individuals would be unable to make informed decisions. The process of learning and discovering new knowledge is itself a valuable exercise of free will, enhancing the moral and intellectual growth of individuals. Moreover, experiencing the effects of natural processes, such as learning that eating certain mushrooms causes illness, provides a firm basis for knowledge that guides future actions. Additionally, acquiring knowledge through experience has great intrinsic value, as it is better justified and more reliable than knowledge that appears without empirical backing. The ability to learn from experience and seek new knowledge is a significant good, allowing humans to understand the world and make informed decisions. This process involves observing natural processes, such as the effects of diseases or environmental changes and drawing conclusions that inform future actions. A similar position can be reached for animal suffering, as it is also able to provide important forms of knowledge. That is, animals learn from their experiences and pass on this knowledge through observation and instinct. This learning process thus helps animals to avoid danger and find resources, contributing to their survival and well-being. In addition to this, animal suffering provides valuable knowledge for humans, offering insights into the consequences of actions and the workings of natural processes.

Natural evil is thus necessary for humans to acquire well-justified knowledge of the effects of their actions. This knowledge is essential for making informed moral choices and exercising free will meaningfully. That is, God provides natural processes that allow humans to learn from experience, thereby ensuring that their beliefs about the world are reliable and justified. The presence of natural evil, while seemingly problematic, thus plays a crucial role in the development of human knowledge and moral agency.

The Evils of Sin and Agnosticism
Sin is a fundamental failure to perform one's obligations to God; however, unlike other evils, sin is inherently tied to God – such that, without God, the notion of sin would not exist. The existence of God thus profoundly impacts the moral landscape, increasing the range of obligatory and wrongful actions. Every act of wrongdoing against others is simultaneously a sinful act against God. Failure to worship and praise God or to pursue one's vocation is also considered

a sin. Moreover, the agnostic's failure to seek knowledge about God's existence is a moral evil, reflecting a neglect of duty with significant moral implications. The possibility of sin thus deepens human responsibility, enabling choices that affect both personal destiny and the destinies of others. This framework allows humans to exercise their free will meaningfully, making the choice to love or hurt God a serious and significant one.

It is important to note that there are two central doctrines of Christianity that show how our sin, despite its evil, enables a great good. The first is the doctrine of the atonement which teaches that Christ's life and death on the cross atone for our sins. As will be noted more fully in later chapters, humans owe God much for giving us our lives, and we must offer reparation if we misuse what he has given us. Since we cannot fully repay God for Christ's life and death, what we can offer back to him is reparation through baptism, the Eucharist and other church ceremonies. The atoning sacrifice of Christ underscores the goodness of generous service, demonstrating God's willingness to take human wrongdoing seriously. While it is not good to sin just so God can forgive one, the possibility of atonement reduces the reason God might have for not creating beings with significant freedom. The willingness to make such a sacrifice gave God more justification for allowing the risk of human wrongdoing.

The second doctrine is the doctrine of the Incarnation, which holds that God became incarnate in Christ, and is relevant to human suffering beyond its role in atonement. As it is beneficial for God to allow humans to experience suffering for the sake of achieving greater goods. Just as parents may impose suffering on their children for their long-term benefit (e.g. a strict diet for health or attending a challenging school for community relations), it is often seen as good for parents to show solidarity by sharing in these hardships. When those who impose suffering also endure it, the suffering is somewhat alleviated, especially if we are aware of their solidarity. This shared suffering can provide encouragement and lessen the overall badness. Hence, if God shares in human suffering to which he subjects us for the sake of greater goods, that indeed reduces the negative impact (badness) of suffering (and thus also reduces the impact had against the overall value of allowing these bad states).

Closely related to the evils of sin, one can also understand that God has the right to impose punishment for sin, and general evils, proportionate to the wrong committed, similar to the way in which humans have the right to seek compensation or impose penalties for personal wrongs. God's punishment (pre- or post-mortem) serves as a deterrent and a means of reform, while also respecting human free will. At a general level, worldly failure and suffering can be taken to have religious value by encouraging individuals to redirect their focus from temporal goods to spiritual goals. The frustration of worldly desires can lead to greater reflection on one's life and priorities, ultimately fostering a deeper connection with God. This redirection is particularly significant in seeking God and engaging in worship, prayer and evangelism. Suffering can thus, again, serve as a catalyst for moral development, helping individuals to overcome excessive attachment to worldly pleasures and to seek higher, eternal goods.

Concerning the issue of agnosticism, which is the lack of awareness or belief in God's existence. One can understand that agnosticism is a form of moral evil if God exists, as it reflects a failure to recognise and fulfil one's duties to God. However, some agnosticism is due to natural evil, as not all humans are equally receptive to arguments or experiences of God – though self-deception and wilful ignorance also play roles in sustaining agnosticism. Closely related to the issue of agnosticism is that of the hiddenness of God, which is able to preserve human free will. That is, a clear and undeniable awareness of God's presence would eliminate the possibility of freely choosing between good and evil. Hence, a certain level of 'epistemic distance' is necessary for humans to make genuine moral choices, including the choice to seek and find God. This distance allows for the exercise of free will in a meaningful way, thus enabling individuals to engage in a cooperative quest for knowledge and a deep relationship with God.

Ultimately, the existence of sin, divine punishment and agnosticism, while seemingly negative, contribute to the possibility of profound moral and spiritual goods. These conditions allow humans to exercise their free will, make significant moral choices and develop a deeper relationship with God. The potential for sin and the reality of suffering are necessary components of a world where humans can achieve the highest goods.

God's Right
As God is the creator and sustainer of all reality – and thus the greatest 'benefactor' of his creation – God has certain 'rights' over his creation. Now, it is right for God to permit bad states for the sake of greater goods, and if the overall value of allowing these bad states is positive. By 'right', it means that it is morally permissible for

someone to perform an action if he does no wrong to others by doing it. Thus, God has a right to allow certain evils if it does no wrong to his creatures. Just as parents have duties to care for their children and rights deriving from these duties, God has far greater duties and rights due to his role as the ultimate source of being for humans. Parents' rights include determining how their children flourish and expecting certain benefits in return, such as obedience. Since God's provision and care are infinitely greater than any human parent's, his rights over humans are similarly extensive.

Now, focussing on the concept of a 'carer', which is an individual who has a duty to care for others and corresponding rights. Carers can include parents, teachers and the state, all of whom have varying degrees of duty and rights based on the extent of their care. Dependents, such as young children or the elderly, may be incapable of making informed decisions about their well-being, requiring carers to make decisions on their behalf. These decisions are guided by principles that balance the dependent's self-determination with his well-being. For individuals who are not fully competent, carers must weigh their well-being against their ability to make autonomous decisions. This balance is thus crucial in making ethical decisions about dependents. So, concerning God's decisions about humans – particularly before they exist and as they become more competent – as the ultimate carer, God must make decisions that are objectively in the best interest of individuals, considering both their current state and potential future well-being. This includes creating humans with a life that is good overall, despite the presence of some bad states. Furthermore, God's rights to cause or allow harm are derived from his role as the ultimate benefactor. God must ensure an overall balance of good in the lives he creates, where the benefits outweigh the harms. This principle applies to both the creation of humans and their experiences throughout life. God's decisions are guided by the need to provide a life that is on balance good, considering the opportunities for moral growth and the potential for eternal compensation. Thus, God must not cause harm that is uncompensated by greater goods, and thus there are limits to his rights. However, determining these limits involves complex moral judgements, but it is insisted that God must remain a benefactor overall. This balance includes opportunities for significant moral choices and the potential for being of use to others, which enhances the overall goodness of life.

However, if the bad states of life are not adequately compensated by the good states experienced, God is obliged to provide compensation in the afterlife. This includes the enjoyment of the beatific vision of God in Heaven and other forms of eternal happiness. The overall balance of good and bad in a person's life must thus be positive, considering both earthly experiences and the potential for eternal compensation. That is, God's right to allow evils is justified if it leads to an overall balance of good in the lives of his creatures, both in this life and in the afterlife.

Weighing Good against Bad

As was expressed in the revised premise two in the first section of this chapter, to produce a theodicy for a certain bad state I, it must be shown that God has the right to allow E to occur, that allowing E is the only morally permissible way to achieve a necessary good (G), that God does everything else possible to bring about G, and that the expected value of allowing E is positive. This framework is essential for justifying the belief in God despite the presence of evil. Moreover, to justify God allowing bad states, the overall balance of good over bad in an individual's life must be positive. However, weighing the bad states against the good states they make possible is indeed challenging – though one can use thought experiments and reflections on real-life experiences to draw comparative judgements about the value of different states. In doing this, it is indeed quite clear that life itself is indeed a tremendous good, one that outweighs many bad states – as, let's say, one were to be given a button that could make one unconscious during periods of pain or boredom, it is intuitively correct to say that few people would use it often. This thus demonstrates the intrinsic value of simply existing as a conscious being (as is also evidenced by the rarity of suicide, which is attributable to the belief that life is generally worth living despite its difficulties). Additionally, as has been argued above, the ability to make meaningful moral choices is a great good. The worst states of the world, such as suffering caused by human malevolence, require the good of having significant moral choices to justify them. Moreover, being of use is intrinsically good, as the suffering of one individual can benefit others, making the sufferer's life meaningful. For example, the suffering of a fawn caught in a thicket can be of use to other animals who learn to avoid similar dangers. This principle extends to human suffering, where individuals can provide opportunities for others to develop virtues such as compassion and courage. Even if the sufferer does not realise the benefits they confer, his or her suffering still has value. Consider the case of an individual who can choose between a short life of pleasure or a short life of pain that leads to the creation of a new human being. It is, again, intuitively correct to say that most people would choose the latter, which highlights the value of being of use. Moreover, Christian revelation also supports the value of service and being of use. That is, New Testament passages emphasise the blessedness of giving over receiving and the greatness of serving others. The New Testament's teachings thus align with the theodicy proposed here, which values free will and being of use as great goods. Therefore, Christian revelation can be taken also to confirm the high value of these goods and provide a framework for understanding the presence of bad states in the world.

Now, it is clear that God could have created a world with reduced pain and suffering, but such a world would lack the moral significance and opportunities for virtue present in our world. While there is a point where the number of bad states makes the world worse overall, it is also quite clear that our world has not reached that point. However, a good God would seek to ensure that the total duration of suffering is limited, that the overall balance of good over bad in each individual's life is positive and a compensatory afterlife also possibly being made available for these individuals (with God, through the incarnation, also bearing in this suffering as well, which will lessen the negative impact of the suffering experienced in an individual's life). The current world order, with its mix of good and bad states, is indeed a temporary experiment that will eventually end. The primary point of human life is to prepare for the next world, where the bad states of this world will be justified by the greater goods they make possible. Hence, a combination of the importance of free will, the value of being of use, the temporary nature of suffering, and the possibility of a compensatory afterlife (and the reality God sharing in human suffering through the incarnation) together justify the presence of evil in a world created by a good God.

Horrendous Evils

An extension of the theodicy constructed here is provided in Swinburne's 2023 article 'A Christian Theodicy' (which also plays a large role in James Sterba and his work, *Could a Good God Permit So Much Suffering? A Debate*).[8] The primary extension provided for the theodicy

---

8. Sterba, James and Richard Swinburne. *Could a Good God Permit So Much Suffering?* Oxford: Oxford University Press, 2024.

is focussed on accounting for horrendous evils because permitting such evils involving great suffering gives humans two kinds of final choices about what sort of being they will be forever. First, it allows those who suffer these evils to freely choose saintly acts of great love and commitment to goodness, even in the face of immense hardship. Becoming a saint necessarily involves a readiness to undertake heroic acts of self-sacrifice and service under very painful circumstances. So, to gain this sanctity, one must actually make the choice to persevere in goodness through severe trials. Thus, those who cement this ultimate commitment are worthy of an endless heavenly life, free of suffering and full of ever-increasing understanding, worship and service. Second, allowing the possibility of horrendous moral evils committed by humans also gives very evil people a final chance either to turn away from their evil path, or to cross a threshold by performing utterly wicked acts and losing their moral conscience completely. A perfectly good God would want to give even the most depraved individuals every opportunity to repent and change before letting them seal their fate. And the suffering caused to victims of such evil acts puts them in a position to respond with saintly endurance that shapes their eternal character, even though it did not result from their own choice. Now, while many may not sympathise with giving cruel and evil people a final chance, God as a loving father is desperate to save even his worst children if possible. The free choice of destiny is a great good, and the stunning example set by those who suffer horrendous evils with love has ripple effects that inspire and improve many other lives. Moreover, an intermediate afterlife may allow those who die without making a definite choice to be purified or make that choice. Ultimately, the opportunity for humans to determine their eternal fate through their own free decisions, especially in the face of severe hardship, is a wonderful gift that arguably justifies God allowing even the worst evils and horrendous suffering.

In conclusion, Swinburne's application of his philosophical framework produces a robust theodicy that demonstrates the possibility of the coexistence of evil and God. By addressing the logical constraints on God's actions, he emphasises the intrinsic value of human free will and the necessity of moral and natural evils for meaningful moral choices and development. Swinburne thus highlights the significance of moral responsibility, the development of a virtuous character and the acquisition of knowledge through experience. Moreover, he underscores the profound impact of sin and agnosticism on the moral landscape and the essential role of divine rights in allowing certain evils for greater goods. Through various theological and philosophical insights, Swinburne emphasises the intricate balance between good and bad states, arguing that the overall balance of good in each individual's life justifies the presence of evil. Swinburne's comprehensive approach provides a nuanced and reasoned defence of theodicy, thus enabling one to reaffirm the coherence of belief in a good God amidst the problem of evil.

Critical Engagements

Providence and the Problem of Evil has drawn significant scholarly attention and various critical engagements from scholars, as Swinburne's work focusses on reconciling the existence of evil with that of a perfectly good God by providing a detailed theodicy that argues that the existence of various evils is necessary for achieving greater goods. Several critics have challenged different aspects of Swinburne's arguments featured in this work. Scholars such as Thomas Flint, John Hick, Philip Quinn, Richard Gale and Paul Draper have raised objections that question the plausibility of a number of Swinburne's claims. This section explores these critical engagements and presents responses that align with Swinburne's philosophical perspective.

Thomas Flint

Critical Engagement. Thomas Flint, in his review article of *Providence and the Problem of Evil*,[9] critiques Swinburne for his extensive reliance on libertarian free will and the concept of 'being of use'. Flint argues that Swinburne's dismissal of middle knowledge is problematic, as it introduces unnecessary risks into God's creation, making it possible for significant moral evils to occur. Flint also points out that Swinburne's criteria for divine permission of evils involve logical and ethical complexities that are not fully addressed.

Critical Response. An adherent of Swinburne's position can offer several responses to Flint's criticisms: first, Flint's concerns about libertarian free

---

9. Flint, Thomas P., 'Review of *Providence and the Problem of Evil* by Richard Swinburne', *The Philosophical Review* 110, no. 1 (2001), pp. 120-22.

will overlook the nuanced philosophical grounding Swinburne provides in his theodicy. That is, Swinburne argues that such freedom is not merely desirable, but essential for the development of moral character and the authentic pursuit of virtue. This view thus engages with fundamental questions in moral philosophy about the nature of ethical growth and responsibility. Second, Swinburne's dismissal of middle knowledge stems from the rigorous analysis he provides of this concept. He contends that the concept is inherently self-contradictory, as it assumes deterministic outcomes for fundamentally indeterministic agents. This argument thus challenges Molinism at its core, questioning its coherence rather than just its plausibility. Third, Swinburne's acceptance of risk in creation reflects a carefully considered axiological stance. He posits that a universe allowing for genuine moral agency, despite its inherent risks, holds greater value than a deterministic one. This perspective offers a more robust theodicy by providing positive reasons for God's choice in creation. Furthermore, the complexity in Swinburne's criteria for divine permission of evils mirrors the complexity of ethical decision making. His approach aligns with sophisticated consequentialist frameworks in normative ethics, engaging with debates about the permissibility of instrumental evils for greater goods. Last, Swinburne's notion of 'being of use' is integral to his ethical framework, not a mere addendum, as it underscores the intrinsic value of moral significance, suggesting that the opportunity to make meaningful ethical choices justifies the potential for moral failure.

After careful consideration, Flint's critique of Swinburne's reliance on libertarian free will and the concept of 'being of use' appears to be somewhat overstated. While Flint raises some interesting points, Swinburne's nuanced engagement with fundamental issues in moral philosophy, his careful analysis of the concept of middle knowledge and his well-reasoned arguments for the value of genuine moral agency provide a substantial defence against many of Flint's criticisms.

John Hick

Critical Engagement. John Hick, in his review article of *Providence and the Problem of Evil*,[10] challenges Swinburne's theodicy by suggesting that it leads to morally questionable conclusions, such as justifying

---

10. Hick, John. "Review of Providence and the Problem of Evil by Richard Swinburne." *International Journal for Philosophy of Religion* 47.1 (2000): 57-61.

slavery and extreme suffering as necessary for greater goods. Hick argues that Swinburne's detailed theodicy overstates the necessity of individual evils and fails adequately to address the disproportionate amount of suffering experienced by some individuals.

Critical Response. An adherent of Swinburne's position can offer several responses to Hick's criticisms: first, Hick's assertion that Swinburne's theodicy leads to morally questionable conclusions misinterprets the nature of Swinburne's argument, as Swinburne does not seek to justify specific evils like slavery, but rather to provide a metaphysical framework for understanding how the possibility of such evils could be consistent with a perfectly good God. This distinction is crucial for appreciating the scope and intent of Swinburne's theodicy. Second, Swinburne's approach to the problem of evil is more nuanced than Hick suggests. Rather than overstating the necessity of individual evils, Swinburne argues for the necessity of the possibility of evil in a world where genuine free will exists. This subtle but important difference allows for a robust defence of God's goodness without endorsing each and every specific instance of suffering. Third, Swinburne's theodicy incorporates a sophisticated understanding of moral development that Hick's critique overlooks. Swinburne contends that the opportunity for significant moral choice, including the choice to resist evil, is a greater good that justifies the risk of evil occurring. This view engages with fundamental questions in virtue ethics about the nature of moral growth and character formation. Furthermore, Swinburne's approach to divine compensation is more philosophically grounded than Hick acknowledges. Rather than being a mere afterthought, the concept of afterlife rectification is integral to Swinburne's overall theodicy, thus addressing concerns about disproportionate suffering within a broader metaphysical framework. Last, Swinburne's theodicy includes a careful consideration of the epistemic limitations of human beings in understanding God's purposes. This epistemic humility, which Hick's critique does not fully address, allows for the possibility that apparently gratuitous evils may serve purposes beyond our current comprehension.

In sum, Hick's critique of Swinburne's theodicy, while emotionally compelling, does not fully appreciate the philosophical nuances of Swinburne's position. By focussing primarily on the apparent moral implications of Swinburne's arguments, Hick does not sufficiently engage with the complexities of Swinburne's approach, such as the distinction between justifying specific evils and providing a metaphysical framework for the possibility of evil. As a result, while Hick's objections serve as a poignant reminder of the existential impact of suffering, they do not comprehensively challenge the cogency of Swinburne's theodicy.

Philip Quinn

Critical Engagement. Philip Quinn, in his review article of *Providence and the Problem of Evil*[11], criticises Swinburne's principle that all suffering, even involuntary, can be justified if it serves a greater good. Quinn finds this principle deeply problematic, particularly when applied to extreme cases such as slavery or the Holocaust. He argues that Swinburne's approach fails to consider adequately the moral repugnance of such conclusions and the implausibility of claiming that all suffering is beneficial for the sufferer.

Critical Response. An adherent of Swinburne's position can offer several responses to Quinn's criticisms: first, Quinn's objection overlooks the distinction that Swinburne makes between the justification of individual instances of suffering and the justification of a world in which suffering is possible. Swinburne's principle, as noted above, is not primarily about validating specific evils, but about providing an explanatory framework for the general possibility of evil in a morally significant universe. Second, Swinburne's approach to extreme cases like slavery or the Holocaust is more ethically nuanced than Quinn suggests. Rather than justifying these atrocities, Swinburne argues that their possibility is an unavoidable consequence of genuine free will, which he considers a greater good. Third, Quinn's critique fails to engage with Swinburne's concept of 'higher-order goods' – those moral virtues that can only be developed through the experience of or response to suffering. This concept is crucial to understanding Swinburne's broader ethical framework.

Thus, Quinn's objections to Swinburne's theodicy, while understandable given the moral repugnance of the examples cited, do not fully consider the nuances of Swinburne's theodicy. Quinn's focus on extreme examples risks oversimplifying the intricate relationship

---

11. Quinn, Philip L., 'Providence and the Problem of Evil by Richard Swinburne', *Faith and Philosophy* 18, no. 3 (2001), pp. 394-98.

between free will, moral development and higher-order goods in Swinburne's argument. Consequently, while Quinn's critique serves as a powerful reminder of the emotional and existential challenges posed by the reality of suffering, it does not provide a comprehensive refutation of the philosophical underpinnings of Swinburne's approach.

Richard Gale

Critical Engagement. Richard Gale, in his review article of *Providence and the Problem of Evil*,[12] questions the coherence of Swinburne's free will defence and his application of rational choice theory to the problem of evil. Gale argues that Swinburne's insistence on the value of free will under severe temptation leads to implausible conclusions about the nature of good and evil. He also critiques Swinburne's reliance on rational choice theory as impractical, given the inscrutability of the utilities and probabilities involved.

Critical Response. An adherent of Swinburne's position can offer several responses to Gale's criticisms: first, Gale's questioning of the coherence of Swinburne's free will defence overlooks the various nuances of his position. Swinburne argues that genuine moral freedom necessitates the possibility of significant moral failings, which is essential for the development of authentic virtue. Second, Swinburne's stance on the value of free will under severe temptation is more sophisticated than Gale suggests. Rather than leading to implausible conclusions, it offers a framework for understanding the development of moral character in challenging circumstances. Third, Gale's critique of Swinburne's use of rational choice theory fails to appreciate its role as a heuristic tool rather than a precise calculus. Swinburne employs this framework to illustrate the complexity of divine decision making, not to provide an exact mathematical model. Furthermore, Swinburne's approach to the problem of evil incorporates a broader metaphysical framework that Gale's criticism does not fully address. This includes considerations of ultimate cosmic justice and the potential for spiritual growth through adversity. Last, Swinburne's reliance on rational choice theory, while admittedly involving inscrutable utilities and probabilities, serves to

---

12. Gale, Richard M., 'Swinburne on Providence', *Religious Studies* 36, no. 2 (2000), pp. 209-19.

highlight the limitations of human understanding in comprehending divine reasoning, rather than providing a definitive solution.

Ultimately, Gale's critique of Swinburne's use of free will and rational choice theory in addressing the problem of evil raises some potential issues, such as Swinburne's insistence on the value of free will under severe temptation and the reliance on inscrutable probabilities. However, these concerns do not necessarily invalidate Swinburne's broader metaphysical framework, which takes into account the complexity of moral decision making and the limitations of human understanding. While Gale's critique points out some areas that require further clarification, it does not conclusively undermine the philosophical basis of Swinburne's theodicy.

Paul Draper

Critical Engagement. Paul Draper, in his review article of *Providence and the Problem of Evil*,[13] critiques Swinburne's reliance on *a priori* reasoning and philosophical analysis to address the problem of evil, suggesting that it overlooks the empirical realities of suffering and the intuitive moral objections many people have. Draper argues that Swinburne's approach is overly theoretical and fails to engage with the lived experiences of those who suffer.

Critical Response. An adherent of Swinburne's position can offer several responses to Draper's criticisms: first, Draper's critique misunderstands the essential role of *a priori* reasoning in constructing a comprehensive theodicy. Swinburne argues that empirical observations of suffering, while important, cannot alone provide a satisfactory framework for understanding the problem of evil. *A priori* analysis is thus necessary to establish the logical possibility and probability of God's existence given the reality of evil. Second, Swinburne's philosophical approach does not ignore empirical realities but rather provides a rational basis for interpreting them. His method involves careful consideration of the nature of good and evil, the value of free will and the potential for moral growth through suffering – all of which inform our understanding of empirical observations. Third,

---

13. Draper, Paul, 'Critical Study of Providence and the Problem of Evil, by Richard Swinburne', *Noûs* 35, no. 3 (2001), pp. 456-74.

Draper's claim that Swinburne fails to engage with lived experiences overlooks the fact that Swinburne's theodicy is deeply concerned with human moral development. Swinburne argues that the experience of overcoming suffering is crucial for the formation of virtues and the realisation of higher-order goods. Furthermore, Swinburne's approach directly addresses intuitive moral objections by providing a rational framework for understanding why a perfectly good God might allow evil. This involves sophisticated arguments about the nature of divine omniscience, the value of free will and the potential for ultimate justice in the afterlife.

It is indeed clear that Draper's critique of Swinburne's *a priori* approach to theodicy emphasises the importance of considering empirical evidence and the lived experiences of those who suffer. While Draper's points are relevant, his critique does not fully acknowledge the value of Swinburne's philosophical framework in providing a rational basis for understanding evil within a theistic worldview. Draper's objections highlight the limitations of purely abstract approaches but do not substantially diminish the philosophical significance of Swinburne's contribution to the ongoing dialogue on the problem of evil. A comprehensive understanding of this complex issue requires both empirical and *a priori* perspectives.

* * *

In all, *Providence and the Problem of Evil* has provoked significant scholarly debate, addressing fundamental issues in theodicy and the nature of divine providence. The critiques by Thomas Flint, John Hick, Philip Quinn, Richard Gale and Paul Draper highlight the challenges and complexities of Swinburne's approach. However, one is able to respond to these issues by emphasising the importance of free will, the role of greater goods and the necessity of a coherent philosophical framework. These engagements enrich the discourse on the problem of evil and demonstrate the ongoing relevance of Swinburne's work in contemporary philosophy of religion.

Conclusion

In conclusion, this chapter has provided a comprehensive guide to Swinburne's *Providence and the Problem of Evil*, outlining the central aim, structure and themes of the work. Swinburne's detailed examination of theodicy demonstrates that the existence of evil can be rationally reconciled with belief in a perfectly good and omnipotent God. By addressing philosophical and theological challenges, Swinburne underscores the compatibility of evil with divine providence, emphasising the importance of human free will, moral growth and the development of good character. His analysis of the necessity of natural and moral evils, the value of rational inquiry in understanding the world, and the role of theodicy in the history of theology highlights the depth and impact of his arguments. As readers explore *Providence and the Problem of Evil* for themselves, they will be better equipped to appreciate Swinburne's rigorous defence of the existence of God, in light of evil, and its significance in contemporary philosophy.

Chapter Four

The Reality of the Soul

This chapter serves as an introduction to Swinburne's *Mind, Brain, and Free Will* (hereafter, *MBFW*), which is a thorough exploration of the nature of human beings and the relationship between the mind, the brain and the freedom of the will. Swinburne focusses on demonstrating that humans are not merely complex machines but possess non-physical souls that interact with their bodies, allowing for genuine free will and moral responsibility. The chapter introduces readers to the central aim and structure of Swinburne's arguments, situating them within the broader context of contemporary debates in the philosophy of mind and neuroscience. It outlines the major sections of the work, including an analysis of ontology and epistemology, the nature of free will and the implications of neuroscience for understanding human agency. By providing this overview, the chapter prepares readers to engage deeply with Swinburne's systematic and rigorous examination of the nature of human beings and the relationship between the mind and the brain, and the implications of this relationship for questions concerning free will, moral responsibility (and, ultimately, the existence of God).

Mind, Brain, and Free Will: Background

Central Aim

The central aim of *MBFW* is to explore the nature of human beings and the relationship between the mind, the brain and free will, specifically addressing whether humans are merely complex machines or whether they possess souls that interact with their bodies. Swinburne seeks to argue that humans are not just physical beings but also possess non-physical souls, and that this dualism allows for genuine free will and moral responsibility. *MBFW* is structured to address various philosophical challenges related to the mind-body problem, the nature of free will and moral responsibility. The work involves a detailed analysis of ontology, epistemology, dualism, agent causation and the implications of neuroscience for understanding free will.

Historical Significance

MBFW was published in 2013 as a work of general philosophy, which built on Swinburne's earlier work, *The Evolution of the Soul*, and thus this work is situated outside the trilogy and tetralogy. It is important to note that, even though *MBFW* is not a work that interacts with theism, the arguments featured within it can be taken to bolster the argument for God's existence from consciousness and providence found in *The Existence of God*, and thus this work should be viewed as a supplementary aspect of the project of bare theism. Now, the immediate historical context of *MBFW* involves broader debates about the nature of consciousness, personal identity and the ethical implications of free will. Philosophers such as Daniel Dennett, in *Consciousness Explained*,[1] and Patricia Churchland, in *Neurophilosophy: Toward a Unified Science of the Mind-Brain*,[2] argued for physicalism, claiming that mental states are entirely reducible to brain states. Dennett's *Elbow Room: The Varieties of Free Will Worth Wanting* and Harry Frankfurt's *The Importance of What We Care About* defended compatibilism by arguing that free will is compatible with determinism.[3] In contrast, *MBFW* defends substance dualism, maintaining that mental states are non-physical and cannot be fully explained by physical processes alone. Moreover, this work also

---

1. Dennett, Daniel C. *Consciousness Explained*. Boston: Little, Brown and Co., 1991.
2. Churchland, Patricia Smith. *Neurophilosophy: Toward a Unified Science of the Mind-Brain*. Cambridge, MA: MIT Press, 1986.
3. Dennett, Daniel C. *Elbow Room: The Varieties of Free Will Worth Wanting*. Cambridge, MA: MIT Press, 1984. Frankfurt, Harry G., ed. *The Importance of What We Care About: Philosophical Essays*. Cambridge: Cambridge University Press, 1988.

provides a robust defence of libertarianism, arguing that free will is incompatible with determinism and that humans possess genuine freedom to choose among morally significant alternatives.

MBFW has thus greatly contributed to the literature by providing a significant philosophical framework for defending substance dualism and the existence of libertarian free will, which is increasingly becoming a minority position in the contemporary field of philosophy.

Literary Structure

The literary structure of *MBFW* is not explicitly divided into parts. However, for a clearer understanding and analysis, it will be helpful to organise it into a dual structure: 'philosophical framework' and 'philosophical application' (the latter is referred to as a 'philosophical' rather than a 'theological' application because the present work focusses on purely philosophical issues). We can thus state this structure more fully as follows:

1. *Philosophical Framework – Ontology and Epistemology*: The first part of *MBFW* focusses on the foundational issues of ontology and epistemology. Swinburne begins by discussing what sorts of things exist (ontology) and how we can know about them (epistemology). He distinguishes between substances (such as electrons, planets and people), properties (such as being spherical or having mass) and times (periods involving substances and their properties). Swinburne then considers the criteria for identity over time for substances, properties and events – with the latter category being reducible to the category of times. Swinburne explores the nature of mental events, arguing that they are distinct from physical events because they involve a subjective aspect that is accessible only to the individual experiencing them. This leads to a discussion of property and event dualism, where Swinburne argues for the existence of both physical and non-physical events. Throughout this discussion, Swinburne explores and utilises an internalist epistemology, focussing on how knowledge is justified from the perspective of the individual knower. He delves into the internal conditions necessary for justification, arguing that access to one's own mental state is crucial for the acquisition of knowledge,

thus providing a robust defence of internalism in the broader context of debates in epistemology.
2. *Philosophical Application – Dualism, Free Will and Responsibility*: The second part of *MBFW* applies the established philosophical framework to the issues of dualism, free will and moral responsibility. Swinburne argues for interactive dualism, where the mind and body interact causally. He defends the idea that humans are composed of two substances: a non-physical soul and a physical body. This dualism provides the basis for agent causation, where individuals (as agents) cause events to occur through their intentions and actions. Swinburne also addresses the implications of dualism for free will. He argues that free will involves the ability to make choices that are not fully determined by prior events, allowing for genuine moral responsibility. Hence, Swinburne provides a discussion of the nature of moral responsibility and the conditions under which individuals can be held accountable for their actions. After this, there is then an (original) application of this framework to support Swinburne's previous theistic conclusions that were reached through his argument from consciousness and providence, ultimately demonstrating how these philosophical insights point towards the necessity of a divine being to explain the holding of various mind-body interactions.

We shall now unpack in greater detail the various areas covered in both parts of *MBFW*.

Themes

Philosophical Framework: Ontology and Epistemology

In this section, Swinburne introduces the philosophical framework for investigating the mind, the brain and free will by examining various ontological and epistemological concepts. Swinburne's objective is to establish a robust framework for understanding the relationship between mental and physical events, the nature of substances and properties, and the principles underlying justified beliefs. Swinburne's detailed analysis thus aims to clarify key philosophical concepts and provide the necessary concepts needed to support subsequent discussions on the interaction between the mind and body, as well as how we can have justified beliefs concerning these notions.

Ontology

The entire history of the world can be comprehensively described using the categories of substances, properties and times (and also causation, though a discussion of this concept will be featured later). A substance, as noted previously, is defined as a particular concrete object, such as a desk or a photon, which can have other substances as parts. A substance exists entirely whenever it exists – that is, it does not partially exist at different times. For example, if a desk exists on a particular day, all parts of it exist on that day. This comprehensive existence distinguishes substances, regardless of their relevance to scientific laws or daily life. In addition to substances, properties are attributes of substances. These properties can be monadic, belonging to a substance independently, or relational, involving multiple substances. Examples include a desk being brown (a monadic property) and John being taller than James (a relational property). Properties are universals, meaning they could be possessed by different substances simultaneously or at different times. Some properties are essential, meaning a substance cannot exist without them, while others are contingent, meaning they can change without affecting the substance's existence. For instance, occupying space is an essential property of a desk, but being brown is contingent. Moreover, the distinction between essential and contingent properties is crucial for understanding the nature of substances and their persistence over time. Essential properties are those without which a substance cannot exist, such as an electron being negatively charged. In contrast, contingent properties can change without altering the substance's fundamental nature. For example, a desk can be painted a different colour and still remain the same desk. To expand on this view, an event can be defined, as noted previously, as the instantiation of a property in a substance at a specific time or the coming into existence or ceasing to exist of a substance. This definition includes both changes and states of affairs, where both are essential for a comprehensive understanding of events. Events often involve relationships between substances and can be temporally extended, such as a desk existing from 1920 to 2026. Using 'event' in this broad sense allows for a more comprehensive categorisation of occurrences in the world. However, it is important to note that events can be reduced to 'times' because they consist of properties possessed or not possessed by substances *at specific times*, or substances existing or not existing *at specific times*. That is, since events are analysable in terms of substances, properties and times, with neither of these three being reducible to the others, times, rather than events, is to be taken as one of the basic categories alongside substances and properties (and also causation).

In terms of laws of nature, different philosophical accounts can be adduced. That is, as noted previously, there is the RBU (relations-between-universals) account, which posits that laws are relations of natural necessitation between universals, such as mass and force in Newton's law of gravity. This account, as also noted previously, is contrasted with the SPL (substances-powers-and-liabilities) account. This account sees laws as regularities in the causal powers and liabilities of substances. According to the SPL account, substances have inherent powers that necessitate certain effects under specific conditions. Now, closely related to the notion of a law of nature is that of causation, where most philosophers since Hume have considered causation as a relation between two events. However, the SPL account's perspective, as stated previously, conceives of causation as holding where substances cause effects due to their inherent liabilities under certain conditions.

Consequently, the objective history of the world is nothing more than a series of events involving substances acquiring and losing properties, entering into and dissolving relations, and coming into and going out of existence. Processes and places can thus be reduced to talk about substances and their properties and times. For instance, a quantum field fluctuating is simply a substance with the property of fluctuating. Similarly, places are defined by their spatial relations to other substances, at a specific time, and motion is understood as changes in these spatial relations, at a specific time. Hence, to tell the entire history of the world, we need only the categories of substance, property and time. Moreover, developing precise terminology to discuss these categories is crucial, as this will allow for a clearer understanding of the relationship between mental and physical events.

Epistemology
The foundation of epistemically justified beliefs involves internalist and externalist perspectives. An epistemically justified belief, as noted previously, is one that is probably true based on the evidence available to the believer, which aligns with the internalist view. This view contrasts

with the externalist view, where justification depends on the belief being produced by a reliable process. However, this dispute can indeed be downplayed as purely semantic, with the focus of our task being on internalist justification, which is crucial for discussing metaphysical possibilities and causal relationships. Building on this, the principle of credulity, as noted previously, asserts that any basic belief is probably true on the believer's evidence unless there is counterevidence. This principle fundamentally supports the reliability of perceptual beliefs. For instance, if it seems to someone that they are seeing a desk, then probably there is a desk unless there is evidence to the contrary. This principle extends to other types of experiences, including memories and logical truths. Denying this principle, as previously noted, leads to extreme scepticism, as it undermines the basis of most ordinary beliefs. Thus, the rational person should be credulous rather than sceptical, assuming that what seems to be true probably is true in the absence of counterevidence. Furthermore, regarding logical modalities, some truths are self-evident and do not require deduction to be justified. For example, the impossibility of a round square is so apparent that it does not need further justification unless challenged by counterevidence. Hence, only when logical status is not obvious is detailed argumentation necessary. A sentence is logically necessary if its negation entails a contradiction, and logically possible if it can be deduced from an obviously possible sentence. Also, thought experiments can serve as tools to illustrate logical possibilities, thus reinforcing the justification of beliefs about logical modalities.

There are three direct sources of justified beliefs about contingent events: experience, memory and testimony. These sources provide non-inferential knowledge about the world, by being underwritten by the principles of memory, credulity and testimony. The principle of memory asserts that what seems to be remembered is probably true unless counterevidence suggests otherwise. Similarly, the principles of credulity and testimony, as noted previously, posit that, first, what people seem to experience is probably true, in the absence of counterevidence and, second, what people seem to report about their experiences or memories is probably true, barring counterevidence. Much of our knowledge, especially concerning our personal experiences, and what we learn in science, history and geography, depends on trusting these sources. For example, scientists depend on observations, calculations and testimonies to establish facts and theories. In addition to these principles, one can also understand that justified beliefs must be causally connected to the events they represent. If evidence suggests that an apparent experience, memory or testimony was not caused by the relevant event, the belief's justification is undermined. For instance, if a belief about seeing a tree is caused by a projected image rather than the actual tree, the belief is unjustified. This causal requirement ensures that beliefs are reliably connected to the events they represent. Justified beliefs about the world necessitate a reliable causal connection, which upholds the principles of memory, credulity and testimony, and this causal criterion is thus essential for maintaining the reliability of our knowledge about contingent events.

Thus, the analysis of epistemology and justified belief revolves around the principles of credulity, memory and testimony, emphasising the necessity of causal connections between beliefs and events to ensure their justification. These principles are thus vital for understanding metaphysical possibilities, logical modalities and the reliability of our knowledge about the world.

In conclusion, Swinburne's philosophical framework offers a comprehensive ontology and epistemology that lays a solid foundation for understanding the nature of existence and the justification of beliefs. By defining substances, properties and times, and emphasising the importance of causal connections, Swinburne provides a robust methodology for analysing the relationship between mental activities and physical events. In addition to this, his principles of memory, credulity and testimony are crucial for establishing epistemically justified beliefs, which are essential for navigating metaphysical possibilities and logical modalities. This all laying the foundation for deeper exploration into the complexities of the nature of human cognition.

Philosophical Application: Dualism, Free Will and Responsibility

In this section, Swinburne applies his philosophical framework to explore complex concepts such as property and event dualism, interactive dualism, agent causation, substance dualism, free will and moral responsibility. By examining the intricate relationships between mental and physical properties, the causal influence of intentions, the nature of personal identity and the basis of moral responsibility, Swinburne aims to provide a comprehensive understanding of the relationship between the mind and body. This exploration enables one to perform a deep analysis of human agency, intentionality and the ethical implications of our actions.

Property and Event Dualism
Mental properties, as noted previously, are those to which a subject has privileged access whenever they are instantiated. This means that the subject is uniquely positioned to know about these properties through direct experience that is not accessible to others in the same way. Physical properties, conversely, are those whose instantiation a subject does not have privileged access to, making them observable ('public') and verifiable through external means. This distinction is crucial for addressing the traditional problem of how mental phenomena relate to physical phenomena. Moreover, pure mental properties are those that do not entail the instantiation of any metaphysically contingent physical properties. For example, the experience of having a headache is a pure mental property because it does not necessarily imply any specific brain state, even though brain states might cause such experiences. Impure mental properties, on the other hand, are those that derive their nature from both mental and physical aspects. An example is the experience of seeing a desk, which involves both the mental state of perceiving and the physical state of the desk being present.

Extending this analysis to events, mental events are those to which the subject has privileged access, such as thoughts, feelings and perceptions. Physical events, by contrast, do not involve such privileged access and are observable externally. Any complete history of the world must account for both types of events, recognising their distinct but interrelated roles. This comprehensive history acknowledges the occurrence of both physical events, like the movement of objects or biological processes, and mental events, such as thoughts and sensations. Mental events are not reducible to physical events, though they may interact in complex ways. To illustrate, consider the mental event of feeling joy and the physical event of certain neural activities in the brain. While these events may be correlated, feeling joy involves a subjective, qualitative experience that cannot be fully explained by describing the neural activities alone. This dualistic perspective maintains that mental events have intrinsic properties that are distinct from any physical description.

Now, a critical examination of physicalism, particularly the 'type-type' identity theory – which posits that every type of mental state corresponds to a specific type of physical state – reveals issues such as the problem of multiple realisability. That is, the same mental state can be realised by different physical states across different organisms, which undermines the type-type identity theory because it cannot account for the diversity in physical states corresponding to the same mental state. In contrast to physicalism, functionalism, a theory proposed by Hilary, asserts that mental states are defined by their causal roles in a system, thus relating inputs (stimuli) to outputs (behaviour)[4]. This view, however, neglects the intrinsic, subjective nature of mental events – this is that, functionalism reduces mental states to their functional roles, thus failing to capture the qualitative aspects of mental experiences. For example, the experience of pain involves more than just the functional role of causing avoidance behaviour – it includes a subjective, qualitative aspect that functionalism does not adequately address. Using the example of pain highlights the inadequacies of functionalism. According to functionalism, pain is identified by its role in causing avoidance behaviour and its relation to other mental states and physical inputs. However, this account misses the essential subjective experience of pain, the qualitative feeling that is central to what it means to be in pain. This subjective experience, or qualia, is a fundamental aspect of mental states that cannot be captured by purely functional descriptions.

The primary argument for property and event dualism rests on the premise that mental properties entail a subjective aspect that cannot be captured by physical descriptions alone. Mental events, such as beliefs, desires and intentions, possess a first-person perspective that is inherently private and inaccessible to external observation. This subjective nature provides strong evidence for considering mental events as fundamentally distinct from physical events. To further support this dualistic framework, one can focus on the concept of supervenience, as detailed previously. Mental properties do not supervene on physical properties, meaning that there is no necessary

---

4. Putnam, Hilary. 'The Nature of Mental States'. In *Mind, Language and Reality: Philosophical Papers*, Volume 2, 429-440. Cambridge: Cambridge University Press, 1975.

physical property that corresponds to every mental property. This lack of supervenience implies that mental properties are not reducible to physical properties. For instance, one can experience pain without there being a specific, corresponding physical state that is universally present in all instances of pain. This independence supports the view that mental properties are distinct and cannot be fully explained by physical properties, and this dualism has significant implications for scientific and epistemological theories. A comprehensive scientific account must incorporate both physical and mental events to fully explain human experience. This means acknowledging the causal relationships and interactions between mental and physical events without reducing one to the other.

For epistemology, dualism emphasises the importance of first-person access to mental events in understanding knowledge and belief. Because individuals have privileged access to their own mental states, any epistemological theory must account for this unique perspective. This approach challenges reductionist theories that attempt to explain all phenomena through physical processes alone. In addition, this dualism also impacts the philosophy of mind and cognitive science, as it suggests that models of the mind must account for the subjective nature of mental events and cannot rely solely on physical descriptions. This perspective thus calls for an integrated approach that considers both the physical and mental dimensions of human experience.

Focussing now on the nuances of pure and impure mental events, pure mental events (such as sensations, thoughts, beliefs, intentions and desires), as with pure mental properties, do not entail any physical occurrences. For example, one can have a headache (a pure mental event) without any specific physical condition being necessarily present. Impure mental events, however, involve both mental and physical components. Seeing a desk, for instance, involves the physical presence of the desk and the mental act of perception. Furthermore, a further (a more novel) distinction can be made between propositional and non-propositional mental events. Propositional events involve an attitude towards a conceivable event under a particular description, such as believing or desiring something specific. Non-propositional events, like sensations, do not involve such attitudes and are purely experiential. Sensory events are a subset of pure mental events, characterised by the instantiation of sensory properties (qualia). These include visual experiences, auditory experiences and other sensory modalities. Sensory events are conscious experiences, inherently known to the subject experiencing them. This intrinsic awareness distinguishes sensory events from physical events, which are known through external observation. Moreover, for intentionality, where intentional actions are those performed with a specific purpose or goal, one can differentiate between intention in action (current intentions) and future intentions (plans or resolutions), which expresses the fact that both involve a conscious decision-making process.

Now, to assess principles about logical modalities, the method of reflective equilibrium needs to be employed. This method, as noted previously, balances common intuitions with theoretical principles to achieve coherence. In normal circumstance, logical possibilities do not always need to be established through detailed argumentation, especially when they are not immediately obvious. For instance, examples like the logical impossibility of a round square illustrate how some truths are self-evident and do not require further justification. However, for less obvious logical statuses, detailed analysis and argumentation are necessary. Reflective equilibrium can thus help to achieve a balance between our intuitions and theoretical commitments, ensuring a coherent understanding of logical possibilities.

Interactive Dualism

Most conscious events, such as perceptions and sensations, are caused by brain events, which themselves are triggered by physical stimuli. For example, the perception of a tree involves both sensation (e.g. the pattern of colours in one's visual field) and belief (e.g. recognising it as a tree). This process is influenced by brain events, which are initiated by light rays stimulating the retina. However, our conscious events, such as intentions, can also cause brain events that lead to physical actions. Following this, one can understand that intentional actions are those performed with a specific purpose in mind, guided by intentions. A distinction, however, can be drawn, as was done before, between instrumentally basic actions and causally basic actions. Instrumentally basic actions are performed without needing to believe in how to do them, such as moving an arm or saying a sentence. These actions are considered basic because they do not require intermediate steps. Causally basic actions, on the other hand, are those that directly cause an effect. For instance, pulling a door handle to open a door is a causally basic action because it directly leads to the door opening. The intentional action of trying to perform an action and having the intention to do it are fundamentally the same. When someone intends to perform an action, this intention causes the corresponding brain events, which then lead to the physical movement. Intentions are thus not merely epiphenomenal but have real causal power, influencing brain events and resulting in bodily movements.

In contrast to this view, epiphenomenalism suggests that, while physical events cause mental events, mental events do not cause any physical events. However, this view is untenable because it fails to account for the apparent causal power of conscious intentions. If epiphenomenalism were true, it would imply that our conscious experiences, such as intentions, have no effect on our actions, which contradicts our everyday experience of intentional actions. Moreover, the core principle of epiphenomenalism – which asserts that conscious events never cause brain events – is indeed problematic, as no one could ever be justified in believing this principle because it contradicts the principle of credulity, as our experience suggests that our intentions do cause our actions and, without strong evidence to the contrary, this experience should be trusted. Therefore, it is highly probable that there is a two-way interaction between conscious events and physical events, where intentions influence brain events, which then lead to actions.

Now, the causal closure of the physical world is the position that all physical events are caused by other physical events, leaving no room for mental events to influence physical events. While brain events often cause sensations and desires, it is unreasonable to deny that conscious events can influence brain events, as the principle of credulity, again, supports the view that our intentions cause our actions. More specifically, neuroscience has shown that specific brain areas are involved in forming intentions, suggesting that brain events contribute to intentional actions. Studies indicate that brain activity can predict actions before individuals are consciously aware of their intentions. However, this does not negate the causal role of intentions. That is, brain events might set the stage for intentions, which then causally influence subsequent brain events and bodily movements. However, even if brain events precede intentions, it does not mean intentions lack causal power. Our experience of intentional actions and the ability to form intentions reflect a genuine interaction between conscious and physical events. Moreover, evidence supports a two-way interaction between conscious intentions and brain events, thus reinforcing the idea that our intentions do cause our actions.

Agent Causation

So, intentions often cause brain events and, thereby, bodily movements; however, it is not merely events within us that cause brain events but rather, we, as agents, cause these brain events by forming intentions to bring about specific effects. To establish these points, the concept of laws of nature, which has been a cornerstone in discussions of causation since the sixteenth century, needs again to be focussed on. Philosophers have long debated whether causation should be analysed in terms of laws of nature or vice versa. According to the event-regularity account derived from Hume, laws of nature, as detailed previously, are regularities observed in events: for instance, if all As are followed by Bs, this constitutes a law of nature. Hume's theory posits that a specific event causes another if it follows a regular pattern, such as one billiard ball moving another upon collision. However, not all regularities qualify as laws of nature – some are merely accidental regularities, such as the extinction of dinosaurs followed by the evolution of mammals. These distinctions lead to a more sophisticated understanding, as developed by David Lewis, who argues, in his paper 'New Work for a Theory of Universals', that true laws are those which form part of the best explanatory system of regularities.[5] However, regularity theories, such as those by Hume and Lewis, cannot adequately explain many instances of ordinary speech about laws and causes. For example, when Newton's law of gravity explains why a planet moves in a certain way, it involves a deeper necessity than mere regular succession. It is thus crucial to understand the laws of nature as relationships involving natural necessity. This contrasts with Hume's concept of empiricism, which claims that we cannot have a coherent concept of natural necessity beyond constant conjunctions of events. This challenge thus asserts that we have direct awareness of exercising causal influence, making the concept of natural necessity intelligible through intentional actions. To elucidate this, one can, again, focus on the nature of intentions, which is a particular kind of causation: forming an intention to cause a bodily movement is essentially the same as causing that movement intentionally. This distinction is pivotal because it shifts the focus from events causing other events to agents causing events through their intentions.

---

5. Lewis, David. "New Work for a Theory of Universals." *Australasian Journal of Philosophy*, vol. 61, no. 4, 1983, pp. 343-377.

Building on this, one can now focus on the notion of agent causation, where humans, as agents, cause brain events by forming intentions. This perspective diverges from regularity theories by emphasising the agent's role in causation. When we form intentions, we are exercising a causal influence that is a direct expression of our agency. This exercise of causal influence is not merely a passive state but an active engagement in bringing about effects. This active engagement aligns with our ordinary understanding of causing events, such as lifting a weight or moving a limb, where we perceive ourselves as the agents making things happen. Furthermore, one can extend this analysis to the powers and liabilities of substances, which are integral to understanding causation. That is, substances, as noted previously, have inherent powers to cause effects and liabilities to exercise these powers under certain conditions. For instance, electrons have the power to repel each other with a force inversely proportional to the square of the distance between them, and they exercise this power whenever they are placed in proximity. Recognising these powers and liabilities thus allows for a more comprehensive understanding of causation, as it accounts for both inanimate and intentional causation. Moreover, concerning intentional actions, these involve agents directly exercising their powers to cause effects. A distinction can be made, however, between basic acts or attempts, which, as noted previously, are instrumentally basic actions that do not require a recipe, and more complex actions that involve a sequence of acts. For example, moving an arm or saying a word are basic acts that agents perform directly. Trying to perform an action is itself a causally basic action, where the agent directly exercises causal influence. This view thus fits with our everyday experience of performing actions intentionally and challenges theories that deny the causal role of intentions.

Substance Dualism
A comprehensive history of the world must incorporate events involving both physical and mental properties – with mental properties being essential for understanding conscious experiences, which cannot be fully explained by physical properties alone. These mental properties, such as beliefs, desires and sensations, are integral to the existence of mental substances, just as, for example, humans, who possess mental properties, are considered mental substances. Now, it is evident from human experience that conscious mental events, such as seeing, hearing and smelling, are often experienced

simultaneously by the same substance. This co-experience indicates that the same mental substance is experiencing these events, which cannot be fully explained by physical properties alone. For instance, when a person simultaneously experiences seeing a tree, hearing a bird and smelling a flower, these experiences are unified within the same consciousness. This unity of consciousness requires the recognition of mental substances as distinct from purely physical substances because different conscious experiences are causally connected to distinct parts of the brain, and these connections are coordinated by a single mental substance. Moreover, any full description of the world must include substances that have all and only co-experienced properties. If a substance has physical properties and physical extension, it must include within its boundaries all parts of the brain whose events are immediate causes or effects of co-experienced conscious events. Neuroscience indicates that different parts of the brain are responsible for different types of conscious experiences, such as visual and auditory sensations. Therefore, the substance that co-experiences these events must encompass the relevant brain parts. However, the mere presence of brain activity does not account for the subjective quality of experiences (qualia) that accompany these brain events.

Contrary to reductionist views, mental properties cannot be treated as non-essential properties of physical substances. A full account of the world must recognise the necessity of mental substances, whose identity is partly determined by mental properties. This perspective challenges the 'animalist' theory of personal identity, which claims that human beings are merely physical substances with contingent mental properties. This view fails to account for the evident unity of conscious experiences, necessitating the inclusion of mental substances in any comprehensive description of the world – with mental substances having essential properties, such as the capacity for beliefs, desires and the disposition to have sensations or thoughts, which are not reducible to physical properties. This underscores the distinct nature of mental substances. Moreover, with regard to the diachronic unity of the human person, which concerns what it means for a person to remain the same over time, mental substances continue to exist over time, experiencing a series of overlapping events that span from one moment to the next. This continuous experience is crucial for maintaining personal identity. For example, the experience of pain or a thought lasts over a period and involves the same substance, experiencing both the beginning and the end of this period.

Now, against the notion that personal identity could be reduced to the continuity of physical or psychological properties alone – which is a view held by many contemporary philosophers such as Derek Parfit, in his work *Reasons and Persons* – one should instead affirm the 'simple' view of personal identity.[6] According to the simple view, personal identity is a separate feature of the world, not analysable in terms of continuity of physical or psychological properties. Each person has a thisness which makes them that person, independent of his physical or psychological properties. This view thus allows for the logical possibility that a person can remain the same even if he has no apparent memory of his past or if his body has undergone significant changes. Also, it can clearly be seen that reductionist theories that attempt to explain personal identity purely in terms of physical continuity or psychological properties are indeed problematic, as these theories fail to account for the subjective experience of being the same person over time – even though Parfit suggests that personal identity consists in psychological connectedness and continuity, including apparent memories and similar character traits. Against this, one should instead affirm the position that each person has a unique thisness that makes them who they are, independently of any physical or psychological properties. This unique thisness is an intrinsic quality that is not dependent on physical or psychological continuity, thus emphasising that, even if all the physical and psychological properties of a person were changed, the person could remain the same mental substance.

In addressing potential counterarguments, such as those posed by Hume, who doubted the existence of a coherent concept of the self, one can understand that our direct experience of overlapping events provides a strong basis for asserting the continuity of the self. This continuity is not derived from physical properties but from the consistent experience of being the same subject of experiences over time. These experiences reinforce the understanding that we are mental substances lasting over time. For instance, the experience of listening to a tune or understanding a long sentence involves overlapping conscious events, providing evidence for the continuous existence of the same mental substance. This notion of the overlapping

---

6. Parfit, Derek, *Reasons and Persons*. Oxford: Clarendon Press, 1984.

of experiences is crucial for demonstrating the persistence of mental substances, as it shows the need to posit a continuous subject of experience over time. To further illustrate this point, one can think of a scenario involving brain transplants, where it is clear that it is logically possible for a person to continue to exist with a totally new brain, provided the replacement happens gradually. Hence, the continuity of overlapping experiences is sufficient to maintain personal identity, even if the brain matter is entirely replaced over time. Additionally, personal memories, which include a belief about the identity of the person who experienced past events, also support the continuity of the self. These memories are not merely about the content of past experiences but also about who had those experiences. Thus, personal memories provide additional evidence for the continuity of mental substances because they include a belief about the self who had the experiences, which, again, supports the notion of a continuous mental substance over time. Thus, humans are mental substances whose identity is partly determined by mental properties. A full history of the world – unlike that posited by certain reductionist views that seek to explain human identity solely in terms of physical or psychological properties – must include mental substances, as purely physical accounts are insufficient to explain the unity of conscious experiences.

Free Will
Humans are rational beings who form intentions based on reasons, which are influenced by their desires and value beliefs. Certain intentions are called 'ultimate intentions', which are the fundamental goals individuals seek to achieve. These ultimate intentions give rise to 'executive intentions', which are specific actions taken to fulfil these broader goals. For example, if one's ultimate intention is to go to bed, the executive intentions might include going to the third floor to find the hotel room and using the lift to get there quickly. However, the dynamic becomes more complex when an agent has multiple ultimate intentions, necessitating a balance between competing goals and beliefs about the most effective means to achieve them. Moreover, desires play a significant role in the formation of ultimate intentions. Desires are inclinations to perform actions for their own sake, without necessarily being tied to achieving other goals. For instance, swearing out of frustration is a short-term desire. However, most desires aim at longer-term goals that are perceived as intrinsically good. Desires

provide reasons for actions and value beliefs, which pertain to the intrinsic goodness or badness of actions. Value beliefs motivate actions directly, and the stronger the value belief, the stronger the inclination to act in accordance with it. Following this, one can understand that individuals often face conflicts between their desires and their moral beliefs. For instance, a person may desire to rest but also believe that it is morally good to help a friend in need. Thus, such conflicts necessitate a decision-making process where the individual must weigh the strength of his desires against his value beliefs. This process underscores the complexity of human intentionality and the scope for rational decision making.

Focussing on the nature of moral beliefs, which are beliefs about the objective intrinsic goodness or badness of actions, these beliefs are held independently of whether the agent desires to perform the action. Most people hold moral beliefs as objective truths, and these beliefs play a significant role in guiding actions, especially in situations involving moral decisions. Moral beliefs, as noted already, are inherently motivating. If an agent believes an action is morally good, this belief provides a reason to perform the action, thereby inclining the agent to act. However, the strength of this inclination can vary, leading to situations where agents must choose between acting on their moral beliefs or yielding to conflicting desires – a phenomenon known as 'weakness of will'. This choice highlights the complex relationship between moral beliefs and desires in the formation of intentions. To illustrate this, one can look at an example concerning the impact of moral beliefs on decision making. For example, a person who believes that telling the truth is morally right may struggle with the desire to lie to avoid punishment. The strength of the moral belief in the importance of truth-telling can motivate the person to act against his desire to lie, demonstrating the power of moral beliefs in shaping actions. Furthermore, concerning the process of deliberation, where agents intentionally consider relevant thoughts and consequences before forming an intention, one can understand that this process involves evaluating the strengths of different desires and moral beliefs, ultimately leading to a decision that reflects the agent's rational evaluation of the best course of action. Moreover, humans are creatures of habit and many of our intentions are influenced by habitual desires and beliefs, which simplifies the decision-making process in familiar situations. Reflective decision making involves consciously deliberating about options, considering various reasons and potential outcomes. Non-reflective decision making relies on established habits and automatic responses. While non-reflective decisions are often quicker and require less cognitive effort, reflective decisions are crucial for handling novel or complex situations that require careful consideration. This reflective deliberation is central to the exercise of free will, as it allows individuals to act in accordance with their considered reasons and intentions rather than being driven by mere impulses or external influences. Additionally, regarding the role of freedom in decision making, one can understand that true freedom involves the ability to act according to one's reasons and intentions without being irresistibly driven by external or internal forces. This conception of freedom is compatible with the existence of causal influences on behaviour, as long as these influences do not completely determine one's actions – with rational agents having the capacity to evaluate and potentially override these influences through reflective deliberation. Free will is thus limited by various factors, including physical ability, knowledge and the strength of desires, and individuals have limited choices and can improve their range of actions through practice and gaining knowledge. By resisting temptations and performing morally good actions, individuals can strengthen their moral character and expand their ability to make free choices. Free will thus involves choosing between actions that one has the power and knowledge to perform. This includes choosing between actions that are equally desired and actions that are believed to be morally best despite conflicting desires. Making morally good choices thus often requires effort and overcoming strong desires to act otherwise. The strengthening of moral character through the consistent exercise of free will and deliberate choice is thus a key aspect of human freedom, as noted previously, as it enhances an individual's ability to act in line with his or her deepest values and rational assessments.

Turning our attention now to the role of neuroscience in understanding free will, certain interpretations of neuroscience experiments, such as those by Benjamin Libet, in his article 'Unconscious Cerebral Initiative and the Role of Conscious Will in Voluntary Action',[7] which suggest that intentions do not cause actions, are indeed problematic,

---

7. Libet, Benjamin. "Unconscious Cerebral Initiative and the Role of Conscious Will in Voluntary Action." *Behavioral and Brain Sciences* 8, no. 4 (1985), pp. 529-566.

as these experiments do not conclusively demonstrate the irrelevance of intentions, as it has already been noted that intentions play a crucial role in causing actions. Moreover, the brain might set up a range of potential actions, with the final decision and conscious intention occurring later in the process. Hence, conscious intentions are genuine causes of actions, even if they occur after some initial brain activity. Humans are thus not merely driven by brain events but actively exercise causal influence through their intentions, which supports the notion of free will in light of the neurological data, challenging deterministic views and highlighting the importance of subjective experience in understanding human action.

Moral Responsibility
Free will is an intrinsic good that is essential for moral responsibility, and people are deemed morally responsible for their intentional actions – culpable for those that are morally wrong and praised for those that are morally right. Moral responsibility is attributed to agents who perform actions with intention; and unintentional actions – where the agent did not foresee or intend the outcomes – do not warrant moral praise or blame. For example, if someone accidentally injures another person without intending to do so and without negligence, they are not morally culpable. In contrast, if the injury was intentional, the agent is morally blameworthy. This distinction is evident in various legal and moral traditions, including the Judaeo-Christian tradition, which differentiates between unintentional and intentional sins, with the latter receiving harsher penalties. Moreover, for an agent to be morally responsible, he must hold moral beliefs about his actions. Moral beliefs, as noted above, inform an individual's understanding of what is right or wrong, and acting against these beliefs constitutes moral culpability. For instance, someone who believes stealing is wrong and still chooses to steal is morally culpable. However, if an agent sincerely believes that an action, such as stealing from the rich to give to the poor, is morally permissible, his culpability is less clear. Moral responsibility is thus tied to the agent's belief about his action's moral quality, rather than the objective morality of the action itself.

Concerning the criteria that determine moral responsibility – intentions – individuals can be taken to be morally responsible not for the success or failure of their actions, but for the intentions behind those actions. An agent thus deserves praise or blame based on what he tried to do, irrespective of whether his efforts were successful. For example, someone who intends to commit a harmful act but is thwarted by external circumstances remains culpable for his intention. Similarly, a person who attempts a morally good act but fails due to unforeseen obstacles still deserves praise for his intention. Furthermore, people are generally not praiseworthy for merely fulfilling their obligations, as these actions are expected. However, supererogatory actions warrant praise because they exceed what is morally required.

Focussing now on the philosophical debate between compatibilism and incompatibilism concerning moral responsibility, incompatibilist theories assert that moral responsibility requires free will, meaning that agents are not fully determined by external causes when forming their intentions. Incompatibilists argue that, for an individual to be morally responsible, he or she must have the freedom to choose his/her actions independently of deterministic forces. Conversely, compatibilist theories contend that moral responsibility does not necessarily require free will in the incompatibilist sense. That is, compatibilists argue that individuals can be morally responsible even if their actions are determined by prior causes, as long as these actions are guided by rational deliberation and align with the individual's reasons and beliefs. Moreover, modern compatibilist theories often include a rationality requirement, suggesting that moral responsibility hinges on the agent's ability to form intentions based on rational deliberation. With regard to modern compatibilist theories, one can look at those of Harry Frankfurt and Gary Watson, who emphasise higher-order desires in moral responsibility. Frankfurt, in his paper 'Freedom of the Will and the Concept of a Person',[8] distinguishes between first-order (basic) and second-order desires (desires about which first-order desires to act on), stating moral responsibility comes from acting on second-order desires. Watson suggests, in his article 'Free Agency',[9] that it depends on aligning actions with moral beliefs. Moreover, J.M. Fischer introduces, in his work *The Metaphysics of*

---

8. Frankfurt, Harry G. "Freedom of the Will and the Concept of a Person." *Journal of Philosophy* 68, no. 1 (1971), pp. 5-20.
9. Watson, Gary. "Free Agency." *Journal of Philosophy* 72, no. 8 (1975), pp. 205-220.

Free Will: An Essay on Control,[10] reasons-responsiveness, requiring agents to recognise and act on reasons, thus differentiating between strong and weak responsiveness. However, these theories can be seen as being too complex and, thus, one should favour the simpler incompatibilist view that moral responsibility requires both free will and moral beliefs.

Now, considering the issue of moral responsibility for past actions – which focusses on how changes in an individual's physical and mental continuity over time affects his responsibility—if human identity were based solely on physical continuity, responsibility for past actions would depend on the degree of physical continuity. Yet, as individuals age and their physical and behavioural patterns change, their responsibility for past actions might diminish. However, the view that humans are essentially pure mental substances, with identity based on the continuity of their soul rather than physical or mental properties, is not plagued by this problem. This perspective implies that individuals remain morally responsible for their actions throughout their lives, regardless of changes in their physical or mental states. Hence, the mere passage of time cannot erase moral responsibility for past actions. The degree of responsibility for past actions depends on the extent of continuity in memory and character. For instance, a person who retains his memory and character over time remains more responsible for his past actions than someone who experiences significant changes in these aspects. Sudden changes, such as memory loss due to brain injury or a significant change in character due to a religious conversion, can affect the degree of responsibility but do not entirely absolve the individual of his past actions.

Additionally, by practising self-control and making morally good choices, individuals can develop habits that make it easier to resist temptations in the future. Conversely, yielding to temptations can weaken one's moral character and make it more difficult to make good choices over time. Thus, while free will is limited, it remains a crucial aspect of moral responsibility. That is, individuals have the capacity to influence their actions and develop their moral character through deliberate choices and efforts. This thus underscores the importance of moral education and self-discipline in fostering a robust sense of moral responsibility. Moral responsibility is thus not merely about

---

10. Fischer, John Martin. *The Metaphysics of Free Will: An Essay on Control.* Oxford: Blackwell, 1994.

the outcome of actions but about the intentions and beliefs behind those actions, which challenges reductionist views that seek to explain human behaviour solely in terms of physical causation – as there is an essential role of conscious intention in shaping actions.

The Argument to God Revisited

The robust position detailed above provides further support for the arguments from consciousness and providence for the existence of God, which both featured in Chapter 2. By unpacking the foundational aspects of ontology, epistemology, dualism, free will and moral responsibility, a comprehensive philosophical framework is built that strengthens the claim of a divine origin for the intricate connections between mind and body.

To start, the detailed exploration of ontology establishes a clear distinction between mental and physical properties, which is critical in arguing that the causal connections between brain events and mental events are improbable without a divine explanation. Mental properties, such as thoughts and sensations, are fundamentally different from physical properties, which are observable and verifiable externally. This distinction underpins the claim that these connections, too specific and detailed to be coincidental, suggest intentional design by God. Thus, by defining substances as entities that exist independently and possess properties, a robust framework is set for understanding how mental properties, tied to conscious experience, differ fundamentally from physical properties that can vary over time. Furthermore, the reliability of perceptual beliefs, emphasised through the principle of credulity, further strengthens the argument. This principle asserts that sensory experiences are probably true unless there is evidence to the contrary, supporting the understanding that our mental states have real causal power over physical brain events. This principle can be extended to argue that, again, the regular causal connections between mental and physical states indicate God's intervention. That is, these experiences and interactions, which science alone cannot fully explain, are best understood through theism. The internalist perspective on justification also supports the idea that the consistent and reliable nature of our mental experiences provides strong evidence for their truth and causal power. This framework thus sets the stage for arguing that the intricate causal relationships between mental and physical events point toward a deliberate design by God rather than random occurrences.

Moreover, the distinction between mental and physical events is essential in the argument for interactive dualism, where mental events, such as intentions, can cause physical brain events. This dualistic perspective challenges reductionist views that attempt to reduce consciousness to mere brain activity. By asserting that mental properties do not supervene on physical properties, the idea is reinforced that mental phenomena are distinct and cannot be fully explained by physical science. This supports the claim that scientific laws are insufficient to account for mind-brain connections, necessitating a personal explanation involving God. By critically examining theories such as physicalism and functionalism and highlighting their limitations in explaining the subjective nature of mental experiences, the necessity of a dualistic framework where mental events possess intrinsic properties not reducible to physical events is also underscored.

In addition, causation is another critical aspect addressed through the SPL account, which sees substances as having inherent powers and liabilities that necessitate specific effects under certain conditions. This perspective supports the view that God endows brain molecules with the ability to produce mental events and respond to intentions. The idea that God can create these mental-physical connections aligns with the dualistic framework, thus providing a coherent account of the observed interactions between the mind and the brain. By asserting that substances have inherent causal powers, the notion is supported that the specific and consistent mind-brain connections observed in human experience are best explained by intentional design, suggesting, again, some form of causal intervention by God. The philosophical framework detailed above thus supports the argument for the divine origin of mind-body connections featured in *The Existence of God* (*EG*). That is, a thorough examination of the nature of mental and physical properties, the reliability of perceptual beliefs and the principles of causation all point towards the necessity of a God in explaining the intricate and specific causal connections between brain events and mental events. The arguments featured above collectively build a case for theism by demonstrating that the complexity and specificity of mind-body interactions, the justified belief in the reliability of mental experiences, and the inherent causal powers of mental events over physical actions cannot be satisfactorily explained by science alone. Instead, these phenomena indicate the involvement of a being, God, who causes these interactions in a way that aligns with human intuition and experience, thus providing a compelling philosophical justification for belief in God.

In addition to the support provided for the argument from consciousness featured in *EG*, one can also see that the concept of free will and moral responsibility featured above also supports the argument from providence that also featured in *EG*. As it has been argued, it is likely that humans possess a form of free will that is not fully determined by prior causes, which allows for undetermined choices, especially in difficult moral situations; and it is the existence of this kind of free will that is crucial for the argument from providence, as it enables humans to make meaningful, morally significant choices. Moreover, the connection between free will and moral responsibility is also important – as the incompatibilist view, which holds that free will is required for moral responsibility, best explains our intuitions about praise, blame, guilt and merit. Thus, this connection between free will and moral responsibility strengthens the providential argument by showing why the free will that God allegedly gives humans is valuable and purposeful. Human decisions and actions are not just apparent but have genuine moral weight and consequences. Furthermore, as it has been argued that it is good for humans to have free will and be morally responsible for their choices, one can also see that this position is also central to the argument from providence, which contends that a good God would create a world where humans have meaningful responsibilities and opportunities. Hence, the concept of free will and moral responsibility detailed above reinforces this claim by explaining the value of these attributes. Ultimately, the conceptualisation of free will and moral responsibility increases the likelihood of theism by making the human condition more probable given the existence of a providential God. If humans possess genuine free will and moral responsibility, then the significant choices and opportunities highlighted in the argument from providence are more to be expected if there is a God who created humans with these capabilities for a purpose. In contrast, a naturalistic universe without a creator is less likely to produce creatures with such libertarian free will and weighty moral responsibilities. Thus, we are provided with further philosophical support for the argument that the human situation points to the existence of a providential God.

In conclusion, Swinburne's application of his philosophical framework offers a robust approach for understanding the relationship between mental and physical phenomena. Swinburne critiques reductionist approaches and emphasises the necessity of recognising the distinct yet interconnected roles of mental and physical properties in shaping human experience. By advocating for a dualistic perspective, Swinburne underscores the importance of subjective experience and intentionality in comprehending human behaviour. His analysis highlights the complexities of personal identity, the exercise of free will, and the foundations of moral responsibility, ultimately providing a nuanced and comprehensive understanding of the mind's relation to the physical world. This approach challenges traditional views and invites further exploration into the philosophical and ethical dimensions of human agency.

Critical Engagements

Mind, Brain, and Free Will has sparked various critical engagements from scholars, as Swinburne's work focusses on demonstrating that humans possess immaterial souls that interact causally with physical bodies and have libertarian free will. However, several critics have challenged different aspects of Swinburne's arguments featured in this work. Scholars such as David Palmer, Nick Holdsworth, C. Stephen Evans, Mara McGuire and Jeffrey Hause, and Ted Poston have raised objections that question the coherence and methodology of Swinburne's claims. This section explores these critical engagements and presents responses that align with Swinburne's philosophical perspective.

David Palmer

Critical Engagement. David Palmer, in his review article of *Mind, Brain, and Free Will*,[11] critiques Swinburne's mind-body dualism and libertarian free will. Palmer finds Swinburne's arguments unpersuasive, particularly the appeal to introspective evidence, which Palmer argues does not decisively support the agent-causal view over non-causal views of free will. He also highlights the problem of 'wild coincidences' in agent-causal libertarianism, as noted by Derk

---

11. Palmer, David, 'Richard Swinburne, Mind, Brain, and Free Will', *Notre Dame Philosophical Reviews*, University of Notre Dame Press, 13 September 2013.

The Reality of the Soul

Pereboom, and the challenge of probabilistic alignment between physical events and agent-caused actions.

Critical Response. An adherent of Swinburne's position can offer several responses to Palmer's criticisms: first, Palmer's dismissal of introspective evidence underestimates its philosophical significance. Swinburne's appeal to introspection aligns with a rich tradition in the philosophy of mind, including recent work on phenomenal consciousness by philosophers such as David Chalmers. This approach recognises that first-person experience provides crucial data for understanding the nature of mind and agency. Second, Palmer's critique fails to appreciate the sophisticated philosophical framework that Swinburne develops to support agent-causal libertarianism. Swinburne's position draws on contemporary developments in action theory, particularly the work of Timothy O'Connor on emergent downward causation, which offers a coherent account of how agent causation can be reconciled with physical laws. Third, the 'wild coincidences' objection raised by Pereboom and echoed by Palmer overlooks Swinburne's nuanced account of rational agency. Swinburne's model of libertarian free will incorporates the role of reason and character in decision making, thus addressing concerns about randomness while preserving genuine alternative possibilities. Furthermore, Swinburne's defence of mind-body dualism can be understood as part of a broader resurgence of interest in dualist approaches within the philosophy of mind. This aligns with recent work by philosophers such as Dean Zimmerman, in his article 'From Property Dualism to Substance Dualism',[12] William Hasker, in his work *The Emergent Self,*[13] and J.P. Moreland and Brandon Rickabaugh, in their work *The Substance of Consciousness,*[14] on the explanatory power of dualism in addressing issues of consciousness and personal identity.

---

12. Zimmerman, Dean W. "From Property Dualism to Substance Dualism." *Aristotelian Society Supplementary* Volume 84, no. 1 (2010): pp. 119-150.
13. Hasker, William. *The Emergent Self.* Ithaca, NY: Cornell University Press, 1999.
14. Rickabaugh, Brandon and Moreland, James P. *The Substance of Consciousness: A Comprehensive Defense of Contemporary Substance Dualism.* Oxford Wiley-Blackwell, 2023.

In all, Palmer's objections to Swinburne's defence of mind-body dualism and libertarian free will, while significant, do not necessarily undermine the overall coherence and explanatory power of Swinburne's framework. Swinburne's approach, grounded in introspective evidence, engagement with contemporary action theory and a nuanced account of rational agency, withstands many of Palmer's criticisms. The 'wild coincidences' problem and the challenge of aligning physical events with agent-caused actions remain important issues for further consideration within Swinburne's view of human agency and free will.

Nick Holdsworth

Critical Engagement. Nick Holdsworth, in his review article of *Mind, Brain, and Free Will*,[15] questions the coherence of Swinburne's substance dualism and the interaction between mental and physical substances. Holdsworth argues that Swinburne's ontology, which separates mental properties from physical properties, fails to account for the empirical data linking brain states to mental events. He also criticises Swinburne's dismissal of the causal closure of the physical world.

Critical Response. An adherent of Swinburne's position can offer several responses to Holdsworth's criticisms: first, Holdsworth's challenge to substance dualism, as with Palmer above, overlooks the sophisticated philosophical framework Swinburne develops to address the interaction problem. Second, Holdsworth's critique fails to appreciate the nuanced way in which Swinburne engages with empirical data. Swinburne's dualism is not a rejection of neuroscientific findings, but rather an interpretation of these findings that preserves the irreducibility of consciousness, in his article 'The Harder Problem of Consciousness'.[16] This approach is consistent with recent developments in neurophilosophy, such as Ned Block's work on the 'hard problem' of consciousness. Third, Swinburne's dismissal of the causal closure of the physical world is not arbitrary but grounded

---

15. Holdsworth, Nick, 'Book Review: Mind, Brain, and Free Will', *Philosophy* 89, no. 4 (2014), pp. 635-42.
16. Block, Ned, 'The Harder Problem of Consciousness', *Journal of Philosophy* 99 (8) (2002): 391-425.

in careful philosophical argumentation – with his position aligning with recent critiques of causal closure by philosophers like E.J. Lowe who argues, in his work *Personal Agency*,[17] that the principle is neither empirically established nor logically necessary. Furthermore, Swinburne's substance dualism can be understood as part of a broader resurgence of interest in non-reductive approaches to consciousness within the philosophy of mind. This aligns with recent work by philosophers like Galen Strawson on panpsychism (featured in his article 'Realistic Monism: Why Physicalism Entails Panpsychism'),[18] and Chalmers on the combination problem (featured in his work *The Character of Consciousness*), which explore alternatives to physicalist accounts of mind. Last, it is important to note that Swinburne's arguments for substance dualism are not intended to provide a complete scientific account of mind-brain interaction, but rather to demonstrate the philosophical coherence and explanatory power of a dualist framework.

In sum, many of Holdsworth's concerns about the interaction problem and the apparent tension between Swinburne's substance dualism and empirical data are addressed by Swinburne's engagement with the hard problem of consciousness, his nuanced interpretation of neuroscientific findings and his alignment with critiques of causal closure. Although the interaction problem remains a challenge for substance dualism, Swinburne's approach offers a sophisticated alternative to reductive physicalism that significantly contributes to contemporary debates in philosophy of mind.

C. Stephen Evans

Critical Engagement. C. Stephen Evans, in his review article of *Mind, Brain, and Free Will*,[19] acknowledges the traditional elements in Swinburne's arguments but suggests he does not sufficiently address how mental substances interact with physical bodies. Evans also notes

---

17. Lowe, E. J. *Personal Agency: The Metaphysics of Mind and Action.* Oxford: Oxford University Press, 2008.
18. Strawson, Galen. "Realistic Monism: Why Physicalism Entails Panpsychism." *Journal of Consciousness Studies* 13, no. 10-11 (2006): pp. 3-31.
19. Evans, C. Stephen, 'Mind, Brain, and Free Will, by Richard Swinburne', *Faith and Philosophy* 31, no. 1 (2014), pp. 105-8.

the lack of discussion about the way in which Swinburne's dualism fits with evolutionary theories of human development.

Critical Response. An adherent of Swinburne's position can offer several responses to Evans' criticisms: first, Evans' critique fails to appreciate the nuanced way in which Swinburne engages with the problem of mental causation. Swinburne's positing of fundamental psychophysical laws is not ad hoc but grounded in careful philosophical argumentation. This approach is consistent with recent developments in the philosophy of science, such as Nancy Cartwright's work on causal powers and the limits of reductionism. Second, the apparent lack of discussion on evolutionary theories in Swinburne's work does not necessarily imply incompatibility, as Swinburne's dualism can be understood within the framework of theistic evolution, which has recently begun to gain traction. Furthermore, Swinburne's substance dualism can be seen as part of a broader philosophical project that seeks to integrate scientific findings with metaphysical insights. This aligns with recent work by philosophers like John Polkinghorne on the relationship between science and religion, exploring ways of reconciling scientific and theological perspectives.

Ultimately, Evans' questions about mental-physical interaction and the compatibility of Swinburne's dualism with evolutionary theory do not fully capture the scope of Swinburne's philosophical project. Swinburne's engagement with the problem of mental causation, potential alignment with theistic evolution and aim of integrating scientific and metaphysical perspectives provide a more comprehensive response to Evans' critique. Further exploration of the relationship between Swinburne's dualism and evolutionary theory could be fruitful, but his approach still offers a nuanced framework for understanding the nature of mind and its place in the world.

Mara McGuire and Jeffrey Hause

Critical Engagement. Mara McGuire and Jeffrey Hause, in their review article of *Mind, Brain, and Free Will*,[20] critique Swinburne's dualism by emphasising the difficulties in reconciling mental causation with established scientific principles. They argue that Swinburne's rejection

---

20. McGuire, Mara, and Jeffrey Hause, 'Richard Swinburne, Mind, Brain, and Free Will', *Review of Metaphysics* 67, no. 3 (2014), pp. 670-72.

of physicalism does not adequately address the empirical evidence supporting the physical basis of mental processes.

Critical Response. An adherent of Swinburne's position can offer several responses to McGuire and Hause's criticisms: first, McGuire and Hause's critique overlooks Swinburne's nuanced engagement with empirical evidence. While acknowledging the correlation between mental and physical events, Swinburne argues that this correlation does not necessitate identity. Second, Swinburne's rejection of physicalism is grounded in his principle of credulity. This principle provides a strong foundation for accepting the reality of mental states as distinct from physical states, aligning with recent work in epistemology on the nature of justified belief. Furthermore, Swinburne's substance dualism offers a compelling solution to the problem of personal identity over time. By positing an enduring mental substance, Swinburne provides an account of personal identity that aligns with our intuitive understanding of self-continuity, addressing challenges that purely physicalist accounts often struggle with. Additionally, Swinburne's approach to mental causation can be understood as a sophisticated form of agent causation, which he argues is necessary for genuine free will and moral responsibility. This aligns with libertarian accounts of free will in contemporary philosophy of action, thus offering a coherent alternative to compatibilist and hard determinist positions. Third, Swinburne's dualism provides a framework for understanding religious experiences and the possibility of life after death, which are important considerations in his broader philosophical and theological project. Thus, while controversial, these aspects of his work demonstrate the explanatory power of dualism in addressing phenomena that lie at the boundaries of scientific inquiry.

It is quite clear that Swinburne's dualist framework offers substantial responses to McGuire and Hause's concerns about reconciling mental causation with scientific principles. By engaging with empirical evidence, grounding dualism in the principle of credulity and aligning with agent-causal theories of free will, Swinburne's approach demonstrates the explanatory power of dualism for addressing questions of personal identity, religious experience and the nature of consciousness, even if the relationship between dualism and science remains a point of contention.

Ted Poston

Critical Engagement. Ted Poston, in his review article of *Mind, Brain, and Free Will*,[21] raises concerns about the coherence of Swinburne's account of mental-physical interaction and the principle of credulity applied to mental causation. Poston questions whether Swinburne's dualism can adequately explain how immaterial mental substances interact causally with physical bodies. He also challenges the principle of credulity as applied to mental causation, suggesting that the apparent signs of mental causation might not be as reliable as Swinburne claims.

Critical Response. An adherent of Swinburne's position can offer several responses to Poston's criticisms: first, Poston's critique underestimates the explanatory power of Swinburne's dualism in accounting for the qualitative aspects of consciousness. Swinburne argues that the subjective, first-person nature of experience is better explained by positing irreducible mental properties, thus addressing the 'hard problem' of consciousness in a way that purely physicalist accounts often struggle to do. Second, as noted above, Swinburne's application of the principle of credulity to mental causation is not naive but is part of a broader epistemological framework. This principle aligns with recent work in social epistemology on the importance of trust in testimony and basic beliefs, as argued by philosophers such as Jennifer Lackey, in her work *Learning from Words: Testimony as a Source of Knowledge*, and Ernest Sosa, in his work *A Virtue Epistemology: Apt Belief and Reflective Knowledge*[22]. Furthermore, Swinburne's account of mental causation is to be understood as a response to the causal exclusion problem in the philosophy of mind. That is, as noted previously, by positing fundamental psychophysical laws, Swinburne offers a solution that preserves mental causation without violating physical causal closure, thus addressing a key challenge to non-reductive physicalism. Third, Swinburne's dualism

---

21. Poston, Ted, 'Richard Swinburne, Mind, Brain, and Free Will', *Journal of Analytic Theology* 4 (2016), pp. 480-84.
22. Lackey, Jennifer, *Learning from Words: Testimony as a Source of Knowledge*, Oxford: Oxford University Press, 2008. Sosa, Ernest, *A Virtue Epistemology: Apt Belief and Reflective Knowledge*, Oxford: Oxford University Press, 2007.

provides a coherent framework for understanding phenomena like intentionality and semantic content, which have proven challenging for purely physicalist accounts. His approach thus aligns well with recent work in the philosophy of language on the irreducibility of meaning, as explored by philosophers like Charles Taylor.

Taking everything into account, Poston's objections concerning the coherence of mental-physical interaction and the application of the principle of credulity to mental causation, while noteworthy, are largely addressed by Swinburne's dualist framework. By engaging with the hard problem of consciousness, grounding the principle of credulity in a broader epistemological context, and responding to the causal exclusion problem, Swinburne provides a robust defence against many of Poston's criticisms. Although the interaction problem remains a point of disagreement, Swinburne's approach offers a nuanced account of mental causation and a compelling framework for understanding intentionality and semantic content.

* * *

In all, *Mind, Brain, and Free Will* has sparked significant debate concerning the cogency of substance dualism, libertarian free will and the epistemological and metaphysical arguments in favour of them. The critiques by David Palmer, Nick Holdsworth, C. Stephen Evans, Mara McGuire and Jeffrey Hause, and Ted Poston highlight the challenges and complexities of Swinburne's approach. However, there are responses that effectively address these criticisms, by focussing on Swinburne's sophisticated philosophical framework, his arguments for mental causation, introspection and psychophysical laws. Overall, these engagements enrich the discourse on various areas of the philosophy of mind, free will and moral responsibility and demonstrate, as with his other works, the ongoing relevance of Swinburne's work.

Conclusion

In conclusion, this chapter has provided a comprehensive guide to Swinburne's *Mind, Brain, and Free Will*, outlining the central aim, structure and themes of the work. Swinburne's detailed examination of ontology, epistemology, dualism, agent causation and the nature of free will demonstrates that humans are not merely physical beings but possess non-physical souls capable of intentional actions and moral responsibility. By addressing philosophical and neuroscientific challenges, Swinburne underscores the compatibility of mental and physical causation, emphasising the importance of rational inquiry in forming justified beliefs about the nature of human beings. His analysis of the relationship between mental and physical properties and the implications for free will and moral responsibility highlights the depth and coherence of his dualistic framework. As readers explore *Mind, Brain, and Free Will* for themselves, they will be better equipped to appreciate Swinburne's rigorous defence of substance dualism, libertarian free will, their evidential relationship to theism and its significance in contemporary philosophy.

Part 2

Ramified Theism

Chapter Five

The Metaphysics of Christian Theism

This chapter serves as an introduction to Swinburne's *The Christian God* (hereafter, *CG*), which is a comprehensive exploration aimed at defending the coherence of the core Christian doctrines, particularly the Trinity and the Incarnation, within the broader context of metaphysics. Swinburne aims to demonstrate that these doctrines are logically coherent and philosophically defensible by delving into the divine attributes and their manifestation in Christian theology. The chapter introduces readers to the central aim and structure of Swinburne's arguments, situating them within the broader context of contemporary debates in the philosophy of religion. It outlines the major sections of the work, including the analysis of the nature of substances, causality, time, necessity and their application to theological concepts such as the divine attributes, the Trinity, and the Incarnation. By providing this overview, the chapter prepares readers to engage deeply with Swinburne's systematic and rigorous examination of the coherence of core Christian metaphysical doctrines within the broader context of theism.

The Christian God: Background

Central Aim

The central aim of *The Christian God* is to articulate and defend the coherence of the core Christian doctrines, particularly the Trinity and the Incarnation, within the broader context of metaphysics.

Building on the groundwork laid in his earlier work, *The Coherence of Theism*, which focussed on the internal coherence of theistic claims, Swinburne's *CG* seeks to demonstrate that these Christian doctrines can be logically coherent and philosophically defensible. The work rigorously examines fundamental metaphysical issues, such as the nature of substance, causality, time and necessity, and applies this metaphysical framework within the theological domain. *CG* assesses the nature of the divine attributes and the specific Christian claims about the Trinity – there being one God and three divine individuals who have the same essence (i.e. the essential property of divinity: pure, limitless intentional power (essential everlasting omnipotence)) – and the incarnation of God as Jesus Christ, to establish whether these doctrines are indeed rational and defensible.

Historical Significance

CG was published in 1994 as the third work within Swinburne's tetralogy on Christian doctrine. The immediate historical context of *CG* involves debates about the logical consistency of the central Christian doctrines of the Trinity and Incarnation within the field of analytic philosophy of religion. Philosophers such as John Hick, in *The Metaphor of God Incarnate*,[1] questioned the coherence of the Incarnation, arguing that the notion of a fully divine and fully human Jesus Christ leads to various logical inconsistencies. Also, Richard Cartwright, in 'On the Logical Problem of the Trinity',[2] critiqued the logical coherence of the Trinity, questioning whether the veracity of the concept of three divine individuals having the same essence could be affirmed without leading to contradictions. *CG* can thus be seen as a response to these challenges by aiming to show that the central Christian doctrines of the Trinity and Incarnation, when grounded on a robust metaphysical foundation, can be formulated in a logically coherent manner.

From the position of hindsight, one can see that *CG* played a pivotal role in bringing about the emergence of a new sub-field within

---

1. Hick, John. *The Metaphor of God Incarnate*. Louisville, KY: Westminster John Knox Press, 1993.
2. Cartwright, Richard. "On the Logical Problem of the Trinity." In *Philosophical Essays*, 187-200. Cambridge, MA: MIT Press, 1987.

analytic philosophy of religion known as analytic philosophical theology, later termed 'Analytic Theology' by Oliver Crisp and Michael Rea, in their work *Analytic Theology: New Essays in the Philosophy of Theology*.[3] This sub-field specifically focusses on using the tools and methods of analytic philosophy to address specific theological questions, bridging the gap between philosophy and systematic theology. Analytic Theology emerged in response to the need for a more rigorous and systematic approach to theological questions, especially those that pertain to the coherence and logical consistency of key religious doctrines. The rigorous approach featured in *CG* exemplified this methodology by applying analytic techniques to unpack and defend complex theological concepts such as the Trinity and the Incarnation. This marked a significant shift from previous theological discussions, which were often more literary or existential in nature, towards a more structured and logical analysis of these theological teachings. *CG*'s influence was crucial in this development because it demonstrated that traditional Christian doctrines could be subjected to the same rigorous scrutiny as other philosophical concepts without losing their theological depth. *CG* (as with the other works within the tetralogy) thus showed that the central Christian doctrines could withstand analytical scrutiny and be articulated in a way that answers contemporary philosophical concerns.

Literary Structure

The literary structure of *CG* is divided into two main parts: 'Metaphysics' and 'Theology'. However, for continuity with the previous chapters in this book, we shall retain the terminology and dual structure as follows:

1. *Philosophical Framework – Metaphysical Foundations*: The first part of *CG* focusses on foundational metaphysical issues. Swinburne discusses the nature of substances, properties, thisness, causation, time and necessity. This thus involves a rigorous examination of how these concepts are to be best conceptualised, providing a basis

---

3. Crisp, Oliver D., and Michael C. Rea, eds. *Analytic Theology: New Essays in the Philosophy of Theology*. Oxford: Oxford University Press, 2009.

for exploring how these concepts apply to the divine nature and the central Christian doctrines.
2. *Theological Application – The Divine Nature and Christian Doctrines*: The second part of CG applies the established metaphysical framework to specific theological claims. Swinburne examines the coherence of the doctrines of the Trinity and the Incarnation. He investigates whether it is logically possible for there to be three divine individuals who share the same essence (i.e. the essential property of divinity: pure, limitless intentional power (essential everlasting omnipotence)) and whether one of those persons could become incarnate as Jesus Christ. Swinburne argues that these doctrines, while complex, can be shown to be coherent through careful philosophical analysis. This involves addressing potential contradictions, ensuring that the definitions used are logically coherent and providing an *a priori* argument for their veracity.

In the following sections, we shall unpack in greater detail the various areas covered in both parts of *CG*.

Themes

Philosophical Framework: Metaphysical Foundations

In this section, Swinburne introduces the philosophical framework that incorporates foundational metaphysical concepts such as the nature of substances, properties, thisness causation, time and necessity. He begins by discussing substances, their properties and their integral role in the world's structure. Swinburne then explores the concept of thisness (*haecceitas*), which distinguishes individual substances from one another. Moving forward, he analyses causation, emphasising the significance of causal powers and intentional actions. The nature of time and its continuous, infinite structure is subsequently examined, along with the implications of causal relationships on temporal order. Finally, Swinburne addresses the concept of necessity, differentiating it from related notions like contingency and possibility and categorising it into logical, ontological and metaphysical necessity. This all provides a comprehensive framework for understanding the nature of the central Christian doctrines.

Substances

The world is comprised of substances, which are particular, concrete objects such as tables, chairs, trees and people. These substances, as noted previously, possess properties, which can be monadic (independent attributes like colour or mass) or relational (attributes that describe their relationship to other substances, like being taller than another object). Properties are also 'abundant', which is that every predicate designates a distinct property, even if some properties do not affect behaviour. Our observational knowledge of the world is fundamentally about recognising which properties are instantiated in substances at specific times. Considering the complexity of substances, they often have an internal structure that is not immediately apparent. For example, material objects consist of form and matter, maintaining their existence through the continuity of their essential properties. Concerning the nature of these components of a substance, substances are concrete and unique, while properties are universals that can be instantiated in multiple things. For instance, being brown is a property that can apply to many items, but a specific table is a unique substance. There is also differentiation that can be established between concrete individuals, such as a table, and abstract individuals, like the number five, which is a construct of language and does not exist concretely. While abstract constructs like numbers are convenient fictions, substances like tables are real. Exploring this further, there is a distinction between 'impure' substances, which are composed of other substances, and 'pure' substances, which do not have parts. For example, a desk has drawers and a top, making it an impure substance. Conversely, there might be pure substances that do not occupy space or have parts, which challenges traditional views on materiality and composition. Furthermore, properties only manifest concretely when instantiated in substances, such as redness existing only when there are red things. Hence, in Aristotelian fashion, properties cannot exist without substances to instantiate them, and substances cannot exist without possessing properties. Substances exist wholly at any moment and persist through time, influencing and being influenced by other substances. Moreover, talk about entities such as smells, sounds and places can also be reduced to discussions about how substances interact with each other and with perceiving beings. And these substances are also involved in events, which as noted previously, are the instantiations of properties in substances at specific times, thus encompassing both static states and changes.

With regard to philosophical classifications, some philosophers argue for a classification based on natural kinds, where substances are identified by essential properties fundamental to their behaviour according to natural laws. However, such classifications are neither exclusive nor exhaustive, as many objects with natural unity do not fit neatly into these categories. One can also make a distinction between 'phase-sortals' and 'substance-sortals' – where the term phase-sortal applies to substances only during certain phases of their existence, while substance-sortals apply throughout. For instance, 'oak tree' is a substance-sortal, but 'sapling' is a phase-sortal. In relation to this, the concept of relative identity, proposed by Peter Geach, posits that an entity can be identical in some respects but not in others, is also to be rejected, as one must maintain that a substance's identity is consistent across all its properties.

Turning to human nature, humans, as noted previously, consist of both a material body and an immaterial soul, with the soul being a pure substance. There is a differentiation between physical properties, which are public and accessible to all, and mental properties, which are private and accessible only to the individual experiencing them. Using thought experiments, one can understand that human identity is more than physical continuity. For example, as alluded to before, if a brain were divided and each half transplanted into different bodies, the resulting individuals would not both be the same person despite sharing parts of the original brain. This thought experiment, as noted previously, demonstrates that something beyond the physical, such as an immaterial soul, is essential to account for the consistency of personal identity over time.

Thisness

Thisness (or haecceity), is a term that refers to the unique individuality of a substance that makes it the particular entity it is. Thisness distinguishes one substance from another, even when they share all other properties. Understanding thisness is thus essential for tracing the continuity of substances over time and for identifying the individual nature of each substance.

A substance's individuality can be due to its unique properties or, alternatively, to its thisness. Thisness thus implies that, even if two substances share all properties, they remain distinct individuals if their 'thisness' differs. The principle of the identity of indiscernibles, which suggests that identical properties entail identical substances, does not hold in cases where thisness is involved.

Now, each substance belongs to a minimum essential kind, a category defined by a set of properties necessary for an entity to be recognised as a substance of that kind. For example, certain properties make an object a desk, and additional, unique properties make it the particular desk it is. This framework helps one identify and refer to substances consistently over time – without a minimum essential kind, it would be impossible to track a substance's continuity, as it could lose all its properties and acquire new ones, yet still be considered the same substance. Revisiting the distinction between monadic and relational properties, monadic properties are those that a substance possesses independently, such as colour or shape. Relational properties, however, depend on the substance's relationship with other entities, like being the son of a blacksmith. Further refinement distinguishes between general relational properties (e.g. living in a city) and particular relational properties (e.g. living in London). There is also a differentiation between hard properties, which belong to an individual solely due to the present state of affairs, and soft properties, which depend on past or future conditions (and which ground hard and soft facts). It is important to note, that no two distinct entities can share all the same properties, and this position can be shown by investigating various forms of the principle of the identity of indiscernibles, which range from very strict forms, requiring all properties to be the same, to weaker forms that only consider certain types of properties. In investigating the holding of these principles, one can see that various scenarios, such as the example of two identical iron spheres in a symmetrical universe, illustrate the complexity of differentiating material objects purely based on their properties.

Turning our attention to the distinction between material objects and human souls, one can ask the question of whether these entities have thisness. While modern physics may challenge the notion of material objects having intrinsic thisness by describing them as fields of force, human souls are stronger candidates for possessing thisness. The uniqueness of an individual's experiences and mental life points to an underlying thisness that is not solely determined by physical properties. One can thus employ the previous hypothesis to explore the logical possibility of identity across different scenarios: the consideration is whether a person with an identical mental and physical history as another could still be a different individual.

The conclusion to be reached is that the unique thisness of a soul is necessary to account for personal identity, as it cannot be solely reduced to properties or physical continuity. Moreover, if material objects were differentiated by their matter, it would lead to implausible conclusions, such as identical objects being considered the same entity if composed of different matter. Also, while theories such as the hylomorphic theory (which combines matter and form) works for material objects, it is less applicable to immaterial entities like souls, which do not undergo fusion or fission like physical matter.

Causation
Causation is an important metaphysical feature within reality, in that substances cause other substances to begin, continue or cease existing or to gain or lose properties. This causation occurs because substances possess causal powers – properties that enable them to bring about events. For example, a stone causes a plate to break due to its power to break objects when dropped from a certain height. Some substances, particularly human souls, may exercise these powers freely, without being causally determined by external forces, thereby affirming the concept of libertarian free will. Substances have liabilities to exercise their causal powers under specific conditions, and these liabilities may be deterministic or probabilistic. For instance, a stone has a deterministic liability to break a plate when dropped from a certain height. However, in the context of quantum mechanics, some liabilities are probabilistic. An atom of radium, for example, has a half-life indicating the probability of decay within a given period. While medium-scale objects generally have deterministic liabilities, quantum indeterminism is significant on very small scales. Moreover, a permissive cause is one that produces an effect because another substance, which could prevent the effect, does not exercise its power. For example, if the decay of a radium atom would prevent an explosion but does not occur, the atom is considered a permissive cause of the explosion. This notion is particularly relevant in the context of intentional causation, where agents can choose to allow or prevent events. Now, the distinction between cause and condition is often arbitrary: for example, if we take a match lit in the presence of hydrogen thereby causing an explosion, it is not always clear whether the match or the hydrogen should be considered the primary cause. Both substances involved in an event can be considered partial causes, whose combined actions

constitute a full cause. Within this perspective one must thus reject the idea that only one substance exerts an active influence, while the other merely provides conditions.

Against the empiricist tradition, which sought to reduce causation to regular successions of events as proposed by Hume, causation, as noted previously, is to be conceived of as a relation between substances and events, not merely events. Substances cause events through their properties and powers. For example, the motion of a brick causing the breaking of a window is better understood as the brick causing the breaking due to its motion, rather than treating the motion and breaking as independent events. This substance-based view of causation is more fundamental and accurate than event-based analyses. Concerning rational agents, these types of entities, as we have seen before, are inclined to act for the sake of the good, as they perceive it. Rational considerations guide their choices, but they are also influenced by desires, which can either support or hinder their pursuit of the good. Furthermore, perfectly free agents, not influenced by non-rational forces, will always pursue the best actions available to them. However, human agents often face conflicting desires, leading them sometimes to act against their better judgement. There is thus a role for reason in guiding actions and also a continuous struggle between reason and desire in human decision making.

Time
Time fulfils a fundamental role in structuring the universe and is best conceived of as a 'continuum' – with a distinction drawn between continuous and dense time. Continuous time can be mapped onto real numbers, encompassing both rational and irrational intervals, while dense time only includes rational intervals.

With regard to the concept of instantaneous events, events perceived to occur instantaneously are better understood as the limits of processes occurring over time. For instance, an individual turning sixty happens at an instant, but this instant is the endpoint of sixty years. Similarly, winning a race is analysed in terms of leading for the final segment of the race's duration. This perspective also applies to scientific contexts, where properties like instantaneous velocity are defined as limits of velocities over increasingly smaller time intervals. Instantaneous properties are not held at an instant but are the limits of properties over periods of time. Focussing on the nature of time's divisibility, any period of time is infinitely divisible, meaning that each period can be broken down into smaller and smaller periods. This infinite divisibility implies, again, that time is a continuum, where instants are the boundaries of periods rather than parts of them. Periods consist of smaller periods that can be subdivided *ad infinitum*, aligning with the mathematical understanding provided by differential calculus and transfinite arithmetic developed in the seventeenth and nineteenth centuries.

Moving on to the structure of time, one can differentiate, as noted before, between the topology and the metric of time. Topology concerns the ordering of events, while metric time deals with the measurement of intervals between them. Time has a metric only if there are laws of nature that enable the measurement of intervals through periodic processes. These processes, when synchronised, confirm natural laws and provide a consistent framework for measuring time. Without such laws, there would be no basis for determining the duration of events, making the concept of temporal intervals meaningless. Now, expanding on the causal structure of time, causation must operate in one temporal direction, with causes preceding effects, thereby ruling out the possibility of backward causation and simultaneous causation. The past is fixed and beyond our influence, while the future remains open to causal intervention. This understanding solidifies the linear structure of time, where the present serves as the boundary between the causally affectable future and the causally fixed past.

Now, concerning the notion of metric-less time – which is the possibility of a universe without periodic processes to keep time – in such a scenario, time would lack a metric and there would be no truth about the duration of events. Within this perspective time must be understood through the relations of events and their causal interactions. In distinguishing temporal truths, within this framework, non-indexical truths describe events by their temporal relations to a specific reference point, like a date on a calendar. Indexical truths, however, describe events relative to the speaker's perspective, such as 'today' or 'yesterday'. Both types of truths are necessary for a complete understanding of time, and indexical facts can only be known at certain periods, which ultimately emphasises the dynamic aspect of temporal knowledge.

Necessity
Necessity is the primary notion from which other modal concepts can be derived: the impossible is necessarily not; the possible is not impossible; and the contingent is neither necessary nor impossible.

Also, different kinds of necessity can be distinguished, with a focus being on two ultimate kinds: 'narrow-logical' necessity and 'broadly-logical' necessity. Starting with narrow logical necessity, this type of necessity is not a deep feature of the world but a characteristic of human language and the way sentences are used. The traditional view that logical necessity is a timeless feature of abstract entities like statements or propositions is thus to be rejected. Instead, narrow logical necessity governs language rather than the world, rooted in how humans construct and use sentences.

Moving on to the concept of broadly logical necessity, one can define it as truth in all possible worlds. However, this form of necessity can be understood without reference to possible worlds by stating that a proposition is necessary if its negation entails a self-contradiction. For instance, the proposition expressed by 'Hesperus is Phosphorus' is necessarily true because 'Hesperus' and 'Phosphorus' both refer to the planet Venus. This necessity is due to the meaning and context in which the names are used. Within this framework broad logical modality is thus reducible to narrow logical modality. Building on this position one can now also contrast the position of 'logical platonism', which posits the existence of timeless entities such as propositions and logical relations, with that of 'logical nominalism', which, as noted previously, views modal truths as grounded in human language. In comparing these two views, a nominalist view is to be favoured, with the claim being made that logical relations and necessary truths can be described without postulating a realm of timeless entities. Instead, these relations are based on the linguistic practices of human beings and the conventions of language.

Now, in transitioning to other forms of necessity, several kinds are able to be distinguished beyond logical necessity. First, accidental necessity refers to statements about the past that cannot be changed by present actions but could have been different at an earlier time. Second, natural necessity pertains to events that occur due to physical causes, such as a bomb explosion. Third, temporal necessity involves substances that continue to exist indefinitely due to their essential powers, unless God ceases to sustain them. Fourth, ontological necessity refers to everlasting events or substances that have no cause, while metaphysical necessity pertains to everlasting events or substances caused by something that itself has no cause and whose properties entail its existence (with both of these latter forms of necessity being different from metaphysical and ontological necessity that featured in Chapter 1). In relation to these forms of necessity, the central metaphysical question is: which substances and properties are ontologically or metaphysically necessary? This question underpins the exploration of the identity of the ultimate nature of reality as that of God or the universe.

In conclusion, Swinburne's philosophical framework provides a detailed, nuanced understanding of the core elements that constitute reality and influence our perception of it. By analysing substances and their properties, he highlights the essential building blocks of the world. The concept of thisness underscores the individuality and continuity of substances, particularly human souls, which possess a unique identity beyond mere physical properties. Swinburne's exploration of causation integrates the roles of causal powers, liabilities and intentional actions, emphasising the importance of rational agency in understanding moral responsibility. His discussion on time reinforces its continuous, infinite nature and the critical role of causal interactions in defining temporal order. Finally, Swinburne's analysis of necessity distinguishes between various kinds of necessity, providing a robust framework for understanding the fundamental aspects of existence and their implications for logical and metaphysical discourse. Through these detailed investigations, Swinburne's framework offers a comprehensive perspective on the philosophical underpinnings of reality, and thus provides a basis for understanding the nature of the central Christian doctrines.

Theological Application: The Divine Nature and Christian Doctrines

In this section, Swinburne applies his philosophical framework to the central Christian doctrines, focussing on the divine properties and nature, the Trinity, the Incarnation and the evidence supporting these beliefs. He begins by exploring the essential attributes of God, emphasising their necessity and coherence within Western religious thought. Swinburne then delves into the nature of divine properties, arguing for their logical consistency and derivability from the concept of 'pure, limitless power'. The discussion then extends to the doctrine of the Trinity, examining its coherence and necessity from a philosophical and theological perspective. Swinburne further investigates the possibility and coherence of the Incarnation and assesses it against certain historical evidence. Through rigorous analysis, Swinburne aims to provide a comprehensive understanding of these complex theological concepts and their implications for the rationality of Christian belief.

Divine Properties

As noted previously, God exists necessarily and eternally as a person who is essentially bodiless (i.e. a spirit), omnipresent, the creator and sustainer of any universe, perfectly free, omnipotent, omniscient, perfectly good and a source of moral obligation. These properties are inseparable from God – such that if he were to lose any of them, he would cease to exist.

More fully, God is a person, a being with beliefs and the capability to perform intentional actions, and God is essentially bodiless, meaning that he does not depend on a body to exist or interact with the world. Unlike humans, who require bodies to perceive and affect their environment, God can act and know without any intermediary. This bodiless nature (i.e. him being a spirit) allows God to be omnipresent, capable of acting anywhere and knowing everything happening everywhere directly. Moreover, God is the creator and sustainer of the universe – in that any substance that exists, apart from God, does so because God causes it to exist and maintains its properties. If the universe began to exist, God caused that beginning; if it has always existed, God continually sustains it. This concept extends to the laws of nature, which operate because God ensures their persistence – one can thus utilise the term 'creator of all' to encapsulate this role. God is also perfectly free, meaning nothing external determines or influences his actions. He chooses how to act at each moment, guided solely by rational considerations. God's freedom thus implies that his actions are not causally determined by previous actions, ensuring his perfect freedom at all times. This perfect freedom is essential to God's nature, as any loss of freedom would contradict his divine properties. Furthermore, God is also omnipotent, in that he is capable of doing anything that is logically possible. This excludes logically impossible actions, such as changing the past or making contradictory states of affairs true. Hence, omnipotence means that God can accomplish any action he chooses, as long as the action itself is logically possible. One must thus reject the notion that God's power includes the ability to perform logically impossible tasks, as such tasks are nonsensical and do not constitute true actions.

Related to this is God's omniscience, which means that he knows all true propositions. This traditionally includes knowledge of all events at all times, both past and future. However, as noted previously, God's omniscience, when correctly understood, must thus be construed in a way that allows for human freedom, implying that God knows all propositions that it is logically possible for him to know without determining human actions. For God's perfect goodness, as also noted previously, one can conceive of this as him being able to perform the best possible actions among those he can do. Furthermore, God's perfect goodness ensures that he does no overall bad actions. In cases where there is no single best action, God's goodness guides him to perform actions within a framework of good options. This perfect goodness limits God's choices to those that align with the best kind of actions, ensuring his moral perfection.

Following this, one can also understand that God is a source of moral obligation, making certain actions obligatory through his commands and forbidding actions to make them wrong. Humans have an obligation to obey God due to his role as their creator and sustainer. This obligation is grounded in the principle that beneficiaries owe duties to their benefactors. God's commands, therefore, establish moral duties for humans, increasing their range of moral responsibilities. For God's eternity, God is everlasting rather than timeless. This means, as was previously stated, that God exists at all times, past, present and future. The idea of God being timeless, existing outside time, makes God less sovereign by him being unable to act within time. However, being everlasting, God is fully sovereign over time and its events, acting at all periods without being constrained by time. Finally, God is a necessary being, existing necessarily rather than contingently. This does not mean that God's existence is logically necessary. Instead, God's necessity is 'metaphysical'. This means that God's existence and properties are inseparable and eternally tied together, making him a necessary being in a certain profound metaphysical sense (a sense that was unpacked in depth in Chapter 1). Hence, God's essential properties ensure his existence as a necessary being and as foundational to the structure of reality.

The Divine Nature: Pure, Limitless Intentional Power
All the divine properties described previously are necessarily interconnected within the individual who possesses them – namely, God – in that, these properties are logically necessary for being God,

which implies that these attributes are essential to God's nature. In other words, a divine being's identity is tied to these properties so intrinsically that, without them, the being would not exist. Moreover, the divine properties, such as omniscience, omnipotence and perfect goodness, are not only essential for being God, but they also naturally fit together. Being a person involves having beliefs and performing intentional actions, which are included in being omniscient and omnipotent. An omniscient being has beliefs about everything and an omnipotent being can successfully perform any intentional action. Moreover, God's bodiless nature ensures that he is not limited by physical constraints, acquiring knowledge and acting upon the world directly. This essential bodilessness also entails omnipresence, enabling God to exercise power and knowledge universally without intermediaries. God's perfect freedom and omniscience entail his perfect goodness. A perfectly free being, unrestrained by non-rational influences, will always pursue the good and being omniscient means having true beliefs about what is good; thus, an omniscient and perfectly free being will inherently be perfectly good. God's role as the creator stems from his omnipotence – such that everything else exists because God permits it, making Him the ultimate creator and sustainer of all. Concerning the implications of this for God's authority, God's complete authority over the universe grants him the right to command its use. This authority, combined with perfect goodness, ensures that God's commands are inherently obligatory. As God is perfectly good and omniscient, he will always command actions that are morally right, establishing moral obligations for humans to follow his directives. Considering God's eternal existence, as the creator and sustainer of all reality, God must also exist eternally. If God began to exist, there would have been a time without his causal influence, contradicting his nature as the sustainer of all. Similarly, if God ceased to exist, events would occur independently of his sustaining power, which is impossible given his nature. Thus, God is eternal and his existence is metaphysically necessary – that is, it is sustained by his pure, limitless intentional power. More specifically, God has pure, limitless intentional power, which means all of God's actions are intentional and carried out with reason. Limitless power indicates that every event other than God's own existence occurs because of his current exercise of power, either directly or permissively. God's limitless power also entails omniscience, as knowing all logically possible actions is integral to his ability to choose between them.

This knowledge includes understanding all past events to accurately determine future actions, thus ensuring God's omniscience. Hence, all divine properties are unified under the concept of pure, limitless intentional power. This unification implies that God's omnipotence, omniscience and perfect freedom are intrinsically connected. (However, it is important to note that this attribute of pure, limitless intentional power is now subsumed in the second edition of *The Coherence of Theism* into the property of essential everlasting omnipotence – and thus all other divine properties are derivable from this one simple property). It is also important to note that the notion of 'divine simplicity' that is found within classical theistic thought is now to be conceived of as the properties being ascribed to God not being separate entities but facets of one unified power – and contrary views such as those of Saint Anselm and Saint Thomas Aquinas, which suggest more complex relationships between divine attributes, are thus to be deemed unnecessary. As, if one sees God's nature as pure, limitless intentional power, this provides a simpler, more coherent understanding. However, in line with Anselm and Aquinas, human understanding of God is indeed limited and analogical. While humans can grasp facets of God's nature through concepts such as pure, limitless intentional power, the full extent of divine simplicity and power likely exceeds human comprehension. In other words, divine properties fit together harmoniously in a way that humans can describe but not fully understand.

The Trinity
An important question to be faced (which was alluded to in Chapter 1) is whether there could be more than one divine being? As noted previously, theoretically there indeed could be multiple divine individuals, as each divine individual, being perfectly good, would act without frustration from the others, thus supporting each other's actions rather than conflicting with them. This mutual support suggests a type of divine harmony that prevents the nullification of omnipotence due to 'volitional conflict'. More specifically, two omnipotent individuals, being perfectly good, would avoid interfering with each other's actions. However, the possibility of conflict remains if both attempt to perform mutually exclusive 'non-rational' acts (such as one omnipotent individual deciding to rotate the Sun on its axis clockwise, whilst, at the same time, the other omnipotent individual deciding to rotate the Sun on its axis anti-clockwise). To prevent this issue, a mechanism ensuring no volitional conflict is necessary,

which could be that of one divine individual prescribing a division of activities, which will ensure harmony and prevent conflicts, thus maintaining omnipotence within a framework of perfect goodness. More fully, unity of action among divine individuals is to be secured by, first, there being a relational dependence between the individuals, where the first divine individual everlastingly causes to exist the second divine individual, and they each cooperate in everlastingly bringing about the third divine individual – which will establish a 'relational hierarchy' in the trinity that can ground the division of spheres of operation. And, second, by each of the divine individuals vowing not to act in certain spheres where the other individuals are operative, which, given that each divine individual is perfectly good, this would be supported by all of the divine individuals, thus ensuring no overlap or conflict. This division of functions will needed to be grounded on the authority of the first divine individual (due to him being the everlasting cause of the other divine individuals), thus allowing for the coexistence of multiple omnipotent beings, each acting within its allocated domain. Such a mechanism would require mutual recognition of duties and limitations, fostering cooperation rather than competition. However, it is not only possible that there could be multiple divine individuals, but it is *necessarily so that there are*: if there is at least one divine individual, there must necessarily be more than one, as perfect goodness necessitates the instantiation of perfect ('worthwhile') love, which requires sharing, thus leading the first divine individual to cause a second. This act of causation is driven by the goodness inherent in sharing love with another divine individual. The second individual, in turn, will cooperate with the first to instantiate the further state of cooperative ('unselfish') love, where the first individual finds another for its beloved (the second individual) to love and be loved by. Given this, the second divine individual would cooperate with the first to everlasting cause a third to exist, thus establishing a Trinity. That is, the goodness of shared (worthwhile) and cooperative (unselfish) love is fully expressed in a Trinity, beyond which additional divine individuals are unnecessary. Why the latter is the case is because no matter how many divine individuals the first and second divine individuals generate, it would always be better if they continued to bring about more. However, as was noted previously, when an infinite series of increasingly better actions is available, it is logically impossible to perform the best action as there is no best action. Therefore, the first and second divine individuals are perfectly good if they perform any one of the good actions within that series. In this context, the perfect goodness of the first divine individual is satisfied by bringing about two additional divine individuals – one to manifest shared love and another to cooperate in sharing in love with the second divine individual. Thus, it is not required for the first divine individual to bring about any additional divine individuals, through cooperating with the second divine individual, to be perfectly good. Any additional divine individuals generated by this cooperative act would not be a necessary *act of their essence* but rather a *creative act of will*. This means any number of divine individuals over the third divine individual would stem from a free-will choice. In other words, any additional divine individuals would not exist necessarily in the same manner as the second and third divine individuals, and thus would not be divine. Therefore, there cannot be any additional divine individual beyond the third divine individual produced by the cooperative act of the first and second divine individuals.

Aligning this now with traditional Christian doctrine, this account matches the assertions of the Nicene and Athanasian Creeds, which emphasise the unity of the Godhead while distinguishing the persons of the Father, Son and Holy Spirit. Furthermore, the doctrine expressed by the creed is not self-contradictory if understood as three divine individuals forming a collective source of all being, who is then identified as the one 'God'. This collective unity ensures that the Godhead is indivisible, with each person necessarily existing in relation to the others. That is, the relational properties of the divine individuals distinguish them from one another, not by thisness but by their relational properties. For instance, the Father is 'uncaused', the Son is 'begotten' (i.e. caused to exist by an uncaused divine individual acting alone (i.e. the Father)) and the Spirit is 'spirated' (i.e. caused to exist by the uncaused divine individual (i.e. the Father) and the divine individual caused to exist by the uncaused divine individual acting alone (i.e. the Son)). These relational properties thus define their unique roles within the Trinity. And the divine essence (i.e. the essential property of divinity: pure, limitless intentional power (essential everlasting omnipotence)), shared by all three, ensures that each individual is fully divine, with the relational properties providing the necessary distinctions without implying difference in essence. This account thus supports a moderate form of 'social trinitarianism', which emphasises both the unity and distinctiveness of the divine individuals – with the persons of the Trinity not being differentiated by thisness but by their relational properties (i.e. *being uncaused, being begotten* and *being spirated*). This approach thus avoids the pitfalls of both strict identity and excessive separation, ultimately presenting a coherent model of divine unity and plurality within the Trinity.

The Possibility of the Incarnation

The Incarnation is a central doctrine within Christianity, which the Council of Chalcedon, in 451 CE, defined by stating that Jesus Christ is a single person who possesses a (true/full) divine nature and (true/full) human nature, without confusion or separation. In assessing the 'Chalcedonian Definition' for internal consistency and compatibility with New Testament descriptions of Christ, one can first understand that the divine nature is essential and ('weakly') immutable, meaning that God cannot cease to be divine. However, human nature, as assumed by Chalcedon, is not essentially immutable, allowing for the possibility that an individual could become human or cease to be human while remaining the same individual. While humans typically have an essential human soul, a divine individual could acquire a human body and sensations through it without altering his divine nature. Although divine omniscience would allow knowledge of the truth despite any misleading sensory data, a divine being could still have desires influenced by a human body. However, these desires would be aligned with true beliefs about the worth of actions, ensuring that any divine desires align with the highest good. Thus, Christ's human desires would not detract from his perfect freedom. It is this separation of divine and human natures that is crucial. Christ could act in ignorance or under temptation but remain sinless, as his divine nature ensures he cannot yield to desires to do wrong. This view maintains that Christ's human experiences, including ignorance and temptation, are genuine, thereby making his life an authentic example for humanity.

In addition to this, Christ's human limitations, as depicted in the New Testament, are also able to be shown to align with Chalcedon's definition for the Scriptures indicate that Christ experienced ignorance, weakness and temptation. For instance, Luke describes Jesus growing in wisdom, and Mark suggests Christ was unaware of certain future divine decisions. However, these human experiences do not contradict Christ's divinity because they occur within his human consciousness, separated from his divine omniscience. This separation explains why Christ, though divine, could experience human limitations. The concept of a 'divided mind' is thus able to reconcile Christ's divine and human experiences. This model suggests that Christ could consciously operate with human limitations while retaining divine knowledge, ensuring his experiences of ignorance and temptation were genuine but did not undermine his divinity. Now, the doctrine of total interpenetration, advocated by John of Damascus, in his work *An Exposition of the Orthodox Faith*– and which posits that Christ's divine nature fully permeates his human nature – is to be rejected[4]. This view suggests that Christ, even as a human, possessed divine omniscience and omnipotence. However, such a view undermines the authenticity of Christ's human experiences. Thus, instead, the idea that Christ's human nature was subject to genuine limitations and temptations is to be affirmed, enabling one to maintain a clear distinction between his divine and human wills. Furthermore, as human nature is a universal set of properties, not an individual concrete particular, Christ's human nature, therefore, should be seen as an acquired set of human properties rather than an independent individual ('concrete') nature. This approach thus avoids the contradictions posed by earlier theological interpretations that treated Christ's human and divine natures as separately differentiated.

For the alternatives to the Chalcedonian definition – namely, that of 'Monophysitism', which claims Christ had only a divine nature, and 'Nestorianism', which posits two separate individuals (divine and human) in Christ – these are thus to be rejected, as the former fails to account for a full human experience, thus undermining the Incarnation's purpose, and the latter reduces the divine-human unity to a mere causal link, which thus lacks the needed metaphysical depth provided by the Chalcedonian union. One can thus reach the position that the Chalcedonian definition and the doctrine of the Incarnation is coherent when understood correctly. By maintaining a clear distinction between Christ's divine and human minds and wills, it is possible to reconcile the New Testament's portrayal of Christ with the doctrine of the Incarnation. Moreover, once the total interpenetration of natures and the hypostatisation of Christ's human nature are rejected – as these interpretations lead to inconsistencies – a view that respects both the integrity of Christ's human experiences

---

4. John of Damascus, Exposition of the Orthodox Faith, in *Nicene and Post-Nicene Fathers, Second Series*, Volume IX, translated by E.W. Watson and L. Pullan, edited by Philip Schaff and Henry Wace, Peabody, MA: Hendrickson Publishers, 1994, pp. 1–101.

and his divine nature can be affirmed, which ensures a coherent and theologically sound understanding of the Incarnation.

The Evidence of Incarnation

Considering the necessity of the Incarnation, it is not necessary for a perfectly good God to become incarnate, nor is it required for him to create human beings. That is, while it is better for God to cause the existence of conscious beings, his perfect goodness does not necessitate the creation of humans or their susceptibility to sin. However, if God does create humans capable of sinning, and they do sin, there has been a debate in Church history about whether God's perfect goodness requires him to become incarnate to offer reconciliation. In exploring two main Christian views, the first, held by Anselm, argued that humans cannot be reconciled to God except through God's incarnation, enabling atonement for sin through a perfect human life and sacrificial death. The second view, supported by Aquinas, Scotus and most Reformers, asserted that God can reconcile humans without becoming incarnate, either by forgiving the penitent without reparation or accepting a lesser atoning act from an ordinary human or an angel. In support of the second view, one can note that a wronged person can forgive without requiring reparation, and this forgiveness is often beneficial as it allows the guilty party to take his wrongdoing seriously by making proper reparation. While a perfect human life can serve as reparation for human sin, God could accept less committed lives as sufficient atonement. However, God's concern for human redemption, though not necessitating incarnation, finds a 'generous propriety' in such an act.

Now, in considering reasons for the Incarnation, one can outline several based on Aquinas' synthesis of Augustine's reasons. First, human nature's unique combination of rational, sensory and physical attributes makes it a fitting nature for God to adopt, showing solidarity with his creation. Second, God's adoption of human nature teaches the dignity of human nature. Third, God Incarnate shows his love for humanity through identification with them. Fourth, an incarnate God provides a living example of how to lead a human life. Finally, although propositional revelation is possible through other means, God's incarnation can increase the force of this revelation. Regarding the historical evidence in support of the Incarnation, the New Testament writings provide public evidence, but this must be supplemented by revelation confirming Christ's perfect goodness and atonement. Christ's Resurrection, given its historical evidence and theological significance, serves as God's seal of approval ('divine signature') on Christ's teachings and life. Furthermore, the Church, founded by Christ's apostles, carries the authority to interpret these teachings and confirm Christ's divine status. While the New Testament might not explicitly state Christ's divinity, it is implicit in his actions and teachings, and this view is affirmed by his disciples post-resurrection. Moreover, the Church's authority, authenticated by God through the Resurrection, supports this interpretation.

In conclusion, Swinburne's application of his philosophical framework helps to demonstrate the coherence of the divine attributes and the central Christian doctrines of the Trinity and Incarnation. By meticulously analysing the essential properties of God, Swinburne establishes their coherence within a robust metaphysical framework, reinforcing the foundational aspects of the divine nature exposited in his earlier work, *The Coherence of Theism*. Moreover, Swinburne's exploration of the Trinity reveals the intricate balance of unity and plurality in the Godhead, arguing for the necessity of multiple divine individuals rooted in perfect goodness and love. In addressing the Incarnation, Swinburne defends the Chalcedonian Definition, demonstrating its coherence and superiority over alternative interpretations. He also emphasises the importance of historical evidence and revelation in supporting Christ's divinity and the Incarnation's theological significance. Overall, Swinburne's analysis integrates philosophical rigour with theological depth, thus offering a robust framework for understanding and affirming the coherence and veracity of the central Christian doctrines of the Trinity and Incarnation.

Critical Engagements

The Christian God has drawn considerable attention and prompted various critical engagements from scholars, as Swinburne's work aims to demonstrate the coherence of Christian doctrines, particularly the Trinity and the Incarnation, through rigorous philosophical analysis. However, several critics have challenged different aspects of Swinburne's arguments featured in this work. Scholars such as Merold Westphal, John Haldane, David Brown, William Hasker and William P. Alston have raised objections that question the coherence of Swinburne's claims. This section explores these critical engagements and presents responses that align with Swinburne's philosophical perspective.

Merold Westphal

Critical Engagement. Merold Westphal, in his review article of *The Christian God*,[5] questions Swinburne's *a priori* argument for the Trinity, suggesting that it undermines the traditional attribute of aseity (self-sufficiency) in divinity. Westphal also critiques Swinburne's treatment of Christ's human soul, arguing that it verges on Apollinarianism by not sufficiently maintaining Christ's full humanity. Additionally, Westphal is sceptical of the extensive reliance on thought experiments to justify his metaphysical claims.

Critical Response. An adherent of Swinburne's position can offer several responses to Westphal's criticisms: first, Westphal's concern about aseity misunderstands the nuanced way Swinburne conceptualises divine self-sufficiency. Swinburne argues that aseity is preserved within the Trinity because the Father, as the ultimate source, eternally generates the Son and (with the Son) spirates the Spirit, with the Trinity that is composed of these three divine individuals (and is identified as the one 'God') lacking any external causation and this is itself a'se. Second, Swinburne's treatment of Christ's human soul is more sophisticated than Westphal's critique suggests. By employing Aristotelian concepts, Swinburne seeks to maintain both Christ's full humanity and full divinity. His approach aims to avoid Apollinarianism by affirming a complete divine and human nature in Christ (of an 'Aristotelian' kind, rather than a 'Platonic' one), while also preserving the unity of Christ's person. Third, Westphal's scepticism about thought experiments overlooks their crucial role in philosophy. Swinburne employs these not as mere speculation, but as rigorous tools for testing the logical coherence and implications of theological doctrines. This approach aligns with long-standing traditions in both philosophy and theology of using analogies and hypotheticals to elucidate complex concepts. Furthermore, Swinburne's *a priori* argument for the Trinity engages deeply with historical Christian

---

5. Westphal, Merold, 'The Christian God by Richard Swinburne', *Review of Metaphysics* 49, no. 2 (1995), pp. 441-42.

doctrine while providing a rational framework for understanding it. His approach offers a philosophical defence of trinitarian theology that addresses various contemporary intellectual challenges.

Although Westphal's critiques of Swinburne's trinitarian theology highlight important issues concerning divine aseity, Christ's human soul and the use of thought experiments, they do not decisively undermine Swinburne's approach. Swinburne's nuanced accounts of divine self-sufficiency, the unity of Christ's person, and the analytical value of hypotheticals, coupled with his incorporation of logical analysis and his engagement with historical doctrine, provide a robust defence of the trinity. While Westphal's challenges merit consideration, Swinburne's philosophical theology remains a sophisticated framework for understanding the Trinity in contemporary intellectual discourse.

John Haldane

Critical Engagement. John Haldane, in his review article of *The Christian God*,[6] challenges several aspects of Swinburne's metaphysical framework. He disputes Swinburne's endorsement of ontological relativism and his rejection of event causation in favour of substance causation. Haldane also questions the coherence of Swinburne's dualist conception of mind and its implications for the Incarnation, suggesting that it fails to account for the unity and complexity of divine and human natures in Christ.

Critical Response. An adherent of Swinburne's position can offer several responses to Haldane's criticisms: first, Haldane's challenge to Swinburne's ontological relativism overlooks its crucial role in providing a flexible metaphysical framework. Swinburne argues that this approach allows for a more nuanced understanding of reality, particularly when dealing with the complexities presented by the central Christian doctrines. It offers a way to reconcile seemingly contradictory attributes within a coherent system. Second, Swinburne's preference for substance ('agent') causation over event causation is not arbitrary but grounded in a sophisticated analysis of agency and responsibility. He contends that substance causation

---

6. Haldane, John, 'The Christian God by Richard Swinburne', *Religious Studies* 32, no. 2 (1996), pp. 281-83.

better accounts for the persistence of identity and the reality of free will, both of which are central to his theological and philosophical arguments. Third, Haldane's concerns about Swinburne's dualist conception of mind underestimate its explanatory power in addressing the challenges presented by the Incarnation. Swinburne's dualism provides a framework for understanding how Christ can possess both divine and human natures without contradiction. It allows for the distinctiveness of these natures while maintaining their unity in the person of Christ. Furthermore, as noted previously, Swinburne's approach to the Incarnation engages deeply with historical Christian doctrine while offering a rational explanation for its coherence. His dualist framework thus seeks to preserve the full divinity and full humanity of Christ, addressing a perennial challenge in Christology.

Ultimately, Swinburne's ontological relativism, preference for substance causation and dualist conception of mind withstand Haldane's critiques and provide a robust philosophical and theological foundation for understanding the Incarnation. Swinburne's approach offers a flexible metaphysical framework, a subtle analysis of agency and responsibility and a cogent explanation for the coherence of Christ's divine and human natures. His account engages deeply with historical Christian doctrine while providing a compelling rational justification for its central claims about the Incarnation.

David Brown

Critical Engagement. David Brown, in his review article of *The Christian God*[7], critiques Swinburne's argument for the Trinity as brief and somewhat simplistic, arguing that it fails to address several key theological concerns. Brown also points out potential issues with Swinburne's Christology, particularly regarding the integration of Christ's divine and human natures without falling into Apollinarianism. Additionally, Brown is critical of the heavy reliance on thought experiments, suggesting that they may not adequately reflect the depth and complexity of theological doctrines.

---

7. Brown, David, 'Review of The Christian God by Richard Swinburne', *The Journal of Theological Studies*, New Series, Vol. 47, no. 1 (1996), pp. 386–389.

Critical Response. An adherent of Swinburne's position can offer several responses to Brown's criticisms: first, *contra* Brown's characterisation of Swinburne's argument for the Trinity as brief and simplistic, Swinburne's approach to the Trinity is grounded in a sophisticated analysis of the divine attributes. His argument, while concise, is the culmination of a rigorous philosophical investigation into the nature and implications of perfect goodness. Second, Swinburne's Christology is more nuanced than Brown's critique suggests. Swinburne employs careful distinctions between essential divine properties and contingent human properties to explain how Christ can be fully divine and fully human without contradiction. This approach, as noted previously, aims to avoid Apollinarianism while maintaining the unity of Christ's person. Third, Brown's criticism of Swinburne's reliance on thought experiments fails to appreciate their specific function in Swinburne's methodology. Rather than being simplistic analogies, these thought experiments, as noted previously, serve as precise logical tools designed to isolate and examine key philosophical principles underlying the Christian doctrines under analysis. Thus, Swinburne uses them to bridge the gap between abstract theological concepts and rationally comprehensible scenarios, thereby subjecting these doctrines to rigorous logical scrutiny.

In sum, Brown's critique of Swinburne's arguments for the Trinity and Christology as simplistic and overly reliant on thought experiments fails to appreciate the depth and rigour of Swinburne's philosophical approach. Instead, Swinburne's analysis of divine attributes, careful distinctions in Christology and use of thought experiments as precise logical tools demonstrate the sophistication of his methodology and overall argumentation.

William Hasker

Critical Engagement. William Hasker, in his review article of *The Christian God*,[8] raises concerns about Swinburne's logical nominalism and its implications for understanding divine properties and the Trinity. He argues that Swinburne's view leads to potential contradictions, especially regarding the omnipotence and interdependence

---

8. Hasker, William, 'The Christian God: Richard Swinburne', *The Journal of Religion* 77, no. 3 (1997), pp. 487-88.

of the divine individuals. Hasker also questions the coherence of Swinburne's explanation of the Incarnation, particularly the division of the divine mind to accommodate human limitations.

Critical Response. An adherent of Swinburne's position can offer several responses to Hasker's criticisms: first, Hasker's concerns about Swinburne's logical nominalism fails to take into account its crucial role within Swinburne's metaphysical framework. Swinburne argues that this approach provides a more flexible and coherent way of understanding divine necessity, thus avoiding the pitfalls of traditional realism. Hence, this nominalist stance is not arbitrary but carefully integrated into Swinburne's broader philosophical system. Second, Swinburne contends that the interdependence of the divine individuals enhances rather than contradicts their omnipotence, as it reflects the perfect love and unity within the Godhead. This view seeks to reconcile the divine attributes with trinitarian doctrine in a logically coherent manner. Third, Hasker's questioning of Swinburne's explanation of the Incarnation underestimates the sophistication of Swinburne's Christology. The concept of a divided mind is not a simplistic solution but a carefully constructed model aimed at preserving both Christ's full divinity and genuine human experience. Swinburne argues that this approach allows for a coherent understanding of how Christ could possess both divine and human knowledge (with its limitations).

All things considered, Hasker's critique of Swinburne's logical nominalism, understanding of divine omnipotence and trinitarian interdependence, and explanation of the Incarnation fails to appreciate fully the coherence and depth of Swinburne's position. Swinburne's nominalist stance, treatment of the divine attributes and concept of a divided mind are carefully integrated into his broader metaphysical framework, providing a sophisticated and logically consistent defence of the Trinity and Incarnation.

William P. Alston

Critical Engagement. William P. Alston, in his article 'Swinburne and Christian Theology',[9] critiques Swinburne's account of the Trinity and Incarnation, suggesting that his explanations may lead to tritheism and fail to capture the full mystery of the doctrines. Alston argues that Swinburne's attempt to make the doctrine of the Trinity intelligible pushes it too far in the direction of tritheism, thereby robbing it of the mystery that has traditionally been considered a distinctive feature of the doctrine. Alston also expresses concerns about Swinburne's approach to the divine properties, particularly the emphasis on the distinctiveness of the divine individuals over their unity, which he believes undermines a robust understanding of monotheism. Additionally, Alston critiques Swinburne's concepts of ontological and metaphysical necessity, arguing that they fail adequately to capture the intuitive notion of ultimate, inevitable existence.

Critical Response. An adherent of Swinburne's position can offer several responses to Alston's criticisms: first, Alston's concern that Swinburne's account of the Trinity veers towards tritheism can be addressed by examining the sophisticated way Swinburne balances unity and distinction within the Godhead. Swinburne argues that the interdependence and necessary coexistence of the divine individuals preserves monotheism, by enabling the formation of the unified collective termed the one 'God' that is made up of these persons. This approach aims to elucidate the doctrine without diminishing its profundity, thus offering a subtle perspective that resists simple categorisation as either tritheism or modalism. Second, Swinburne's emphasis on the distinctiveness of the divine individuals is not at the expense of their unity, but rather an attempt to provide a logically coherent account of the trinitarian relations. He contends that this framework allows for a deeper understanding of the relationship of the persons within the Trinity, thus, again, enhancing rather than undermining monotheism. Third, Alston's critique of Swinburne's concepts of ontological and metaphysical necessity highlights an area where Swinburne has indeed revised his position. In the latest edition

---

9. Alston, William P., 'Swinburne and Christian Theology', *International Journal for Philosophy of Religion* 41, no. 1 (1997), pp. 35-57.

of *The Coherence of Theism*, Swinburne adopts a more mainstream understanding of necessity, aligning with the insights of Saul Kripke and Hilary Putnam. This demonstrates Swinburne's willingness to refine his arguments in light of philosophical developments and critiques. Thus, Swinburne's revised approach to divine necessity, which proposes an intermediate account (that was unpacked in Chapter 1), seeks to address the very concerns Alston raises. This new framework aims to capture the intuitive notion of ultimate, inevitable existence, while maintaining its rigour and coherence.

In the final analysis, Alston's criticisms of Swinburne's account of the Trinity and understanding of necessity, while important, do not decisively undermine the coherence and value of Swinburne's approach. Swinburne's nuanced balance of unity and distinction within the Godhead and his willingness to revise his position demonstrate the robustness and adaptability of his framework, with his revised approach to divine necessity ultimately addressing Alston's concerns.

* * *

In all, *The Christian God* offers a comprehensive philosophical defence of the central Christian doctrines of the Trinity and Incarnation, addressing complex metaphysical issues in order to demonstrate their overall coherence. The critical engagements by scholars such as Westphal, Haldane, Brown, Hasker and Alston highlight significant challenges, but the responses to these challenges, focused on the nature of necessity, the explanatory power of dualism and the importance of thought experiments for logical reasoning, underscore the robustness and intellectual rigour of his approach. These engagements contribute to an ongoing dialogue that enriches the understanding of the central Christian doctrines of the Trinity and Incarnation.

Conclusion

In conclusion, this chapter has provided a detailed guide to Swinburne's *The Christian God*, outlining its central aim, structure and themes. Swinburne's meticulous examination of various metaphysical concepts and their application within theology underscores the logical coherence of Christian beliefs. By addressing fundamental issues such as the nature of substances, causation, time, necessity and their relevance to theological thinking, Swinburne establishes a robust framework for understanding the Trinity and the Incarnation.

His analysis affirms that these doctrines, while complex, can be defended through rigorous philosophical inquiry. Swinburne's work thus remains a pivotal text in Analytic Theology, influencing contemporary debates and enriching the discourse on the rationality of Christian belief. As readers explore *The Christian God* for themselves, they will be better equipped to appreciate Swinburne's rigorous defence of the Christian doctrine of the Trinity and the Incarnation, and its significance in contemporary philosophy.

Chapter Six

The Plausibility of the Atonement

This chapter serves as an introduction to Swinburne's *Responsibility and Atonement* (hereafter, *RA*), which is a robust exploration of plausibility of the Christian doctrine of the atonement. Swinburne aims to establish a coherent framework for understanding certain concepts in both mundane human contexts and within the context of this traditional Christian doctrine. The chapter outlines the central aim and structure of Swinburne's arguments, situating them within the broader context of contemporary debates in the philosophy of religion. It introduces readers to the major sections of the book, including an analysis of moral responsibility, the role of free will and the application of these principles to Christian doctrines such as sin, redemption and sanctification. By providing this overview, the chapter prepares readers to engage deeply with Swinburne's systematic and rigorous examination of the Christian doctrine of the atonement.

Responsibility and Atonement: Background

Central Aim

The central aim of *RA* is to explore and establish a coherent framework for understanding the Christian doctrine of the atonement, which is grounded upon certain ethical and theological concepts such as responsibility, guilt, merit, punishment, the process of atonement and forgiveness. Swinburne seeks to elucidate how individuals acquire moral merit or guilt through their actions and how these notions are applicable to the doctrine of the atonement, including sin, redemption, sanctification and final judgement. RA is structured to address various philosophical challenges related to the application of these moral concepts to both human and divine interactions. Through rigorous analysis, Swinburne aims to demonstrate that the Christian doctrine of the atonement is morally plausible when interpreted through the lens of these ethical concepts, thus countering claims that it is inherently implausible or incoherent.

Historical Significance

RA was published in 1989 as the first work in Swinburne's tetralogy on Christian doctrine. The immediate historical context of RA involves debates about the cogency of various moral concepts related to the Christian doctrine of the atonement. Philosophers such as Herbert McCabe, most recently in works such as *Faith Within Reason*,[1] critically examined the moral implications of Christian teachings on sin and redemption. Also, Eleonore Stump, in various writings (and most recently in her work, *Atonement*),[2] examined the way in which the concepts of forgiveness and reconciliation are central to the Christian understanding of atonement and how these can be philosophically articulated to address issues of justice and mercy.

RA can thus be seen as part of this broader effort, engaging with the work of these and other philosophers, to build a robust framework for understanding the ethical and theological dimensions of the Christian doctrine of the atonement. As with Swinburne's other works, RA's publication greatly contributed to the continued scholarly engagement and debate on the plausibility of this important Christian teaching.

Literary Structure

RA is not explicitly divided into parts. However, for continuity with the previous chapters in this book, we shall retain the terminology and dual structure as follows:

---

1. McCabe, Herbert. *Faith Within Reason*. London: Continuum, 2007.
2. Stump, Eleonore. *Atonement*. Oxford: Oxford University Press, 2019.

1. *Philosophical Framework – Moral Goodness and Responsibility*: The first part of *RA* focusses on the philosophical analysis of moral goodness, responsibility and related concepts. Swinburne examines the nature of moral goodness, moral responsibility, weakness of will, merit, reward, guilt, atonement, forgiveness and punishment. He explores the conditions under which individuals acquire moral merit or guilt through their actions and how these concepts interrelate. This involves a rigorous examination of the principles underlying moral praise and blame, the role of free will and the implications of these principles for human interactions.
2. *Theological Application – Christian Atonement*: The second part of *RA* applies the established philosophical framework to specific Christian theological claims concerning the atonement. Swinburne investigates the coherence and moral plausibility of doctrines such as sin and original sin, redemption, sanctification and the concepts of Heaven and Hell. He examines how these doctrines can be understood in light of the moral concepts discussed in the first part, arguing that traditional Christian claims can be shown to be plausible and morally defensible. This thus involves addressing potential objections and demonstrating how these theological concepts can be integrated into a coherent moral framework.

We shall now unpack in greater detail the various areas covered in both of these parts of *RA*.

Themes

Philosophical Framework: Moral Responsibility and Atonement

In this section, Swinburne introduces the philosophical framework behind various aspects of moral philosophy, focussing on objective moral goodness, moral responsibility, free will, merit and reward, guilt and forgiveness, punishment and the human moral condition. He begins by examining the distinct nature of moral goodness, differentiating it from other forms of goodness and emphasising the importance of both objective and subjective moral values. Swinburne then delves into moral responsibility, highlighting the significance of intentions and the role of overcoming contrary desires. He defends the necessity of libertarian free will for true moral accountability, thus rejecting compatibilist views. The discussion extends to the concepts of merit and reward, stressing the importance of recognising and rewarding supererogatory actions. Swinburne also examines the processes of guilt, atonement and forgiveness, underscoring the relationship between personal responsibility and communal support. This all finally leads to an analysis of the nature of punishment and the complex nature of the human moral condition, exploring the inherent conflicts in human desires and the influence of genetic and social factors on moral behaviour.

Objective Moral Goodness

The concept of moral goodness is distinct from other forms of goodness, such as aesthetic or practical goodness. Moral goodness specifically applies to agents and their actions. Objective moral goodness refers to the inherent moral value of an action, regardless of the agent's beliefs. Actions like paying debts or visiting the lonely possess objective moral goodness because they fulfil universally recognised moral duties. Subjective moral goodness is tied to the agent's beliefs about the morality of his actions. Subjective moral goodness occurs when an agent performs an action he believes to be morally right, even if that belief is mistaken. This form of goodness values the agent's intention and effort to act morally according to his understanding. For instance, if a person gives money to someone he mistakenly believes is in need, the act retains subjective moral goodness due to the intention behind it. Despite the diversity of moral beliefs, there is underlying agreement on many moral issues, as moral beliefs are rooted in universal properties recognised by many people, such as causing pleasure or avoiding harm. However, disagreements arise from different weightings of these properties rather than from fundamentally different moral frameworks.

One can divide the goodness of character into three types: goodness of desires, goodness of beliefs and goodness of will. Goodness of desires involves having a natural inclination to perform good actions. Hence, an agent who is naturally generous or honest exemplifies this type of goodness. Goodness of beliefs refers to holding correct moral beliefs, while goodness of will is about having a strong desire to do good as such, even if one's specific beliefs about what is good are incorrect. In relation to this, there is also the distinction which we have previously focussed on between obligatory actions, which are moral duties, and supererogatory actions, which go beyond what is required. Obligatory actions – such as keeping promises and feeding one's children – are essential for maintaining moral order. On the other hand, supererogatory actions, such as giving all one's possessions to feed the starving, represent acts of exceptional moral value but are not required. While fulfilling obligations is crucial, supererogatory acts are significant because they demonstrate an individual's commitment to moral goodness beyond mere duty. Moreover, performing good actions despite contrary desires is praiseworthy. That is, an action is more praiseworthy if it is done in the face of temptation or difficulty. For example, helping a friend despite a strong desire to rest showcases a higher level of moral goodness than helping when it is easy. This struggle against contrary desires enhances the moral value of the action. Furthermore, whilst the goodness of an action is partly determined by its consequences, the agent's intentions are equally important. That is, an agent who tries to do good but fails due to circumstances beyond his control still possesses moral goodness. This is because the intentional effort to do good reflects the agent's moral character.

Moral Responsibility and Weakness of Will

An agent is morally responsible in the sense that he is praiseworthy or blameworthy for his intentional actions. That is, an agent is morally responsible for his actions when he intentionally chooses to perform them – with praise being due for actions considered good and blame appropriate for actions deemed bad. More fully, an agent is praiseworthy for actions he believes to be good, regardless of the objective moral value of those actions. This traditional view holds that moral praise is accorded to those who try to do what they believe is good. Hence, praise is particularly due to actions performed despite significant contrary desires. However, there is an asymmetry when it comes to blame: an agent is blameworthy for doing what he believes is wrong, rather than for performing an objectively bad act. Moreover, refraining from obligatory acts is blameworthy, and doing the right thing in the face of great temptation is praiseworthy. The effort required to overcome contrary desires enhances the moral value of an action, making it more deserving of praise. Following this, one can also understand that praise and blame are appropriate *only* for chosen intentions, and thus not for accidental outcomes. This view aligns with the traditional perspective that moral worth is intrinsic to the agent's intentional actions. Blame is due when an agent intentionally tries to do what he believes is wrong, and praise is due when he tries to do what he believes is supererogatory good, especially in the face of contrary desires.

Transitioning to another crucial aspect, while agents are responsible for their actions in accordance with their moral beliefs, they are also responsible for cultivating their character over time. A good character, which consists of desires and beliefs aligned with moral goodness, is praiseworthy. Conversely, a bad character, marked by inclinations towards bad actions, is blameworthy. Moral responsibility thus involves both immediate actions and the long-term development of one's character. To further elaborate, one can understand that weakness of will, where agents often act against their better judgement due to stronger contrary desires, is a real phenomenon; yielding to temptation is a genuine aspect of human experience. Agents are often influenced by desires that conflict with their moral beliefs, leading to actions that are not in line with what they believe to be best. This struggle between reason and desire is central to understanding moral responsibility. However, moral assessment should not focus solely on the outcomes of actions, as proposed by some philosophers. Instead, true moral worth lies in the agent's intentions and efforts to act in accordance with his moral beliefs. Thus, praise and blame should be based on the agent's attempts to fulfil his moral duties, rather than the objective results of his actions.

The Relevance of Free Will
For agents to be morally responsible, they must have the power to choose, independently of all causal influences. This traditional view of free will – libertarian free will – which was introduced previously, can be contrasted with various forms of compatibilism and incoherentism. Compatibilism, as noted previously, is the belief that moral responsibility is compatible with determinism, while incoherentism claims that the notion of free will required for moral responsibility is fundamentally flawed and incoherent. Now, moral responsibility is only applicable if an agent's actions are not predetermined by prior states or external causes. If an agent's actions are causally determined by his brain state, which in turn is determined by external factors, then the agent could not have acted otherwise. However, this would negate the agent's moral responsibility, as true moral responsibility requires the possibility of acting differently under the same circumstances.

An agent's contribution to his actions must originate within himself and not be made inevitable by other causes. Moreover, an agent must possess moral beliefs to be held morally responsible. These beliefs guide the agent's choices and actions, providing a framework for determining right and wrong. An agent with free will but no moral beliefs cannot be morally responsible, as his actions would lack the necessary moral context. Thus, moral responsibility requires both free will and moral beliefs. However, compatibilists argue that agents can be morally responsible for their actions even if those actions are causally determined. Compatibilists thus redefine free will to mean the ability to act according to one's desires and intentions, regardless of whether those desires and intentions are themselves determined. This view is to be rejected, however, because true moral responsibility requires the freedom to choose between alternatives without being causally necessitated.

In exploring this more deeply, one form of compatibilism, known as the 'straight rule of responsibility', asserts that agents are responsible for all intentional acts, regardless of causal determination. This, however, can be challenged by highlighting scenarios where agents are driven by irresistible desires, such as addiction or coercion, arguing that moral responsibility cannot be attributed in such cases. If an agent's actions are inevitable due to prior causes, then the agent cannot be held morally responsible, as he lacks the genuine freedom to choose otherwise. In a deterministic universe, actions would still be good or bad, right or wrong. However, agents would not be blameworthy or praiseworthy for their actions, as they would be fully determined by prior causes. This undermines the basis for moral responsibility, as agents would lack the freedom to choose differently. Moral responsibility thus requires the ability to act independently of deterministic causes. Given this, one should thus hold to an incompatibilist view of freedom, the view that free will (and thus moral responsibility) is incompatible with determinism. That is, libertarian free will, which posits that agents have the genuine ability to choose between alternatives, provides agents with an ability that is not constrained by causal determinism, which thus allows for true moral responsibility. Accepting libertarian free will requires rejecting determinism, but this is necessary to preserve the concept of moral responsibility. An alternative perspective concerns that of the notion of second-order desires, which, as noted previously, was introduced by Harry Frankfurt. Second-order desires are desires about one's desires, such as wanting to want to be generous. Frankfurt argues that free will involves aligning one's first-order desires with one's second-order desires. However, this view is also to be rejected as 'genuine' free will involves the power to choose independently of all desires and external influences. Again, it is libertarian free will that is essential for holding agents accountable for their actions, ultimately allowing for genuine praise and blame and, as humans possess this kind of free will, they are therefore capable of moral responsibility.

Merit and Reward

Supererogatory actions, actions that go beyond moral obligations, can be classified into two categories: favours and creative acts. Favours are acts that directly benefit other individuals, while creative acts primarily benefit the agent, though they may also indirectly benefit the community that has nurtured the agent. Both types of supererogatory actions create obligations for others. For example, a favour creates an obligation for the recipient to express gratitude, and a creative act creates an obligation for the community to respect and acknowledge the agent's efforts. Building on this, one can understand that fulfilling one's obligations simply clears a debt and does not generally create a situation that requires positive action from others. However, supererogatory actions do create such situations. Moreover, accepting favours is often good because it allows the donor to become part of the recipient's personal relationships, fostering friendship and love. Rejecting favours can imply that the donor's contributions are worthless, potentially damaging the relationship. However, there are circumstances where it is good or even obligatory to refuse favours, such as when accepting them could lead to negative consequences or misunderstandings. When a favour is accepted, it creates a new situation where the beneficiary should respond with gratitude. Expressing gratitude is not merely good but obligatory, as unreciprocated friendship can be painful for the donor. The obligation to express gratitude arises because accepting a gift encourages a friendship that should be reciprocated. This reciprocity can include returning favours, which helps to develop and strengthen friendships. However, for significant favours, merely saying 'thank you' is insufficient – that is, the expression of gratitude must sometimes be costly to demonstrate genuine appreciation. In addition to favours, creative acts, which do not have immediate beneficiaries, also create new obligations. It is good for individuals to acknowledge and appreciate the achievements of others. This recognition is important as it gives public acknowledgement of significant truths and confers a favour on those who performed the creative acts. Individuals who perform creative acts indirectly benefit their community by fulfilling the community's efforts to educate and nurture them. The community, in turn, has an obligation to respect and acknowledge these achievements, as they enrich the community as a whole.

Turning now to a related concept, the concept of merit, which supererogatory actions bestow upon the agent. One can understand that merit can be objective or subjective. Objective merit belongs to an agent who performs a supererogatory act, regardless of whether the agent believes the act to be supererogatory. For instance, an agent might work hard to achieve something that benefits others without realising its broader impact. Subjective merit, on the other hand, arises from an agent's intention to perform what he believes to be a supererogatory act, even if he is mistaken – and full acknowledgement and reward are appropriate only when there is both objective and subjective merit. Recognising the achievements of others is inherently good. Acknowledging someone's creative or supererogatory acts provides public recognition of significant contributions and benefits the agent who performed the acts. By acknowledging these achievements, the community honours the efforts of those who contributed to the agent's development. It is good for the community to show gratitude and respect for these contributions, as it fosters a sense of belonging and mutual respect. To further elaborate, special obligations arise from benefits received, such as the responsibilities owed to parents, grandparents and members of one's nurturing community. These obligations are often involuntary but are based on the benefits conferred, such as life, nurture and education. People need to feel a sense of belonging, and recognising and fulfilling these special obligations is crucial for maintaining strong, supportive relationships within the community.

Guilt, Atonement and Forgiveness
Guilt is the status acquired by an agent who fails to fulfil his or her moral obligations. Further, there is a distinction to be drawn between objective guilt, which arises from failing to meet moral duties regardless of the agent's beliefs, and subjective guilt, linked to an agent's intentional failure to act according to his perceived

obligations. Objective guilt is a status akin to uncleanliness, whereas subjective guilt involves a personal acknowledgement of wrongdoing and a failure of personal trust. Objective guilt occurs when an agent does something wrong, such as failing to educate his children properly, even if he believes his actions are right. This type of guilt reflects a breach of moral law, independent of the agent's awareness. However, subjective guilt arises when an agent knowingly fails to fulfil his obligations. For example, if a person believes he should repay a debt but neglects to do so, he is subjectively guilty. Subjective guilt is more severe as it involves deliberate intent or negligence. One can also draw a distinction between subjective guilt and shame – with the latter involving regret for the type of reason behind an action, rather than its consequences. Similarly, pride pertains to being pleased with the reasons behind an action. Subjective guilt may exist without shame, as an agent might recognise his wrongdoing without feeling ashamed. Conversely, an agent may feel ashamed for actions he does not consider morally wrong but that fail to meet his personal ideals.

Now, to address these forms of guilt, the process of atonement is necessary. There are four components of atonement: repentance, apology, reparation and penance. Repentance involves acknowledging the wrongdoing and resolving to amend one's behaviour. Apology is the public expression of this repentance to the victim. Reparation entails making amends for the harm caused, while penance involves performing additional acts to demonstrate sincerity and remorse. These steps help the wrongdoer distance himself from the past wrongdoing and align his current intentions with moral goodness. Turning our attention now to the role of the victim: forgiveness is a crucial part of this process. Forgiveness is the act of the victim accepting the wrongdoer's atonement efforts, thereby helping to remove the wrongdoer's guilt. Forgiveness is thus a performative act that signifies the victim's willingness to move past the wrongdoing. Without the victim's forgiveness, the wrongdoer remains guilty despite his efforts at atonement. However, if the victim refuses to forgive despite substantial atonement, the wrongdoer's guilt can eventually dissipate as he has done all he can to make amends.

With regard to the communal aspect of these concepts, special obligations arise from benefits received, such as responsibilities towards family members and the nurturing community. These obligations are often involuntary but are based on the mutual benefits

The Plausibility of the Atonement 255

and support within a community. Failing to fulfil these obligations harms not only the direct victim but also the community that has invested in the agent's moral development. Additionally, individuals may bear some responsibility for the actions of others, particularly when they have influenced or failed to deter the wrongdoer. This responsibility is most significant within close relationships, such as family and community members. While individuals are not guilty for others' actions, they have a duty to help those they influence to make atonement for their wrongdoings.

Punishment

Punishment is the right of a victim to exact reparation if a wrongdoer does not voluntarily make amends. This reparation should compensate not only for the original harm but also for additional inconveniences such as trauma and anxiety caused by the wrongful act. However, the concept of punishment extends beyond mere reparation to include an element of penalty for the wrongdoer's harmful attitude or malevolent intent, which is termed retribution. In building on this foundation, one can understand that though individuals have the right to exact retribution, they may transfer this right to the state, either explicitly or implicitly. The state, acting as an agent for the victim, administers punishment. Neither the victim nor the state is obliged to punish, although there are often good utilitarian reasons for doing so, such as prevention, deterrence and reform.

    The primary justification for punishment is as a substitute for revenge, preferable when an authority acts on behalf of the victim. If the state punishes wrongdoers, it must act within the limits of retributive justice, having the right to administer punishment only when functioning as an agent for the victim. Moreover, the utilitarian justification of punishment, focussing solely on deterrence, prevention and reform, can be viewed as being problematic for it can lead to morally unacceptable consequences, such as punishing the innocent or excessively punishing the guilty. One can thus differentiate between punishment and revenge – with punishment by an official authority normally being viewed positively, while revenge by the victim or someone close to him normally being viewed negatively. The primary difference between these two concepts lies in the authority and broader social context. That is, punishment by the state is meant to be impartial and serve the greater good, while revenge is personal and subjective. Punishment includes a performative element – a public reprimand expressing moral condemnation and reinforcing the social stigma attached to the wrongdoing. Concerning limitations of retribution and the virtue of mercy, while victims have the right to exact retribution, there is no obligation to do so. Mercy, which involves refraining from punishing, is often considered a supererogatory act – an act that goes beyond duty. Showing mercy can be objectively good and sometimes necessary to achieve greater moral ends. However, the right to exact retribution is fundamental and should not be dismissed lightly. Moreover, individuals can implicitly consent to the state's authority by accepting the benefits of living within a regulated society. This consent is presumed unless explicitly revoked. The state's right to punish derives from its role as an agent of the victims, exercised through legal and judicial processes designed to ensure fairness and impartiality. Also, the systematic use of punishment by the state is more effective and just than individual acts of revenge.

Man's Moral Condition
Human desires often conflict with their moral beliefs, and this inherent conflict leads to temptation and a propensity for wrongdoing – termed 'original sinfulness', which can be both subjective (acting against one's conscience) and objective. More precisely, many desires, especially those for personal enjoyment, power and admiration, are self-centred and often clash with others' desires. While humans also possess altruistic desires, these are often weaker compared to selfish ones. This fundamental conflict is a natural aspect of human desires, not a result of education or upbringing. Now, conflicting desires can arise logically or circumstantially. Logical conflicts occur when two people desire mutually exclusive outcomes, such as both wanting to be the sole ruler. Circumstantial conflicts depend on external factors, such as limited resources. Human nature and the world's conditions ensure that such conflicts are inevitable. The inherent selfishness in human desires leads to a propensity for objective wrongdoing. This selfishness often tempts individuals to satisfy their desires through immoral means. The strongest of these selfish desires is sloth, the desire to avoid effort – and as fulfilling moral obligations requires effort, which humans are naturally inclined to avoid, this results in moral failure. Humans could theoretically be free of conflicting desires, existing in harmony like a highly intelligent ant colony. However, human nature is fundamentally different, driven by self-centred desires.

These desires make humans prone to wrongdoing, both objectively (without realising it) and subjectively (being aware of the wrongdoing but unable to resist the temptation). Subjective wrongdoing, which is the more important form of wrongdoing, occurs when individuals act against their moral beliefs due to strong conflicting desires. This is often compounded by self-deceit, where individuals refuse to acknowledge their moral beliefs or the consequences of their actions. An example is the obedient official in the Holocaust, who hides from himself the true nature of his actions. This self-deceit turns moral weakness into what appears as deliberate wickedness.

The evolutionary emergence of moral beliefs marks the transition from animal behaviour to moral agency. The ability to make moral distinctions transformed early humans into moral agents. This development introduced objective and subjective wrongdoing, as humans began to understand moral duties and were tempted to act against them. Moreover, the transmission of moral beliefs is also a cultural phenomenon, while the propensity for wrongdoing is biologically transmitted through genes. This genetic predisposition to wrongdoing is activated by the acquisition of moral beliefs, leading to a continuous relationship between nature and nurture. In addition to this, false moral beliefs also further corrupt human character. That is, inadequate or incorrect moral teachings fail to guide individuals towards the good and can even encourage bad actions. A corrupt moral system can weaken an individual's resolve to pursue the good, reinforcing bad desires and increasing both objective and subjective wrongdoing. Social influence and example play significant roles in shaping moral behaviour. Good examples can reinforce the pursuit of the good, while bad examples can make it easier to yield to temptation. An ideal education system would thus teach and exemplify good moral behaviour, therefore, counteracting the natural propensity for wrongdoing.

In conclusion, Swinburne's philosophical framework provides a nuanced understanding of the various dimensions of moral goodness and responsibility. The importance of both objective and subjective moral values has been shown, with an emphasis being provided concerning the role of intentions and the struggle against contrary desires in moral evaluation. Swinburne defends the traditional view of libertarian free will as essential for genuine moral responsibility, arguing against compatibilist perspectives. His analysis of merit and reward highlights the significance of recognising and rewarding supererogatory actions, while his exploration of guilt, atonement and forgiveness reveals the complex relationship between personal responsibility and communal support. Swinburne's discussion of punishment emphasises the necessity of retributive justice while acknowledging the role of mercy. Finally, his exploration of the human moral condition delves into the inherent conflicts in human desires and the influence of genetic and social factors, providing a thorough understanding of the challenges and complexities of moral behaviour. Through this detailed examination, Swinburne offers valuable insights into the nature of moral philosophy and the principles guiding moral evaluation and responsibility.

2.2 Theological Application: Christian Atonement

In this section, Swinburne applies his philosophical framework to the central elements that make up the Christian doctrine of the atonement. He begins by discussing the implications of God's existence on moral obligations and the potential for supererogatory acts. Swinburne then focuses on the concept of original sinfulness, examining the hereditary transmission of a propensity for wrongdoing and its theological significance. He further addresses the doctrine of redemption, highlighting the necessity of Christ's sacrifice for human atonement. This then continues with an exploration of sanctification and the process of moral purification, followed by an analysis of the afterlife focussed on Heaven and Hell. Through these discussions, Swinburne integrates his philosophical insights with key aspects of this central Christian doctrine, providing a comprehensive understanding of Christian moral and philosophical theology.

Morality under God

It is assumed here that there exists an omnipotent, omniscient, perfectly free and perfectly good God, who created and sustains the universe. This God became incarnate in Jesus Christ, lived a saintly life, died to atone for humanity's sins and rose from the dead. Christ founded the Church to continue his work and seeks humanity's eternal well-being in friendship with him. This detailed assumption is necessary for discussing the implications of Christian doctrines on human moral responsibility and destiny. As noted in previous chapters, moral obligations are taken to exist independently of

God's commands – certain minimal duties, such as truth-telling and refraining from murder, are obligatory regardless of God's existence. However, if God exists, humans have a greater duty to obey his commands due to their total dependence on him. This dependence means that failing in any duty to fellow humans also constitutes a failure towards God, which is termed sin. Thus, while God's existence increases the scope of obligations, it does not eliminate the potential for supererogatory (beyond duty) good deeds. Within this context the (infamous) 'Euthyphro dilemma' is thus able to be presented, which questions whether actions are obligatory because God commands them or if God commands them because they are obligatory, is examined. In response to this, a middle ground can be proposed, which is some moral truths are necessary and independent of God's will, while others depend on God's commands. Moreover, God's commands can refine and deepen our understanding of moral obligations without completely redefining them. While God, as the creator, has the right to command certain actions, there are limits to what can be morally permissible. For example, God cannot command actions that impose unjustifiable harm on others. A perfectly good God would not subject humans to excessively restrictive moral obligations, allowing them some freedom in how they use their lives. This perspective supports the idea that there remains room for supererogatory acts even within a theistic moral framework: while God's commands create many obligations, they do not cover every aspect of life, leaving space for supererogatory goodness. This doctrine has traditionally been more accepted in Catholic thought and contrasts with Protestant views, which often reject the idea of supererogation. Nevertheless, a generous God would not demand total servitude, allowing humans to choose how to use their lives within certain limits.

In delving deeper, one can turn to the doctrine of sanctity, which holds that only those with wills firmly dedicated to the good will attain salvation. This doctrine, common to both Catholic and Protestant thought, emphasises the necessity of a profound commitment to God's will. While this doctrine implies that sanctity is required for salvation, it does not negate the possibility of supererogatory acts. Hence, individuals are not obliged to pursue the most direct path to salvation but are encouraged to strive towards it, leaving room for personal choice and supererogatory goodness.

Original Sinfulness

Original sinfulness is a moral disease transmitted genetically, not merely through social or environmental influence. As the Council of Trent (1545 - 1563CE) asserted in the *Decree on Original Sin* (Fifth Session), this transmission occurs by 'propagation, not imitation',[3] which countered the Pelagian view that sinfulness is primarily a result of social factors. This proneness to sin inclines individuals towards sinning without necessitating it. Some theologians, such as Saint Augustine and his Protestant successors, argued that humans necessarily sin without divine grace, while others, such as the Early Church Fathers and Eastern Orthodox theologians, emphasised human free will and the potential to avoid sin.

Focussing on Augustine's perspective, Augustine suggested, in his work *On Original Sin*, that humans are inherently inclined to sin because of the original sin inherited from Adam[4]. Without sufficient grace, humans necessarily sin, as their will is corrupted and unable to choose good on its own. However, with sufficient grace, humans necessarily do good, as grace transforms the will, enabling it to choose rightly. Augustine's ambivalence on free will has led to various interpretations, with some seeing his views as deterministic and others interpreting them as compatible with a form of conditional free will that operates under the influence of grace. John Calvin's doctrine of total depravity, presented in his work *Institutes of the Christian Religion*, takes Augustine's ideas further by asserting that humans are utterly devoid of all good without divine grace[5]. According to Calvin, every aspect of human nature is corrupted by sin, rendering humans completely incapable of choosing good or seeking God on their own. Divine grace is thus not just necessary but also irresistible, compelling the elect towards salvation and good works. This position, however, has deterministic implications, as it suggests that human

---

3. Decree Concerning Original Sin. Session V, 17 June 1546. In *Decrees of the Ecumenical Councils*, edited by Norman P. Tanner, vol. 2, Sheed & Ward and Georgetown University Press, 1990, p. 666.
4. Augustine of Hippo, On Original Sin, in T*he Works of Saint Augustine: A Translation for the 21st Century*, translated by John E. Rotelle, New York: New City Press, 1997.
5. Calvin, John, *Institutes of the Christian Religion*, translated by Henry Beveridge, Peabody, MA: Hendrickson Publishers, 2008, Book II, Chapter 3.

will is entirely overridden by divine intervention, leaving no room for genuine human freedom or moral responsibility. One can thus contrast these positions with the more moderate positions of theologians such as Duns Scotus, who argued for the coexistence of free will and divine grace. Scotus maintained that humans have the capacity to choose good or evil freely, but divine grace assists the will without coercing it. Scotus believed that God's grace makes it possible for humans to perform good actions, but it does not force them to do so, thus preserving human free will. Scotus' position suggests that God's greatness is not diminished by allowing creatures to determine their own destiny. Instead, it highlights a collaborative relationship between divine grace and human freedom, where grace enables but does not compel, thus supporting the notion of human free will and moral responsibility.

With regard to the role of the first human, Adam, he is posited as representing the emergence of moral agency in the evolutionary process. This first moral agent, capable of distinguishing between right and wrong and making free choices, committed the first subjective sin. However, Augustine's view of Adam as a perfect being endowed with original righteousness is not correct; instead, Adam's sin was a natural result of his human nature, which was inherited from his non-human ancestors. This perspective thus aligns with a gradualist view of evolution, where moral capacities developed slowly over time. Considering the implications of Adam's sin, the 'monogenist' view that all humans descended from a single pair can be questioned and, instead, moral concepts and proneness to sin can be taken to have arisen independently in different human groups. Thus, the desires leading to sin are genetically inherited, while moral beliefs are socially transmitted. That is, Adam's sin set a precedent for the social transmission of corrupt morality, but the genetic predisposition to sin was already present in pre-human ancestors.

In further exploring inherited sin, one can consider the doctrine of original guilt, which asserts that Adam's descendants inherit guilt for his sin. Most early Christian theologians rejected or were unaware of this doctrine; and one can understand that guilt cannot be inherited but is linked to personal responsibility. Moreover, biblical texts, such as the teachings of Jeremiah and Ezekiel, reject the notion of children bearing the iniquity of their parents. While humans inherit a debt or moral obligation from Adam, they do not inherit guilt for his sin.

Redemption

A distinction can be drawn between objective sin, which is almost unavoidable due to moral ignorance and carelessness, and subjective sin, which involves yielding to temptations such as sloth, greed, lust and envy. However, for both forms of sin, the guilt from our sins requires substantial atonement towards God, and there is an obligation to assist others in their atonement – with the significant burden of sin being underscored through the example of Saint Paul, who deeply felt the weight of moral obligations and his own sinfulness despite his dedication to the law of God.

Now, with regard to the need for atonement, human sinners must make atonement for their own sins and help others with their atonement. This specific view of the atonement under focus aligns with Anselm's 'satisfaction' theory, as further developed by Aquinas. Within this view, one can understand that, while repentance and apology are personal acts, others can assist by providing means for reparation and penance. Hence, Jesus Christ, who owed nothing to God due to his divine nature, offered his life and death as reparation and penance for humanity's sins. Now, a good God would not simply forgive sins without requiring reparation and penance, as overlooking serious harm would mean not taking the perpetrator seriously. Thus, while some theologians, such as Aquinas, acknowledged that God could forgive without demanding reparation, repentance and apology are essential. Our freedom to do good or ill involves the responsibility to rectify wrongs. So, providing the opportunity to make amends allows individuals to affirm their identities as responsible agents, similar to a parent who gives a teenager the means (e.g., money) to repair the neighbour's window that they had broken, allowing the child to take responsibility for its actions.

In further exploring Christ's role, Christ's sacrifice is unique in that, while no one can make atonement for another's sins directly, individuals can assist others in making atonement. Thus, Christ's life and death serve as a means for humanity to offer reparation and penance to God. This aligns with the concept of sacrifice in the Bible, where a valuable offering is made to God, often shared with worshippers. Christ's voluntary sacrifice – despite being foreseen to result in death – provides a perfect life that can be offered as reparation and penance for human sins.

Now, in relation to other models of atonement, such as Christus Victor, ransom and penal substitution theories, one can understand that these theories lack explanatory power and coherence. As the Christus Victor model fails to explain why a costly struggle was necessary, the ransom model implies an illogical prior agreement with the Devil and the penal substitution model, which sees Christ's suffering as punishment in place of humanity's, makes the process too mechanical and less personal. These models, thus, do not adequately address the relational aspect of reconciliation between God and humanity. The sacrifice model is thus found to be the most satisfactory, particularly as expressed in the epistle to the Hebrews. This model views Christ's life and death as a valuable gift to God, whose benefits flow to others through the Resurrection. Thus, as noted already, in this model, Christ's life and death are available for humans to offer as reparation and penance – this interpretation aligning with biblical passages where forgiveness and redemption are linked to the individual's active participation in Christ's sacrifice, such as at baptism and the Eucharist.

Sanctification and Corruption

Sanctification is the purging of oneself from past wrongdoing by pleading the atonement made by Christ. This involves fulfilling obligations and performing supererogatory acts in the present. Sanctification requires forming true moral beliefs and cultivating a natural inclination to conform to them. The Church plays a crucial role in this process by facilitating the formation of good character through teaching, example and encouragement to worship and theological study. An individual who seeks to do good is likely to question his moral beliefs and seek true beliefs. This quest thus leads to the understanding that actions should be done for their own sake, not just because they are good. The pursuit of a good character thus involves developing a natural love for people and things, with the ultimate goal being the beatific vision of God in Heaven. By habitually performing good actions, an agent becomes naturally inclined to do them in the future, thus reducing the need for agonising choices. This process enhances the likelihood of consistently doing good actions. However, while it is good to form one's own character for good, it is not always good to form the character of others. Depriving someone of the choice to pursue the good by eliminating contrary desires can be problematic. Yet, fostering a good character in oneself through deliberate steps is crucial. This involves training oneself to resist desires that deter the pursuit of the better and cultivating a holy will through practices such as ascetic disciplines. The Church's precepts thus provide guidance on moulding desires for good; and the support of the Church and its teachings plays a vital role in sanctification. However, the natural inclination towards good can be corrupted through repeated wrongdoing and self-deception. That is, yielding to desires for what one believes to be wrong leads to a gradual dulling of conscience – with self-deception, where an agent suppresses his moral beliefs, being a significant factor in this process. This can lead to a loss of moral sensitivity, where the agent no longer perceives the moral value of actions and becomes driven solely by desires. Hence, the process of corruption involves the suppression of moral beliefs and the reinforcement of bad desires. Over time, this can result in the complete loss of moral beliefs and the dominance of self-centred desires. This state is thus likened to losing one's soul, where the individual becomes an arena of conflicting desires without the guidance of reason. This total corruption is a gradual process that requires repeated acts of self-deception and suppression of conscience. However, external influences can play a significant role in the process of corruption: a corrupt society can significantly contribute to the development of wrong moral beliefs and evil desires. Conversely, a supportive environment can promote the formation of good character. Thus, the Church's role in providing positive influences through teaching and example is crucial in counteracting the natural propensity for wrongdoing and fostering sanctification.

Heaven and Hell
Humans, as noted previously, consist of both body and soul, with the essence of a person not being the body, as it can be replaced, but the soul, which initiates intentional actions, experiences consciousness and carries character traits. Although the soul typically functions with a body, God can sustain the soul without a body or provide it with a new one. The soul's desires and beliefs, however, are often expressed through bodily means, making human souls inherently suited for human bodies. Consequently, the Christian belief that God will eventually provide new bodies to souls is to be affirmed.

Now, for the fate of 'saints' – who are individuals whose wills are firmly directed towards the good – one can understand that a saint is someone already partially blessed, finding happiness in performing good actions and experiencing good things. True happiness stems from fulfilling desires, which, in the case of saints, align with moral goodness. Saints derive happiness from virtuous actions, even if such actions involve struggles against contrary desires. A good God would complete the saint's character formation and remove any conflicting desires, allowing the saint to perform good deeds naturally and easily. This eternal well-being in union with God is seen as a merited reward, though it is to be emphasised here that a good God must have further reasons for granting such a reward, by recognising the infinite value of a good character. Contrastingly, a benevolent God would not impose the beatific vision on a totally corrupt being, as such an individual would be incapable of enjoying it. Instead, the totally corrupt, having destroyed their moral awareness and left themselves with competing desires, would receive punishment proportional to their sins. Hence, the traditional Christian notion of eternal sensory punishment is to be disaffirmed – as it is excessively vindictive. Instead, annihilation or elimination could be a more just fate for the totally corrupt, as maintaining their existence serves no purpose. Alternatively, if kept alive, their pleasures would be limited to those that do not involve moral goodness.

In considering various fates for those with half-formed characters, one possibility is elimination, given the lack of a fully developed character worth preserving. Another is reincarnation, offering them another chance to form their character. A third option is Purgatory, where individuals with a basic inclination towards good can perfect their character. This aligns with the Catholic doctrine, which holds that those in Purgatory will eventually reach Heaven, though the duration and effort required depend on each individual's prior choices and actions.

Two guiding intuitions concerning all of this are thus to be emphasised: the fate of individuals for eternity often depends on their choices in this life; and no one is deprived of the fate they truly seek. One could affirm Aquinas' view that the wicked in Hell, if genuinely penitent, would be forgiven by God. However, such repentance is unlikely, because of the fixed nature of their impenitence. Nevertheless, a good God would give individuals the opportunity to achieve the beatific vision if they seek it but would also respect their freedom to reject it, thus granting them the fate they have chosen through their actions and desires.

In conclusion, Swinburne's application of his philosophical framework provides a precise definition of the Christian doctrine of the atonement, in light of various principles of moral philosophy. He argues that the existence of an omnipotent, omniscient and perfectly good God amplifies human moral obligations while preserving the potential for supererogatory acts. Swinburne's examination of original sinfulness highlights the hereditary transmission of the propensity for wrongdoing, thus emphasising the role of free will and individual moral responsibility. His discussion on redemption underscores the necessity of Christ's sacrificial atonement for human sins, thus aligning with the biblical and theological teaching. The process of sanctification is portrayed as a deliberate effort to cultivate moral goodness, supported by the Church's teachings and community. Finally, Swinburne's exploration of the afterlife in the form of Heaven and Hell reflects a balanced understanding of divine justice and human moral choices. Overall, Swinburne's integration of moral philosophy with Christian theology offers a profound insight into the workings of the Christian doctrine of the atonement, the moral implications of religious belief and the pursuit of a virtuous life.

Critical Engagements

Responsibility and Atonement has garnered significant attention and sparked various critical engagements from scholars, as Swinburne's work focusses on demonstrating that the concept of moral responsibility and the doctrine of the atonement, as traditionally understood in Christianity, are indeed philosophically defensible. However, several critics have challenged different aspects of Swinburne's arguments featured in this work. Scholars such as Paul Helm, H.P. Owen, Colin Gunton, Eleonore Stump and Steven S. Aspenson have raised objections that question the plausibility of Swinburne's claims. This section explores these critical engagements and presents responses that align with Swinburne's philosophical perspective.

Paul Helm

Critical Engagement. Paul Helm, in his review article of *Responsibility and Atonement*,[6] critiques Swinburne's moral objectivism and his *a priori* assumptions about moral principles. Helm argues that Swinburne's reliance on moral objectivism, where certain moral truths hold in every possible world, leads him to make overly confident assertions about what God can and cannot do. Helm also criticises

---

6. Helm, Paul, 'Responsibility and Atonement by Richard Swinburne', *Religious Studies* 26, no. 3 (1990), pp. 431-33.

Swinburne's method of filtering Christian doctrines through his moral principles, which can result in the dismissal of significant theological doctrines on *a priori* moral grounds.

Critical Response. An adherent of Swinburne's position can offer several responses to Helm's criticisms: first, Helm's critique of Swinburne's moral objectivism fails to consider its essential role in forming a coherent framework for understanding divine nature and action. Swinburne argues that moral truths that hold across all possible worlds provide a necessary foundation for comprehending God's goodness and actions. Second, Swinburne's method of filtering Christian doctrines through moral principles is not aimed at dismissing theological doctrines, but rather at ensuring their logical and ethical coherence. This approach seeks to demonstrate that Christian beliefs can withstand rigorous philosophical scrutiny. Third, Swinburne's confidence in making assertions about what God can and cannot do stems from his understanding of divine perfection and omnipotence. He argues that God's nature as a perfectly good being necessarily constrains divine action in ways that align with objective moral truths. Furthermore, Swinburne's moral objectivism provides a basis for understanding the universality of divine commands and the rationality of religious ethics. This framework offers a philosophical grounding for the belief that God's moral nature is consistent across all possible worlds.

All things considered, while Helm's critiques of Swinburne's moral objectivism and method of doctrinal analysis raise important questions, Swinburne's approach remains a sophisticated attempt to reconcile philosophical rigour with theological insight. His moral objectivism provides a coherent framework for understanding divine nature and action, and his doctrinal analysis seeks to demonstrate the logical and ethical coherence of the Christian doctrine of the atonement.

H.P. Owen

Critical Engagement. H.P. Owen, in his review article of *Responsibility and Atonement*[7], raises concerns about Swinburne's interpretation of key Christian doctrines, particularly regarding original sin and Christ's redemptive work. Owen questions Swinburne's rejection of the Augustinian view of original sin and his interpretation of atonement as a form of sacrifice. He also highlights potential inconsistencies in Swinburne's view of substitutionary atonement, noting that Swinburne's approach may not fully account for the traditional understanding of Christ's all-sufficient sacrifice.

Critical Response. An adherent of Swinburne's position can offer several responses to Owen's criticisms: first, Owen's concern about Swinburne's rejection of the Augustinian view of original sin does not address the philosophical and ethical challenges posed by traditional interpretations. Swinburne's reinterpretation aims to maintain the essence of the doctrine while addressing issues of inherited guilt and moral responsibility. Second, Swinburne's approach to atonement as a form of sacrifice seeks to provide a rational framework for understanding Christ's redemptive work. This interpretation aligns with biblical metaphors, while offering a philosophically coherent account of how Christ's death affects human salvation. Third, the apparent inconsistencies in Swinburne's view of substitutionary atonement can be addressed by examining his nuanced understanding of Christ's sacrifice as both representative and transformative. Swinburne argues that Christ's death serves as a catalyst for human repentance and moral transformation, rather than a simple transaction. Furthermore, Swinburne's reinterpretation of these doctrines aims to make them more accessible to contemporary philosophical inquiry without compromising their theological significance. His approach seeks to demonstrate the rational credibility of these core Christian beliefs.

In the final analysis, Swinburne's reinterpretation of original sin and atonement represents a thoughtful attempt to articulate these doctrines in philosophically defensible terms, even though it departs from traditional formulations. By addressing philosophical and

---

7. Owen, H.P., 'Review of Responsibility and Atonement by Richard Swinburne', *New Blackfriars*, 72, no. 846 (1991), pp. 99–101.

ethical challenges posed by traditional interpretations, Swinburne offers fresh insights into these central Christian beliefs, thus inviting deeper reflection on their meaning and implications.

Colin Gunton

Critical Engagement. Colin Gunton, in his review article of *Responsibility and Atonement*,[8] criticises Swinburne's treatment of the humanity of Christ and the role of the Holy Spirit in the process of atonement. Gunton argues that Swinburne's focus on moral and legal aspects of atonement leads to a somewhat mechanical understanding of redemption. He also questions the adequacy of Swinburne's discussion of sanctification and the transformative power of the Holy Spirit, suggesting that Swinburne's approach may overlook the relational and dynamic aspects of atonement.

Critical Response. An adherent of Swinburne's position can offer several responses to Gunton's criticisms: first, Gunton's concern about Swinburne's focus on moral and legal aspects of atonement ignores the philosophical necessity of establishing a clear rational framework for understanding redemption. Swinburne's approach aims to provide a logically coherent account of how Christ's death affects human salvation. Second, while Swinburne's treatment may appear mechanical, it seeks to elucidate the objective basis for atonement. This approach does not negate the relational aspects but provides a foundation for understanding them within a broader philosophical context. Third, regarding the role of the Holy Spirit and sanctification, Swinburne's work implicitly addresses these through his emphasis on moral transformation and the human response to divine initiative. His focus on repentance and reparation inherently involves the transformative power traditionally attributed to the Holy Spirit. Furthermore, Swinburne's approach to atonement, while emphasising moral and legal dimensions, does not preclude the relational and dynamic aspects. Rather, it provides a framework within which these aspects can be understood and articulated.

---

8. Gunton, Colin, 'Responsibility and Atonement, by Richard Swinburne', *The Journal of Theological Studies*, New Series, 42, no. 2 (1991), pp. 801-4.

Ultimately, Swinburne's treatment of atonement and the role of Christ's humanity represents a rigorous attempt to provide a philosophically coherent account of these doctrines, even if it faces challenges raised by Gunton. Although his approach focusses on moral and legal aspects, it offers a foundation for understanding the broader implications of Christ's redemptive work.

Eleonore Stump

Critical Engagement. Eleonore Stump, in her festschrift essay 'Love and Forgiveness: Swinburne on Atonement',[9] critiques Swinburne's account of forgiveness, arguing that his emphasis on conditional forgiveness is inconsistent with the unconditional nature of divine forgiveness as depicted in the Gospels. Stump suggests that Swinburne's view fails to capture the fullness of Christ's teachings on forgiveness, which emphasise unconditional love and mercy. She also criticises Swinburne's interpretation of atonement, claiming that it does not adequately address the relational and transformative aspects of Christ's redemptive work.

Critical Response. An adherent of Swinburne's position can offer several responses to Stump's criticisms: first, Stump's critique of Swinburne's conditional forgiveness disregards the moral complexity involved in genuine reconciliation. Swinburne argues that his view of forgiveness respects the moral agency of both wrongdoer and victim, thus aligning with principles of justice and personal responsibility. Second, while Swinburne's account may seem at odds with unconditional divine forgiveness, it seeks to explain how such forgiveness can be morally justified. His approach aims to reconcile divine mercy with moral accountability, therefore providing a framework for understanding forgiveness that does not compromise moral integrity. Third, regarding the relational and transformative aspects of atonement, Swinburne's theory implicitly addresses these through its emphasis on repentance and moral transformation. The process of seeking forgiveness and making reparation inherently involves a relational dimension and personal change. Furthermore, Swinburne's interpretation of atonement, while, as noted previously, focussed on moral and legal aspects, does not

---

9. Stump, Eleonore, 'Love and Forgiveness: Swinburne on Atonement', in M. Bergmann and J.E. Brower (eds), *Reason and Faith: Themes from Richard Swinburne* (Oxford: Oxford University Press, 2016), pp. 148-70.

negate the role of divine love and mercy. Rather, it seeks to explain how these operate within a framework of moral objectivity and personal responsibility.

In sum, Swinburne's treatment of forgiveness and atonement represents a nuanced attempt to provide a philosophically robust account of these doctrines, although it faces challenges raised by Stump. His approach, though emphasising conditions for forgiveness, offers insights into the moral dynamics of reconciliation and transformation.

Steven S. Aspenson

Critical Engagement. Steven Aspenson, in his article 'Swinburne on Atonement',[10] critiques Swinburne's use of philosophical concepts to explain theological doctrines, particularly the notion of atonement. Aspenson argues that Swinburne's approach may be too abstract and detached from the lived experience of faith. He also questions whether Swinburne's philosophical framework can fully capture the depth and mystery of Christ's atoning work.

Critical Response. An adherent of Swinburne's position can offer several responses to Aspenson's criticisms: first, Aspenson's concern about the abstractness of Swinburne's approach misses the importance of philosophical rigour in defending and explaining theological doctrines. As Swinburne's use of philosophical concepts aims to provide a rational foundation for faith, complementing, rather than replacing, lived religious experience. Second, while Swinburne's framework may seem detached from experiential faith, it seeks to offer intellectual support for believers grappling with doubts or seeking deeper understanding. His approach provides tools for articulating and defending Christian beliefs in a pluralistic intellectual landscape. Third, regarding the depth and mystery of Christ's atoning work, Swinburne's philosophical analysis does not claim to exhaust its meaning. Rather, it aims to demonstrate the logical coherence and plausibility of atonement, thus providing a framework within which its profound implications can be explored. Furthermore, Swinburne's philosophical treatment of atonement serves to bridge the gap

---

10. Aspenson, Steven S., 'Swinburne on Atonement', *Religious Studies* 32, no. 2 (1996), pp. 187-204.

between faith and reason, offering a rational basis for belief that can enhance, rather than diminish, the spiritual significance of Christ's redemptive work.

* * *

In the end, Swinburne's philosophical analysis of atonement represents a thoughtful attempt to articulate this central Christian doctrine in philosophically defensible terms, even though it faces challenges raised by Aspenson. His approach offers a way to engage with the intellectual aspects of faith without negating its experiential and mystical dimensions.

Conclusion

In conclusion, this chapter has provided a comprehensive guide to Swinburne's *Responsibility and Atonement*, exploring the ethical and theological concepts of responsibility, guilt, merit, punishment, atonement and forgiveness. Swinburne sought to establish a coherent framework for understanding these concepts in both human interactions and within the context of traditional Christian doctrines. The chapter outlined the central aim and structure of Swinburne's arguments, situating them within the broader context of contemporary debates in the philosophy of religion. It introduced readers to the major sections of the work, including an analysis of moral responsibility, the role of free will and the application of these principles to the Christian doctrine of the atonement and related notions such as sin, redemption and sanctification. As readers explore *Responsibility and Atonement* for themselves, they will be better equipped to appreciate Swinburne's rigorous defence of the plausibility of the Christian doctrine of the atonement and its significance in contemporary philosophy.

Chapter Seven

The Probability of the Resurrection

This chapter serves as an introduction to Swinburne's *The Resurrection of God Incarnate* (hereafter, *RGI*), which is a comprehensive investigation into the resurrection of Jesus Christ. Swinburne aims to demonstrate that the resurrection of Jesus is a probable event, supported by both philosophical argumentation and historical evidence. The chapter introduces readers to the central aim and structure of Swinburne's arguments, situating them within the broader context of contemporary debates in the philosophy of religion. It outlines the major sections of the work, including an analysis of the principles for evaluating evidence, God's reasons for becoming incarnate, and the historical evidence for Jesus' life, death and resurrection. By providing this overview, the chapter prepares readers to engage deeply with Swinburne's systematic and rigorous examination of the resurrection of Jesus Christ.

The Resurrection of God Incarnate: Background

Central Aim

The central aim of *RGI* is to examine and provide evidence for the resurrection of Jesus Christ. Swinburne seeks to demonstrate that the resurrection of Jesus is probable, given the historical evidence and the broader philosophical context of Christian theism. Moreover, Swinburne argues that the Resurrection serves as a divine signature on the teachings of Jesus, validating his claim to divinity and the doctrines of the Church he founded. *RGI* is thus structured to address philosophical and theological challenges related to the Resurrection, which, therefore, involves a detailed analysis of the principles for weighing evidence, God's reasons for becoming incarnate and the historical evidence for Jesus' life, death and resurrection.

Historical Significance

RGI was published in 2003 as a work outside the trilogy and tetralogy, which, nonetheless, continued Swinburne's broader project of applying a rigorous philosophical method to an important theological teaching. The immediate historical context of *RGI* involves broader debates about the nature and credibility of the Resurrection as a historical event. Philosophers, such as David Hume, in *An Enquiry Concerning Human Understanding*, had famously challenged the credibility of miracles, arguing that the evidence for miracles is always outweighed by the evidence against them. Additionally, John Hick, in *The Metaphor of God Incarnate*, offered a metaphorical interpretation of the Incarnation, suggesting that this doctrine should be understood symbolically rather than literally, or as a doctrine grounded upon history. *RGI* thus directly addresses the challenges raised by individuals such as Hume and Hick by providing a structured framework for evaluating the historical evidence for the Resurrection (and thus the veracity of the Incarnation as well), ultimately arguing that it is indeed the most probable explanation of the evidence surrounding the life of Jesus Christ. Since its publication, *RGI* has profoundly shaped discussions about the credibility of the Resurrection and the rationality of religious belief. It has set a high standard for subsequent debates in the philosophy of religion on the resurrection of Jesus, thus prompting continuous scholarly engagement concerning the question of the probability of this central teaching within Christianity.

Literary Structure

The literary structure of *RGI* is divided into three main parts: 'General Background Information', 'Prior Historical Evidence' and 'Posterior Historical Evidence'. However, for continuity with the previous chapters in this book, we shall retain the terminology and dual structure as follows:

1. *Philosophical Framework – Principles and Incarnational Reasons*: The first part of *RGI* focusses on the philosophical principles for weighing evidence related to the Resurrection. Swinburne begins by discussing the types of evidence available, including general background evidence about the existence of God and specific historical evidence related to Jesus' life and death. He emphasises the importance of considering both types of evidence to assess the probability of the Resurrection. Swinburne assesses the specific reasons why God would want to become incarnate – namely, (i) to provide atonement for human sins, (ii) to identify with human suffering and (iii) to reveal moral truths – and the five marks that an incarnate God would need to possess in order to be identified as such – (i) living a perfect life, (ii) expressing a belief in his own divinity, (iii) teaching that his life is an atonement for sin, (iv) providing moral and theological teaching and (v) founding a Church to continue his work. Moreover, he also examines arguments against the possibility of miracles, addressing Hume's scepticism and defending the rationality of believing in supernatural events given adequate evidence.
2. *Theological Application – The Historical Jesus and the Resurrection*: The second part of *RGI* applies the established philosophical framework to specific theological claims about Jesus and the Resurrection. Swinburne investigates the historical sources that provide evidence for Jesus' life, teachings, death and post-death appearances. He evaluates the moral and theological implications of Jesus' life, arguing that Jesus led the sort of life that God would have reason to validate through a miraculous Resurrection. Moreover, Swinburne also addresses potential objections and rival theories about what happened after Jesus' death. He examines the empty tomb, the reported appearances of the risen Jesus and the transformation of the disciples, arguing that the Resurrection provides the best explanation for these historical facts. Swinburne concludes that, given the background evidence for the existence of God and the

specific historical evidence, it is significantly probable that Jesus rose from the dead.

We shall now unpack in greater detail the various areas covered in both parts of *RGI*.

Themes

Philosophical Framework: Principles and Incarnational Reasons

In this section, Swinburne introduces the philosophical framework for assessing historical evidence and discusses four main types of evidence – memory, testimony, physical traces and background evidence – and how they can systematically be evaluated using probability reasoning. Moreover, Swinburne examines why God might choose to become incarnate and what characteristics would mark God Incarnate, and emphasises that, despite the seeming improbability of miracles, a structured analysis of these evidence types can provide a reasonable basis for believing in the historicity of such events.

Principles for Weighing Evidence

In establishing the methodology for evaluating historical evidence, four main types of evidence can be identified: testimony, memory, physical traces and background evidence. First, apparent testimony claims should be taken as genuine unless counterevidence suggests otherwise. For example, if someone claims to have seen an event, this should generally be believed unless there is a reason to doubt his or her reliability. If Jesus rose from the dead, this would be a miracle – a violation of natural laws brought about by God. If there is no God, such a violation cannot occur. However, if evidence from natural theology suggests the existence of God, then the positive testimony about the Resurrection can make it probable. Hence, the role of testimony in establishing historical facts is crucial and, as the principle of testimony is essential for gaining knowledge beyond our own experiences, one should again trust all testimony in the absence of counterevidence. Thus, while testimony can be unreliable, this determination must rely on the trustworthiness of other forms of testimony – with there being an importance given to multiple, independent testimonies for strengthening the credibility of an event (as long as they do not derive from a common unreliable source). Second, memories, or more precisely, apparent personal memories, should be trusted in the absence of counterevidence. While memories can be confirmed by generalisations about the world, the trustworthiness of memory itself is a fundamental *a priori* principle. This principle is crucial because if memory could not be trusted, we would have no knowledge beyond immediate perception. Hence, all memory should be trusted unless there is specific evidence to the contrary, such as known tendencies to misremember certain events or strong evidence that contradicts the memory. Third, physical traces, such as fingerprints or archaeological finds, are also important forms of evidence. Moreover, the connection between physical traces and their causes is established inductively through observed regularities and theories about how the world works. For example, fingerprints found at a crime scene can strongly suggest the presence of a particular individual, based on the established uniqueness and transferability of fingerprints. Finally, background evidence involves understanding the general likelihood of events based on broader theories or patterns observed in the world. However, background evidence is not causal evidence like testimony or physical traces but helps assess the probability of certain events. For instance, if a person known for honesty testifies to witnessing a rare event, his character serves as background evidence supporting his claim.

Now, in evaluating miraculous claims, which seem to violate natural laws, one must understand that all claims about natural laws and historical events are, in fact, corrigible, meaning they can be revised in light of new evidence. That is, while scientific laws have strong predictive power, occasional anomalies – *contra* Hume – should not lead to outright dismissal of those laws but rather an understanding that these laws cannot account for the anomaly (without being rendered as complex) and thus divine intervention is indeed possible. Hence, detailed historical evidence for events such as the Resurrection must be considered in the broader context of the available background evidence, including the existence of God and the likelihood of divine intervention. Moreover, given the principle of testimony, one should trust the testimony to a miracle, in the absence of any counterevidence against it. Hence, one does not have good grounds for rejecting a miracle claim outright as Hume argued for one to. Rather, a rigorous analysis of each claim indeed needs to be performed (as will now be done for the Resurrection).

God's Reasons for Becoming Incarnate

If evidence from natural theology supports the existence of a God who is omnipotent, omniscient, perfectly free and perfectly good, then this God will always strive to do the best possible act. However, as has been noted before, there may not always be a single best possible act, but rather a range of equally good acts. Thus, while God cannot always do the best, he can always fulfil all his obligations. Obligations typically arise from commitments or benefits received, such as the obligation to keep promises, care for parents and do no harm to others. Now, God had no obligation to create humans, as obligations presuppose the existence of beings to whom one is obliged. However, once God creates humans, he has obligations to ensure that their lives, on balance, are good. So, a perfectly good being will always fulfil these obligations. Having created humans, God has obligations to ensure their overall well-being. These obligations include making sure that human lives are, on balance, good, though not necessarily devoid of suffering. God's obligations do not entail making life devoid of challenges but ensuring that these challenges contribute to a greater good. For example, God might allow natural disasters to foster human virtues such as courage and generosity. Moreover, God's inability to perform the absolute best act (because of the infinite potential for good) does not contradict his perfect goodness. Instead, God's perfect goodness is demonstrated by fulfilling his obligations and performing many good acts, even if there are always more good acts he could perform.

Now, based upon this understanding of God's perfect goodness, there are three *a priori* reasons for God to perform the action of becoming incarnate within his creation: to provide atonement for human sins, to identify with human suffering and to reveal moral truths. More fully, the first *a priori* reason for God's incarnation is to help humans achieve atonement. As noted in the previous chapter, the process of atonement typically involves four components: repentance, apology, reparation and penance. Repentance and apology allow a person to distance themselves from wrongdoing both internally and externally. Reparation helps restore the status quo by addressing the effects of the wrongdoing. And for more serious offences, penance, a small gift or service, serves as a token of sorrow for failing in one's obligations. The process of atonement is completed when the victim forgives the wrongdoer, treating him as if he had not wronged him.

Now, as also previously noted, humans have inherited an 'original sinfulness', a propensity for wrongdoing that has led them to wrong God, or sin, in both direct and indirect ways. Direct wrongdoing includes failing to show God the reverence and gratitude due to the ultimate source of their existence. Indirect wrongdoing involves abusing free will and responsibility by wronging others, thereby hurting God's creation. This all results in guilt. Additionally, humans inherit a form of guilt from their ancestors, who failed in their obligations to God and are thus indebted to Him. This inherited guilt imposes an obligation on descendants to help their ancestors atone for their sins. Given the propensity to sin, humans face a daunting task in fulfilling their obligation to atone and clear their moral debt to God. A perfectly good God would thus likely respond by helping humans make proper atonement. Since the central aspect of the moral debt to God is failing to live good lives, the required atonement is a good life offered to God as reparation. However, humans, given their moral debts, are unlikely to provide this on their own. Therefore, God could become incarnate, live a perfect human life and offer it to God as reparation. This perfect human life, lived by God incarnate, would be a sufficient reparation, as the victim (God) determines when reparation is sufficient. By associating their repentance and apology with the reparation provided by God Incarnate, humans can achieve full atonement and obtain forgiveness from God. Thus, given the sinfulness of humanity, there is a strong *a priori* reason to expect God to become incarnate to help humans deal with their sin.

The second *a priori* reason for God's incarnation is to identify with human suffering. A perfectly good God would choose to share in the suffering of his creation to demonstrate solidarity and love. Similarly, as noted previously, parents often subject their children to suffering for a greater good, such as making them attend a challenging school to build community relations. It is thus good, but not obligatory, for parents to share in their child's suffering in such cases. However, when the suffering is severe, sharing in it becomes a moral obligation. For example, if a country is unjustly attacked and conscription is introduced, parents might veto their child's conscription if they are under 18. However, if a parent (under 50) refuses the veto due to the attack's severity, they have a moral obligation to volunteer themselves and share their child's suffering. This parallels the Incarnation: the suffering God permits humans to endure obliges him to share in it. Given God's perfect goodness, this obligation to share in our suffering will be fulfilled through the Incarnation, which provides the second *a priori* reason for this event taking place.

The third *a priori* reason for God's incarnation is to guide humans to live morally good lives. A perfectly good God would provide revelatory information to help humans achieve this end and become saints. This information includes knowledge about God's nature and actions, such as his incarnation, and the future of humanity. This helps humans worship God correctly, use the means for atonement that has been provided and stay motivated in their pursuit of goodness. Additionally, moral guidance on which actions are obligatory is crucial. Humans, inheriting a propensity for wrongdoing (original sinfulness), may misinterpret moral truths. Given this and humans' failure to live good lives based on natural moral awareness, God would intervene to provide necessary moral instruction. Furthermore, a living example of perfect moral behaviour is essential, as it is easier for humans to understand and apply moral information when they have a concrete example. Thus, by becoming incarnate and living a perfect life, God provides such an example and encouragement for others to emulate. Given God's desire for humans to become saints, this provides the third *a priori* reason to expect God to become incarnate.

So, God would seek to become incarnate in order to dispense an obligation to share in human suffering, to provide a reparational sacrifice that can be utilised by humans to make an atonement and to provide theological and moral instruction by living a perfect human life. Each of these reasons can be taken to be, at a minimum, an 'equal best action'. However, intuitively, the second action is indeed a 'unique best action', and the first and the third action might plausibly be so as well. An action is a unique best action if it is an overriding action, which is an action that is 'sensible', 'appropriate', 'reasonable' and 'rational' to do. That is, taking all reasons into account, it is better to perform the action than not to perform it, because there is no other action that has these specific features (i.e. no other action that is as sensible, appropriate, reasonable and as rational to do). Thus, by an action having these specific features, God would be inclined to perform the action, if he is unimpeded by non-rational forces to choose a less good action. However, as God is essentially perfectly free, he would not be so impeded and, as he is also essentially omniscient, he will know the moral truth value of an action, resulting in him inevitably performing a unique best action if there is one (and performing no bad actions). Thus, taking these three reasons into account, there is strong reason to believe that, if there is a God, as a unique best action, he will become incarnate in order to identify with our suffering and for at least one of the other two reasons.

The Marks of God Incarnate

If God were to become incarnate, the life led by God Incarnate must exhibit certain characteristics to fulfil the purposes of atonement, identification with human suffering and revelation of moral truths. If a God were to become incarnate for these three reasons, he would need to live a life as a 'prophet' that is marked by five specific qualities. The first mark is living a perfectly good life, which includes demonstrating supererogatory goodness, going beyond basic moral requirements to exemplify extraordinary virtue. Second, the prophet must show that he believes himself to be God Incarnate. This belief does not need to be declared outright at the beginning of his ministry but must eventually be evident through his teachings and actions, revealing his understanding of his divine nature. Third, the prophet must teach that his life is an atonement for sin and provide healing in ways beyond ordinary human capacities, addressing physical, psychological or societal suffering and evils. Fourth, the prophet needs to teach deep moral and theological truths, offering guidance on how to live a good life, worship properly and understand the afterlife. These teachings must be plausibly true and deep, guiding humanity in ways that align with divine intentions. Fifth, the prophet must establish a 'Church' (i.e. an authoritative community) to continue his work and teachings. This Church must perpetuate his teachings, provide forgiveness of sins and spread the message to new generations and cultures, ultimately ensuring that the benefits of the Incarnation are accessible beyond the initial community.

In addition to these five marks (termed the 'prior historical evidence'), the life of an incarnate God must be authenticated by a 'super-miracle'. This is crucial because a super-miracle, defined as a clear and extraordinary violation of natural laws, would serve as a divine signature on the prophet's life, confirming his divine identity and mission. Without such a miracle – such as a resurrection – it could be argued that the prophet's achievements might be the result of natural processes or human effort rather than divine intervention. Therefore, the super-miracle provides indisputable evidence (termed the 'posterior historical evidence') that the prophet's life and work are indeed of divine origin. And thus, as it will be shown below, the historical evidence concerning the life, teachings and actions of Jesus of Nazareth align with these five marks, and the evidence for his resurrection, conceptualised as a super-miracle, sets him apart as the unique candidate for being God Incarnate.

In conclusion, Swinburne's philosophical framework provides a rigorous methodology for evaluating historical evidence, emphasising the importance of memory, testimony, physical traces and background evidence – that includes three *a priori* reasons for God becoming incarnate and five marks for identifying him as such. By utilising this framework for performing this type of historical analysis, Swinburne argues that it is possible to reasonably support the historicity of the Resurrection. This structured approach offers a logical framework for assessing extraordinary historical claims, demonstrating that belief in the resurrection of Jesus can be grounded in a careful and systematic analysis of the available evidence.

Theological Application: The Historical Jesus and the Resurrection

In this section, Swinburne applies his philosophical framework to that of an historical and theological analysis of the person of Jesus of Nazareth and his purported resurrection. He evaluates the reliability of historical sources, examines the nature of Jesus' life and teachings and assesses the evidence for the Resurrection. Swinburne aims to demonstrate that the historical accounts of Jesus and the Resurrection are credible and to provide a strong foundation for the belief in Jesus' divinity and the truth of the Resurrection. This analysis focusses on the authenticity of the New Testament documents, the coherence of Jesus' actions and teachings, with the five marks identified previously, and the overall probability of the Resurrection as a historical event.

Historical Sources
Almost all the evidence about Jesus' life and teachings comes from written testimonies, with the most significant evidence contained in the books of the New Testament. Moreover, the majority of scholars agree that most of these books were written within 110 years of the

events they describe, primarily focussing on the last three years of Jesus' life and what followed. Now, the genre of the New Testament writings is crucial in assessing their reliability as historical sources. While some books of the Old Testament, like Jonah and Daniel, are understood as fictional stories intended to encourage or teach, the New Testament books are predominantly intended as historical accounts. The epistles of Saint Paul, for example, are seen as paradigm examples of letters with historical content that are intended to be taken literally. Furthermore, several of Paul's epistles are attributed to him by nearly unanimous scholarly consensus, dating them between 49 CE and 58 CE. Paul's letters, especially the more personal ones, reflect his honesty and compassion, which supports the fact that Paul intended his brief narratives to be taken as literal historical truths.

Turning to the Gospels and Acts, these texts also purport to be historical accounts. Acts reads like contemporary works of history, especially its later parts, which contain detailed and matter-of-fact descriptions of events. This narrative style, along with the internal references to other historical documents and the use of first-person accounts in some passages, thus supports their historical intent. The synoptic Gospels (Matthew, Mark and Luke) approach recording history with an intent that blends historical narrative and theological reflection. That is, these Gospels were intended as historical narratives, despite occasional theological reflections within them. The gospel of Luke, in particular, explicitly states its intention to provide an orderly and accurate account of events. Thus, while acknowledging that some elements, such as the infancy narratives, may contain theological embellishments, the primary aim of these texts is historical documentation. Moreover, the gospel of John also contains both historical narratives and theological reflections. Some stories in John, such as the miracle at the pool of Bethesda and the raising of Lazarus, might be intended more for theological illustration than as literal historical accounts. However, despite this, John's gospel still purports to present historical events, particularly those surrounding the passion and resurrection of Jesus. Other early Christian writings, such as the first epistle of Clement and the epistles of Ignatius of Antioch – dating from the late first and early second centuries – also provide additional corroboration for the historical accounts in the New Testament, thus reinforcing the reliability of the primary sources.

Now, while discrepancies and theological embellishments do exist, they do not undermine the overall historical framework, as the substantial agreement among the synoptic Gospels, despite minor differences, supports their reliability. Furthermore, the consistency of key events, such as Jesus' baptism, crucifixion and resurrection, across multiple sources – including non-Christian references – further affirms their credibility. Thus, the New Testament writings, particularly the Gospels and Acts, should be regarded as fundamentally reliable historical sources. Despite occasional theological reflections and minor discrepancies, their primary intent and substantial agreement on key events affirm their reliability. Hence, on the basis of the principle of testimony, which holds, as noted previously, that one should trust testimony unless there is counter evidence against it, one should indeed affirm the reliability of the New Testament. As this principle suggests that we should generally accept the accounts presented in the New Testament as truthful unless we have specific reasons to doubt them. And thus these texts, being written testimonies from individuals close to the events they describe, should thus be considered reliable historical sources under this principle, unless proven otherwise.

A Perfect Life and Moral Teaching
To consider Jesus as God Incarnate his life must have been a perfect human life, one that could be offered as reparation for human sin and serve as a moral exemplar. The evidence of Jesus' public behaviour, such as his association with tax collectors and sinners as well as with the Pharisees, supports the claim that he led a perfect life. Géza Vermes, the eminent Jewish historian, highlights, in his work *Jesus the Jew: A Historian's Reading of the Gospels,* Jesus' unique approach to social outcasts – ultimately emphasising that Jesus did not merely defend the poor and oppressed but actively sought out and befriended those despised by society.[1] Furthermore, Jesus' willingness to eat with sinners and tax collectors and to touch lepers – actions that offended the pious Jews of his time – demonstrates a profound love for outcasts. Jesus led the life of a wandering teacher, with no permanent home, teaching publicly about God's love and how people should live. This lifestyle, combined with Jesus' deep prayer life and sense of divine calling, exemplifies a life dedicated to fulfilling God's will. In

---

1. Vermes, Géza. *Jesus the Jew: A Historian's Reading of the Gospels.* SCM Press, 1983, pp. 223-224.

addition to his behaviour, Jesus provided deep moral teachings and demonstrated his divinity through miraculous acts. The Gospels report numerous miracles performed by Jesus, primarily healings, which were acts of love and compassion. These miracles, such as healing the blind, deaf and lepers, as well as raising the dead, suggest that Jesus' life was characterised by miraculous interventions that align with divine intervention. While some healings could have natural explanations, others appear to be genuine violations of natural law, further supporting Jesus' divinity. Moreover, Jesus' miracles were seen as signs of the Kingdom of God breaking into the world. For instance, Jesus' response to accusations that he cast out demons by the power of Beelzebub was to assert that if he did so by the Spirit of God, then the Kingdom of God had come to his audience. Jesus' healings and exorcisms – whether understood as literal miracles or as profound psychological healings – thus reflect divine intervention and serve to affirm his divine mission. Additionally, Jesus' crucifixion was a key element of his perfect life. That is, a prophet leading a perfect life could not have been justly condemned. The charges against Jesus included accusations of blasphemy by Jewish authorities for claiming divine prerogatives and condemnation by Roman authorities for claiming to be the king of the Jews. Jesus' claims to divine authority and Messiahship were necessary for his role as God Incarnate and these claims were true. Thus, significantly, Jesus' crucifixion, as an innocent person condemned unjustly, was the culmination of a life of atonement. Jesus' acceptance of his fate and his prayer for forgiveness for his executioners, as reported in the gospel of Luke, exemplify supreme acts of supererogation. Jesus' life and actions, including his willingness to suffer and die unjustly, demonstrate the kind of perfect life expected of God Incarnate. Furthermore, the profound moral teachings of Jesus focussed on God's love for humanity, the importance of forgiveness and the call to show supererogatory love. Jesus' teachings on the love of God for humans, exemplified in parables like the prodigal son and the lost sheep, and the call for humans to forgive others as God forgives them, are encapsulated in the Lord's Prayer, which emphasises the need for forgiveness. Moreover, Jesus also taught the importance of supererogatory love, as highlighted in the Sermon on the Mount and the parable of the sheep and the goats. Jesus commended reliance on God, the practice of prayer, fasting and almsgiving with humility and the urgency of spiritual reform. While there is some debate over the interpretation of Jesus' teachings, the core message of love, forgiveness and the expectation of divine judgement is clear. In addition to this, the controversial teaching of Jesus regarding the Last Judgement, in which the good are rewarded and the bad are punished, reflects the belief in the ultimate separation of the good and the bad, with the bad suffering in the afterlife. This separation respects human free will, allowing individuals to determine their eternal destiny through their choices. The permanence of this separation is justified by the moral development of individuals and their persistent rejection or acceptance of God.

The life and teachings of Jesus align with what one would expect from God Incarnate. That is, Jesus' perfect life, deep moral teachings, miraculous acts and willingness to suffer and die unjustly all support the claim that he was God Incarnate.

Jesus Implied His Divinity

An explicit claim by Jesus that he was God would have been misunderstood by first-century Jews. Thus, instead of making a direct statement, Jesus left many clues that, upon reflection, led his followers to recognise his divinity. These clues included accepting worship, forgiving sins, claiming a unique intimacy with God and actions that led to accusations of blasphemy during his trial. Jesus had to be subtle about his divinity because claiming to be God outright would have been inconceivable to his contemporaries and could have defeated the purposes of the Incarnation. Moreover, Jesus often taught in ways that made those in his audience think and reach conclusions on their own. This method included refusing to answer questions directly and instead asking questions that led his followers to consider their beliefs deeply. For instance, when questioned about his authority, Jesus asked about John the Baptist's authority, making the audience reflect on the source of his own. Similarly, Jesus' actions, such as riding into Jerusalem on Palm Sunday and cleansing the Temple, were symbolic acts meant to prompt reflection and recognition of his divine authority.

Additionally, various actions of Jesus implied his divinity. Jesus performed miracles, such as healing the sick and raising the dead, which indicated divine power. Jesus also forgave sins, which bystanders understood as a divine prerogative, and claimed authority to interpret and amend Mosaic law, as seen in his teachings on the Sabbath and other legal matters. These actions led his opponents to accuse him of blasphemy, a charge based on Jesus arrogantly assuming divine privileges. Now, after his resurrection, Jesus' divinity was more openly recognised. For example, the gospel of Matthew ends with Jesus commanding his disciples to baptise in the name of the Father, the Son and the Holy Spirit, placing himself on a level with God the Father. Also, in the gospel of John, doubting Thomas addresses the resurrected Jesus as 'My Lord and my God', a clear acknowledgement of his divine status, and other New Testament passages describe the disciples worshipping Jesus, an act reserved for God, indicating their recognition of his divinity.

There are two important utterances of Jesus that might suggest that he believed himself to be less than divine. The first is Jesus' statement in Mark that he does not know the day or hour of the end times, knowledge that the Father alone possesses. However, in a divided Incarnation, as was explained in Chapter 5, God Incarnate would not necessarily know all things and would act and speak based on human limitations. Thus, it is indeed possible for him not to know the hour of the end times. The second is Jesus' cry of dereliction on the cross, 'My God, my God, why have you forsaken me?' Now, this might indicate a momentary feeling of abandonment; however, this does not necessarily imply a permanent lack of divine self-awareness. Furthermore, concerning the important verse about Jesus accepting John's baptism, which was for the forgiveness of sins, one can understand that Jesus' baptism did not imply that he believed himself to be a sinner but rather that he identified with Israel's need for repentance and was setting an example. Also, regarding the temptations of Jesus, these temptations were to do less than the best, rather than to do wrong, and overcoming these temptations demonstrated Jesus' perfect moral character. Additionally, various New Testament writers implicitly or explicitly acknowledged Jesus' divinity. The gospel of John, the epistle to the Hebrews and the Pauline epistles all contain passages that ascribe divine attributes to Jesus, suggesting pre-existence and a role in creation. Moreover, the infancy narratives in Matthew and Luke, which describe Jesus' virginal conception, imply a unique divine status from birth. These writings reflect a developing understanding among early Christians that Jesus was indeed God Incarnate.

Jesus thus left sufficient clues during his life that, upon reflection, led his followers to recognise his divinity. These clues included his actions, teachings and post-resurrection acknowledgements, which collectively pointed to his unique relationship with God. The early Christian understanding of Jesus as God Incarnate, despite initial Jewish and pagan expectations, was based on a careful interpretation of his life and teachings – with this gradual revelation being necessary to ensure that Jesus' followers could come to a true understanding of his divine nature without misconceptions.

Jesus Taught His Atonement
Jesus intended, through his life and death, to replace the existing system of Temple worship, which relied heavily on animal sacrifices for atonement. This intent is evident in the accusations made against Jesus during his trial, specifically the claim that he would destroy the temple 'made with hands' and rebuild it 'in three days'. That is, Jesus' statement about destroying the Temple and rebuilding it in three days was understood by the early Christian community as referring to Jesus' body, which, again, indicated a substitution of Jesus' body for the Temple. The destruction of the Temple and its replacement with the body of Jesus symbolised a new covenant, with Jesus' life and death serving as the ultimate sacrifice. This interpretation aligns with the broader Christian understanding of Jesus' death as an atoning sacrifice, providing a foundation for the new covenant between God and humanity. Now, while Jesus did not outright condemn the sacrificial system practised in the Temple, his actions, such as the cleansing of the Temple, indicated a desire to reform or replace it. By driving out those who sold animals for sacrifices and overturning the money changers' tables, Jesus symbolically rejected the current system, thus promoting a new understanding of atonement. Furthermore, at the event of the Last Supper, during which Jesus instituted a new ceremony with his disciples, using the phrases 'my body' and 'my blood'. This ceremony implied that Jesus was offering himself as a sacrifice, replacing the traditional animal sacrifices of the Temple. This new covenant, which was symbolised by the Last Supper, was intended to establish a new form of atonement centred on Jesus' own sacrifice. Furthermore, the words spoken by Jesus at the Last Supper, as recorded in the Gospels and Paul's letters, allude to his body and blood being given for many, underscoring the sacrificial nature of his death.

Additionally, within the broad scheme of the New Testament, Jesus' death as an atoning sacrifice is a recurring theme. Various passages where Jesus' death is described in sacrificial terms suggest that the early Christian community understood his death as fulfilling the role of Temple sacrifices. This interpretation is further reinforced by Jesus' prediction of his own death and the understanding of his resurrection as the ultimate validation of his sacrificial act. The pervasive theme of atonement through Jesus' death in different New Testament writings points to a common origin in Jesus' own teachings. Moreover, the notion of sacrifice was central to Jewish worship, and Jesus' actions and teachings must be understood within this context. As already noted, the centrality of animal sacrifice in the Temple was a key element of Jewish religious practice, and Jesus' actions suggested a radical shift. The cleansing of the Temple was a significant act that demonstrated Jesus' intention to replace the existing sacrificial system with a new form of worship centred on his own sacrifice.

The evidence from the New Testament thus supports the claim that Jesus taught his life and death as an atoning sacrifice, as the institution of the Last Supper, Jesus' actions in the Temple and the consistent theme of atonement in early Christian writings all point to this understanding.

Jesus Founded a Church

Jesus formed a community based on twelve leaders, which symbolised the foundation of a new Israel. This new community, the Church, was meant to reconstitute Israel, thus signifying a new covenant. By establishing this new community, Jesus aimed to absorb the old Israel and hoped that the latter would convert the Gentiles. Importantly, one can thus understand that Jesus intended to found a church that would persist beyond his lifetime: his commissioning of the Twelve Apostles was not a temporary measure but rather a foundational act for a lasting institution. This is evident from the involvement of the twelve in key events, such as the Last Supper, by which Jesus established the practice of the Eucharist. Within only a few years of Jesus' death, Christian communities celebrating the Eucharist had been established in various parts of the Middle East, indicating a continuity of practice and belief that stemmed from Jesus' intentions.

In addition to this, while the evidence of Jesus explicitly intending baptism as an admission ceremony for the Church is not direct, it quickly became a central rite in early Christianity. Baptism symbolised repentance and the washing away of sins, and its rapid adoption indicates that it was seen as a continuation of Jesus' teachings. Thus, the institution of the Eucharist clearly demonstrated Jesus' intention to establish a lasting community, with baptism playing a complementary role in this foundation. Moreover, Jesus founded the Church not just for Israel but for all peoples. Although Jesus' own mission was primarily directed at the Jews, his teachings and actions implied a broader mission. Passages where Jesus acknowledges the future inclusion of gentiles, such as the Parable of the Great Banquet where guests from all directions are invited, point to this broader mission. This is further evidenced by the early Church's eventual outreach to Gentiles that, despite initial hesitation, included gentiles and the acceptance of converts without circumcision, which indicated a shift towards a universal mission.

Now, the Early Church's teachings and practices must align with Jesus' teachings to ensure that the benefits of his life and death are available to future generations. And thus God, in endorsing Jesus' life and teachings, ensured that the core elements of Christian doctrine, such as the sacraments of baptism and Eucharist, and the doctrines of atonement and Incarnation, were preserved. These teachings and practices, central to almost all Christian traditions, reflect the continuity and fidelity to Jesus' original message. For example, the doctrine of the Trinity, while not explicitly taught by Jesus, has roots in his teachings. That is, Jesus distinguished himself from God the Father and spoke of the Holy Spirit, laying the groundwork for the Trinitarian doctrine developed later by the Church. The doctrine of the Trinity, as articulated in the Nicene Creed, thus does not contradict Jesus' teachings but rather extrapolates from them, therefore, aligning with the Church's role in interpreting and teaching Jesus' message.

So, Jesus' actions and teachings, particularly his institution of the Eucharist and the commissioning of the Twelve, demonstrate his intention to found a church that would persist and carry his message to all peoples. This Church, with its universal mission and continuity of core teachings, was intended to perpetuate the benefits of Jesus' life and death, ensuring that his message would be available to future generations.

The Resurrection (i): The Appearances

Despite differences in details concerning the resurrection appearances of Jesus, all sources agree on the fundamental fact that Jesus rose from the dead and appeared to his followers. Moreover, this consistency across multiple accounts provides a strong foundation for the historicity of the resurrection. Now, the most reliable account is the credal statement given by Saint Paul in 1 Corinthians 15, which lists official witnesses such as Peter, the Twelve and James. Paul's account, grounded in the early Christian creed, is seen as having the greatest historical reliability due to Paul's character and direct interactions with other apostles. In this account, Paul focusses on key witnesses who had official standing within the early Christian community, but this does not exclude others from having seen the risen Jesus. Appearances to non-apostles, such as the two disciples on the road to Emmaus and Mary Magdalene, were likely omitted from Paul's list because they did not hold the same official status. Furthermore, if Jesus rose bodily from the dead and intended his Church to know about it, two primary expectations follow: that the disciples would see and interact with him, and that the tomb would be empty. The various reports of Jesus' appearances should be considered veridical unless significant discrepancies undermine their credibility; and discrepancies in detail do not significantly detract from the core truth shared by all accounts. For instance, Matthew reports appearances to Mary Magdalene and the other Mary, and to the eleven disciples in Galilee, while Luke emphasises appearances around Jerusalem, including to the two disciples on the road to Emmaus and to the apostles. John's gospel adds unique appearances, such as to Thomas and to seven disciples by the Sea of Galilee. These differences, however, can be harmonised without compromising the overall reliability of the Resurrection narratives. This could be a sequence starting with the appearance of Mary Magdalene at the tomb, followed by the appearance of the two disciples on the road to Emmaus, then to Peter and subsequently to the gathered apostles. So, Jesus appeared to different groups at different times, both in Jerusalem and Galilee, culminating in his ascension witnessed by the apostles. Moreover, despite this harmonisation process, one can understand that discrepancies are expected in oral traditions passed down over decades. However, the core message of Jesus' resurrection remained consistent, which is more important than the exact details of each appearance. Minor differences likely resulted from the theological motivations of the Gospel writers and the natural variations in oral transmission. The resurrection of Jesus is thus supported by substantial historical evidence, based upon the consistency of the core message across diverse sources and the reliability of key witnesses such as Paul.

The Resurrection (ii): The Empty Tomb and the Observance of Sunday

The concept of resurrection in first-century Judaism inherently implied bodily resurrection. Therefore, the empty tomb is a crucial piece of evidence supporting the claim that Jesus rose from the dead. The Gospels portray Jesus appearing in an embodied form after his resurrection. This was crucial because the Jewish understanding of resurrection required a physical body. Luke explicitly states that Jesus ate fish in front of his disciples to prove he was not a ghost. The insistence on Jesus being embodied highlights the significance of the empty tomb – if Jesus had risen in a new, unrelated body, the tomb's emptiness would not be necessary. Moreover, first-century Jews would have naturally associated Jesus' resurrection with an empty tomb. If the tomb had still contained Jesus' body, the early Christians, including Paul, would have faced significant challenges in convincing others of the Resurrection. Thus, the fact that there is no record of such objections suggests that the empty tomb was an established part of the Resurrection belief from the beginning. There is, indeed, a scholarly debate over whether the empty tomb narratives were later additions to the Gospel accounts to support the Resurrection appearances. However, it can be argued that, if the early Christians believed the tomb still contained Jesus' body, Paul and other early apostles would have had to address this in their teachings and writings. The absence of such discussions in Paul's letters thus indicates that the early Christians took the empty tomb for granted as part of the Resurrection belief. Furthermore, the Gospels all start their accounts of the resurrection with women discovering the empty tomb, which strengthens its historical reliability, given the low status of women in the first century. Luke and John further confirm this by mentioning that Peter, and in John's account, the beloved disciple, also found the tomb empty.

In addition to this, the early Christian practice of celebrating the Eucharist on Sundays, the first day of the week, provides strong evidence for the belief that Jesus rose from the dead on a Sunday. This tradition must have been established very early, as it was universally practised by the time of the earliest Christian communities. The consistent celebration of the Eucharist on Sundays thus indicates that the early Christians believed that the Resurrection occurred on that day. New Testament evidence, such as Acts 20:7, which mentions the breaking of bread on the first day of the week, and 1 Corinthians 16:2, where Paul instructs Christians to set aside money on the first day of the week, show that Sunday had significant theological importance for early Christians. Additionally, post-New Testament writings, such as the *Didache* and Justin Martyr's *First Apology*, confirm the practice of Sunday Eucharist, thus further supporting the idea that it was rooted in the belief in the Resurrection on Sunday. In relation to this, the phrase 'on the third day' was integrated into early Christian creeds, as seen in 1 Corinthians 15:4. This phrase likely became part of the tradition due to its alignment with the observed events rather than as a result of scriptural prophecy. Thus, again, the early practice of Sunday Eucharist, commemorating the Resurrection, provides substantial evidence for the historical basis of the third-day tradition. The historical evidence for the empty tomb and the early Christian practice of celebrating the Eucharist on Sundays thus strongly supports the claim that Jesus rose from the dead. That is, the empty tomb was a necessary component of the Resurrection belief, and the early Christian tradition of Sunday observance reflects the conviction that the Resurrection did indeed occur on that day.

Rival Theories of What Happened
If Jesus was not raised bodily from the dead, then an alternative theory must explain what happened to his body. Five alternative theories can possibly achieve this task: that Jesus did not die on the cross, that the body remained in the tomb but was misidentified, that enemies stole the body, that grave robbers stole the body, or that friends of Jesus stole the body. First, with regard to the theory that Jesus did not die on the cross but was only half-dead and later revived in the cool of the tomb, one can see that there are significant difficulties with this theory, including the certainty of death ensured by Roman soldiers and those who buried Jesus. Also, Jesus, in an enfeebled state, could not have escaped from the linen cloth and moved the stone from the tomb without assistance, which implies deceit by his disciples. Furthermore, Jesus' weakened condition would not have allowed him to inspire the Resurrection appearances, which often involved miraculous elements like

passing through doors. This theory also requires an explanation of what happened to Jesus afterwards, which is not supported by the historical evidence.

Second, for the theory that the disciples misidentified the tomb, the consistent testimony across the Gospels is that Joseph of Arimathea, a respected member of the council, buried Jesus in a new tomb hewn out of rock. Moreover, it is, indeed, extremely improbable that the women who followed the burial would misidentify the tomb; and the disciples would also have conducted their own inquiries to confirm the tomb's location. Additionally, the theory also fails to account for the Resurrection appearances. Third, for the theory that enemies of Jesus stole the body to prevent an honourable burial or to quash a potential cult, if enemies had stolen the body, they would have produced it once the Christian movement gained momentum to disprove the Resurrection claims. Hence, the absence of any such action from Jesus' enemies significantly weakens this theory. Additionally, the story of the disciples stealing the body circulated by Jewish authorities, as mentioned in Matthew, suggests that enemies did not possess the body.

Fourth, regarding the theory that grave robbers stole the body, grave robbing was common in the ancient world but primarily targeted valuable items buried with the deceased. However, Jesus' burial was hurried, and it is likely that there were no valuables in his tomb. Thus, if grave robbers had stolen the body, they would not have left the burial cloths behind and a naked body would thus have been found, which is not reported in the Resurrection narratives. Also, the presence of the grave clothes in the tomb, as described in the gospel of John, contradicts this theory. Fifth, the theory that friends of Jesus, possibly the women who discovered the empty tomb, stole the body to give it a more honourable burial; while this theory might initially seem plausible, it involves significant deceit. Such an act would likely have been detected by other disciples, including James, Jesus' brother, who later became a leader in the Christian community. Hence, the improbability of successfully hiding the body and the lack of motivation for the women to conceal their actions further weaken this theory.

Given all of this, the traditional account of Jesus' bodily resurrection is taken to be the simplest and most plausible explanation for the evidence. Each alternative theory requires implausible assumptions and additional complexities that make them less likely. Also, the consistent testimony of the empty tomb, the Resurrection appearances, and the early Christian belief in the Resurrection align best with the traditional account. Thus, while the Resurrection involves a significant violation of natural laws, its improbability should be weighed against the prior historical evidence supporting divine intervention. In other words, the account does not suffer from the complexities and improbabilities that plague the rival theories, making it the most probable explanation for the events surrounding Jesus' death.

The Significance of the Resurrection

The Jewish understanding of miracles and divine intervention would have allowed them to see the Resurrection as a sign of God's approval and validation of Jesus. The Old Testament provided categories for recognising divine actions, such as the fulfilment of prophecies and the performance of extraordinary miracles. The Resurrection, as an unprecedented event, would have been seen as God's definitive endorsement of Jesus' mission and teachings: the bodily resurrection of Jesus, if it occurred, would (as a 'super miracle') be God's authenticating signature on Jesus' life, ultimately signifying God's acceptance of his atoning sacrifice. That is, the Resurrection would demonstrate God's approval of Jesus' perfect life and his sacrificial death. Jesus thus offered his life to God, and God accepted this gift by raising Jesus from the dead, thereby validating the atonement made for human sins. In addition to this, under various atonement theories, the Resurrection signifies that the penalty or ransom has been paid. For example, in the penal substitution theory, the Resurrection indicates that Jesus' sacrifice was sufficient to pay for humanity's sins, similar to the release of a prisoner after the sentence is served. This acceptance and validation by God are crucial for the significance of the Resurrection, as it demonstrates that Jesus' sacrifice was effective and complete. Moreover, the Resurrection serves to vindicate Jesus' teachings – as this divine endorsement indicated that Jesus' teachings were true and authoritative. Thus, belief in the Resurrection was the driving force behind the spread of the Gospel and, if God raised Jesus, it constituted an intervention in history to ensure the success of Jesus' life and message. This act of raising Jesus would have been seen by his contemporaries as a validation of his claim to be the Son of God and his teachings about the Kingdom of God and the afterlife. The Resurrection was thus the ultimate demonstration of God's power and approval, confirming that Jesus was indeed the Messiah and Son of God.

The cumulative argument detailed above asserts that the overall balance of evidence strongly supports the occurrence of the Resurrection. While natural theology moderately supports the existence of God and his reasons for becoming incarnate, there is significantly more evidence that Jesus led a life characteristic of God Incarnate, culminating in the unparalleled super-miracle of the Resurrection. The historical evidence for the Resurrection is consistent with what one would expect if Jesus truly rose from the dead and, importantly, no other prophet in history (such as Muhammad) has significant evidence of such a super-miracle. This unique combination of evidence for Jesus' life and Resurrection makes it overwhelmingly probable that Jesus was God Incarnate, as it would be highly improbable for such evidence to exist if Jesus were not God Incarnate, because that would constitute a deception by God, which is inconsistent with his nature. That is, God's nature as a perfectly good being would preclude him from engaging in deception. Thus, God would not falsely put his divine signature on the life of a prophet who was not God Incarnate, as this would be a massive deception similar to leaving someone's fingerprints at the scene of a crime he did not commit. Hence, such an act would be inconsistent with the perfect goodness and truthfulness expected of God. The historical evidence thus renders the resurrection of Jesus, God Incarnate, as significantly probable.

Appendix: Formalising the Argument

The main argument featured above can now be formalised using the traditional calculus of probability. As noted previously, probability can be understood in three ways: physical probability, statistical probability and logical probability. Physical probability refers to how past events determine the likelihood of future events, as suggested by natural laws. Statistical probability is a proportion in a class, such as the probability of a coin toss resulting in heads. Logical probability, the focus here, measures how likely one proposition makes another, based on the evidence available. Focussing now on the later form of probability, as expressed through the usage of Bayes' theorem, in order to determine the probability that Jesus was God Incarnate who rose from the dead, several steps and probabilities need to be considered. First, we define the key elements as follows: k represents the evidence of natural theology, e is the detailed historical evidence about Jesus, $h1$ is the hypothesis that God became incarnate in Jesus, $h2$ is the hypothesis that Jesus rose from the dead, h is the combined hypothesis ($h1$ and $h2$), and t is theism, the claim that there is a God. Now, starting with the initial probabilities, we assign $P(t/k) = 0.5$ to the probability of theism given natural theology (which is modest given the results reached in Chapter 2). Next, we consider the probability of incarnation, c, given theism and natural theology, $P(c/t.k) = 0.5$, leading to $P(c/k) = 0.5 \times 0.5 = 0.25$.

We then examine the conditional probabilities: $P(f/c.k) = 1/10$ for the probability of evidence (f) given incarnation and natural theology, $P(\neg c/k) = 0.75$ for the probability of no incarnation given natural theology, and $P(f/\neg c.k) = 10^{-6}$ for the probability of evidence (f) given no incarnation and natural theology. Here, f represents the conjunction of three pieces of evidence: $f1$ (evidence of Jesus' teachings, life, and the founding of a church), $f2$ (evidence that his life was culminated by a super-miracle, such as the Resurrection), and $f3$ (evidence that neither the prior nor the posterior requirements for being God Incarnate were satisfied in any other prophet in human history in any way comparable to Jesus). The very low value of $P(f/\neg c.k) = 10^{-6}$ above reflects the extreme improbability of finding evidence of a prophet satisfying both the prior and posterior requirements for being God Incarnate, including a super-miracle like the Resurrection, if there was no divine incarnation (and on the basis of God's perfect goodness not allowing for mass deception) – this thus accounts for the uniqueness of the case of God incarnate in human history. Now, combine these probabilities, we calculate the total probability of evidence: $P(f/k) = (1/10 \times 0.25) + (10^{-6} \times 0.75)$, which simplifies to $P(f/k) = 0.025 + 0.00000075 \approx 0.025001875$. Using Bayes' theorem, we find the probability of incarnation given the evidence: $P(c|f \ \& \ k) = P(f|c \ \& \ k) \ P(c|k) \ / \ P(f|k)$. Substituting the values, we get $P(c|f \ \& \ k) = 0.025 \ / \ 0.025001875$, which is a number very close to 1. Finally, we adjust for the detailed historical evidence about Jesus, e, and the conjunction of hypotheses $h1$ and $h2$. This leads us to conclude that $P(h/e$ and $k)$ is approximately 0.97. The initial probability $P(c/f.k)$, which is very close to 1, considered the probability of incarnation given evidence and natural theology, while the final probability $P(h/e.k)$ of approximately 0.97 takes into account the detailed historical evidence about Jesus, making the hypothesis slightly less certain but still highly probable. Hence, given the combined detailed historical evidence and natural theology, it is highly probable (approximately 0.97) that Jesus was God Incarnate who rose from the dead. Thus, while precise numerical values are not possible, the rough probabilities featured here illustrate that the Resurrection is indeed highly probable.

In conclusion, Swinburne's application of his philosophical framework demonstrates that the New Testament documents, especially the Gospels and Paul's epistles, offer robust historical evidence for the life, teachings and resurrection of Jesus. He asserts that the Resurrection is the most probable explanation for the empty tomb and the post-resurrection appearances reported by multiple sources. By analysing the intent and context of these narratives, Swinburne demonstrates that Jesus' life exemplified the qualities of God Incarnate, and the Resurrection served as divine confirmation of his mission. This thorough examination substantiates the belief in Jesus' resurrection and divinity, ultimately presenting a compelling case for the foundation of the Christian faith.

Critical Engagements

Swinburne's *The Resurrection of God Incarnate* has sparked extensive scholarly discussion and critique. Swinburne's work aims to demonstrate that the resurrection of Jesus is highly probable based on a combination of historical evidence and philosophical argumentation. However, several critics have challenged different aspects of Swinburne's arguments featured in this work. Scholars such as Paul K. Moser, John Haldane, Michael Martin, Paul J. Griffiths and Chris Jackson have raised important objections against Swinburne's position. This section explores these critical engagements and presents responses that align with Swinburne's philosophical perspective.

Paul K. Moser

Critical Engagement. Paul K. Moser, in his critical notice 'Philosophy of Religion and Christian Resurrection',[2] raises several issues about Swinburne's use of testimony, the need for epistemic distance and

---

2. Moser, Paul K., 'Critical Notices: Philosophy of Religion and Christian Resurrection: The Resurrection of God Incarnate by Richard

the absence of the Holy Spirit in Swinburne's account of resurrection evidence. Moser challenges Swinburne's principle of testimony, arguing that merely reporting an event without counterevidence is insufficient for belief unless the reporters are in a position to know what they report with justifying evidence. Furthermore, Moser questions Swinburne's assertion that clear evidence of God's presence would undermine human free will and responsibility. Lastly, Moser criticises Swinburne for overlooking the role of the Holy Spirit in affirming the Resurrection to believers.

Critical Response. An adherent of Swinburne's position can offer several responses to Moser's criticisms: first, Moser's challenge to Swinburne's principle of testimony fails to consider the nuanced application of this principle to the Resurrection accounts. Swinburne argues that the early Christian witnesses were indeed in a position to know what they reported, given their direct encounters with the resurrected Jesus and their willingness to face persecution for their claims. Second, regarding epistemic distance, Swinburne's position is more subtle than Moser suggests, as Swinburne contends that, while certainty might undermine free will, the kind of probabilistic evidence he proposes maintains a balance between divine hiddenness and revelation, preserving human freedom while providing rational grounds for belief. Third, while Swinburne may not explicitly focus on the Holy Spirit's role in affirming the Resurrection, his approach does not preclude this aspect. Rather, his philosophical analysis aims to complement spiritual experiences by providing a rational foundation for belief. Furthermore, Swinburne's emphasis on testimony and historical evidence serves to ground faith in verifiable facts, thus offering a bridge between subjective religious experience and objective historical inquiry.

All things considered, Moser's challenges to Swinburne's principle of testimony and understanding of epistemic distance raise important questions. However, Swinburne's approach remains an effective attempt at providing a rational foundation for belief in the Resurrection. His application of the principle of testimony to the early Christian witnesses, his balancing of divine hiddenness and revelation, and

---

Swinburne', *International Journal of Philosophical Studies* 12, no. 1 (2004), pp. 61-82.

his emphasis on grounding faith in verifiable facts all contribute to a philosophically robust case for the Resurrection.

John Haldane

Critical Engagement. John Haldane, in his review article of *The Resurrection of God Incarnate*,[3] critiques Swinburne's reliance on precise numerical probabilities in assessing the likelihood of the Resurrection and Incarnation. He argues that the application of Bayesian probability to theological claims may seem overly precise and that the assignment of specific numerical values to probabilities might appear arbitrary or underdetermined. Haldane also questions the principles underlying Swinburne's inductive reasoning, particularly the preference for simplicity in causal hypotheses.

Critical Response. An adherent of Swinburne's position can offer several responses to Haldane's criticisms: first, Haldane's concern about the precision of numerical probabilities in Swinburne's work neglects the methodological value of such an approach. Swinburne employs Bayesian probability not as an exact measure, but as a tool to illustrate the relative strength of competing hypotheses. Second, while the assignment of specific numerical values may seem arbitrary (though there are no numerical values and calculations utilised in the main text of *RGI* and thus only in the appendix), Swinburne's calculations are based on careful analysis of historical evidence and philosophical reasoning. These values serve to quantify the cumulative weight of evidence rather than claiming absolute precision. Third, Swinburne's preference for simplicity in causal hypotheses aligns with well-established principles in both science and philosophy. This approach, based on the principle of Ockham's razor, is, as noted previously, widely accepted as a valid criterion for theory selection. Furthermore, Swinburne's use of Bayesian probability provides a structured framework for evaluating complex theological claims, allowing for a more rigorous assessment of the resurrection and incarnation hypotheses.

In the end, Haldane's concerns raise valid questions about the precision of numerical probabilities in Swinburne's work. Nevertheless, Swinburne's application of Bayesian probability to theological claims

---

3. Haldane, John, 'The Resurrection of God Incarnate', *Mind*, New Series, 113, no. 450 (2004), pp. 397-401.

represents a sophisticated attempt to bring analytical rigour to questions of faith. Moreover, his use of probability as a tool to illustrate the relative strength of competing hypotheses, his grounding of calculations in careful analysis of evidence and reasoning, and his alignment with well-established principles such as Ockham's razor all contribute to a philosophically compelling approach.

Michael Martin

Critical Engagement. Michael Martin, in his review article of *The Resurrection of God Incarnate*,[4] criticises Swinburne's estimation of the probability that God would become incarnate, die and be resurrected as being too high. He also questions the coherence of the atonement theory Swinburne adopts, suggesting that alternative means of atonement could have been more fitting. Additionally, Martin points out potential moral and logical issues with Jesus' actions and teachings, including the lack of independent confirmation of the Resurrection from non-Christian sources.

Critical Response. An adherent of Swinburne's position can offer several responses to Martin's criticisms: first, Martin's objection to Swinburne's high-probability estimate for the Incarnation and Resurrection overlooks the cumulative nature of Swinburne's argument. Swinburne's estimation is based on a careful analysis of multiple factors, including the nature of God, the human condition and the historical evidence. Second, regarding the coherence of Swinburne's atonement theory, one can argue that, while alternative means of atonement might be conceivable, the sacrificial account of the atonement that was presented provides a uniquely effective solution to the problem of human sin, balancing divine justice and mercy in a way that other hypothetical means might not. Third, Martin's concerns about the moral and logical issues in Jesus' actions and teachings can be addressed by considering the cultural and historical context of the Gospels, as well as the complexities involved in divine revelation through human agency. Moreover, the lack of independent non-Christian confirmation of the Resurrection does not significantly undermine its credibility. Given the social and political context of early

---

4. Martin, Michael, 'The Resurrection of God Incarnate: Richard Swinburne', *Religious Studies* 40, no. 3 (2004), pp. 367-71.

Christianity, the absence of such sources is not unexpected and does not negate the substantial evidence provided by Christian accounts.

Ultimately, Martin's objections to Swinburne's high-probability estimate for the Incarnation and Resurrection, his concerns about the coherence of Swinburne's atonement theory, and his questions about the moral and logical issues in Jesus' actions fail to provide effective challenges to Swinburne's position. Thus, Swinburne's treatment of these central Christian doctrines remains a sophisticated attempt to provide a rational foundation for belief.

Paul J. Griffiths

Critical Engagement. Paul J. Griffiths, in his review article of *The Resurrection of God Incarnate*,[5] critiques Swinburne's use of Bayesian probability and evidentialist internalism. He finds the numerical precision in Swinburne's probability estimates specious and argues that the epistemological framework assumed by Swinburne may not be compelling to all rational agents. Griffiths also questions the practical utility of Swinburne's argument, suggesting it fails to persuade non-believers while being unnecessary for those already committed to the Christian faith.

Critical Response. An adherent of Swinburne's position can offer several responses to Griffiths' criticisms: first, Griffiths' concern about the numerical precision in Swinburne's probability estimates underestimates the methodological value of such an approach. That is, Swinburne's use of Bayesian probability is not intended to provide absolute certainty, but rather to offer a structured framework for comparing the relative plausibility of different hypotheses. Second, while Swinburne's evidentialist internalism may not be compelling to all rational agents, it provides a robust philosophical foundation for evaluating religious claims. This approach allows for a systematic examination of evidence that can be valuable to both believers and sceptics alike. Third, regarding the practical utility of Swinburne's argument, one can contend that it serves multiple purposes. For believers, it offers intellectual support for faith, while for non-believers, it presents a rational

---

5. Griffiths, Paul J., 'Richard Swinburne, The Resurrection of God Incarnate', *The Journal of Religion* 84, no. 2 (2004), pp. 308-10.

case for reconsidering Christian claims. Furthermore, Swinburne's approach bridges the gap between faith and reason, demonstrating that religious beliefs can be subject to rational scrutiny and defendable on rational grounds. This can be particularly valuable in academic and intellectual contexts. Last, Swinburne's method, while rigorous and analytical, does not aim to replace faith but to complement it, offering a way to understand the rational basis of Christian beliefs.

In all, *contra* the criticisms raised by Griffiths, Swinburne's use of Bayesian probability and evidentialist internalism represents a rigorous methodology for assessing the truth value of the central teaching of the Christian faith. Although Griffiths' critiques highlight the potential limitations and applicability of such methods in theology, Swinburne's work makes a significant contribution to the dialogue between faith and reason, by providing a robust and structured framework for comparing the relative plausibility of different religious truth claims.

Chris Jackson

Critical Engagement. Chris Jackson, in his review article of *The Resurrection of God Incarnate*,[6] critiques Swinburne's use of Bayesian probability and the concept of predictive power. Jackson argues that Swinburne's application of Bayes' theorem is flawed because it assumes prior probabilities that may not be reliably estimated and uses 'predictions' that are theological assumptions rather than genuine predictions. Jackson also highlights that Swinburne's handling of recalcitrant data, such as morally troubling scriptural content and failed prophecies, is inadequate. Additionally, Jackson points out that Swinburne fails to adequately address plausible rival hypotheses, such as the legend and temporary-burial hypotheses.

Critical Response. An adherent of Swinburne's position can offer several responses to Jackson's criticisms: first, Jackson's concern about Swinburne's use of prior probabilities misses the careful reasoning behind these assignments. Swinburne's priors are not

---

6. Jackson, Chris, 'Book Review: Revelation: From Metaphor to Analogy and The Resurrection of God Incarnate', *Essays in Philosophy* 19, no. 2 (2018), pp. 364-82.

arbitrary but are based on a comprehensive analysis of background knowledge, including philosophical arguments about the nature of God and what, given this nature, God is likely to do within his creation. Second, while Jackson characterises Swinburne's 'predictions' as theological assumptions, one can argue that these are logical consequences derived from the hypothesis of God's existence and nature. That is, they serve as a means to test the explanatory power of theism against the available evidence. Third, regarding recalcitrant data such as morally troubling scriptural content and failed prophecies, Swinburne's approach does not ignore these issues. Rather, it seeks to interpret them within a broader theological framework, considering factors such as progressive revelation and the complexities of divine communication through human authors. Furthermore, Swinburne's treatment of rival hypotheses, while perhaps not as extensive as Jackson would prefer, does address major alternative explanations. His argument is that the resurrection hypothesis, when properly understood, has greater explanatory power and scope than competing theories. Last, Swinburne's probabilistic approach to the Resurrection is part of a cumulative case that incorporates multiple lines of evidence and argument. Hence, it is not intended to stand alone but to contribute to a broader philosophical case for Christian theism.

In sum, even though Jackson's concerns about Swinburne's use of prior probabilities, his characterisation of Swinburne's 'predictions' as theological assumptions, and his emphasis on recalcitrant data and rival hypotheses pose significant challenges, Swinburne's careful reasoning behind his probability assignments, his derivation of logical consequences from the hypothesis of God's existence and nature, and his incorporation of multiple lines of evidence and argument all contribute to a philosophically robust case for the Resurrection.

* * *

In all, *The Resurrection of God Incarnate* has provoked significant scholarly debate, addressing fundamental issues in historical theology, philosophy and religious epistemology. The critiques by Paul K. Moser, John Haldane, Michael Martin, Paul J. Griffiths and Chris Jackson highlight the challenges and complexities of Swinburne's approach. However, it has been possible to show that the issues raised by these scholars can be adequately addressed by emphasising the importance of reliable testimony, the role of probabilistic reasoning, the theological coherence of the atonement and the philosophical rigour of Bayesian analysis. Overall, these engagements enrich the discourse on the probability of the Resurrection and demonstrate, as with his other works, the ongoing relevance of Swinburne's work.

Conclusion

In conclusion, this chapter has provided a comprehensive guide to Swinburne's *The Resurrection of God Incarnate*, outlining the central aim, structure and themes of the work. Swinburne's detailed examination of the principles of evidence and historical documentation demonstrates that belief in the resurrection of Jesus is a rational response to the available data. By addressing philosophical and theological challenges, Swinburne underscores the compatibility of the Resurrection with historical enquiry, emphasising the importance of rigorous analysis in forming justified religious beliefs. His exploration of the historical evidence and its support through *a priori* philosophical argumentation highlight the depth and veracity of the Resurrection claim. As readers explore *The Resurrection of God Incarnate* for themselves, they will be better equipped to appreciate Swinburne's rigorous defence of the resurrection of Jesus and its significance in contemporary philosophy.

Chapter Eight

The Authenticity of Revelation

This chapter serves as an introduction to Swinburne's *Revelation: From Metaphor to Analogy* (hereafter, *RMA*), which is a detailed examination of divine revelation in Christian theology. Swinburne aims to demonstrate how one can recognise and establish the veracity of divine revelation, specifically that of the Christian revelation. The chapter introduces readers to the central aim and structure of Swinburne's arguments, situating them within the broader context of philosophical and theological challenges related to divine communication. It outlines the major sections of the work, including philosophical methodology, which focusses on the philosophy of language and the function of religious language, and theological application, which examines the content and development of Christian revelation. By providing this overview, the chapter prepares readers to engage deeply with Swinburne's systematic and rigorous examination of the veracity of divine revelation, particularly within the context of Christian theology.

Revelation: From Metaphor to Analogy: Background

Central Aim

The central aim of *RMA* is to explore the nature of divine revelation within Christian theology, demonstrating how revelation, and specifically that of the Christian revelation expressed within the Bible and Church tradition, can be assessed for its authenticity. Swinburne's work seeks to provide a rigorous methodology for recognition of a true revelation from God and the grounds for acknowledging both the original teachings of Jesus and subsequent Christian doctrines derived from them. *RMA* thus involves a detailed analysis of religious language, focussing on how theological truths are conveyed through metaphors and analogy and how these can be interpreted coherently.

Historical Significance

RMA was published in 1992 as the second work in Swinburne's tetralogy on Christian doctrine. The immediate historical context of *RMA* involves broader debates about the nature and coherence of religious language and the authenticity of divine communication. Theologians such as Karl Barth, in his *Church Dogmatics*[1], and Hans Urs von Balthasar, in *The Glory of the Lord*[2], had provided a less precise analysis of the notion of revelation, employing a more literary and theological style. Barth emphasised the transcendence and mystery of God's self-disclosure, while von Balthasar focussed on the aesthetic dimensions of divine revelation. Their approaches, which are part of a tradition of thought that were subject to the charge by Swinburne of 'loose and sloppy style of argument',[3] contrasted with *RMA*'s rigorous philosophical method, which aimed to bring a new level of precision and clarity to the understanding of how divine revelation, expressed metaphorically or analogically, can be interpreted rationally.

The ongoing influence of *RMA* necessitated a second edition in 2007, in which Swinburne incorporated more thorough linguistic and historical analysis, and responded to contemporary critiques, further supporting the cogency of the arguments featured in the first edition.

---

1. Barth, Karl, *Church Dogmatics*, edited by G.W. Bromiley and T.F. Torrance, translated by Geoffrey W. Bromiley, Edinburgh: T&T Clark, 1936–1969.
2. von Balthasar, Hans Urs, *The Glory of the Lord: A Theological Aesthetics, Vol. 1: Seeing the Form*, translated by Erasmo Leiva-Merikakis, San Francisco: Ignatius Press, 1982.
3. Swinburne, Richard. *The Coherence of Theism: Second Edition*. Oxford: Oxford University Press, 2016, p. 7.

Literary Structure

The literary structure of *RMA* is divided into three main parts: 'Meaning', 'Evidence of a Christian Revelation' and 'The Christian Revelation'. However, for continuity with the previous chapters in this book, we shall retain the terminology and dual structure as follows:

1. *Philosophical Framework – Meaning and Evidence*: The first part of *RMA* focusses on the philosophy of language, discussing how words and sentences convey propositions. Swinburne examines the use of metaphor and analogy in religious language, arguing that, while metaphors are useful for expressing complex divine truths, analogies provide a clearer and more precise understanding. This involves a rigorous analysis of how language functions in both mundane and theological contexts, ensuring that the propositions expressed are logically coherent.
2. *Theological Application – The Christian Revelation*: The second part of *RMA* applies the established philosophical framework to specific claims concerning the Christian revelation. Swinburne outlines the criteria for recognising a genuine divine revelation, presenting tests for evaluating purported revelations based on content, method of expression, transmission and development by the Church. Additionally, Swinburne examines the content of the original revelation of Jesus and his apostles, and the role of the Church in developing and interpreting this revelation. This part also includes a discussion on the moral teachings of Christianity and how they can be seen as part of the divine revelation.

We shall now unpack in greater detail the various areas covered in both parts of *RMA*.

Themes

Philosophical Framework: Meaning and Evidence

In this section, Swinburne introduces the philosophical framework that is necessary for understanding meaning and language use in communication. Swinburne begins by defining key terminologies crucial for discussing how messages assert truth claims. Moreover, Swinburne explores the role of presuppositions in communication, examining how shared beliefs and context influence the truth value of statements. He further differentiates between literal and metaphorical meanings, emphasising the importance of context and the evolution of language. Finally, Swinburne analyses the concept of genre, highlighting how different literary and non-literary forms convey complex information and how their truth values are assessed within their respective frameworks.

Terminology

A statement is often expressed through a token declarative sentence, which is a sentence uttered by a particular person in a specific circumstance. For instance, 'It is raining now', uttered in England at 6.00 pm on 25 January 2025, is a token sentence. Different token sentences can convey the same information if they express the same proposition, even if uttered by different people at different times. For example, 'Rex mortuus est', 'Le roi est mort' and 'The king is dead' all express the same proposition. Now, a crucial distinction exists between a 'statement' and a 'proposition'. A proposition is the element of the claim made by a token sentence that is also made by any other token sentence synonymous with it. In contrast, a statement is the claim made by the token sentence in its particular context. For example, 'I am ill', 'You are ill' and 'He is ill', when uttered in the same context, all express the same statement, though not the same proposition. This distinction helps in understanding the precise claim made in a given context. Furthermore, referring expressions include indexicals, definite descriptions and proper names. Indexicals, such as 'I', 'you' and 'he', pick out different individuals in different contexts based on the speaker or writer. That is, definite descriptions like 'the king of Spain' pick out an individual in virtue of possessing some property, while proper names such as 'Aristotle' are rigid designators that refer to the same individual regardless of the properties they might gain or lose over time. The truth value of a statement is invariant, depending only on the properties of individuals at particular times, independent of how these are picked out.

Whether a given token sentence is true or false depends on three facets of reality: the conventions of the language, the referential context and the remaining truth-relevant conditions. For example, the truth of 'You are ill' depends on the meaning of the words, who is being addressed and whether that person is actually ill. While propositions retain the mode of presentation, statements do not, making their truth absolute. Thus, token sentences express both propositions and statements, with the former being dependent on referential contexts and the latter on truth-relevant conditions. Moreover, there is a differentiation between 'sentence meaning' and 'speaker's meaning'. Sentence meaning refers to the statement expressed by a token sentence, while the speaker's meaning pertains to the speaker's intended meaning, which may include indirect information or hints beyond the literal statement. However, not all communication is verbal – in that, natural gestures and symbolic acts can express statements, commands or questions based on psychological or conventional recognition within a society. Examples of this include gestures such as kisses and grimaces, or symbolic acts like raising a flag to claim territory. These non-verbal communications are deeply embedded in cultural contexts and traditions, which illustrates how actions can convey complex messages without words.

Presupposition and Statement

Presuppositions play a crucial role in communication, such that using shared presuppositions often makes it easier to convey information succinctly and intelligibly. For instance, when one says, 'The eighty-first floor feels the wind', the focus is not on the floor number but on the belief that the office is on that floor. This technique thus leverages shared beliefs to convey a message effectively. Similarly, one might use another person's belief, even if not shared, to communicate more acceptably. For example, saying, 'He looks happier since he resigned from the bank', leverages the listener's belief about the person's resignation, even if the speaker believes he was dismissed. In analysing the truth value of statements involving false presuppositions, such as 'the man drinking Martini', who is actually drinking sherry, some philosophers, such as Bertrand Russell, in his essay 'On Denoting', argue that such a statement is false since the presupposition is incorrect.[4] Others, like Peter Strawson, in his paper 'On Referring', argue it is neither true nor false because the referring expression fails.[5] A middle position, which one should accept, however, is that, if the intended reference is clear to the audience, the truth value of

---
4. Russell, Bertrand. "On Denoting." *Mind* 14, no. 56 (1905): pp. 490.
5. Strawson, P. F. "On Referring." *Mind* 59, no. 235 (1950): pp. 330-331.

the statement remains intact despite the false presupposition. This is particularly compelling when the false description is a cultural presupposition. For example, in illustrating this point, one can see that Roman historians (such as Tacitus in *The Annals* (*Annales*)) writing about 'the divine Augustus',[6] or biographers of Gautama ('the Buddha') use presuppositions common to their cultures.[7] Thus, even if modern readers do not share these presuppositions, the statements about their actions remain true if understood within their cultural context. This approach respects the role of presuppositions in communication, ensuring that the primary message is not obscured by culturally specific assumptions. Separating presuppositions from statements allows for clearer communication – for example, if one was pointing to a lake and calling it a river, or referring to someone's stepfather as his father, while these presuppositions are false, the intended message remains clear. That is, if the culture has a shared understanding that allows these presuppositions to be separated from the main message, the statement should be judged based on the intended information, not the false presupposition. Furthermore, cultural presuppositions also influence the clarity and meaning of sentences, especially in new or unforeseen situations. To use another hypothetical example, imagine a culture with only two words for colour, 'blue' and 'green', when it faces new colours that do not fit neatly into these categories. In this instance, the truth value of statements such as 'Everything is either blue or green' becomes unclear. The meaning of such statements is vague because the culture lacks the presuppositions to address these new situations clearly. Importantly, however, empirical terms often cannot cover all possible scenarios due to the limitations of human imagination and cultural presuppositions. This leads to vagueness in the application of concepts like 'adultery' when new forms of relationships or practices are considered. While some cultures may have clear definitions for

---

6. Tacitus. *The Annals*. Translated by J. C. Yardley. Oxford: Oxford University Press, 2008. See, for example, Book 1, Chapter 10, where Tacitus refers to Augustus as 'the divine Augustus' (*divus Augustus*).
7. For biographies of the Buddha that reflect presuppositions common in ancient Indian Buddhist culture, see: Aśvaghoṣa. *The Buddhacarita*. Translated by E. H. Johnston. Lahore: University of the Panjab, 1936. And *The Mahāvastu*. Translated by J. J. Jones. 3 vols. London: Luzac & Company, 1949-1956.

specific situations, many do not, resulting in ambiguous guidance for behaviour.

Now, the context of utterance affects the accuracy required for statements to be considered true. In practical communication, sentences are often used in a context where strict accuracy is not necessary. For example, describing an object as 'round' does not require it to meet the geometric definition of roundness if the context makes the intended meaning clear. Similarly, general statements such as 'All As are B' can be considered true in everyday contexts despite exceptions, which is unlike that of mathematical contexts where precision is paramount. Hence, the standard of accuracy appropriate to the context determines the truth value of statements. Thus, by analysing these aspects of presupposition, it becomes clear how cultural context, shared beliefs and practical communication standards, influence the interpretation and truth value of statements. This understanding ultimately helps in assessing the coherence and clarity of messages across different contexts and cultural frameworks.

Analogy and Literal Meaning

The literal sense of a word is determined by its semantic and syntactic criteria, such as that of the word 'bank', which can refer to the edge of a river or a financial institution. These uses can be categorised as univocal (same sense), analogical (similar sense) or equivocal (dissimilar sense). Distinguishing these categories is useful and aligns with historical uses of these terms, though different authors might use them differently. To explain these distinctions further, the concept of a 'predicate scheme' can be introduced – which is that of a set of words that can replace a given word in a sentence while maintaining its well-formedness. For example, 'boy' in 'The boy asked for a job' can be replaced with 'girl', 'old man' or 'plumber', but only some of these substitutions are meaning-relevant. Words are used univocally if they have the same predicate scheme, analogically if they have overlapping schemes and equivocally if their schemes do not overlap significantly. A further example using the word 'charged' illustrates this point, as the word 'charged' in 'He charged the gun' is equivocal to 'He charged the jury', given that they share no common synonyms or contraries. However, 'charged' in 'He charged his assistants' is analogous to 'He charged her with information', as they share some synonyms but not others. Cases where words are used in an abstract sense, such as 'The arch carries the weight of the roof' and 'The first premise carries the weight of the argument', demonstrate how the same word is used analogically to describe different types of support.

Now, both semantic and syntactic criteria are essential to determine the sense of a word. For example, two uses of the word 'red' must apply to the same group of objects to have the same sense. Hence, agreement on verification conditions is essential for determining the sameness of sense. Thus, words are used univocally if they share the same semantic and syntactic criteria, analogically if they largely share these criteria and equivocally if they largely differ. For a denominative analogy, where a word is used to describe something related to the objects or situations to which it normally applies – such as a diet is 'healthy' if it causes good health, and urine is 'healthy' if it indicates good health – while there is a connection in their meaning, the use of 'healthy' in these contexts is not saying something similar about diet and urine.

With regard to the concept of metaphor, it is best defined as the use of a word to designate a feature believed to be distinctive of the objects it normally denotes. Thus, metaphorical meaning arises from the context and the word's previous literal sense. For example, a statement such as 'Wittgenstein paints in oils rather than watercolours' metaphorically describes Wittgenstein's style of argument. Moreover, metaphors often have wide border areas where their truth value is neither clear nor precise. That is, metaphorical sentences often have truth values, although these can be vague. The truth conditions of metaphors are largely similar to those of their corresponding similes. For instance, 'Cynthia proved to be a hedgehog' could be true if Cynthia exhibits hedgehog-like characteristics, even if hedgehogs are not actually prickly. Language thus evolves through the use of metaphors, as certain new words or senses of words often arise from metaphorical uses that become established over time. This process ultimately helps to create precise meanings for abstract concepts, scientific phenomena and philosophical ideas.

Genre
The context of meaning and truth value of sentences within a work is of great importance. The literary context (surrounding sentences), social context (authorship and intended audience) and cultural context (wider societal beliefs and conventions) collectively help to clarify whether sentences should be taken literally or metaphorically and determine the standards of accuracy relevant to their truth. In addition to the identification of the context of a given work,

various written works can also be classified into different genres based on three main aspects: subject matter, style and conventions of reference. These aspects determine how a work is perceived and interpreted. For instance, genres such as history or philosophy differ significantly from poetry or fiction, not only in content but also in the use of metaphor and background knowledge. Understanding the genre of a work is thus essential to grasp its truth value and overall message. While individual sentences in non-literary genres (e.g. history, philosophy) can be assessed for their truth value, the unit of communication in such works is the whole piece. A work is entirely true if all its sentences are true, and false to the extent that it contains false sentences. However, in literary genres such as fiction and poetry, individual sentences often lack a truth value because their referring terms do not pick out anything in the real world. The truth value of the whole work in fiction is often irrelevant – instead, such works are evaluated for their depth, insight and the overall message they convey. Furthermore, parables or poems, which may commend certain behaviour or depict situations as typical, can be described as true if they accurately reflect the nature of the behaviour or situation. Leigh Hunt's poem 'Abou Ben Adhem' illustrates this point well, as the poem's message, which emphasises the importance of loving one's fellow men, is considered true based on the truth of its underlying message, not the literal existence of its characters or events. Now, identifying the message of a literary work to assess its truth can indeed be challenging, but it is evident in some cases. For the genre of models, which describes underlying essences using familiar yet inadequate comparisons, examples can be provided from science – such as water waves and sound waves – to explain how models work by highlighting positive, negative and neutral analogies between the model and the process it describes. This contrasts with allegories, which are fictional stories with characters and events that correspond to real-life individuals and situations. George Orwell's *Animal Farm* and John Bunyan's *Pilgrim's Progress* are examples of allegories that convey real-life truths through fictional narratives.

Another genre is that of fables, which can take the form of moral fables, metaphysical fables and historical fables. First, moral fables are short fictional stories designed to commend or discourage certain behaviour – an example of this is Nathan's fictional story to King David in the Bible which serves as a means of criticising David's actions in pursuing Bathsheba. In assessing the truth value of a moral fable, they are to be assessed as true if the behaviours they commend are indeed good. Second, metaphysical fables are fictional stories that convey deep metaphysical or epistemological truths. Ancient myths and stories often served this purpose by providing metaphorical insights into the human condition and the nature of reality. Third, historical fables are a blend of historical events with fictional details to convey the essence of the events, and thus they aim to provide a deeper understanding of historical figures and their motives. A fable can have a double meaning – both a literal historical meaning and a deeper, often allegorical, meaning. Alfred Lord Tennyson's *Idylls of the King* is an example of a work with this type of dual meaning – with it being identifiable both as a historical narrative and a metaphysical fable about the human condition. In general, understanding the genre and context is crucial for accurately interpreting and assessing the truth of any work, whether it is literary or non-literary.

In conclusion, Swinburne's philosophical framework provides a comprehensive background for understanding meaning and the various ways language is used in communication. By defining essential terminology and examining the role of presuppositions Swinburne highlights how context and shared beliefs influence the interpretation of statements. His analysis of analogy, metaphor and genre underscores the dynamic nature of language and the importance of context in determining meaning and truth value. Moreover, Swinburne's insights into how different genres convey messages and are evaluated for their truth contribute to a deeper understanding of communication – essential for both philosophical inquiry and everyday discourse. This all lays a solid foundation for further exploration within a theological context of how meaning is constructed and conveyed by revelation.

Theological Application: The Christian Revelation

In this section, Swinburne applies his philosophical framework to that of the Christian revelation, thus exploring its necessity, authenticity and interpretation within a Christian framework. He begins by discussing the need for revelation, asserting that divine communication is essential for humans to understand truths about God's nature, moral directives and historical events that they could not ascertain independently. Swinburne then outlines the criteria for evaluating the authenticity of a revelation, emphasising the importance of content, miracles, church fidelity and developed doctrine. He further examines the original Christian revelation, the role of the Church in maintaining doctrinal continuity and the complexities of interpreting theological definitions and biblical texts. Swinburne concludes by discussing the moral teachings derived from revelation and the processes by which the Church interprets and applies these teachings to guide believers.

The Need for Revelation

The existence of God makes the occurrence of revelation highly probable, as God, being omnipotent and perfectly good, would want to reveal truths to humanity that it could not discover on its own due to limitations in its persistence, honesty and capability. Now, recognising a divine message requires understanding the context – who sends the message, to whom it is sent and against what background of shared assumptions it is communicated. Hence, a revelation is essential for conveying crucial information that humans need but cannot ascertain independently. Thus, if it is probable that God exists, as has been argued previously, it follows that revelation from God becomes likely, particularly if it serves purposes that are beneficial to humanity. More specifically, there are four kinds of truths that would be beneficial for humans to know through revelation: first, truths concerning God's nature that help humans interact with him appropriately. For instance, the concept of God as a Trinity is something that humans could not have deduced without revelation, yet it significantly enhances the understanding of God's nature and fosters more appropriate worship. The second kind of truths concern historical details about significant events such as the Incarnation. That is, if God became incarnate to address human sin and suffering – as was argued in the previous chapter – it is crucial for humans to know when, where and how this occurred. So historical details provide context and validate the significance of such events, making the Incarnation's purposes – atonement for sins and identification with human suffering – clearer. In other words, detailed historical revelation ensures that such pivotal events serve their intended purposes effectively. Third, there are certain moral truths that are difficult to discern – that is, while humans can discover some moral truths through reflection and reasoning, many moral issues remain contentious and unresolved without divine guidance. A revelation thus helps to clarify what actions are good or bad, obligatory or supererogatory, and beyond human debate and cultural differences. Contemporary moral debates, such as those on abortion and euthanasia, are areas where divine revelation can provide definitive guidance, thus helping humans align their actions with divine will and moral truths. Fourth are truths that serve to encourage humans to pursue good actions and avoid evil by informing them about the consequences of their actions, such as rewards and punishments. That is, just as parents guide their children with incentives and deterrents, God uses revelation to guide humans towards moral behaviour. Thus, revelation is able to offer insights into the rewards of Heaven and the dangers of Hell, thereby motivating humans to strive for moral excellence and spiritual well-being. This process thus helps individuals form virtuous characters naturally inclined towards goodness.

It is important to note, however, that revelation must be accessible and relevant across different cultures and time periods. Yet, there is indeed a challenge in transmitting a divine message that remains clear and applicable despite changes in cultural, scientific and philosophical contexts. To address this, one can provide a combination of culture-specific and culturally independent revelations. This approach thus ensures that, while the core message remains consistent, it is communicated in a way that resonates with different cultural backgrounds and evolving understandings. Now, the specific mechanisms through which revelation can be preserved and interpreted across generations can take different forms. For example, it can take the form of an infallible authority within a religious community that is able to provide definitive interpretations of divine revelation. Alternatively, it could take the form of a consensus method, where truth emerges over time through collective reflection and discussion within the religious community. Either way, if a specific mechanism is established that can accompany the revelation provided by God, then the core tenets of revelation are able to be maintained, even as interpretations evolve to address new cultural and intellectual challenges.

The Four Tests for a Revelation
On the basis of the significant evidence supporting the existence of God, specific tests must be applied to candidate revelations to ascertain their authenticity. These tests parallel those used to authenticate a human letter, which includes the content, method of expression and transmission. However, for a divine revelation, these tests need to

be adapted – in that, the content must be what God would choose to reveal, the method of expression must be uniquely attributable to God, and the transmission test is to be replaced by additional tests that are pertinent to divine communication. More fully, the first test examines whether the content of the purported revelation aligns with what God would choose to reveal. Such content must address matters beyond human capability to ascertain independently, such as theological truths, moral truths and God's plans for humanity. For instance, revelations about God's nature and moral directives, such as the Christian concept of the Trinity, are truths humans could not deduce without divine intervention. Importantly, however, these revelations must be true and not contradict clear moral intuitions – as falsehoods would discredit their divine origin. For example, if a revelation condoned acts like rape or murder, it would be deemed false. The second test involves the method of expression, which must include a divine signature – typically a miracle. A miracle is defined as a violation of natural laws that only God could perform. For example, the biblical story of Elijah calling down fire from heaven is considered a divine act because it violates natural expectations and was interpreted as God's endorsement of Elijah's message. Similarly, events such as the Resurrection or instantaneous healing are viewed as miracles validating the divine origin of a revelation, as the occurrence of such events, supported by strong historical evidence, serves as God's authentication of the revelation. The third test evaluates whether the revelation includes guidance on establishing an authoritative body (i.e. the Church) to interpret and elaborate on the teachings. A genuine revelation must provide a framework for continuous interpretation, thus ensuring the message remains relevant across cultures and eras. This, therefore, involves identifying the original teachings and distinguishing them from their presuppositions. The Church must thus interpret these teachings plausibly, reflecting the original revelation's intent. For example, the Christian Church's role in interpreting and developing doctrines over centuries demonstrates the necessity of such an institution. The fourth test assesses whether the Church's interpretations align with what God would likely teach humanity. This includes evaluating the content for its plausibility and consistency with the original revelation. The Church's developed doctrines must concern significant topics and be reasonably probable, and evidence of further miracles accompanying the Church's proclamations would reinforce the authenticity of its interpretations.

However, overwhelming evidence could undermine the purpose of revelation, which is to guide sincere seekers of truth without coercing belief through undeniable proofs. Thus, if a revelation satisfies all four tests, it is likely genuine. Now, among major religions, the Christian revelation uniquely meets these criteria – in that Christianity claims miracles, particularly the resurrection of Christ, as evidence of divine endorsement. In contrast, other religions such as Islam, which denies the divinity of Jesus and the Resurrection, or Judaism, which does not provide the same level of miraculous evidence, do not meet the second test as convincingly. Thus, the coherence and cumulative evidence of Christianity make it the most probable candidate for a true revelation from God.

The Original Revelation

The Christian revelation includes the teachings of God to the Israelites, as recorded in the Old Testament, ultimately culminating in the teachings of Jesus Christ. These teachings involve not only Jesus' direct instructions but also the significance of his actions, as interpreted and communicated by his apostles. The central aspect of this revelation is thus propositional, meaning it includes specific claims about theological and moral truths that Jesus and his apostles imparted. More specifically, the original propositional revelation comprises God's teachings to the Israelites and the teachings of Jesus about his actions' significance, as well as the apostles' teachings. The apostles, especially the Twelve commissioned by Jesus, had the authority to interpret and expand on Jesus' teachings – and Acts chapter fifteen exemplifies this authority, where the apostles and elders made decisions about gentile converts, beginning their proclamations with 'It has seemed good to the Holy Spirit and to us', thus signifying their perceived divine authority. Now, the sources for understanding the content of the original revelation include the New Testament books, especially the four Gospels, Acts of the Apostles, the Pauline and other apostolic letters and the book of Revelation. These texts, written in various styles and genres, collectively offer insights into the teachings and actions of Jesus and the apostles. These documents must thus be analysed critically to discern their historical and theological content. With regard to the genre of the collection of texts that make up the Christian revelation, many of them – such as the letters of Saint Paul – are paradigm examples of ancient letters intended to convey historical claims and certain theological teachings. Acts is seen as a work of history that details the early Church's growth and the apostles' actions; and the gospels of Matthew, Mark, Luke and John are treated as historical narratives, though they include elements of theological interpretation and symbolic acts. These texts, by and large, aim to record the historical teachings and actions of Jesus and the apostles. Jesus' teachings focus on five key areas: his divinity, atonement for sins, the founding of a church with divine authority, moral teachings on how to live and promises of eternal life or specific warnings of alienation from God. Now, despite scholarly scepticism, there is, as noted in the previous chapter, substantial historical evidence to support the claim that Jesus taught about his divinity. That is, while Jesus did not explicitly state 'I am God' during his lifetime, his actions and implicit teachings, coupled with post-resurrection proclamations, support this claim – specifically, Jesus' forgiving of sins, being accused of blasphemy and accepting worship are indirect claims to divinity. In addition to this, as also noted previously, Jesus' life and actions also served as an atonement for sins – with the significance of the Last Supper, at which Jesus instituted the Eucharist with the words 'This is my body' and 'This is my blood', indicating his life as a sacrificial offering. Moreover, Jesus' deliberate actions leading to his crucifixion, such as him challenging the Jewish authorities and allowing himself to be captured, further emphasise this atoning role – with the apostles' unanimous teaching that Jesus died for humanity's sins underscoring this doctrine's centrality.

The apostles played a crucial role in spreading and developing Jesus' teachings, as these individuals, who were considered authoritative leaders by the Early Church, were believed to be guided by the Holy Spirit in their teachings and decisions. Again, Acts of the Apostles and various epistles illustrate the apostles' belief in their divine mandate to teach and guide the Church – this being expressed by them interpreting Jesus' teachings, making doctrinal decisions and establishing early Christian communities. As noted previously, the apostles extended Jesus' teachings to gentiles without requiring circumcision, which reflected their belief in the universal applicability of Jesus' message. The apostles' establishment of church practices, such as the Eucharist, and their decisions on doctrinal matters demonstrate their authoritative role in shaping early Christianity. This authority was seen as divinely sanctioned, ensuring the correct interpretation and transmission of Jesus' teachings. It was miracles, however, that served the role of authenticating the Christian revelation. Miracles – particularly that of the resurrection of Jesus – are to be taken as God's signature to validate the teachings of Jesus and the apostles. Moreover, the Resurrection, supported by historical evidence, is presented as a 'cornerstone ('super') miracle' that reinforces the credibility of the Christian revelation. However, other miracles reported in the New Testament, such as healings and exorcisms, further authenticate the divine origin of Jesus' message. The historical reliability of the New Testament accounts, coupled with the evidence for miracles, thus supports the authenticity of the Christian revelation and the consistency of these accounts with what one would expect from a divine revelation lends credibility to the claims of Jesus' divinity, atonement and the founding of the Church.

The Church

Jesus' actions and teachings were fundamental in establishing a new religious community, referred to as the Church. Jesus appointed twelve apostles, which was a symbolic act representing the reformation of Israel. This new community, or Church, was marked by certain performative actions – particularly, as noted previously, the institution of the Eucharist. Hence, the celebration of the Eucharist became a central practice of early Christian communities, ultimately signifying the new Israel that derives from the twelve apostles. Within the scriptures, Jesus is explicitly seen to have appointed Simon Peter as the leader of this new Church, signifying his role by giving him the name 'Peter' or 'Cephas', meaning rock – with this specific renaming being significant, as it indicated Peter's foundational role in the Church. However, despite this, there indeed is some controversy regarding the extent of Peter's leadership and whether his authority was meant to be infallible and perpetuated through successive leaders of the Church. Nevertheless, for a church to be considered the true Church founded by Jesus, it must meet twofold criteria: criteria of connectedness and continuity in both organisation and doctrine. Connectedness of organisation means being organised in a way similar to the apostolic Church, while continuity involves gradual and legitimate changes over time. These specific criteria focussed on connectedness and continuity of organisation help in determining the authenticity of an ecclesial body's claim to be part of the Church Jesus founded. Now, significant splits in Church history, such as those between Catholics, Nestorians and Monophysites, and later between Roman Catholics and Orthodox Christians, as well as the various Protestant denominations, demonstrate the complexities of maintaining connectedness and continuity. However, despite these divisions, there has been substantial continuity in aims and organisation across different Christian bodies, which is essential for identifying the true Church. Moreover, connectedness and continuity of doctrine are crucial for the true Church. Connectedness of doctrine involves teaching the same core doctrines as the apostolic Church, while continuity means that any doctrinal developments must be legitimate extensions of the original revelation. Although historical evidence of the apostolic Church's teachings is limited, it is enough to establish a baseline for evaluating the continuity of later ecclesial bodies. Moreover, the role of miracles and the 'purity of life' can be considered additional tests for the true Church. That is, while miracles can reinforce a church's claim to authenticity, they are not as crucial as the original miracle of the Resurrection – furthermore, too much reliance on miracles might attract people for the wrong reasons, though occasional miracles can support a church's authority. With regard to the purity of life, some movements, such as Donatism, have argued that the true Church must be a society of saints, free from impurity. However, this view misunderstands the Church's role as a sanctifying agent, which is meant to mould sinners into saints. The Church must teach and encourage holiness, but it is not necessary for all members to be fully sanctified at all times.

So, the identity of the Church influences its ability to interpret the original revelation. That is, the Church's role is to interpret, not to create new revelations, ensuring that the original message is understood and applied correctly in new cultural contexts. The true Church, which maintains connectedness and continuity with the apostolic Church, is best positioned to provide reliable interpretations of the original revelation.

Theological Definitions
Theological definitions in documents such as the Nicene Creed are meant to be clear and precise, with each sentence contributing to the overall truth of a given document. These definitions, issued by

The Authenticity of Revelation

councils or groups of humans at particular times, represent their understanding of divine revelation rather than direct quotations from God. While creeds do not claim to contain hidden meanings for future generations, the Bible, which is considered God's word for all ages, is often interpreted with the expectation that its full meaning may only be realised over time. This distinction is thus crucial for understanding how creeds and scriptural texts are treated differently in terms of interpretation and authority.

To derive doctrines from the original revelation, one must utilise public and rational procedures to validate certain doctrinal developments. That is, these procedures must show that these beliefs are indeed involved in the original revelation, allowing theologians and councils to reject implausible interpretations. Thus, Christian tradition involves accepting or rejecting doctrines based on such rational procedures, ultimately ensuring that the posited doctrines remain true to the original revelation. Now, proper interpretation of the original revelation requires consistency with historical evidence and logical coherence. That is, interpretations must be plausible, meaning there is a modest probability that they are correct. This involves distinguishing the record of the original revelation from its presuppositions, identifying analogies and metaphors, and understanding different genres within the texts. The specific sub-field of theology called Systematic Theology, is thus crucial in producing coherent interpretations that align with the original message. Moreover, Church councils and theologians play a crucial role in interpreting the original revelation and resolving new disputed issues. Their interpretations should be trusted, especially when they are familiar with the prophet's teachings or have divine guidance. God guides the Church to discover the correct interpretation of the prophet's teachings, ensuring that the Church's interpretations remain faithful to the original revelation. However, wildly implausible interpretations by the Church would indicate a failure in the truth of the revelation itself. One can thus take certain examples as cases that illustrate the process of deriving doctrines from the original revelation – the doctrinal development of the Trinity and the Incarnation involved various theological interpretations before the Church settled on the most plausible ones. The Council of Nicaea's formulation that the Son was 'of the same substance' as the Father was chosen over Arius' view that the Son was 'of like substance' because it better satisfied the criteria for doctrinal development. Hence, these interpretations, while not deductively derived from Scripture, are the most plausible interpretation available, given the historical and theological context. Thus, proper interpretation of the original revelation requires a systematic approach that considers historical evidence, logical coherence and divine guidance. The true Church, characterised by connectedness and continuity of doctrine, plays a central role in maintaining and interpreting these teachings. Hence, by adhering to rational procedures and ensuring consistency with the original message, the Church ensures that its doctrines remain faithful to the divine revelation.

The Bible
The Old and New Testaments of the Bible are considered integral to the 'deposit of faith'. The high status of the Bible was recognised by the Early Church, which established by the end of the second century that any claims about revealed doctrine must derive from the Scriptures. The New Testament itself affirms the divine inspiration of the Old Testament, particularly in passages such as 2 Timothy 3:16, which states, 'All Scripture is inspired by God and profitable for teaching, for reproof, for correction, and for training in righteousness.' However, despite its esteemed status, the Old Testament posed certain challenges for early Christians due to perceived discrepancies between its teachings and those of Jesus. This tension led figures like Marcion of Sinope to reject the Old Testament as part of the Christian canon. However, orthodox defenders such as Saint Irenaeus of Lyon reasserted its value, arguing that certain aspects were temporary or metaphorical. Origen of Alexandria further advanced this by emphasising certain metaphorical interpretations, thus suggesting that many parts of the Bible should be understood in a non-literal sense in order to align with Christian doctrine.

Now, concerning the nature of the Bible, there are two principal views regarding the authorisation of the Bible: the 'strong' view, which holds that God ensured every sentence in the Bible is part of a unified, true message; and the 'moderate' view that posits that, while God ensured the essential messages were true, some minor errors by human authors might exist. Both views can be considered central to Christian doctrine. Within both frameworks, one's interpretation of the Bible heavily depends on identifying appropriate units within the text and recognising its various genres, which, as noted previously, dictate whether passages should be taken literally or metaphorically.

The Authenticity of Revelation

However, the complexities inherent in interpreting the Bible are indeed significant, as certain sentences are not intended to be understood literally – thus necessitating reading the Old Testament in light of the New Testament and established Church doctrines. Hence, the role of Church tradition is crucial in biblical interpretation, as it helps to establish Church doctrine, and discern which books are canonical and how they should be understood – with the Councils' decisions on the canon also based on the connectedness and continuity of doctrine with the original revelation. Importantly, however, one must affirm that there is also a two-way process where doctrine is derived from Scripture, and Scripture is interpreted in light of existing doctrines. In interpreting this revelation, the recognition of the various genres within the Bible is essential for understanding its messages accurately. That is, biblical texts are often composed of smaller units, each with distinct social, cultural and literary contexts. Thus, understanding these contexts is crucial for interpreting the Bible's sentences and identifying their original meaning. For example, Psalm 21, originally used in a New Year festival for enthroning a king, has specific historical references that must be considered for proper interpretation. Yet, many biblical passages have false scientific or historical presuppositions, which, however, do not affect the truth value of the main message when interpreted metaphorically. An example of this is Psalm 104, which praises God for setting the earth on its foundations, based on the ancient belief that the earth is stationary. However, the metaphorical interpretation of this passage suggests that God ensures the earth's stability, which is the intended message. Thus, understanding when to interpret passages metaphorically is key to resolving apparent contradictions and maintaining the coherence of the Bible's overall message – this being so if interpreting a given verse literally leads to it contradicting science, history, certain moral truths and established Christian doctrines. Moreover, with regard to the genre of prophecy, one must distinguish between unconditional and conditional prophecies. That is, biblical prophecies were often understood conditionally, meaning they would come true unless certain actions were taken to prevent them. This conditional nature is evident in passages like Ezekiel's prophecies, which contain implicit conditional clauses. Hence, understanding the conditional nature of these prophecies helps to clarify their intended messages and the context in which they were delivered. Interpreting the Bible thus requires a nuanced understanding of its complex composition and historical context. The Church's role in defining and interpreting Scripture ensures that its teachings remain faithful to the original revelation – and the Bible's high status in Christian doctrine is able to be maintained through careful exegesis, with the recognition of the metaphorical nature of many passages, and an understanding of the genre and context of each book. This comprehensive approach thus ensures that the Bible continues to serve as a central pillar of the Christian faith, ultimately guiding believers in their understanding of God's revealed truth. Moreover, by adhering to these interpretative principles, the Church maintains the integrity of its doctrinal teachings and provides a coherent framework for understanding the Bible in the modern world.

Moral Teaching
The Christian revelation encompasses not only theological truths but also moral truths about human behaviour – with these moral truths being integral to understanding which good acts are required for securing redemption. Theological truths are to be taken as existing independently of revelation, whereas moral truths can be created by divine command. That is, God's command to perform certain actions makes them obligatory, unlike theological truths, which are true regardless of revelation. Revelation of moral truths thus has a unique capacity to create new moral obligations. As noted previously, certain moral truths can be categorised into necessary moral truths; now, however, one can also add other categories of moral truths, such as conditionally necessary moral truths, divine command obligations and context-specific obligations. Necessary moral truths are obligations that are universal, such as the duty to obey God's commands, including honouring parents and not lying. Conditionally necessary moral truths are obligations that apply universally unless God permits exceptions, such as prohibitions against killing, adultery and theft. These are generally binding unless explicitly permitted by God. Divine command obligations are obligations created directly by God's command, such as loving one's neighbour, which elevate certain good acts to obligatory status, transforming what would otherwise be supererogatory actions into duties. Context-specific obligations are obligations specific to certain groups or individuals, such as the commandment to observe the Sabbath, which may be binding on specific communities (e.g. ancient Israelites) but not universally applicable.

Now, interpreting moral teachings from the Bible involves recognising the human authorship of the biblical books, where moral

The Authenticity of Revelation

instructions often appear as personal commands. Despite this, the divine authorisation of these books implies that the moral instructions they contain are from God. Thus, interpreting moral teachings from the Bible requires applying the same interpretive rules used for other biblical sentences: distinguish presuppositions from statements, interpret literally, where possible, and otherwise, metaphorically. For example, Psalm 137:9, which speaks of dashing infants against rocks, should be understood metaphorically as destroying wicked inclinations through Christ, because it contradicts established Christian moral doctrine. Furthermore, identifying the category of a moral teaching involves determining whether it can be discerned by natural reason or whether it requires divine revelation. On top of this, New Testament teachings should be prioritised over Old Testament laws of sacrifice and ritual, which are no longer binding post-Christ. Core Christian ethics are thus derived from Jesus' general teachings, particularly those in the Sermon on the Mount. These include worshipping God, forgiving others and showing generous love to all. These teachings align with universal moral goods recognised even by atheists, though interpretations vary as to whether Jesus meant these as obligatory or merely commendable. The Catholic tradition, as has been shown a number of times before, distinguishes between obligatory and supererogatory good acts, thus suggesting that, while fulfilling obligations might lead to Heaven eventually, supererogatory acts could lead to immediate entrance. It is to be appreciated that a good God would encourage but not mandate constant moral obligations. Moreover, contentious moral issues, such as prohibitions against adultery, fornication and homosexual acts, are rooted in the belief that sex is a gift from God for the stability of the family. These teachings, supported by centuries of tradition and biblical texts, constitute central Christian doctrines and are morally plausible. Other moral issues such as abortion and euthanasia are to be understood in light of traditional moral teachings – which emphasise that of prohibition – while also considering contemporary ethical debates and scientific advancements concerning these nuanced issues.

Christian moral teachings, derived from both scripture and tradition, thus meet the tests of a true revelation by providing consistent, rational guidelines for behaviour. These teachings – while sometimes requiring divine command for their full moral weight – align with the broader framework of Christian doctrine and the goal of guiding believers towards holiness and moral integrity. The consistency and continuity of these moral teachings over time, supported by Church authority and tradition, thus provide a reliable foundation for moral behaviour and spiritual growth within the Christian faith.

One can thus reaffirm the position reached here that evidence from natural theology suggests the existence of God is not improbable, and it is reasonable to expect that God would reveal essential truths to humanity. These revelations, which humans could not reach unaided, include God's nature, the Incarnation, atonement for sins and moral guidance. The teachings of Jesus and his apostles, particularly Jesus' perfect life, divinity, atonement through his death and establishment of the Church, align with what one would expect from divine revelation. Jesus' teachings about the end of the world, final judgement, Heaven and Hell and detailed moral instructions advocate for a life of supererogatory goodness. Also, the possibility of Hell or extinction is consistent with God's nature, by emphasising the command to live righteously and generously.

Furthermore, the Christian revelation's credibility hinges on a divine signature being provided, identified as the resurrection of Jesus, which has significant historical evidence in support of this (as was shown in the previous chapter). Though the current form of the Christian revelation has been refined by the Church over centuries, there has been a maintenance of doctrinal continuity with the apostolic Church. Central doctrines, such as those in the Nicene Creed and correct biblical interpretations, have been consistently upheld by major ecclesial bodies claiming apostolic continuity. Peripheral doctrines, such as geo-centrism and the ordination of women, have been debated, with some deemed non-essential. The ongoing refinement of Christianity, guided by the Holy Spirit, thus involves removing false presuppositions and applying the original message to new contexts. This dynamic process of doctrinal development underscores the coherence and historical authenticity of the Christian revelation, making it a plausible candidate for the divine revelation provided by God.

Appendix: Formalising the Argument
The main argument featured above can now be formalised using the traditional calculus of probability. As noted previously, probability can be understood in three ways: physical probability, statistical probability, and logical probability. Focusing on logical probability, as expressed through Bayes' theorem, we can formalise the argument

The Authenticity of Revelation

about the probability of the Christian revelation. We define key elements as follows: k represents the evidence of natural theology, t is theism (the hypothesis that there is a God), and r is the occurrence of a revelation of the requisite kind authenticated by miracle and developed in a church. Based on previous arguments, we assume $P(t/k) = 0.5$, meaning the probability of theism given natural theology is 0.5. If there is a God, there is a strong reason to expect a revelation, so we assign $P(r/t.k) = 0.5$. Given $P(t/k) = 0.5$, the probability of a revelation given the background evidence becomes $P(r/k) = P(r/t.k) \times P(t/k) = 0.5 \times 0.5 = 0.25$. The historical evidence, d, about Jesus and the Church he founded is divided into two parts: $d1$ (evidence of Jesus' teachings, life, and the founding of a church) and $d2$ (evidence relevant to whether there was a prophet whose life was culminated by a super-miracle, and whether that prophet was identical with Jesus). Using Bayes' theorem, we calculate the probability of the revelation given this evidence: $P(r/d.k) = 1 / (1 + 3 \times (P(d/\neg r.k) / P(d/r.k)))$. We then assess $P(d/r.k)$ and $P(d/\neg r.k)$. For $d1$: $P(d1/r.k) = 1/4$; $P(d1/\neg r.k) = 1/20$. For $d2$: $P(d2/d1.r.k) = 1/2$; $P(d2/d1.\neg r.k) = 1/50$. Combining these, we get: $P(d/r.k) / P(d/\neg r.k) = (P(d2/d1.r.k) \times P(d1/r.k)) / (P(d2/d1.\neg r.k) \times P(d1/\neg r.k)) = (1/2 \times 1/4) / (1/50 \times 1/20) = 125$. Therefore: $P(r/d.k) = 1 / (1 + (3 / 125)) = 125 / 128 \approx 0.9766$. This indicates that, given the evidence of natural theology and the historical evidence about Jesus and his Church, the probability that there has been a revelation is approximately 0.9766. Finally, considering the evidence that this revelation occurred through Jesus (denoted as j), we know that $P(r/d.k) = P(j/d.k) + P(\neg j/d.k)$. As it plausible for one to assign a very low probability to the revelation occurring through another prophet, one can set $P(\neg j/d.k) = 0.0066$. Thus, we can calculate: $P(j/d.k) = P(r/d.k) - P(\neg j/d.k) \approx 0.9766 - 0.0066 = 0.97$. The historical evidence gives a 0.97 probability to the core teaching of Jesus developed by the Church being a true revelation from God.

This value aligns with the probability that Jesus was God Incarnate and that he rose from the dead, as calculated in *The Resurrection of God Incarnate*. These probabilities are similar because if God became incarnate to identify with our suffering, to atone for our sins, and to reveal truth to us, he would have ensured that those truths continued to be available to us. However, it's crucial to emphasise that these precise numerical values are used to give artificially precise values to such expressions as 'very probable' and 'more probable than not' simply to illustrate the force of the arguments. The real conclusion is that the Christian Revelation, Jesus being God Incarnate, and Jesus rising from the dead are all very probably true.

In conclusion, Swinburne's application of his philosophical framework highlights the critical role of revelation in conveying essential truths about God, morality and significant historical events. He argues that the existence of God makes revelation highly probable and outlines rigorous criteria for assessing its authenticity. Moreover, Swinburne demonstrates how the Christian revelation, particularly through the life and teachings of Jesus and the apostles, provides a coherent and plausible account of divine truth, supported by historical evidence and miraculous authentication. The Church's role in interpreting and maintaining doctrinal continuity ensures that these teachings remain relevant and true to the original revelation. Ultimately, Swinburne asserts that the Christian Revelation, with its unique combination of evidence and coherence, stands as a credible and essential communication from God, guiding believers toward moral and spiritual fulfilment.

Critical Engagements

Revelation: From Metaphor to Analogy has stimulated extensive scholarly critique due to its rigorous philosophical defence of the authenticity of Christian revelation. Swinburne's work focusses on providing a detailed framework for understanding and justifying the Christian revelation. However, several critics have challenged different aspects of Swinburne's arguments featured in this work. Scholars such as Bradley H. McLean, Chris Jackson, Graham Gould, Richard S. Briggs and John Lamont have raised objections that question the plausibility of Swinburne's position. This section explores these critical engagements and presents responses that align with Swinburne's philosophical perspective.

Bradley H. McLean

Critical Engagement. Bradley H. McLean, in his review article of *Revelation*,[8] critiques Swinburne for his philosophical methodology, which disengages from the historical and socio-cultural contexts of

---

8. McLean, Bradley H., 'Lessons Learned from Swinburne: A Critique of Richard Swinburne's Revelation: From Metaphor to Analogy', *Toronto*

biblical texts. McLean argues that Swinburne's distinction between 'sentences' and 'statements' reverts to an outdated form/content dichotomy and neglects the complexities of biblical scholarship. He asserts that Swinburne's use of seventeenth-century understandings of miracles, influenced by John Locke, is anachronistic and fails to account for the cultural specificity of the Western Christian tradition. Furthermore, McLean highlights the exclusionary nature of Swinburne's four tests for revelation, which prioritise Christian revelation and dismiss non-Christian religions.

Critical Response. An adherent of Swinburne's position can offer several responses to McLean's criticisms: first, McLean's critique of Swinburne's distinction between 'sentences' and 'statements' fails to take into account the philosophical utility of this differentiation. This distinction allows Swinburne to engage with the enduring truth claims of biblical texts while acknowledging their historical context. Second, while Swinburne's approach to miracles may draw from earlier philosophical traditions, it provides a coherent framework for analysing divine intervention that remains relevant to contemporary discussions. Third, the alleged exclusionary nature of Swinburne's four tests for revelation can be seen as a necessary feature of rigorous philosophical inquiry. These criteria aim to identify the most rationally compelling revelation, not to dismiss other traditions arbitrarily. Furthermore, Swinburne's methodology, while perhaps less focussed on historical-critical approaches, offers a complementary philosophical perspective that can enrich biblical scholarship.

Ultimately, McLean's critique of Swinburne's distinction between 'sentences' and 'statements', his approach to miracles and the alleged exclusionary nature of his four tests for revelation does not significantly undermine the robustness and insight of Swinburne's philosophical methodology. Swinburne's approach remains a valuable way to engage with biblical texts and the concept of revelation from a rational, analytical perspective, offering a means to explore the philosophical implications of the Christian revelation.

Chris Jackson

Critical Engagement. Chris Jackson, in his review article of *Revelation*,[9] criticises Swinburne's probabilistic approach, particularly his application of Bayes' theorem. Jackson points out that Swinburne's estimates for prior probabilities often exclude relevant recalcitrant data, such as morally troubling scriptural content and failed prophecies. Jackson also argues that Swinburne's criteria for what constitutes a revelation are overly restrictive and inherently biased towards Christian claims. He further critiques Swinburne's misunderstanding of the nature of predictions, suggesting that Swinburne's so-called 'predictions' for identifying an incarnate God are not necessary or universally applicable.

Critical Response. An adherent of Swinburne's position can offer several responses to Jackson's criticisms: first, Jackson's concern about Swinburne's exclusion of recalcitrant data overlooks the methodological necessity of establishing a baseline probability before addressing more complex issues. Swinburne's approach allows for a systematic evaluation of evidence, with the possibility of adjusting probabilities as additional data is considered. Second, as noted previously, while Swinburne's criteria for revelation may seem restrictive, they serve as a necessary framework for rigorous philosophical analysis. These criteria aim to provide a rational basis for evaluating religious claims, rather than arbitrarily favouring Christian beliefs. Third, Jackson's critique of Swinburne's 'predictions' misunderstands their purpose. These are not meant to be universally necessary conditions, but rather logical expectations based on the nature of a perfectly good God, thus serving as a heuristic tool for identifying genuine revelation.

In the final analysis, Jackson's concerns about Swinburne's exclusion of recalcitrant data, the restrictiveness of his criteria for revelation and the nature of his 'predictions' do not diminish the robustness and success of Swinburne's probabilistic approach and criteria for revelation. Rather, Swinburne's methodology provides a rigorous framework for systematically evaluating the evidence

---

9. Jackson, Chris, 'Book Review: *Revelation: From Metaphor to Analogy* and *The Resurrection of God Incarnate*', *Essays in Philosophy* 19, no. 2 (2018), pp. 364-82.

for revelation, facilitating rational discussion of the veracity of this important theological issue.

Graham Gould

Critical Engagement. Graham Gould, in his review article of *Revelation*,[10] notes that Swinburne's expanded second edition of Revelation includes a new chapter on Christian moral teachings, which Gould finds vulnerable to the charge of begging the question. Gould argues that Swinburne's reliance on Christian tradition to define philosophical criteria potentially biases his conclusions and limits engagement with contemporary moral debates.

Critical Response. An adherent of Swinburne's position can offer several responses to Gould's criticisms: first, Gould's concern about Swinburne's reliance on Christian tradition to define philosophical criteria misses the necessity of starting from a specific theological standpoint when evaluating religious claims. Swinburne's approach acknowledges this foundation while still aiming for philosophical rigour. Second, while the new chapter on Christian moral teachings may seem to beg the question, it can be seen as an attempt to demonstrate the internal consistency and rational defensibility of Christian ethics within its own framework. Third, Swinburne's use of traditional Christian concepts does not preclude engagement with contemporary moral debates. Rather, it provides a stable foundation from which to address modern ethical issues. Furthermore, Swinburne's approach invites dialogue between traditional Christian ethics and contemporary moral philosophy, potentially enriching both fields through critical engagement.

Despite Gould's objections regarding Swinburne's reliance on Christian tradition, potential circularity of arguments, and use of traditional concepts, Swinburne's approach successfully bridges traditional Christian ethics with philosophical analysis. By grounding Christian moral concepts in tradition while subjecting them to rational scrutiny, Swinburne's approach contributes to a fruitful interchange between religious ethics and moral philosophy, offering new perspectives and insights into the philosophical foundations of Christian moral teachings.

---

10. Gould, Graham, 'Revelation: From Metaphor to Analogy, Second Edition by Richard Swinburne', *The Journal of Theological Studies* 59, no. 1 (2008), pp. 454.

Richard S. Briggs

Critical Engagement. Richard S. Briggs, in his review article of *Revelation*,[11] critiques Swinburne for imposing metaphorical interpretations on biblical texts where a literal interpretation seems more straightforward. Briggs argues that Swinburne's approach can obscure the intended meaning of these texts and lead to forced interpretations that undermine their credibility. He also questions Swinburne's criteria for evaluating revelations, suggesting they are overly rigid and fail to account for the diversity of religious experiences.

Critical Response. An adherent of Swinburne's position can offer several responses to Briggs' criticisms: first, Briggs' concern about Swinburne's use of metaphorical interpretations fails to recognise the philosophical necessity of reconciling apparent contradictions in biblical texts. Swinburne's approach aims to preserve the coherence of Christian doctrine while respecting the texts' historical context. Second, while metaphorical readings may seem forced in some cases, they often serve to uncover deeper theological truths that align with the broader Christian message. This approach acknowledges the complexity of religious texts and their potential for multiple layers of meaning. Third, Swinburne's criteria for evaluating revelations, though potentially rigid, provide a necessary framework for rational assessment of religious claims. Their apparent inflexibility is a feature of their philosophical rigour rather than a flaw. Furthermore, Swinburne's approach to biblical interpretation invites a dialogue between literal and metaphorical readings, potentially enriching our understanding of these texts. Last, while Swinburne's criteria may not fully account for the diversity of religious experiences, they offer a starting point for systematic evaluation of revelations that can be further refined and expanded.

Thus, Swinburne's endeavour to bring philosophical rigour to the study of religious texts and experiences remains valuable, notwithstanding Briggs' concerns about metaphorical interpretations, inflexible evaluation criteria, and limited accounting for diverse religious experiences. Swinburne's methodology engages with biblical texts, respecting their historical context while being open to deeper

---

11. Briggs, Richard S., 'Revelation: From Metaphor to Analogy (Second Edition), by Richard Swinburne', *Heythrop Journal* 53, no. 2 (2012), pp. 283-84.

theological insights, thus enriching the dialogue between biblical studies and philosophy of religion.

John Lamont

Critical Engagement. John Lamont, in his article 'Stump and Swinburne on Revelation',[12] raises several objections against Richard Swinburne's views on revelation. Lamont critiques Swinburne's deistic conception of revelation, arguing that it creates an unnecessary separation between the original divine message and its transmission through history. He points out that Swinburne's approach might imply that sophisticated historical knowledge is necessary to understand divine revelation, thereby contradicting the purpose of revelation, which is to communicate important information to all people. Additionally, Lamont challenges the practical application of Swinburne's criteria for identifying the true Church, questioning whether historical scholarship alone can establish continuity of doctrine and organisation. Lamont suggests that Swinburne's rigid framework fails to account for the dynamic nature of religious experience and the ongoing role of divine guidance in interpreting revelation.

Critical Response. An adherent of Swinburne's position can offer several responses to Lamont's criticisms: first, Lamont's characterisation of Swinburne's view as 'deistic' misunderstands the nuanced way Swinburne balances divine action and human interpretation. Swinburne's approach aims to preserve the integrity of the original revelation while acknowledging the role of the Church in its transmission and interpretation. Second, while Swinburne's emphasis on historical knowledge might seem to limit access to divine revelation, it can be seen as an attempt to ground religious claims in verifiable evidence, making them more accessible to rational inquiry. Third, Swinburne's criteria for identifying the true Church, though challenging to apply, provide a rational framework for evaluating claims of ecclesiastical authority. This approach seeks to balance historical continuity with doctrinal consistency. Furthermore, Swinburne's method does not exclude ongoing divine guidance but rather

---

12. Lamont, John, 'Stump and Swinburne on Revelation', *Religious Studies* 32, no. 3 (1996), pp. 395-411.

provides a means to distinguish authentic revelation from later accretions or distortions.

In the end, Swinburne's project to reconcile divine communication with historical and rational inquiry retains its significance and sophistication, despite Lamont's critiques of his 'deistic' view, concerns about revelation accessibility, and challenges in applying criteria for identifying the true Church. Swinburne's approach, which engages with religious claims while respecting tradition and remaining open to critical examination, makes a valuable contribution to the ongoing conversation between philosophy, theology and historical studies, thus offering new insights into the nature of divine revelation and its transmission through history, as well as providing a rational framework for evaluating claims of religious authority.

* * *

In all, *Revelation: From Metaphor to Analogy* has provoked significant scholarly debate, addressing fundamental issues in philosophy, theology and biblical studies. The critiques by Bradley H. McLean, Chris Jackson, Graham Gould, Richard Briggs and John Lamont highlight the challenges and complexities of Swinburne's approach. However, one is able to respond to the issues raised by affirming the importance of a coherent philosophical framework, the use of probabilistic reasoning and the role of tradition in understanding revelation. These engagements enrich the discourse on the plausibility the of Christian revelation and demonstrate, as with his other works, the ongoing relevance of Swinburne's work.

Conclusion

In conclusion, this chapter has provided a comprehensive guide to Swinburne's *Revelation: From Metaphor to Analogy*, outlining its central aim, structure, and themes. Swinburne's meticulous examination of philosophical methodology and theological application underscores the rationality of the Christian revelation. By addressing fundamental issues such as the use of metaphor and analogy in religious language, the criteria for recognising genuine divine revelations, and the role of the Church in interpreting and maintaining doctrinal continuity, Swinburne establishes a robust framework for understanding and evaluating purported revelations. His analysis thus demonstrates that the central Christian doctrines, while complex, can be defended through rigorous philosophical inquiry. As readers explore *Revelation* for themselves, they will be better equipped to appreciate Swinburne's rigorous defence of the Christian revelation and its significance to contemporary philosophy.

Chapter Nine

The Rationality of Faith

This chapter serves as an introduction to Swinburne's *Faith and Reason* (hereafter, *FR*), which is a comprehensive exploration aimed at demonstrating that religious faith can be rational and justified through philosophical investigation. Swinburne aims to show that faith and reason are not mutually exclusive but can be reconciled. The chapter introduces readers to the central aim and structure of Swinburne's arguments, situating them within the broader context of contemporary debates in the philosophy of religion. It outlines the major sections of the work, including an analysis of the nature and rationality of belief, the value of rational religious belief, and the role of faith in religious practice. By providing this overview, the chapter prepares readers to engage deeply with Swinburne's systematic and rigorous examination of the rationality of religious faith.

Faith and Reason: Background

Central Aim

The central aim of *FR* is to explore the relationship between faith and rationality in the context of religious belief. *FR* seeks to demonstrate that religious faith can be rational and that the practice of religion can be justified through reason. Specifically, *FR* examines the nature of belief, the rationality of religious belief, the value of rational religious belief and the role of faith in religious practice. This thus involves a detailed analysis of how faith interacts with evidence, reason and religious creeds. *FR* is, therefore, structured to address various philosophical and theological challenges regarding the rationality of faith. Thus, on the basis of rigorous argumentation, *FR* aims to show that faith is not contrary to reason but can be a rational response to evidence and experience.

Historical Significance

FR was first published in 1981 as the third work within Swinburne's trilogy on theism. It is important to note that, even though *FR* is part of the trilogy on theism, the focus of the work is on specifically showing the rationality of Christian belief and faith. It thus (at least in the second edition) takes into account a lot of the results featured in the tetralogy (and in *The Resurrection of God Incarnate*) and therefore it fits better with the project of ramified theism, rather than that of bare theism. Now, the immediate historical context of *FR* involves debates about whether religious belief and faith are inherently irrational. Philosophers such as Alvin Plantinga, in *Warranted Christian Belief*,[1] argued for the rationality of Christian belief through the concept of properly basic beliefs, suggesting that belief in God can be rational without evidence. Meanwhile, John Hick, in *An Interpretation of Religion*,[2] argued for the equal moral worth of different religious ways of living, challenging the exclusivity of Christian truth claims. Swinburne's work responds to these positions by arguing for the rationality of Christian belief specifically, while also addressing the broader implications for religious epistemology.

The wide-ranging influence of *FR* led to the publication of a second edition in 2005, where Swinburne refined his arguments in light of ongoing discussions and new philosophical developments (which, amongst other things, included the expanded content interacting with the work of Plantinga and Hick).

---

1. Plantinga, Alvin. *Warranted Christian Belief*. New York: Oxford University Press, 2000.
2. Hick, John. *An Interpretation of Religion: Human Responses to the Transcendent*. New Haven: Yale University Press, 1989.

Literary Structure

The literary structure of *FR* is not explicitly divided into parts. However, for continuity with the rest of this book, we shall retain our terminology and dual structure as follows:

1. *Philosophical Methodology – The Nature of Belief and Rational Belief*: The first part of *FR* focusses on the philosophical analysis of belief, including an examination of the nature of belief and the conditions that make a belief rational. That is, Swinburne examines different types of rationality (i.e. internalist and externalist accounts) and criteria for rationality, and performs an examination of the principles of logical (inductive/epistemic) probability, evidence and the probabilistic nature of belief formation.
2. *Theological Application – The Nature and Justification of Religious Belief and Faith*: The second part of *FR* applies the established philosophical framework to specific theological claims about religious belief and faith. Swinburne investigates the conditions of rationality that apply to religious belief and the nature of faith in the context of Christian belief, addressing the relationship between faith and reason, the role of divine grace and the justification for holding religious beliefs. Swinburne thus explores how faith can be a rational response to religious experience and evidence, and how it interacts with the doctrines and practices of the Christian creed, with a comparison of this creed to other religious creeds being provided.

We shall now unpack in greater detail the various areas covered in both of parts of *FR*.

Themes

Philosophical Framework: The Nature of Belief and Rational Belief

In this section, Swinburne introduces the philosophical framework underpinning his exploration of the rationality of religious belief and faith. He begins by examining the nature of belief, emphasising its contrastive and probabilistic characteristics, and its influence on actions and decision making. Swinburne argues that beliefs are not binary but exist on a spectrum influenced by perceived probabilities and contextual alternatives. He further explores the relationship between belief and evidence, highlighting the foundational role of basic propositions derived from experiences and intuition. Building on this, Swinburne defines rational belief and action, distinguishing between subjective criteria (rational$_1$) and objective criteria (rational$_2$) of rationality. Swinburne introduces the concepts of diachronic justification and the necessity of thorough investigation for beliefs to be considered justified. Swinburne also addresses the importance of knowledge as justified true belief, advocating for beliefs grounded in objective criteria to increase their likelihood of truth.

The Nature of Belief
Belief is inherently contrastive, meaning it is always relative to alternatives. For instance, to believe that today is Monday is to believe that it is more probable than not that today is Monday. Belief in a proposition typically means believing it is more probable than its negation – with this probabilistic understanding of belief extending to complex scenarios where multiple alternatives are to be considered. Thus, to maintain a clear concept of belief, it is useful to adopt the view that belief in a proposition means believing it is more probable than any alternative. The relative nature of belief highlights its dependence on context and available alternatives. For instance, believing in the existence of God involves considering the probability of God's existence compared to the probability of atheism or agnosticism. Belief is thus not a binary state but a spectrum influenced by the perceived probabilities of various alternatives.

The connection between belief and action posits that belief influences the way individuals pursue their goals. If someone believes a certain road leads to London, he will take that road to achieve his goal of reaching London. This practical consequence of belief is a key aspect of understanding belief itself. Belief about the probability of different actions attaining a goal will guide a person's actions, assuming he has no other conflicting purposes. Beliefs also play a crucial role in decision making and behaviour. Beliefs about the likelihood of success in various endeavours shape how people act. For example, a person who believes prayer is effective may pray regularly, while someone who doubts its efficacy may not. This link between belief and action thus underscores the practical importance of belief in shaping human behaviour and decision-making processes. It is also important to note that belief is complex and influenced by multiple factors. That is, people may have many beliefs that never affect their actions but, if a situation arises where those beliefs are relevant, they will influence behaviour. Individuals may have multiple purposes, and their actions will depend on the relative strength of these purposes and their beliefs about the probability of achieving them through different means. The relationship between different beliefs and goals further compounds this complexity. For example, a person might believe in both the effectiveness of prayer and the importance of medical treatment, leading to a combined approach to seeking health. Beliefs are thus not isolated but part of a broader network of convictions and purposes that interact in complex ways.

Now, concerning the relationship between belief and evidence one can distinguish between different types of probability – with inductive probability being crucial in understanding belief. That is, belief is relative to the evidence available to an individual, and a person believes a proposition if he believes the evidence makes it more probable than any alternative. Hence, evidence plays a foundational role in shaping belief. Specifically, how people assess evidence and its impact on their beliefs is crucial. Rational belief is grounded in the assessment of evidence, which involves weighing the support that various pieces of evidence provide for different propositions. This process of evidence evaluation is central to forming justified beliefs.

Turning from the role of evidence, it is thus important now to consider the nature of 'basic propositions'. Basic propositions, which are beliefs not solely based on other beliefs but on experiences or apparent memories, form the foundation of a person's belief system and influence other beliefs. These propositions are not necessarily infallible but are held with varying degrees of confidence. Basic propositions are crucial because they underpin more complex belief structures. For example, the belief that 'I am experiencing pain' is a basic proposition that influences beliefs about medical treatment and personal well-being. Moreover, intuition and reason also contribute to belief, as many beliefs about logical or mathematical truths are based on intuition rather than empirical evidence. These intuitive beliefs form part of the basic propositions that underpin a person's overall belief system. Further elaborating on this concept, intuition provides immediate, non-inferential knowledge that complements empirical evidence. For instance, the belief in the basic principles of arithmetic or geometry is often grounded in intuitive understanding. Hence, both intuition and reason are thus essential in forming a coherent and comprehensive belief system.

The Nature of Rational Belief

Rational actions can be defined by distinguishing between actions that are rational according to an agent's criteria and those that are rational based on objective criteria. An action is rational$_1$ if it is the best action to take given the agent's criteria and evidence. For instance, if someone believes that buying a lottery ticket is the best action, despite the low probability of winning, it is considered rational$_1$ if it aligns with his understanding of the values and probabilities involved. However, agents can have false beliefs about what risks are worth taking. Thus, rational$_2$ actions are those that are objectively the best to take, given the correct probabilities and the agent's evidence about his circumstances. For example, buying a lottery ticket might be rational$_2$ if the agent has ample financial resources but irrational if he cannot afford the loss.

This type of analysis can now be extended to beliefs, which produces different forms of justification (or 'rationality') as follows: a belief is rational$_1$ if it is based on evidence that, by the agent's criteria, makes it probable. This involves internal coherence within the agent's system of beliefs. However, a belief can also be rational$_2$ if it is supported by correct criteria of probability and evidence, regardless of the agent's subjective criteria. Furthermore, a differentiation can be made between beliefs that are justified at a specific moment (synchronically) and those justified over time (diachronically). Diachronic justification is where a belief must be adequately investigated to be justified. This involves seeking more evidence and reassessing existing evidence. A belief that has undergone such rigorous investigation is termed rational$_3$ if it aligns with the agent's criteria, rational$_4$ if it aligns with the correct criteria, and rational$_5$ if it meets both subjective and objective criteria. Investigation is important in achieving justified beliefs, where an action is rational$_3$ if it is based on beliefs that the agent regards as adequately investigated. The failure to investigate adequately can lead to irrational actions and beliefs, both from the agent's perspective and an objective standpoint. Moreover, a failure to investigate can occur in various ways, such as neglecting to gather enough representative evidence or failing to recognise the importance of investigation. Such failures can render beliefs and actions irrational$_4$ or irrational$_5$, depending on whether the failure is judged by the agent's criteria or objective criteria.

The concept of knowledge is closely related to justified true belief, where for a belief to constitute knowledge, it must be not only true (and thus 'defeat free') and strongly held but also justified. This justification, as noted above, can be 'internalist', where the agent's evidence and criteria support the belief, or 'externalist', where the belief is produced by a reliable process. Unpacking these types of justification in more depth, for an internalist, what makes a belief justified are 'internal' factors, that is, ones of which the believer can become aware by introspection if she chooses. This primarily means her basic propositions (the evidence from which she starts or should start if she reflects on the matter) and the criteria by which she judges (or can judge, if she reflects on which criteria she should use) that such-and-such propositions are evidence for such-and-such a further proposition. For an externalist, however, a belief being justified depends on the process by which it is produced being of the right kind, quite independently of whether the believer is, or can become, aware of whether the belief has been produced by a process of the right kind. The process of production being of the right kind is normally spelt out in terms of the process being a reliable one (that is, one which usually produces true beliefs). One can critique externalism, however, from several angles. First, 'pure' externalist theories make the rationality of our beliefs something to which we have no access. This implies that we cannot improve our beliefs based on reflection and introspection, which contradicts the intuitive idea that we can enhance our epistemic situation through internal scrutiny. Second, externalism faces the problem of specifying the type of process that confers justification. For example, reliabilism, a prominent family of theories within externalism, needs a principled way of selecting the type to which a token process of belief production should be referred. Without this, the theory lacks content and practical applicability. Third, most externalist theories include internalist elements, such as the notion of defeaters, which are accessible pieces of evidence that render a belief logically improbable. This reliance on internalist criteria suggests that externalism cannot stand alone and must incorporate internal aspects to be functional.

Now, Plantinga's theory of warrant is another notable externalist approach. Plantinga, in his work *Warrant and Proper Function*[3], defines 'warrant' as the quality that turns true belief into knowledge, which depends on the proper functioning of cognitive faculties according to a design plan aimed at truth. In other words, for Plantinga, a belief is warranted if it is produced by cognitive faculties functioning properly in an appropriate epistemic environment. One can, as with general externalist theories, also push back against Plantinga's position. That is, in addition to the issues already raised against general externalist theories, and despite the simplicity of Plantinga's theory, one can first note that his theory presupposes the existence of God, which limits its acceptance to those who share this theistic belief. For non-theists, this reliance on a divine design plan is problematic and makes the theory less universally applicable. In addition to this, despite its externalist framework, Plantinga's theory relies on internalist criteria when dealing with defeaters and assessing evidence. This hybrid approach thus reveals the necessity of internalist elements even within an externalist theory, thus challenging the purity of externalism and Plantinga's version of it. So, in turning our attention to internalism, an internalist theory of justification emphasises the importance of internal access to justificatory factors, such as that of a belief system that is introspectively accessible and improvable. In defining this further, one can again distinguish between synchronic and diachronic justification, however, now within an internalist context. Synchronic justification means a belief is justified at a particular time if it is based on the subject's total evidence at that time, which renders the belief probable. This evidence can be subjective (the subject's actual basic propositions) or objective (the propositions which the subject is right to hold as basic). Hence, for the former, a belief is synchronically subjectively justified (rational$_1$) if it is based on and rendered probable by the subject's total actual evidence given his inductive criteria. Diachronic justification, on the other hand, means a belief is justified if it is a response to adequate investigation over time. There are various internalist kinds of diachronic justification, including a belief being based on what the subject regards as adequate investigation by his own criteria (rational$_3$), being probable given the

---

3. Plantinga, Alvin. *Warrant and Proper Function*. New York: Oxford University Press, 1992.

subject's criteria and based on adequate investigation by these criteria (rational$_4$), and being based on correct criteria of adequacy (rational$_5$).

In conclusion, Swinburne's philosophical framework provides a robust foundation for understanding belief and rationality within a general epistemological context. Swinburne emphasises that belief is inherently probabilistic and context-dependent, influencing actions and decisions based on perceived probabilities and available evidence. Swinburne also underscores the importance of basic propositions and intuition in forming a coherent belief system and highlights the necessity of thorough investigation for achieving justified beliefs. By distinguishing between subjective and objective criteria of rationality, Swinburne lays the groundwork for assessing rational actions and beliefs. His exploration of knowledge as justified true belief reinforces the significance of grounding beliefs in objective criteria to enhance their truth value.

Theological Application: The Nature and Justification of Religious Belief and Faith

In this section, Swinburne extends his philosophical framework to explore the importance of true religious belief, the nature of faith, the purpose of religion, the role of creeds and a comparative assessment of religious creeds. Swinburne emphasises the intrinsic significance of true religious beliefs for understanding our obligations and achieving lasting well-being. He distinguishes between propositional belief and faith, highlighting faith as a deeper personal commitment. The purpose of religion, according to Swinburne, is to attain salvation and deep well-being, with Christianity offering a comprehensive path through worship, ethical behaviour and service. The role of creeds in guiding believers towards religious goals is also examined, with a particular focus on the Christian creed's framework. Swinburne underscores the necessity of thorough investigation and rational belief in comparing religious creeds, arguing that the Christian creed provides a robust path to achieving religious goals. Finally, he asserts that faith is a voluntary act involving the deliberate pursuit of understanding and alignment with religious goals, with the Christian faith, in particular, being the specific form of faith to adopt in one's pursuit of the true religious way.

The Importance of True Religious Belief

Beliefs about whether there is a God and what properties God has, or what actions he has performed, are fundamental to understanding our obligations and how to live our lives. If God exists, we owe him gratitude, worship and obedience. Thus, having true beliefs about God is crucial for fulfilling these obligations. Moreover, many religions offer the possibility of attaining a deep well-being, or salvation, which is a great good. True beliefs about the means of achieving salvation are, therefore, of immense value. That is, mundane pleasures are temporary and often unsatisfying, while the deep well-being promised by religious salvation can provide lasting fulfilment. Consequently, it is crucial to investigate and acquire true beliefs about religious matters to avoid wasting time on fruitless pursuits and to fulfil potential obligations to God. Also, it is rational investigation that is essential for forming true religious beliefs. That is, rational investigation, which involves considering evidence and applying correct inductive criteria, is the best way to achieve beliefs that are probably true and people have an obligation to investigate religious matters adequately, given their significant implications for how we should live and what obligations we might have to God.

Concerning various non-rational reasons for holding religious beliefs, some writers in Christian thought have suggested that there are reasons to believe in the Christian 'creed' beyond its probable truth. These reasons may give rise to obligations to cultivate belief or simply make it good to do so. For instance, there might be a duty to believe informants who claim to have had religious experiences, provided their claims are not too improbable. Moreover, there is a moral obligation to investigate religious matters and cultivate rational beliefs. This obligation extends to ensuring that those dependent on us, such as our children, are also informed about their religious duties and the way to salvation. Thus, having true beliefs about God and his properties is important, as these beliefs shape our actions and understanding of our place in the universe. The pursuit of true religious beliefs is not only a personal duty but also a responsibility to others, as our beliefs can influence those around us. Therefore, there is a great importance for rational inquiry and the investigation of religious truths to fulfil these obligations and attain true well-being.

The Nature of Faith

Propositional belief pertains to the acceptance that certain propositions are true, and faith is fundamentally about trust in a person, particularly God or Christ, who possesses certain properties and has performed specific actions. This distinction is essential because faith, unlike mere belief, involves a deeper personal commitment. With regard to the nature of faith there are three different views that present themselves: first is the Thomist view of faith, which has its roots in the works of Saint Thomas Aquinas and has been widely held within and outside Christianity. According to this view, faith in God is primarily a belief that God exists. Aquinas adds that faith also involves believing certain other propositions about God and his actions based on divine revelation. And Aquinas also differentiates faith from scientific knowledge, as faith is a firm belief in something that surpasses human understanding and cannot be proven by reason alone. This view, however, raises questions about the merit of faith, as Aquinas argues that even devils have faith since they believe in God's existence. For Aquinas, as featured in his work *Summa Theologica* II-II, Q. 2, Art. 1-10,[4] meritorious faith must be voluntary and formed by love, which involves a commitment to actions inspired by love for God. Nevertheless, faith is more an intellectual assent to the existence of God and the truths of divine revelation, albeit not necessarily accompanied by an understanding or personal trust. This view thus underscores belief in doctrinal truths as the primary component of faith, where faith might exist without a deep, personal trust in God's active benevolence. Second is the Lutheran perspective, which emphasises, based on the writings of Martin Luther – such as his *Commentary on Romans* – that faith involves both belief and trust in God.[5] Luther stressed that faith is not only about intellectual assent to propositions but also about personal trust in God's mercy and promises. This view posits that true faith combines knowledge, assent and trust. Trust, in this context, means

---

4. Aquinas. *Summa*. Second Part of the Second Part, Question 2, Articles 1-10.
5. Luther, Martin. *Lectures on Romans: Glosses and Scholia*. Edited by Hilton C. Oswald. Translated by Walter G. Tillmanns and Jacob A. O. Preus. Vol. 25 of Luther's Works. St. Louis: Concordia Publishing House, 1972. See especially Luther's comments on Romans 1:17 and 3:21-28.

acting on the assumption that God will fulfil his promises, even when evidence suggests otherwise. This trust must be accompanied by good purposes aligned with the love of God, making it an active, not merely intellectual, faith. It is important to note that the historical debate concerning these two views on faith can be plausibly seen in reality as that of a verbal dispute because both traditions ultimately converge on the idea that faith is not merely an intellectual assent but requires a transformative commitment that leads to action (faith formed by love in Catholic terms). That is, each tradition uses 'faith' with nuanced emphases – Lutherans stressing the trust aspect and Catholics (Thomists) the intellectual assent, yet both acknowledge the necessity of a faith that results in love and good works. Thus, the dispute can be viewed more as a difference in emphasis and theological starting points rather than in the essential nature of what constitutes saving faith. Both views advocate for a faith that moves beyond mere belief, incorporating a robust commitment to living out the implications of faith through love and good deeds. This suggests that the historical conflict over the term 'faith' could stem more from semantic and doctrinal emphases rather than a fundamental theological divergence. Third, the Pragmatist view of faith, which is influenced by thinkers such as William James, explored in his lecture 'The Will to Believe',[6] and Søren Kierkegaard, in his work *Fear and Trembling*,[7] suggests that faith can exist without firm propositional belief. Instead, it involves acting *as if* religious propositions are true because of the potential benefits, such as eternal well-being. This view allows for faith to be a rational choice, made in the face of uncertainty, by prioritising the hoped-for outcomes of religious actions. Hence, the Pragmatist view posits that, even without a strong belief in the truth of religious propositions, a person can still live a religiously faithful life, by acting as if his specific religion is true and thus engaging in practices and actions that express trust in God.

---

6. James, William. "The Will to Believe." In *The Will to Believe and Other Essays* in Popular Philosophy, 1-31. New York: Longmans, Green, and Co., 1896.
7. Kierkegaard, Søren. *Fear and Trembling*. Translated by Alastair Hannay. London: Penguin Books, 1985.

Now, early Christian writers such as Clement of Alexandria, in his work *Stromata*,[8] and Cyril of Jerusalem, in his work *Catechetical Lectures*,[9] depicted faith both as firm conviction and as trust in uncertain hopes. Hence, early Christians likely understood faith as a marginally stronger belief in the Christian system compared to alternatives, coupled with a commitment to act on that belief. Over time, especially post-Renaissance, the conditions for belief and faith evolved. The rise of agnosticism and scepticism has led to different interpretations of what constitutes genuine faith. Modern Protestant theology, for instance, sometimes emphasises a non-propositional view of faith, focussing on experiencing and interpreting the world as God's creation. However, this can still be expressed in propositional terms, as it involves a belief that the world is as God reveals it. Hence, different Christian traditions emphasise various aspects of faith, but all agree on its profound importance in shaping religious life and practice. True faith, while deeply personal, is also inherently rational and purposeful, guiding believers in their relationship with God.

The Purpose of Religion

Religions aim to achieve salvation, which is conceived of, as noted previously, as a deep well-being. This deep well-being involves performing good actions in a desirable situation while understanding and desiring to be in that situation. Christianity provides a comprehensive package for salvation that includes understanding the universe, living a worthwhile life, and ultimately achieving a deep and everlasting well-being in Heaven. Unpacking this more fully, religions offer salvation by providing an understanding of the universe and a way of life that leads to well-being. Christianity, for example, teaches that the world depends on God, and pursuing the Christian way leads to forgiveness, reconciliation and a meaningful life of worship and service. Hinduism and Buddhism also offer salvation but differ significantly from Christianity. That is, they emphasise reincarnation and eventual escape from the cycle of

---

8. Clement of Alexandria. *Stromata*. In Ante-Nicene Fathers, Vol. 2, edited by Alexander Roberts, James Donaldson, and A. Cleveland Coxe, 299-568. Buffalo, NY: Christian Literature Publishing Co., 1885.
9. Cyril of Jerusalem. *Catechetical Lectures*. In Nicene and Post-Nicene Fathers, Second Series, Vol. 7, edited by Philip Schaff and Henry Wace, 1-203. Buffalo, NY: Christian Literature Publishing Co., 1894.

death and rebirth, rather than forgiveness and reconciliation with a personal deity. Specifically, for one to follow the Christian way, one must obey the Ten Commandments, the Sermon on the Mount, and the teachings of Saint Paul. Christianity thus involves a way of life that combines worship, ethical behaviour and service to others. This lifestyle is not only beneficial for the individual but also contributes to the salvation of others, as God desires everyone to be saved through the actions of believers.

Now, there are three primary reasons for pursuing a religious way: to render proper worship and obedience to God; to attain one's own salvation; and to help others attain their salvation. The pursuit of these goals reflects the love of God, which is central to the Christian faith, and these reasons are interrelated and mutually supportive – in that worshipping God and living according to his will naturally involves helping others and, in turn, securing one's own salvation. Moreover, humans have an obligation to acknowledge and worship their benefactors, especially if the benefactor is the perfectly good source of all being. This duty of worship is paramount and should be performed with gratitude and obedience, reflecting the nature of God as described in the Christian creed. So, from this viewpoint, as noted previously, well-being involves performing good actions in a desirable situation and knowing and desiring to be in that situation. This world is inherently good and pursuing the Christian way provides a depth of well-being that constitutes a limited form of salvation. It is important to seek forgiveness from God for failing to fulfil one's obligations and to live a life of worship and service. Furthermore, it is good to help others achieve a life of worship and service to God, leading them to Heaven. While it is important to encourage others to make the right choices, it is not appropriate to force anyone to do so. Instead, each individual must exercise his or her free will in making moral decisions.

It is again important to note that the three reasons for pursuing the Christian way are not in competition but rather complement each other. The love of God leads believers to worship him properly, seek their own and others' salvation, and perform actions that reflect this love. The Christian way thus provides a comprehensive path to deep well-being and ultimate salvation.

The Role of Creeds in Christianity

Different religions propose various paths to achieve their distinct religious goals, making the selection of the right religious path crucial for attaining these goals. Believers need to trust that the religious way they follow is more likely to achieve their goals than any other. In this context, the Christian creed provides a framework for worshipping and obeying God. This creed encompasses the belief in the Trinity – God the Father, Son and Holy Spirit. This Trinitarian doctrine underscores God's omnipotence, omniscience and perfect goodness, with the Father, Son and Holy Spirit unified in love and action, making God deserving of worship and obedience. The Christian creed also emphasises Jesus Christ's incarnation, life, death and resurrection, which offer a means of atonement for human sins and demonstrate God's solidarity with human suffering. Building on this foundational framework, the Nicene Creed is one of the most widely accepted creeds in Christianity. It begins by affirming God as the creator of all things, highlighting the duty to worship and obey him. The creed further asserts the oneness of Jesus Christ with God, affirming his divinity and role in creation. And the Nicene Creed declares Christ's incarnation and redemption of humanity, stressing his suffering, crucifixion and resurrection. This declaration provides a basis for worshipping Jesus as God and recognising his redemptive work.

In further exploring the practical implications of these beliefs, the Christian way involves performing actions in line with God's commandments and teachings, encapsulated in the Bible. The Christian creed provides a detailed account of these commandments and teachings, guiding believers in their worship and service to God and others. Living a life of service is inherently good and fulfils the obligations to God and fellow humans, who are also God's creation. When compared with other religious frameworks, the Christian creed offers a more comprehensive understanding of God's nature and commands. That is, other religions do not worship God for all the attributes that the Christian creed recognises, such as the love within the Trinity and the Incarnation. Thus, following the Christian way is more likely to achieve the goals of rendering proper worship and obedience to God than other religious ways.

Regarding the ultimate goal of such religious practices, salvation through the Christian way involves worship, service, repentance and seeking forgiveness for sins. Salvation also includes gaining a deep understanding of the world and one's place in it, which is facilitated by the teachings of the Christian creed. This understanding and the relationship with God will deepen in Heaven, where believers who follow the Christian way will ultimately be taken. Thus, belief in the Christian creed is important for pursuing the Christian way. This belief does not need to be absolute conviction but should involve a trust that the Christian way is the most probable means to achieving religious goals. This belief, combined with a strong commitment to following the Christian way, can lead to the development of a character suited for Heaven and a good God would not deny Heaven to someone with the right character, even if his belief was not strong due to no fault of his own. Hence, by following the Christian way, believers can achieve proper worship and obedience to God and attain their own salvation. And the Christian creed's detailed account of God's nature and commands sets it apart from other religious creeds, making it a more reliable path to achieving the goals of religion.

Comparing Creeds and Assessing Religious Beliefs

The necessity of seeking true beliefs, as noted previously – especially in the realm of religious creeds – is of great importance. Rational belief, termed $rational_5$ belief, is achievable only through adequate investigation, which requires a deep and comprehensive exploration of the claims and teachings of various religions. This thorough investigation is necessary to avoid a superficial understanding and to ensure that one's beliefs are well-founded. In performing this investigation, it is important to focus on the great world religions, which have garnered the dedication of many serious and knowledgeable people throughout history. Moreover, paying attention to religious creeds introduced by personal contacts is also suggested, as these may hold significant personal relevance. This approach ensures a balance between broad understanding and personal relevance, providing a solid foundation for forming rational beliefs. To underscore the impact of our modern resources, given the unprecedented access to information in the modern era, thorough investigation is necessary to form well-founded beliefs. Hence, rational beliefs about the relative probabilities of religious creeds must be supported by substantial evidence and rigorous investigation. This process involves evaluating personal religious experiences, the testimony of others and historical evidence supporting religious claims. Hence, $rational_5$ belief requires positive arguments and evidence from both personal experiences and the testimony of others – with this comprehensive approach ultimately helping to establish a robust and rational belief system. Ultimately, by performing this investigation, individuals can form well-founded beliefs that guide them towards personal salvation and a meaningful life.

Now, in further delving into the specifics of the nature of this type of investigation, in the context of the Abrahamic religions – Christianity (the 'Christian creed'), Judaism (the 'Judaic creed') and Islam (the 'Islamic creed') – all three assert that God has revealed truths to humanity but they differ significantly in the specifics of these revelations. Christianity claims that God became incarnate in Jesus Christ and provided atonement for human sins, a doctrine denied by both Judaism and Islam. Judaism maintains that God's revelations were directed towards the people of Israel, while Islam posits that Muhammad is the final prophet with the ultimate revelation in the Quran. These differences highlight the unique claims of Christianity about the nature of God (as a Trinity) and the historical events (such as the Resurrection) that are foundational to its faith. Moreover, Judaism and Islam present challenges to Christianity by denying the doctrines of the Trinity and the Incarnation, arguing for a strictly monotheistic view of God without the tripersonal aspect found in Christianity. This critique emphasises the logical and theological complexities within the Christian understanding of God as triune. Additionally, Islam's claim that Jesus did not die on the cross directly contradicts the central Christian tenet of the Resurrection, posing another significant theological divergence. In comparing the explanatory power of these creeds, Christianity argues that its doctrines better account for the historical evidence of Jesus' life, death and purported resurrection, which, as detailed in Chapter 7, are to be seen as verifiable public events. The miracles and teachings of Jesus, corroborated by historical documents and eyewitness accounts, are, as also noted previously, to be presented as empirical support for Christian claims. In contrast, the miracles associated with other religions, such as those in Islam and Judaism, often rely on less direct historical evidence, which can be seen as a limitation in establishing their credibility through rational inquiry. Furthermore, Christianity, as noted in Chapters 7 and 8, emphasises the need for revelation to be accompanied by miraculous events that serve as divine signatures authenticating the message. This is particularly evident in the case of Jesus' resurrection, which is argued to be a clear divine endorsement

The Rationality of Faith

of his teachings and sacrifice. Hence, the Resurrection is seen not only as a miraculous event but also as a fulfilment of prophecies and essential grounds for affirming Jesus' claims. In all, the Christian creed is thus held to be more probable than the Judaic and Islamic creeds.

The final step in showing the Christian creed (or some other theistic creed) to be more probable than any rival religious creed would be to show that it is more probable than any non-theistic creed. How can the Christian creed be compared with the creed of a non-theistic religion such as Buddhism? As they are so different, each must be assessed separately for its probability as a whole. The Christian creed, containing both the existence of God and detailed Christian claims, is probable to the extent to which it is probable *a priori* (which is a matter of the simplicity of the claim that there is a God, and how probable that makes the other doctrines – so that overall they fit together into a simple system) and has greater explanatory power than any equally simple system – that is, predicts better both the data of natural theology (the existence and orderliness of the world etc.) and the New Testament data, as well as data adduced by rival systems. Buddhism, as a prominent non-theistic religion, posits the fundamental law of karma, which asserts that virtuous actions create future pleasure and that non-virtuous actions create future pain. However, karma cannot explain why there is a universe at all or why the universe is governed by natural laws of a very simple kind that led to the evolution of animal and human bodies. Furthermore, the doctrine of reincarnation, which is essential to Buddhism, adds complexity without empirical evidence to support the cycle of rebirth and karma's influence across lifetimes. In comparing this all to Christianity, the Christian creed argues for the existence of a personal God who created and sustains the universe, offering a simpler and more probable explanation for the existence and orderliness of the universe than that offered by Buddhism. Moreover, Christianity provides, again, not only philosophical arguments but also historical evidence through the life, death and resurrection of Jesus, making its claims more accessible to rational inquiry and empirical validation in comparison to that of the purported historical claims of Buddhism. In sum, the Christian creed is thus also to be held to be more probable than the non-theistic creeds such as Buddhism.

However, not all religions posit creeds like the ones that have been analysed, and also do not have detailed practices and large followings like the religions of these creeds. That is, some are proposed by individual thinkers and share elements with traditional religions, often recommending similar ways of life. These 'philosophical religions' must be judged on their own merits. They cannot appeal to a prophet's revelation for their doctrines unless they also endorse all other teachings of that prophet. If they teach one doctrine based on prophetic authority, they must consistently teach the others as well, or rely solely on independent grounds for their beliefs. John Hick's position concerning religious pluralism falls into this type of category. Hick's position, defended in his work *An Interpretation of Religion*, emphasises the idea of 'the Real', a transcendent divine reality that underlies all religious experiences. Hick posits that the world's major religions are different human responses to the same ultimate reality, which he terms the Real. He argues that, although religious traditions conceptualise the Real in diverse ways – whether as a personal God in theistic traditions or as an impersonal ultimate reality in non-theistic ones – these different portrayals are culturally shaped interpretations of the same foundational truth. Hick maintains that religious experiences across different faiths are valid and lead towards the same ultimate goal of salvation, which he describes as the transformation from self-centredness to reality-centredness. However, one can critique Hick's position based on the vagueness and lack of substantive content in his concept of the Real. Hick's description of the Real as a 'noumenon', something beyond human comprehension and conceptual frameworks, makes it so abstract that it becomes practically meaningless. Without more concrete attributes or characteristics, the Real cannot fulfil the role Hick assigns to it in uniting diverse religious experiences. Furthermore, one can challenge the notion that all religious paths are equally valid or effective in achieving salvation. Different religions have inherently different understandings and goals regarding salvation, some focussing on personal liberation, others on divine worship, which complicates the claim that all are simply different routes to the same ultimate end. This all suggests that Hick's framework, while aiming for inclusivity and respect for all traditions, ultimately oversimplifies the profound doctrinal differences between religions.

In all, the Christian creed, with its strong historical foundation and rational arguments, is a more probable and convincing framework for understanding the nature of reality and achieving the goals of religion compared to the other theistic and non-theistic creeds on offer.

Faith Is Voluntary

Faith, particularly Christian faith, is a voluntary act. That is, while beliefs themselves are not directly chosen, the decision to seek beliefs through adequate inquiry into religious truths is a voluntary action. Faith is thus not merely an intellectual assent but a deliberate pursuit of understanding and aligning oneself with religious goals. Individuals have the freedom to choose their goals, whether they seek their own earthly well-being, that of their family, or broader goals like the well-being of humanity and the worship of God. Moreover, natural human instincts drive people to seek basic well-being, including food, drink, companionship and respect for those who deserve it. This natural inclination extends to showing gratitude and repentance, which are foundational to religious practice. The desire for deeper and longer-term well-being, including religious goals, is a natural extension of these earthly desires. It is indeed important to dedicate time to investigate the goals offered by different religions and assessing their worth. This process involves examining the probability of achieving these goals through various religious ways. A rational belief, formed through thorough investigation, can lead to the conclusion that one religion offers goals worth pursuing more than others and this rational belief takes into account the likelihood of the truth of different religious creeds and the value of their respective goals.

Now, balancing the worth of the goals with the probability of their attainment is crucial when deciding which religious way to pursue. That is, if an individual concludes that the Christian goals are highly valuable and that the probability of the Christian creed being true is sufficiently high, then it is rational to follow the Christian way. Conversely, if the probability of any religion being true is deemed very low, it may be reasonable to focus on pursuing mundane goods instead. This balancing act ensures that one's actions are guided by a rational assessment of both the worth of the goals and the likelihood of achieving them. However, the concept of free will in the acquisition of faith is also important. As noted earlier, there is a distinction between libertarian free will, which allows individuals to choose between different actions despite external influences, and compatibilist free will, which is compatible with predetermined actions. It is clear that faith is voluntary in the sense that individuals can choose, in a libertarian sense, to seek beliefs through adequate investigation and act on the assumptions that align with their findings. This voluntary aspect of faith involves trust in God and the pursuit of religious goals, which are rational$_5$ actions if supported by adequate evidence.

It is important to note, however, that the process of investigating religious truth and pursuing a religious way is continuous. Individuals should remain open to new evidence and willing to reinvestigate their beliefs throughout their lives. This openness ensures that one's faith remains rational$_3$, based on current evidence and understanding. Such a dynamic approach to faith allows for deeper religious experiences and a more profound understanding of God's nature and purposes.

Faith is thus a voluntary and rational pursuit, grounded in a thorough investigation of religious truths and a balanced assessment of the worth of religious goals. Faith involves not only intellectual assent but also a committed pursuit of understanding and aligning one's life with religious teachings. Thus, this comprehensive approach to faith ensures that individuals seek the best possible path to well-being and fulfilment, guided by a rational and voluntary choice. If the Christian way is found to have highly valuable goals and a sufficiently high probability of truth, as it has been argued here (and in the previous chapters), it is indeed the rational path to follow.

In conclusion, Swinburne's application of his philosophical framework underscores the critical role of true religious belief in understanding our obligations and achieving deep well-being. Swinburne distinguishes faith as a deeper personal commitment beyond mere propositional belief, emphasising the importance of rational inquiry and evidence in forming these beliefs – with the purpose of religion, particularly Christianity, being framed as achieving salvation and well-being through a life of worship, ethical behaviour and service. Swinburne further highlights the Christian creed as a comprehensive guide for believers, arguing that its detailed understanding of God's nature and commands sets it apart from other religious creeds. He stresses the necessity of thorough investigation and rational belief to ensure that one's religious path is well-founded and capable of guiding one towards true well-being and salvation. Lastly, Swinburne asserts that faith is a voluntary and rational pursuit, grounded in a committed effort to understand and align with religious truths, ensuring that individuals seek the best possible path to fulfilment and well-being, which has been argued to be that of the Christian way.

Critical Engagements

Faith and Reason has garnered significant attention and sparked various critical engagements from scholars, as this work focusses on demonstrating that religious faith, particularly Christian faith, is rational and can be justified through philosophical reasoning. However, several critics have challenged different aspects of Swinburne's arguments featured in this work. Scholars such as Eleonore Stump, John F. Post, Robert Merrihew Adams, Richard L. Sturch and John L. Schellenberg have raised objections that question the coherence and methodology used in supporting Swinburne's claims. This section explores these critical engagements and presents responses that align with Swinburne's philosophical perspective.

Eleonore Stump

Critical Engagement. Eleonore Stump, in her review article of *Faith and Reason*,[10] critiques Swinburne's handling of the Reformation controversy and his definitions of faith and salvation. She argues that Swinburne's claim that the dispute between Catholics and Reformers over faith and works is merely verbal fails to acknowledge the substantive theological differences. Stump highlights that for Reformers, faith alone justifies, whereas, for Catholics, both faith and good works are necessary. This distinction, according to Stump, significantly impacts the practical and theological understanding of salvation.

Critical Response. An adherent of Swinburne's position can offer several responses to Stump's criticisms: first, while Stump correctly identifies the substantive theological differences between Catholic (Thomist) and Reformed (Lutheran) views on faith and works, Swinburne's approach aims to highlight the underlying agreement on their necessity for salvation. Second, Swinburne's characterisation of the dispute as 'merely verbal' can be understood as an attempt

---

10. Stump, Eleonore, 'Faith and Reason', *Philosophical Review* 93, no. 2 (1984), pp. 308-12.

to bridge the theological gap by emphasising commonalities rather than differences. Third, Swinburne's probabilistic model of faith, which incorporates both belief and trust, provides a nuanced framework that can accommodate insights from both Catholic and Reformed traditions. Furthermore, Swinburne's approach invites a deeper dialogue between these traditions, potentially leading to a more unified understanding of faith and salvation. Last, by focussing on the practical outcomes of faith and works, Swinburne's analysis offers a way to move beyond historical disputes towards a more ecumenical perspective.

In the final analysis, while Stump's critique highlights important theological distinctions between Catholic and Reformed views on faith and works, Swinburne's approach, which aims to emphasise underlying agreements and bridge the theological gap, remains a valuable contribution to the dialogue. Moreover, his probabilistic model of faith, incorporating both belief and trust, provides a nuanced framework that can accommodate the important insights from both traditions.

John F. Post

Critical Engagement. John F. Post, in his review article of *Faith and Reason*,[11] criticises Swinburne's conclusion that it is immoral to cultivate an irrational belief in God. Post contends that Swinburne's reliance on rational evidence and probability to justify religious faith does not adequately account for the deeply personal and experiential aspects of faith. He argues that Swinburne's emphasis on rational justification may undermine the intrinsic value of faith as trust in God.

Critical Response. An adherent of Swinburne's position can offer several responses to Post's criticisms: first, Post's concern about Swinburne's emphasis on rational evidence misses the complementary nature of reason and personal experience in Swinburne's approach to faith. Second, Swinburne's focus on rational justification does not aim to replace the personal aspects of faith, but to provide

---

11. Post, John F., 'Faith and Reason by Richard Swinburne', *Journal of the American Academy of Religion* 51, no. 4 (1983), pp. 707-8.

a solid foundation that can enhance and deepen one's trust in God. Third, the claim that cultivating irrational belief is immoral stems from Swinburne's commitment to intellectual honesty, which he sees as crucial for genuine faith. Furthermore, Swinburne's approach can be seen as an attempt to integrate faith and reason, offering believers a way to engage with their beliefs intellectually without diminishing their theological significance. Last, by providing rational grounds for faith, Swinburne's method may actually strengthen the intrinsic value of faith by making it more resilient to intellectual challenges.

Ultimately, despite Post's concerns about Swinburne's emphasis on rational evidence, Swinburne's approach successfully integrates reason and personal experience in understanding faith. His focus on rational justification does not diminish the personal aspects of faith but rather provides a solid foundation that can enhance and deepen one's trust in God. Swinburne's commitment to intellectual honesty and his attempt to reconcile faith and reason thus offer believers a way to engage with their beliefs intellectually without compromising their religious significance.

Robert Merrihew Adams

Critical Engagement. Robert Merrihew Adams, in his review article of *Faith and Reason*,[12] objects to Swinburne's conception of religious faith as probability assignment. Adams argues that belief is more fundamental and primitive than any process of justification, and that Swinburne's approach may lead to a superficial understanding of faith. He also questions whether it is religiously appropriate to place such a heavy emphasis on rational justification for faith, suggesting it might detract from the sincerity of religious commitment.

Critical Response. An adherent of Swinburne's position can offer several responses to Adams' criticisms: first, Adams' objection to faith as probability assignment overlooks the particular way Swinburne integrates this concept with more fundamental aspects of belief and trust. Second, while belief may indeed be more primitive than justification, Swinburne's approach aims to provide

---

12. Adams, Robert Merrihew, 'Faith and Reason by Richard Swinburne', *Noûs* 19, no. 4 (1985), pp. 626-33.

a framework for evaluating and strengthening these basic beliefs. Third, the emphasis on rational justification in Swinburne's work is not intended to replace sincerity of commitment, but to complement and reinforce it. Furthermore, Swinburne's probabilistic approach to faith can be seen as a tool for articulating and examining beliefs, rather than a replacement for the core experience of faith itself. Last, by subjecting faith to rational scrutiny, Swinburne's method may actually deepen religious commitment by demonstrating its coherence and plausibility.

In all, Adams' critique of Swinburne's conception of religious faith does not diminish its value as a sophisticated attempt to bridge the gap between rational inquiry and religious commitment. Swinburne's probabilistic approach to faith provides a robust framework for evaluating and strengthening one's basic religious beliefs; and his method of subjecting faith to rational scrutiny may actually deepen religious commitment by demonstrating its overall veracity.

Richard L. Sturch

Critical Engagement. Richard L. Sturch, in his review article of *Faith and Reason*,[13] critiques Swinburne's intellectual view of faith, arguing that it overlooks the emotional and relational dimensions. Sturch finds Swinburne's comparisons between religions to be thin and not fully representative of the depth and richness of religious experiences across different faiths. He suggests that Swinburne's analysis may be too impersonal and dry, lacking the passionate love of God evident in many believers' lives.

Critical Response. An adherent of Swinburne's position can offer several responses to Sturch's criticisms: first, Sturch's concern about the intellectual view of faith overlooking emotional and relational dimensions fails to recognise Swinburne's intention to provide a comprehensive framework that can accommodate these aspects. Second, while Swinburne's comparisons between religions may seem thin, they serve as a starting point for more in-depth analysis and

---

13. Sturch, Richard L., 'Faith and Reason, Second Edition, by Richard Swinburne', *The Journal of Theological Studies*, New Series, 57, no. 2 (2006), pp. 822-24.

provide a rational basis for interfaith dialogue. Third, the apparent impersonality of Swinburne's approach is not a neglect of passionate faith, but an attempt to articulate its rational foundations. Moreover, as noted above, Swinburne's rigorous analytical method can be seen as complementary to, rather than replacing, the lived experience of faith, thus offering believers tools to understand and articulate their beliefs.

In sum, Sturch's critique of Swinburne's intellectual approach to faith does not appreciate its value in providing a rational foundation for religious belief. Swinburne's analytical method complements the emotional and relational dimensions of faith, offering believers tools to understand and articulate their beliefs.

John L. Schellenberg

Critical Engagement. John L. Schellenberg, in his festschrift essay 'Working with Swinburne: Belief, Value, and the Religious Life',[14] raises a nuanced objection to Richard Swinburne's emphasis on the necessity of propositional beliefs in religious faith. Schellenberg argues that Swinburne's insistence on the need for comparative epistemic beliefs about the truth of religious creeds is overly intellectualised and neglects the practical, evaluative and emotional dimensions of faith. He posits that it is possible for a person to live a robust religious life, committed to religious goals and practices, without holding specific propositional beliefs about the likelihood of the truth of religious doctrines. Schellenberg illustrates this with the example of Esther, a hypothetical Christian who, despite losing her explicit beliefs in Christian doctrines, continues to engage in Christian practices due to her strong evaluative and emotional attachment to Christian ideals and goals.

Critical Response. An adherent of Swinburne's position can offer several responses to Schellenberg's criticisms: first, Schellenberg's objection to the necessity of propositional beliefs misses the

---

14. Schellenberg, John L., 'Working with Swinburne: Belief, Value, and the Religious Life,' in M. Bergmann and J.E. Brower (eds), *Reason and Faith: Themes from Richard Swinburne* (Oxford: Oxford University Press, 2016).

foundational role these play in Swinburne's understanding of rational religious commitment. Second, while Schellenberg's example of Esther illustrates the possibility of religious practice without explicit beliefs, Swinburne might argue that such practice lacks the depth and consistency provided by a well-grounded epistemic framework. Third, Swinburne's emphasis on comparative epistemic beliefs does not negate the importance of emotional and evaluative aspects of faith, but rather provides a rational structure within which these can be meaningfully directed. Furthermore, Swinburne's approach can be seen as an attempt to integrate the intellectual and practical dimensions of faith, thus offering a more holistic understanding of religious commitment. Last, by insisting on the importance of propositional beliefs, Swinburne's work provides a basis for critically engaging with different religious traditions, fostering informed dialogue and decision making.

Thus, despite Schellenberg's critique of Swinburne's emphasis on propositional beliefs, his framework for religious faith remains a cogent and comprehensive approach to religious commitment. Swinburne's approach, while insisting on the foundational role of beliefs, acknowledges the importance of emotional and evaluative aspects of faith and thus provides a rational structure within which these can be meaningfully directed.

* * *

In all, *Faith and Reason* offers a rigorous philosophical defence of the rationality of religious faith, provoking thoughtful critiques from various scholars. The objections raised by Eleonore Stump, John F. Post, Robert Merrihew Adams, Richard L. Sturch and John L. Schellenberg address fundamental aspects of Swinburne's methodology and arguments. In response, to these issues one can highlight the importance of epistemic justification, the role of rational belief and the integration of emotional and relational dimensions of faith. These responses collectively reinforce the rationality of faith and demonstrate Swinburne's commitment to a robust and intellectually rigorous defence of general theistic and Christian faith.

Conclusion

In conclusion, this chapter has provided a comprehensive guide to Swinburne's *Faith and Reason*, outlining the central aim, structure and themes of the work. Swinburne's detailed examination of belief and rationality demonstrates that religious faith can be a rational response to evidence and experience. By addressing philosophical and theological challenges, Swinburne underscores the compatibility of faith with reason, emphasising the importance of rational inquiry in forming true religious beliefs. His analysis of the Christian creed and its role in guiding believers towards salvation and well-being highlights the depth and cogency of the Christian faith. As readers explore *Faith and Reason* for themselves, they will be better equipped to appreciate Swinburne's rigorous defence of the rationality of faith and its significance in contemporary philosophy.

Bibliography

Biographies of Richard Swinburne

'An interview with Richard Swinburne'. Richard Swinburne interviewed by Max Baker-Hytch. (Religious Studies, 2024), 1-14

'Science and Religion: Exploring the Spectrum', Richard Swinburne interviewed by Paul Merchant, 27 October 2015 to 3 March 2016 Transcript, British Library, National Life Stories Collection, C1672/15

'Natural Theology and Orthodoxy', in Rico Vitz (ed.), Turning East: Contemporary Philosophers and the Ancient Christian Faith (New York: St Vladimir's Seminary Press, 2012), 47–78

'The Vocation of a Natural Theologian', in Kelly James Clark (ed.), *Philosophers Who Believe: The Spiritual Journeys of Eleven Leading Thinkers* (Downers Grove, IL: InterVarsity Press, 1993), 179-202

Works of Richard Swinburne

Books (in chronological order)

Space and Time (London: MacMillan & Co. London, 1968; 2nd edn, 1981)

The Concept of Miracle, New Studies in the Philosophy of Religion (London: MacMillan & Co., 1971)

An Introduction to Confirmation Theory (London: Methuen, 1973)

The Coherence of Theism, Clarendon Library of Logic and Philosophy (Oxford: Oxford University Press, 1977; 2nd edn, 2016)

The Existence of God (Oxford: Oxford University Press, 1979; 2nd edn, 2004)

Faith and Reason (Oxford: Oxford University Press, 1981; 2nd edn, 2005)

The Evolution of the Soul (Oxford: Oxford University Press, 1986; rev. edn, 1997)

Responsibility and Atonement (Oxford: Clarendon Press, 1989)

Revelation (Oxford: Oxford University Press, 1991; 2nd edn, 2007)

The Christian God (Oxford: Oxford University Press, 1994)

Is There a God? (Oxford: Oxford University Press, 1996; rev. edn, 2010)
Simplicity as Evidence of Truth, The Aquinas Lecture in Philosophy (Milwaukee, WI: Marquette University Press, 1997)
Providence and the Problem of Evil (Oxford: Oxford University Press, 1998)
Epistemic Justification (Oxford: Oxford University Press, 2001)
The Resurrection of God Incarnate (Oxford: Oxford University Press, 2003)
Was Jesus God? (Oxford: Oxford University Press, 2008)
Mind, Brain, and Free Will (Oxford: Oxford University Press, 2013)
Are We Bodies or Souls? (Oxford: Oxford University Press, 2019)
Could a Good God Permit So Much Suffering? (with James Sterba) (Oxford: Oxford University Press, 2024)

Edited volumes (in chronological order)

The Justification of Induction, Oxford Readings in Philosophy (London: Oxford University Press, 1974)
Space, Time and Causality (Dordrecht: Reidel, 1983)
Personal Identity (co-edited with Sydney Shoemaker) (Oxford: Blackwells, 1984)
Miracles (New York: MacMillan, 1989)
Bayes's Theorem, Proceedings of the British Academy, Vol. 113 (Oxford: Oxford University Press, 2002)
Free Will and Modern Science (Oxford: Oxford University, 2011)
Natural Theology in the Eastern Orthodox Tradition (co-edited with David Bradshaw) (St Paul, MN: IOTA Publications, 2021)

Articles in journals and contributions to edited volumes (in chronological order)

'Three Types of Thesis about Fact and Value', *Philosophical Quarterly* 11 (1961), 301-7
'The Presence-and-Absence Theory', *Annals of Science* 18 (1962), 131-45 (repr. in Notes from the Editors to facsimile edition of W. Bateson, *Mendel's Principles of Heredity* [Birmingham, AL: Gryphon Editions, 1990])
'Privacy', *Analysis* 24 (Supplement No. 2) (1963-64), 127-36
'Falsifiability of Scientific Theories', *Mind* 73 (1964), 434-36
'Times', *Analysis* 25 (1964-65), 185-91
'Galton's Law-Formulation and Development', *Annals of Science* 21 (1965), 15-31
'The Timelessness of God', *Church Quarterly Review* (1965), 323-37 and 472-86
'Conditions for Bitemporality', *Analysis* 26 (1965-66), 47-50
'Knowledge of Past and Future', *Analysis* 26 (1965-66), 166-172
'Affecting the Past', *Philosophical Quarterly* 16 (1966), 341-47

'The Beginning of the Universe', *Proceedings of the Aristotelian Society*, Supplementary Volume 40 (1966), 125-38
'Horizons', *Philosophy of Science* 33 (1966), 210-14
'Grue', *Analysis* 28 (1967-68), 123-28
'The Argument from Design', *Philosophy* 43 (1968), 199-212
'Miracles', *Philosophical Quarterly* 18 (1968), 320-28
'Primary and Secondary Tests', *Analysis* 29 (1968-69), 203-5
'The Christian Wager', *Religious Studies* 4 (1969), 217-28
'Projectible Predicates', *Analysis* 30 (1969), 1-11
'Vagueness, Inexactness, and Imprecision', *British Journal for the Philosophy of Science* 19 (1969), 281-99
'Whole and Part in Cosmological Arguments', *Philosophy* 44 (1969), 339-40
'Choosing between Confirmation Theories', *Philosophy of Science* 37 (1970), 602-13
'Physical Determinism', in G.N.A.Vesey (ed.), *Knowledge and Necessity* (London: MacMillan, 1970)
'Popper's Account of Acceptability', *Australasian Journal of Philosophy* 49 (1971), 167-76
'Probability, Credibility, and Acceptability', *American Philosophical Quarterly* 8 (1971), 275-83
'The Probability of Particular Events', *Philosophy of Science* 38 (1971), 327-43
'The Paradoxes of Confirmation – A Survey', *American Philosophical Quarterly* 8 (1971), 318-30
'The Argument from Design – A Defence', *Religious Studies* 8 (1972), 193-205
'Cohen on Evidential Support', *Mind* 81 (1972), 244-48
'Confirmability and Factual Meaningfulness', *Analysis* 33 (1972-73), 71-76
'Omnipotence', *American Philosophical Quarterly* 10 (1973), 231-37
'Sense and Nonsense in Physics and Theology', Inaugural Lecture, University of Keele, 1973
'Personal Identity', *Proceedings of the Aristotelian Society* 74 (1973-74), 231-47
'Duty and the Will of God', *Canadian Journal of Philosophy* 4 (1974), 213-27
'Meaningfulness without Confirmability – A Reply', *Analysis* 35 (1974-75), 22-27
'Analyticity, Necessity and Apriority', *Mind* 84 (1975), 225-43
'The Objectivity of Morality', *Philosophy* 51 (1976), 5-20
'Persons and Personal Identity', in H.D. Lewis (ed.), *Contemporary British Philosophy* (Fourth series) (London: Allen & Unwin, 1976)
'Reply to Wallace's "On Making Actions Morally Wrong"', *Canadian Journal of Philosophy* 3 (1976), 551-52

'The Problem of Evil', in S.C. Brown (ed.), *Reason and Religion* (Ithaca, NY: Cornell University Press, 1977)

'Natural Evil', *American Philosophical Quarterly* 15 (1978), 295-301

'The Cosmological Argument' (in German), in N. Hoerster (ed.), *Glaube und Vernunft: Texte zur Religions Philosophie* (Munich: Deutscher Taschenbuch-Verlag, 1979)

'God's Action in the World', *Epworth Review* 6 (1979), 89-100

'Conventionalism about Space and Time', *British Journal for the Philosophy of Science* 31 (1980), 255-72

'Properties, Causation, and Projectibility: Reply to Shoemaker', in L.J. Cohen and M. Hesse (eds), *Applications of Inductive Logic* (Oxford University Press: Oxford, 1980)

'The Evidential Value of Religious Experience', in A.R. Peacocke (ed.), *The Sciences and Theology in the Twentieth Century* (Notre Dame, IN: University of Notre Dame Press, 1981)

'Are Mental Events Identical with Brain Events?', *American Philosophical Quarterly* 19 (1982), 173-81

'Science Is Both Inductive and Realist', in D.R. Gregory (ed.), *The Questions Behind the Answers* (Washington DC: University Press of America, 1982)

'Causality' and 'Theism', in John Bowden (ed.), *Dictionary of Christian Theology* (London: SCM Press, 1983)

'Mackie, Induction, and God', *Religious Studies* 19 (1983), 385-91

'A Theodicy of Heaven and Hell', in A.J. Freddoso (ed.), *The Existence and Nature of God* (Notre Dame, IN: University of Notre Dame Press, 1983)

'Verificationism and Theories of Space-Time', in Swinburne (ed.), *Space, Time and Causality*

'Analytic/Synthetic', *American Philosophical Quarterly* 21 (1984), 31-42

'Desire', *Philosophy* 60 (1985), 429-45

'Original Sinfulness', *Neue Zeitschrift für Systematische Theologie und Religionsphilosophie* 27 (1985), 235-50

'Thought', *Philosophical Studies* 48 (1985), 153-71

'Indeterminism of Human Actions', *Midwest Studies in Philosophy* 10 (1986), 431-49

'Analogy and Metaphor', in G.J. Hughes (ed.), *Philosophical Assessment of Theology* (Tunbridge Wells: Search Press, 1987)

'Knowledge from Experience and the Problem of Evil', in W.J. Abraham and S. Holtzer (eds), *The Rationality of Religious Belief* (Oxford: Clarendon Press, 1987)

'The Origin of Consciousness', in J.M. Robson (ed.), *Origin and Evolution of the Universe* (Montreal: McGill-Queen's University Press, 1987)

'The Structure of the Soul', in A. Peacocke and G. Gillett (eds), *Persons and Personality: A Contemporary Enquiry* (Oxford: Blackwell, 1987)

'The Christian Scheme of Salvation', in Thomas V. Morris (ed.), *Philosophy and the Christian Faith* (Notre Dame, IN: University of Notre Dame Press, 1988)

'Could There be More Than One God?' *Faith and Philosophy* 5 (1988), 225-41

'Does Theism Need a Theodicy?' *Canadian Journal of Philosophy* 18 (1988), 287-312

'The Free Will Defence', *Archivio di Filosofia* 56 (1988), 585-96

'Meaning in the Bible', in S. Sutherland and T.A. Roberts (eds), *Religion, Reason and the Self* (Cardiff: University of Wales Press, 1989)

'The Argument from the Fine Tuning of the Universe', in J. Leslie (ed.), *Physical Cosmology and Philosophy* (New York: MacMillan, 1990)

'Could God Become Man?', in G.N.A. Vesey (ed.), *The Philosophy in Christianity* (Cambridge: Cambridge University Press, 1990)

'Faith and the Existence of God', in A.P. Griffiths (ed.), *Key Themes in Philosophy* (Cambridge: Cambridge University Press, 1990) (Many amended versions published under various titles elsewhere.)

'God's Necessary Being', in M.M. Olivetti (ed.), *L'Argumento Ontologico* (Milan: Cedam, 1990)

'The Limits of Explanation', in D. Knowles (ed.), *Explanation and Its Limits* (Cambridge: Cambridge University Press, 1990)

'Tensed Facts', *American Philosophical Quarterly* 27 (1990), 117-30

'Necessary *a Posteriori* Truth', *American Philosophical Quarterly* 28 (1991), 113-23

'Revelation', in K.J. Clark (ed.), *Our Knowledge of God* (Norwell, MA: Kluwer Academic Publishers, 1992)

'God and Time', in E. Stump (ed.), *Reasoned Faith* (Ithaca, NY: Cornell University Press, 1993)

'Interpreting the New Testament – Comments on the paper of Attridge', in E. Stump and T.P. Flint (eds), *Hermes and Athena: Philosophical Theology and Biblical Exegesis* (Notre Dame, IN: University of Notre Dame Press, 1993)

'Reply: Further Defence of Christian Revelation', *Religious Studies* 29 (1993), 395-400

'Body and Soul', in T. Szubka and R. Warner (eds), *The Mind-Body Problem: The Present State of this Debate* (Oxford: Blackwell, 1994)

'The Content of Propositional Revelation', in M.M. Olivetti (ed.), *Filosofia della Rivelazione* (Milan: Cedam, 1994)

'Eschatology', 'Eternity', 'Evil, The Problem of', 'God', 'Hell', 'Immortality', 'Religion, Philosophy of, Problems of', in T. Honderich (ed.), *Oxford Companion to Philosophy* (Oxford: Oxford University Press, 1995)

'The Problem of Evil', in P. Koslowski (ed.), *Jahrbuch für Philosophie des Forschungsinstituts für Philosophie Hannover* (Vienna: Passagen Verlag, 1995)

'Theodicy, Our Well-being, and God's Rights', *International Journal for the Philosophy of Religion* 38 (1995), 77-93

'Thisness', *Australasian Journal of Philosophy* 73 (1995), 389-400; and (in German) in J. Brandl, A. Kieke and P.M. Simons (eds), *Metaphysik: Neue Zugänge zu alten Fragen* (Baden-Baden: Academia Verlag, 1995)

'The Beginning of the Universe and of Time', *Canadian Journal of Philosophy* 26 (1996), 169-89

'Dualism Intact', *Faith and Philosophy* 13 (1996), 68-77

'God and Morality', in M.M. Olivetti (ed.), *Philosophie de la religion: Entre éthique et ontologie* (Milan: Cedam, 1996)

'Reply to Stump and Kretzmann', *Faith and Philosophy* 13 (1996), 413-14

'Some Major Strands of Theodicy', in D. Howard-Snyder (ed.), *The Evidential Argument from Evil* (Bloomington, IN: Indiana University Press, 1996)

'Evidence for the Resurrection', in S.T. Davis, D. Kendall and G. O'Collins (eds), *The Resurrection* (Oxford: Oxford University Press, 1997)

'The Irreducibility of Causation', *Dialectica* 51 (1997), 79-92

'Predictivism', *Trames* (Estonian journal) 2 (1997), 99-108

'Response to Derek Parfit', in P. van Inwagen and D.W. Zimmerman (eds), *Metaphysics: The Big Questions* (Oxford: Blackwell, 1998)

'Revelation' and 'Soul', in Edward Craig (ed.), *Routledge Encyclopedia of Philosophy* (London: Routledge, 1998)

'The Bible as Inspired Text' and 'The Bible as Historical Evidence of the Resurrection', in Bible, Latvian Bible Society (1999)

'Many Kinds of Rational Theistic Belief', in G. Brüntrup and R.K. Tacelli (eds), *The Rationality of Theism* (Boston: Kluwer, 1999)

'The Modal Argument Is Not Circular', *Faith and Philosophy* 15 (1999), 371-72

'La Teologia Naturale Oggi', in F. Mercadante and V. Lattanzi (eds), *Elogia della Filosofia* (Proceedings of a Conference in Honour of Antonio Rosmini) (Rome: Fondazione Nazionale Giuseppe Capograssi, 2000)

'Reply to Grunbaum', *British Journal for the Philosophy of Science* 51 (2000), 481-85

'Reply to Richard Gale', *Religious Studies* 36 (2000), 221-25

'Evidence for the Incarnation', in M. Meyer and C. Hughes (eds), *Jesus Then and Now* (Harrisburg, PA: Trinity Press International, 2001)

'Natural Theology in the Light of Modern Cosmology and Biology', in *Science and the Future of Mankind: Proceedings of Working Group 12-14 November 1999, Jubilee Plenary Session 10-13 November 2000* (Vatican City: Pontifical Academy of the Sciences, 2001)

'Philosophical Theism', in D.Z. Phillips and T. Tessin (eds), *Philosophy of Religion in the 21st Century* (Basingstoke: Palgrave, 2001)

'Plantinga on Warrant', *Religious Studies* 37 (2001), 203-14

'Christianity and the Discourse of the World Religions – The Contribution of Philosophical Theology', in P. Koslowski (ed.), *Philosophischer Dialog der Religionen statt Zusammenstoss der Kulturen im Prozess der Globalisierung* (Munich: Fink, 2002)

'Contemporary Anglo-American Philosophy of Religion' (in Russian), in A. Kyrlezhev (ed.), *The Holy Trinity* (Moscow: Patriarchate of Moscow, 2002); and (in English) in M.Y. Stewart (ed.), *The Trinity: East/West Dialogue* (Boston: Kluwer, 2003)

'A New Programme of Natural Theology' (in French), in S. Bourgeois-Gironde, B. Gnassounou and R. Pouivet (eds), *Analyse et théologie* (Paris: J. Vrin, 2002)

'Response to My Commentators', *Religious Studies* 38 (2002), 301-15

'The Argument to God from Fine-Tuning Reassessed', in N. Manson (ed.), *God and Design: The Teleological Argument and Modern Science* (London: Routledge, 2003)

'Morality and God', *Revue Internationale de Philosophie* 3, no. 225 (2003), 315-28; published in Spanish in A.L. Cuenca (ed.), *Resistiendo al oleaje* (Madrid: Cuaderno Gris, 1999)

'What Is So Good about Having a Body?', in T.W. Bartel (ed.), *Comparative Theology* (London: SPCK, 2003)

'The Argument from Laws of Nature Reassessed', in M. Ruse and W. Dembski (eds), *Debating Design: From Darwin to DNA* (Cambridge: Cambridge University Press, 2004); repr. in M. Stone (ed.), *Reason, Faith and History: Essays in Honour of Paul Helm* (Farnham: Ashgate, 2008)

'Natural Theology, Its "Dwindling Probabilities" and "Lack of Rapport"', *Faith and Philosophy* 21 (2004), 533-46

'Prior Probabilities in the Argument from Fine-Tuning', *Faith and Philosophy* 22 (2005), 641-53

'The Probability of the Resurrection', in A. Dole and A. Chignell (eds), *God and the Ethics of Belief* (Cambridge: Cambridge University Press, 2005)

'Second Reply to Grunbaum', *British Journal for the Philosophy of Science* 56 (2005), 919-25

'The Value and Christian Roots of Analytical Philosophy of Religion', in H.A. Harris and C. Insole (eds), *Faith and Philosophical Analysis* (Farnham: Ashgate, 2005)

'Relations between Universals or Divine Laws?', *Australasian Journal of Philosophy* 84 (2006),179-89

'Sobel on Arguments from Design', *Philosophia Christi* 8 (2006), 227-34

'Wodurch ich bin – Eine Verteidigung des Substanzdualismus', in B. Niederbacher and E. Runggaldier (eds), *Die menschliche Seele* (Frankfurt: Ontos Verlag, 2006)

'Cosmic Simultaneity', in W.L. Craig and Q. Smith (eds), *Einstein, Relativity and Absolute Simultaneity* (London: Routledge, 2007)

'From Mental/Physical Identity to Substance Dualism', in P. van Inwagen and D. Zimmerman (eds), *Persons: Human and Divine* (Oxford: Clarendon Press, 2007)

'The Requirements for a Satisfactory Theodicy' (in Russian), in V. Shokhin (ed.), *The Problem of Evil and Theodicy*, Institute of Philosophy, Russian Academy of the Sciences (Moscow: Nauka, 2007)

'The Revival of Natural Theology', *Archivio di Filosofia* 75 (2007), 303-22

'A Simple Theism for a Mixed World – Response to Bradley', *Religious Studies* 43 (2007), 271-77

'Che cosa mi rende me? Una difesa del dualismo delle sostanze', in A. Lavazza (ed.), *L'Uomo a due dimensione* (Milan: Bruno Mondadori, 2008); and in A. Lavazza (ed.), *Contemporary Dualism: A Defence* (London: Routledge, forthcoming)

'Christ's Atoning Sacrifice', *Archivio di Filosofia* 76 (2008), 81-87

'God and Morality', *Think* 20 (2008), 7-15

'What Difference Does God Make to Morality', in R.K. Garcia and N.L. King (eds), *Is Goodness without God Good Enough?* (Lanham, MD: Rowman & Littlefield, 2008)

'Authority of Scripture, Tradition, and the Church', in T.F. Flint and M. Rea (eds), *Oxford Handbook of Philosophical Theology* (Oxford: Oxford University Press, 2009)

'How the Divine Properties Fit Together: Reply to Gwiazda', *Religious Studies* 45 (2009), 495-98.

'Substance dualism', *Faith and Philosophy* 26 (2009), 501-13

'God as the Simplest Explanation of the Universe', *European Journal for Philosophy of Religion* 2 (2010), 1-24; and in A. O'Hear (ed.), *Philosophy and Religion, Royal Institute of Philosophy Supplement 68* (Cambridge: Cambridge University Press, 2011)

'In Defence of Logical Nominalism', *Religious Studies* 46 (2010), 311-30

'What Does the Old Testament Mean?', in M. Bergmann, M. Murray and M. Rae (eds), *Divine Evil? The Moral Character of the God of Abraham* (Oxford: Oxford University Press, 2010)

'What Makes a Scientific Theory Probably True', 'The Argument to God from Laws of Nature', and 'The Argument to God from Fine-Tuning', in M.Y. Stewart (ed.), *Science and Religion in Dialogue*, Vol. 2 ([in Chinese] Shanghai: Fudan University Press, 2008; and [in English] Oxford: Wiley-Blackwell, 2010)

'The Coherence of the Chalcedonian Definition of the Incarnation', in A. Marmodoro and J. Hill (eds), *The Metaphysics of the Incarnation* (Oxford: Oxford University Press, 2011)

'Could Anyone Justifiably Believe Epiphenomenalism?', *Journal of Consciousness Studies* 18, nos 3/4 (2011), 196-216

'Dualism and the Determination of Action', in Swinburne (ed.), *Free Will and Modern Science* (largely the same as 'The Impossibility of Proving that Human Behaviour Is Determined', in T. Crisp, S. Porter and G.A. Ten Elshof [eds], *Neuroscience and the Soul* [Grand Rapids, MI: Eerdmans, 2016], which includes a 'Reply to Speak')

'Evidence', in T. Dougherty (ed.), *Evidentialism and Its Discontents* (Oxford: Oxford University Press, 2011)

'Gwiazda on the Bayesian Argument for God', *Philosophia* 39, no. 2 (2011), 393-96

'Bayes, God, and the Multiverse', in J. Chandler and V. Harrison (eds), *Probability in the Philosophy of Religion* (Oxford: Oxford University Press, 2012)

'How to Determine Which Is the True Theory of Personal Identity', in G. Gasser and M. Stefan (eds), *Personal Identity – Complex or Simple?* (Cambridge: Cambridge University Press, 2012)

'The Vocation of a Natural Theologian', in R. Vitz (ed.), *Turning East: Contemporary Christian Philosophy and the Ancient Christian Faith* (New York: St Vladimir's Press, 2012); and (in Polish) under the title, *My Spiritual Autobiography: The Vocation of a Natural Theologian* (Poznań: Poznańskie Studia Teologiczne, 2012)

'What Kind of Necessary Being Could God Be?', *European Journal for Philosophy of Religion* 4, no. 2 (2012), 1-18; and in M. Szatkowski (ed.), *Ontological Proofs Today* (Frankfurt: Ontos Verlag, 2012)

'Why Hume and Kant Were Mistaken in Rejecting Natural Theology', in T. Buchheim, F. Hermanni, A. Hutter and C. Schwöbel (eds), *Gottesbeweise als Herausforderung für die moderne Vernunft* (Tübingen: Mohr Siebeck, 2012)

'*A Posteriori* Arguments for the Trinity', *Studia Neoscholastica* 10 (2013), 13-27

'Does God Permit Massive Deception?', *Philosophia Christi* 15 (2013), 265-70

'Gregory Palamas and Our Knowledge of God', in A. Schumann (ed.), *Logic in Orthodox Christian Thinking* (Frankfurt: Ontos Verlag, 2013); and in *Studia Humana* 3, no. 1 (2014), 3-12

'Häggström om Swinburne och sannolikheten för Guds existens', *Filosofisk Tidskrift* 4 (2013), 3-11

'The Probability of the Resurrection of Jesus', *Philosophia Christi* 15 (2013), 239-52

'Responsibility, Atonement, and Forgiveness', in J.P. Moreland, K.A. Sweis and C.V. Meister (eds), *Debating Christian Theism* (Oxford: Oxford University Press, 2013)

'Précis of *Mind, Brain, and Free Will*' and 'Response to Reviewers', *European Journal for Philosophy of Religion* 6, no. 2 (2014), 1-3 and 51-63

'Second Response to Cavin and Columbetti', *Philosophia Christi* 16 (2014), 419-22

'Time and Causality', *American Philosophical Quarterly* 51 (2014), 233-45

'The Argument from Souls to God', *Religious Studies* 51 (2015), 293-305

'Could God Be a Necessary Being?', *Oxford Studies in Philosophy of Religion* 6 (2015), 224-44

'The Implausibility of Physical Determinism', in R.N. Williams and D.N. Robinson (eds), *Scientism: The New Orthodoxy* (London: Bloomsbury, 2015)

'The Inevitable Implausibility of Physical Determinism', *Journal of Consciousness Studies* 22, nos 11/12 (2015), 43-59

'Necessary Moral Principles', *Journal of the American Philosophical Association* 1 (2015), 617-34

'Reply to Vladimir Shokhin' (in Russian), synopsis of and reply to a critical notice of the Russian edition of *The Existence of God*, *Voprosi Filosophii* 2 (2015), 63 and 77-82

'How God Makes Life a Lot More Meaningful', in S. Goetz and J. Seachris (eds), *The Meaning of Life* (London: Bloomsbury Academic, 2016)

'The Impossibility of Proving that Human Behaviour Is Determined' and 'A Rejoinder to Speak', in Thomas M. Crisp, S. Porter and G.A. Ten Elshof (eds), *Neuroscience and the Soul* (Grand Rapids, MI: Eerdmans, 2016)

'Causation, Time, and God's Omniscience', *Topoi* 36, no. 4 (2017), 675-84

'In Defence of Open Theism', *Science, Religion & Culture* 4, no. 2 (2017), 56-62

'Response to My Commentators', *Religious Studies* 53 (2017), 403-18

'Why the Life of Heaven Is Supremely Worth Living', in T. Ryan Byerley and Eric J. Silverman (eds), *Paradise Understood: New Philosophical Essays about Heaven* (Oxford: Oxford University Press, 2017)

'The Argument from Consciousness', in J. Walls and T. Dougherty (eds), *Two Dozen (or So) Theistic Arguments* (Oxford: Oxford University Press, 2018)

'The Argument to the Soul from Partial Brain Transplants', *Philosophia Christi* 20, no. 1 (2018), 13-19

'Mental Causation Is Really Mental Causation' in M.P. Guta (ed.), *Consciousness and the Ontology of Properties* (London: Routledge, 2018)

'Phenomenal Conservatism and Religious Belief', in Matthew A. Benton, J. Hawthorne and D. Rabinowitz (eds), *Knowledge, Belief, and God: New*

Insights in Religious Epistemology (Oxford: Oxford University Press, 2018)

'The Social Theory of the Trinity', *Religious Studies* 54 (2018), 419-37

'God's Omnipotence', in Benedikt P. Goecke and C. Tapp (eds), *The Infinity of God* (Notre Dame, IN: University of Notre Dame Press, 2019)

'The Implausibility of the Causal Closure of the Physical', *Organon F* 26 (2019), 25-39

'Stump on Forgiveness', *Faith and Philosophy* 36 (2019), 81-101

'The Criterion of Simplicity in Metaphysics and Ethics', in J. Hermann, J. Hopster, W. Kalf and M. Klenk (eds), *Philosophy in the Age of Science* (Lanham, MD: Rowman & Littlefield, 2020)

'How to Define "Moral Realism"', *Journal of Philosophical Theological Research* (Iranian journal) 22, no. 85 (2020); and *New Blackfriars* 105, no. 2 (2024)

'The Structure of Probabilistic Arguments for the Existence of God', in R. Silvestre, B.P. Göcke, J.-Y. Béziau and P. Bilimoria (eds), *Beyond Faith and Rationality: Essays on Logic, Religion, and Philosophy* (Cham: Springer, 2020)

'Forgiving as a Performative Utterance', in M. McKenna, D. Nelkin and B. Warmke (eds), *Forgiveness and Its Moral Dimensions* (Oxford: Oxford University Press, 2021).

'God and Revelation', in B.M. Mezei, F.A Murphy and K. Oakes (eds), *The Oxford Handbook of Divine Revelation* (Oxford: Oxford University Press, 2021)

'You Are Your Soul', *Think* 57 (2021), 53-67

'Natural Theology for Today', in Swinburne and Bradshaw (eds), *Natural Theology in the Eastern Orthodox Tradition*

Biographical memoir of John Lucas, in *Biographical Memoirs of Fellows of the British Academy*, 2022

'God's Moral Goodness', *Philosophia Religii* (Russian journal) (2022); and 'Response to Papers Critiquing "God's Moral Goodness"', *Philosophia Religii* (2023)

'Natural Theology', 'Philosophy of Religion', 'Teleological Argument' and 'Theism', in A. Louth (ed.), *The Oxford Dictionary of the Christian Church*, 4th edn (Oxford: Oxford University Press, 2022)

'What We Cannot Know about God', in G. Gasser and S. Kittle (eds), *The Divine Nature: Personal and A-Personal Perspectives* (London: Routledge, 2022)

'A Christian Theodicy', *Forum Philosophicum* 27, no. 1 (2023), 9-25

'A Cartesian Argument for Substance Dualism', *Belgrade Philosophical Annual* 36, no. 1 (2023), 33-48

Response to a symposium on 'How to Define "Moral Realism"' (*Journal of Philosophical Theological Research* [Iranian journal] 22, no. 85 [2020];

and *New Blackfriars* 105, no. 2 [2024]), *Date Palm Compote* (a Russian philosophical journal) (forthcoming)

Secondary Literature

Critical Engagements

1 *The Coherence of Theism*

Daher, Adel, 'Richard Swinburne, *The Coherence of Theism*', *International Journal for Philosophy of Religion* 12, no. 4 (1981), 245-8

Hepburn, Ronald W., '*The Coherence of Theism* by Richard Swinburne', *Philosophy* 54, no. 207 (1979), 125-7

Inwagen, Peter van, 'Review of *The Coherence of Theism* by Richard Swinburne', *The Philosophical Review* 88, no. 4 (1979), 668-72

Penelhum, Terence, '*The Coherence of Theism* by Richard Swinburne', *The Journal of Philosophy* 77, no. 8 (1980), 502-8

Penelhum, Terence. 'Review of The Coherence of Theism'. *The Journal of Philosophy* Vol. 77, No. 8 (Aug., 1980), pp. 502-508

Philipse, Herman, *God in the Age of Science? A Critique of Religious Reason* (Oxford: Oxford University Press, 2012)

2 *The Existence of God*

Golding, Joshua, 'Richard Swinburne, *The Existence of God*, 2nd ed.', Notre Dame Philosophical Reviews, University of Notre Dame Press, 4 April 2005

Grünbaum, Adolf, 'The Poverty of Theistic Cosmology', *British Journal for the Philosophy of Science* 55, no. 4 (2004), 561-614

Philipse, Herman, *God in the Age of Science? A Critique of Religious Reason* (Oxford: Oxford University Press, 2012)

Stump, Eleonore, 'Richard Swinburne: *The Existence of God*', *The Thomist* 46, no. 3 (1982), 478

Sturch, Richard L., '*The Existence of God*, Second Edition, by Richard Swinburne', *The Journal of Theological Studies* 57, no. 1 (2006), 401-5

3 *The Problem of Evil*

Draper, Paul, 'Critical Study of *Providence and the Problem of Evil*, by Richard Swinburne', *Noûs* 35, no. 3 (2001), 456-74

Flint, Thomas P., 'Review of *Providence and the Problem of Evil* by Richard Swinburne', *The Philosophical Review* 110, no. 1 (2001), 120-22

Gale, Richard M., 'Swinburne on Providence', *Religious Studies* 36, no. 2 (2000), 209-19

Hick, John, 'Richard Swinburne, *Providence and the Problem of Evil*', *International Journal for Philosophy of Religion* 47, no. 1 (2000), 57-61

Quinn, Philip L., '*Providence and the Problem of Evil* by Richard Swinburne', *Faith and Philosophy* 18, no. 3 (2001), 394-98

4 The Reality of the Soul

Evans, C. Stephen, '*Mind, Brain, and Free Will*, by Richard Swinburne', *Faith and Philosophy* 31, no. 1 (2014), 105-8

Holdsworth, Nick, 'Book Review: *Mind, Brain, and Free Will*', *Philosophy* 89, no. 4 (2014), 635-42

McGuire, Mara, and Jeffrey Hause, 'Richard Swinburne, *Mind, Brain, and Free Will*', *Review of Metaphysics* 67, no. 3 (2014), 670-72

Palmer, David, 'Richard Swinburne, *Mind, Brain, and Free Will*', Notre Dame Philosophical Reviews, University of Notre Dame Press, 13 September 2013

Poston, Ted, 'Richard Swinburne, *Mind, Brain, and Free Will*', *Journal of Analytic Theology* 4 (2016), 480-84

5 The Metaphysics of Christian Theism

Alston, William P., 'Swinburne and Christian Theology', *International Journal for Philosophy of Religion* 41, no. 1 (1997), 35-57

Brown, David, '*The Christian God* by Richard Swinburne', *The Journal of Theological Studies* 47, no. 1 (1996), 386-89

Haldane, John, '*The Christian God* by Richard Swinburne', *Religious Studies* 32, no. 2 (1996), 281-83

Hasker, William, '*The Christian God*: Richard Swinburne', *The Journal of Religion* 77, no. 3 (1997), 487-88

Westphal, Merold, '*The Christian God* by Richard Swinburne', *Review of Metaphysics* 49, no. 2 (1995), 441-42

6 The Plausibility of the Atonement

Aspenson, Steven S., 'Swinburne on Atonement', *Religious Studies* 32, no. 2 (1996), 187-204

Gunton, Colin, '*Responsibility and Atonement*, by Richard Swinburne', *The Journal of Theological Studies*, New Series, 42, no. 2 (1991), 801-4

Helm, Paul, '*Responsibility and Atonement* by Richard Swinburne', *Religious Studies* 26, no. 3 (1990), 431-33

Owen, H.P., '*Responsibility and Atonement* by Richard Swinburne', *New Blackfriars* 72, no. 846 (1991), 99-101

Stump, Eleonore, 'Love and Forgiveness: Swinburne on Atonement', in M. Bergmann and J.E. Brower (eds), *Reason and Faith: Themes from Richard Swinburne* (Oxford: Oxford University Press, 2016), 148-70

7 The Probability of the Resurrection

Griffiths, Paul J., 'Richard Swinburne, *The Resurrection of God Incarnate*', *The Journal of Religion* 84, no. 2 (2004), 308-10

Haldane, John, '*The Resurrection of God Incarnate*', *Mind*, New Series, 113, no. 450 (2004), 397-401

Jackson, Chris, 'Book Review: *Revelation: From Metaphor to Analogy* and *The Resurrection of God Incarnate*', *Essays in Philosophy* 19, no. 2 (2018), 364-82

Martin, Michael, '*The Resurrection of God Incarnate*: Richard Swinburne', *Religious Studies* 40, no. 3 (2004), 367-71

Moser, Paul K., 'Critical Notices: Philosophy of Religion and Christian Resurrection: *The Resurrection of God Incarnate* by Richard Swinburne', *International Journal of Philosophical Studies* 12, no. 1 (2004), 61-82

8 The Authenticity of Revelation

Briggs, Richard S., '*Revelation: From Metaphor to Analogy* (Second Edition), by Richard Swinburne', *Heythrop Journal* 53, no. 2 (2012), 283-84

Gould, Graham, '*Revelation: From Metaphor to Analogy*, Second Edition by Richard Swinburne', *The Journal of Theological Studies* 59, no. 1 (2008), 454

Jackson, Chris, 'Book Review: *Revelation: From Metaphor to Analogy* and *The Resurrection of God Incarnate*', *Essays in Philosophy* 19, no. 2 (2018), 364-82

Lamont, John, 'Stump and Swinburne on Revelation', *Religious Studies* 32, no. 3 (1996), 395-411

McLean, Bradley H., 'Lessons Learned from Swinburne: A Critique of Richard Swinburne's *Revelation: From Metaphor to Analogy*', *Toronto Journal of Theology* 29, no. 2 (2013), 369-87

9 The Rationality of Faith

Adams, Robert Merrihew, '*Faith and Reason* by Richard Swinburne', *Noûs* 19, no. 4 (1985), 626-33

Post, John F., '*Faith and Reason* by Richard Swinburne', *Journal of the American Academy of Religion* 51, no. 4 (1983), 707-8

Schellenberg, John L., 'Working with Swinburne: Belief, Value, and the Religious Life,' in M. Bergmann and J.E. Brower (eds), *Reason and Faith: Themes from Richard Swinburne* (Oxford: Oxford University Press, 2016)

Stump, Eleonore, 'Faith and Reason', *Philosophical Review* 93, no. 2 (1984), 308-12

Sturch, Richard L., '*Faith and Reason*, Second Edition, by Richard Swinburne', *The Journal of Theological Studies*, New Series, 57, no. 2 (2006), 822-24

Festschrifts

Bergmann, Michael, and Jeffrey E. Brower, *Reason and Faith: Themes from Richard Swinburne* (Oxford: Oxford University Press, 2016)

'In Honour of Richard Swinburne', *Religious Studies* 53, Special Issue 3 (2017)

Mößner, Nicola, Sebastian Schmoranzer and Christian Weidemann (eds), *Richard Swinburne: Christian Philosophy in the Modern World* (Ontos Verlag, 2008)

Padgett, Alan, *Reason and the Christian Religion: Essays in Honour of Richard Swinburne* (Oxford: Clarendon Press, 1994)

Introductions

Chartier, Gary, 'Richard Swinburne', in Ian S. Markham (ed.), *The Student's Companion to the Theologians* (Malden, MA: Wiley-Blackwell, 2013), 415-23

Langtry, Bruce Richard, 'Swinburne', in Graham Oppy and Nick Trakakis (eds), *The History of Western Philosophy of Religion*, Vol. 5 (Durham: Acumen Publishing, 2009), Chapter 23, 329-43

Ozioko, Johnson Uchenna, *Rationality of the Christian Faith in Richard Swinburne* (Rome: Urbaniana University Press, 2019)

Welty, Greg, 'Richard Swinburne', in Benjamin K. Forrest, Joshua D. Chatraw, and Alister E. McGrath (eds), *The History of Apologetics: A Biographical and Methodological Introduction* (Grand Rapids, MI: Zondervan Academic, 2019), 667-84

Index

Adams, Robert Merrihew, 361
Agents, 18, 33, 46, 48, 99, 108, 111, 117, 120, 122, 125–126, 133–134, 150, 153, 156, 171, 181, 191–192, 196–200, 222–223, 248, 250–252, 257, 262, 302, 343
Agnosticism, 126–127, 156, 163, 165, 170, 341, 350
Alston, William P., 67, 242
Analogy, 12, 26, 51, 86, 303, 306–308, 312–313, 315, 330, 332–334, 336
Animals, 98, 111, 117, 124, 126, 131, 150–152, 159, 161, 163, 167, 288
Anselm of Canterbury, 90, 104
Apollinarianism, 237, 239–240
Aquinas, Thomas, 13, 18, 22–23, 66, 75, 79, 83, 89–91, 104, 118–120, 147, 230, 235, 262, 265, 348
Atonement, 12, 20, 26, 50–51, 164, 235–236, 245–249, 251, 253–255, 257–259, 261–263, 265–272, 275, 278–281, 285, 288–290, 295, 301–302, 305, 316, 320–321, 328, 352, 354
Augustine, 21, 79, 148–149, 235, 260–261

Barth, Karl, 307
Basic propositions, 341–342, 344–346
Bayesian probability, 135–136, 300, 302–303
Beauty, 45, 143, 148–151
Beliefs, 14–15, 17, 21, 23, 28, 37–40, 43–49, 51, 56, 58–60, 68, 70–72, 80, 102, 104, 111, 113, 115–116, 122, 134, 150–153, 158, 160–163, 181–185, 187–188, 192–193, 195–196, 198–202, 210, 212, 226–227, 229, 233, 243, 248, 250–251, 253, 256–257, 261, 263–264, 267–269, 271, 286, 303, 305, 309–310, 312–313, 315, 323, 332, 339–344, 346–347, 352–354, 356–358, 361–365
Bible, 85, 149, 262, 306, 314, 323–327, 352
Boethius, 85
Brain, 11, 27, 51, 121–122, 161, 178–179, 181, 186, 189–193, 195, 197–198, 200–202, 204, 206–208, 210–212, 220, 250
Braithwaite, R.B., 68
Briggs, Richard S., 334

Causation, 18, 29, 31–34, 37, 49, 74–76, 109, 179, 181–183, 185, 191–192, 201–202, 205, 208–212, 217–218, 222–224, 226, 231, 237–239, 243
Church, 3–5, 13–15, 65, 148, 164, 235–236, 258, 260, 263–264, 266, 273, 275, 281, 289–291, 297, 306–308, 316, 318, 320–330, 335–336
Consciousness, 9, 92, 99, 105, 114, 119, 121, 132, 179, 181, 193, 201–203, 205–207, 209–211, 233, 264
Cosmological argument, 18–19, 117–119
Credulity, 38, 43–44, 49, 130, 137–138, 184–185, 190, 201, 209–211

Daher, Adel, 97

Index

Dawkins, Richard, 12
Death, 9, 19–20, 70, 124–127, 150, 162, 164, 209, 235, 262–263, 268–269, 273–275, 288–290, 293, 295, 328, 351–352, 354–355
Defeaters, 38, 44, 344–345
Desires, 47–48, 71–72, 123, 145, 147, 150–151, 154–155, 157, 159–160, 165, 187–188, 190, 192–193, 195–197, 199, 223, 233, 248–252, 256–258, 261, 263–265, 351, 357
Determinism, 20, 79, 179–180, 250–251
Diachronic justification, 39, 341, 343, 345
Divine attributes, 10, 23, 55, 58, 67–68, 70, 93, 96, 98, 215–216, 230, 236, 240–241, 287
Divine simplicity, 230
Draper, Paul, 142, 175
Dualism, 11–12, 19, 27, 51, 99, 179–181, 185–189, 192, 201–202, 204–212, 239, 243

Emotions, 125, 151
Epistemic distance, 126, 165, 298–299
Epistemology, 8, 11, 22–23, 28, 37–38, 40, 43–45, 47, 49, 94–95, 98, 100, 134–135, 137, 178–181, 183, 185, 188, 201, 209–211, 304, 339
Eternal, 32, 71, 84–87, 91–93, 165–167, 169, 229, 258, 265, 286, 320, 349
Ethics, 8, 11, 23, 28, 45, 48–50, 100, 171–172, 267, 327, 333
Event dualism, 180, 185–187
Evil, 10–12, 20, 22–23, 25–27, 50, 79–80, 94, 105, 114, 122, 125–127, 129, 131–132, 141–145, 147–149, 151, 153, 155–165, 167–177, 261, 263–264, 317
Evolution, 9, 11, 27, 88, 106, 120, 149, 179, 191, 208, 261, 309, 355
Existence of God, 1, 6–8, 11, 13, 18, 21–22, 25, 50, 57, 90, 98, 103–105, 107–109, 111–117, 119, 121–135, 137, 139–140, 142–143, 145–146, 163, 177–179, 201–202, 275–277, 296, 316–317, 328, 330, 341, 345, 348, 355
Experience, 10, 13, 35, 62–64, 68, 71–72, 96, 103, 105, 118, 122, 126, 128–130, 155, 157–158, 161–164, 169, 173, 176, 184–188, 190, 192–195, 198, 201–205, 209–210, 233–234, 241, 250, 271, 299, 335, 339–340, 360–363, 365

Faith, 1–2, 4, 6, 8, 10–12, 14–16, 18, 20–22, 24–26, 28, 30, 32, 34, 36, 38, 40, 42, 44, 46, 48, 50–51, 56, 58, 60, 62, 64, 66, 68–70, 72, 74, 76, 78, 80, 82, 84, 86, 88, 90, 92, 94, 96, 98, 100, 102, 104, 106, 108, 110, 112, 114, 116, 118, 120, 122, 124, 126–128, 130, 132, 134, 136, 138, 140, 142, 144, 146, 148, 150, 152, 154, 156, 158, 160, 162, 164, 166, 168, 170, 172–174, 176, 180, 182, 184, 186, 188, 190, 192, 194, 196, 198, 200, 202, 204, 206–208, 212, 216, 218, 220, 222, 224, 226, 228, 230, 232, 234, 236, 238, 240, 242, 244, 246, 248, 250, 252, 254, 256, 258, 260, 262, 264, 266, 268, 270–272, 274, 276, 278, 280, 282, 284, 286, 288, 290, 292, 294, 296, 298–304, 308, 310, 312, 314, 316, 318, 320, 322, 324, 326, 328, 330, 332, 334, 336, 338–365
Fall, 75, 88, 112, 129, 146, 148
Flint, Thomas, 170–171, 176
Free will, 19–20, 32, 51, 79–82, 118, 124, 141–142, 144, 148, 152–153, 155–157, 159, 162–163, 165, 168–176, 178–181, 185, 197–200, 203–204, 206–212, 239, 247, 250–252, 260, 266, 272, 279, 286, 299, 351, 357

Gale, Richard, 174
God, 1–2, 6–13, 17–27, 50–51, 55–57, 63–68, 70–75, 77–95, 97–101, 103–105, 107–137, 139–159, 161–172, 175–179, 201–203, 215–216, 225–230, 232–233, 235–240, 242–244, 258–267, 273–282, 284–288, 290, 295–305, 307, 315–321, 323–330, 332, 339, 341, 345, 347–358, 360–362
Good and evil, 79, 122, 126–127, 129, 144, 157, 161, 165, 174–175
Gospels, 11, 270, 283–285, 288, 292, 294, 298, 301, 319–320
Grünbaum, Adolf, 138

Haecceitas, 218
Haldane, John, 238, 300

Hasker, William, 205, 240
Heaven, 90, 167, 247, 258, 263–266, 317–318, 327–328, 350–351, 353
Hell, 247, 258, 264–266, 317, 328
Hepburn, Ronald W., 95
Hick, John, 171, 216, 339
Hiddenness, 105, 126–127, 131, 165, 299
History, 11, 31, 69, 86, 91, 105, 109, 118, 127, 131, 138–139, 148, 177, 182–184, 186, 192, 195, 221, 235, 274, 283, 295–297, 314, 320, 322, 325, 335–336, 353
Hume, David, 33, 74, 104

Identity, 9–10, 19, 30–31, 37, 61–63, 72–73, 87–88, 102, 179–180, 186–187, 193–195, 200, 204–205, 209, 220–222, 226, 229, 233, 239, 281, 322
Immutability, 78, 84, 86
Incarnation, 9, 13, 15, 20, 26, 51, 126–127, 164, 168, 215–218, 226, 233–236, 238–239, 241–244, 274, 278–281, 286–287, 290, 297, 300–302, 316, 328, 352, 354
Inductive probability, 17, 108, 342
Interactive dualism, 181, 185, 189, 202

Jackson, Chris, 303, 332
James, William, 349
Justice, 10, 20, 84, 158, 174, 176, 246, 255, 258, 266, 270, 301

Kant, Immanuel, 67, 91
Kierkegaard, Søren, 349
Knowledge, 4, 15, 17, 19, 28, 36, 38, 41–45, 49, 66, 72, 76, 78–82, 85–87, 94, 110–111, 113, 115, 123, 131, 133, 137, 139, 153–154, 156–158, 161–165, 169–171, 180, 184–185, 188, 197, 210, 219, 224, 228–230, 233–234, 241, 276–277, 280, 287, 304, 314, 335, 341, 343–346, 348
Kripke, Saul, 35

Lamont, John, 335
Laws of nature, 32, 74, 84, 86, 88, 109–110, 112, 118–121, 127, 183, 191, 224, 227
Lewis, David, 74, 191
Liabilities, 29, 32–34, 74, 109, 120–121, 127, 183, 192, 202, 222, 226

Libet, Benjamin, 197
Logical necessity, 35, 37, 60, 63, 225
Love, 20, 83, 92, 117, 144, 148, 151–152, 164, 169, 231–232, 235–236, 241, 252, 263, 270, 279, 284–286, 327, 348–349, 351–352, 362

Mackie, J.L., 7, 142
Maimonides, 95
McCabe, Herbert, 246 McLean, Bradley H., 330 McMullin, Ernan, 137
Mental events, 71, 121–122, 129, 180, 186–188, 190, 192, 201–202, 206
Mental properties, 71–73, 87, 186–188, 192–193, 195, 200–202, 206, 210, 220
Miracles, 25, 105, 112, 114, 127–128, 131–132, 274–276, 285–286, 295, 316, 318–319, 321–322, 331, 354
Modal logic, 139
Modality, 29, 34–36, 57–60, 70, 94–95, 225
Molinism, 81–82, 171
Monophysitism, 234
Monotheism, 242
Moral Evil, 125, 144–145, 148, 156–160, 164–165
Moral responsibility, 19–20, 27, 48–49, 51, 79–80, 82, 126, 169, 178–179, 181, 185–186, 198–201, 203–204, 209, 211–212, 226, 245, 247, 249–252, 257–258, 261, 266, 268, 272
Moser, Paul K., 298

Natural evil, 11
Natural law, 285
Natural Theology, 8, 132, 136, 297
Necessary, 19–20, 29, 32–35, 37, 46–47, 56–57, 59–63, 72, 77, 82–84, 87, 89–91, 94, 97–98, 113, 120, 122–126, 141–144, 146, 150, 156–159, 161–163, 165, 167, 170, 172, 175, 180–181, 184, 187, 189, 207, 209, 221–222, 224–226, 228–230, 232, 235, 242, 251, 254, 256, 258–260, 263, 267, 280, 285, 288, 292–293, 308, 312, 322, 326, 331–332, 334–335, 353, 359

Necessity, 19–20, 22, 29, 34–35, 37, 47, 49, 57–63, 70–72, 74, 89–92, 96, 98, 109, 118–119, 141, 143–144, 156,

Index

160–161, 169, 172, 176–177, 181, 185, 191, 193, 202, 204, 215–218, 224–226, 228, 235–236, 241–243, 248, 258–259, 266, 269, 315, 318, 332–334, 341, 345–346, 349, 353, 358–359, 363
Neoplatonism, 84, 147
Nestorianism, 234
Neuroscience, 12, 178–179, 190, 193, 197
Nominalism, 34, 225, 240–241

Omnipotence, 24, 55, 57, 70, 72, 75–78, 86–87, 89, 92–93, 101, 115–116, 128, 142, 145, 147, 154, 216, 218, 227, 229–232, 234, 240–241, 267, 352
Omniscience, 39, 55, 57, 70, 72, 76–83, 86–87, 93, 101, 115–116, 128, 176, 228–230, 233–234, 352
Ontology, 29, 34, 49, 178–182, 185, 201, 206, 211
Oppy, 12
Original sinfulness, 256, 258, 260, 266, 279–280
Otto, Rudolf, 92
Owen, H.P., 268

Pain, 9, 125, 142, 145–147, 159–162, 167–168, 187–188, 193, 342, 355
Paul of Tarsus, 262, 283, 291, 319, 351
Penelhum, Terence, 72, 100
Perfect Goodness, 55, 57, 63, 70, 82–83, 86–87, 92–93, 115–117, 126, 128, 145, 147, 154, 228–229, 231–232, 235–236, 240, 278–279, 296–297, 352
Personal identity, 9, 19, 72–73, 87, 102, 179, 186, 193–195, 204–205, 209, 220, 222
Philipse, Herman, 12, 98
Phillips, D.Z., 69
Physical events, 108, 118, 123, 180–181, 183, 185–190, 201–202, 205–206, 209
Plantinga, Alvin, 8, 22, 80, 339, 345
Platonism, 225
Post, John F., 360
Powers, 29–30, 32–34, 74, 109, 111, 116, 120–121, 127, 134, 154, 183, 192, 202, 208, 218, 222–223, 225–226
Prayer, 155, 165, 284–285, 341–342
Presupposition, 310–312

Probability, 5, 7, 11, 13, 17, 19, 21, 23, 25–26, 37, 39–43, 50–51, 96, 98, 103, 105–118, 121–123, 128, 130–136, 140, 175, 222, 273–277, 279, 281–283, 285, 287, 289, 291, 293, 295–297, 299–305, 323, 328–329, 332, 340–343, 355, 357–358, 360–361
Properties, 29–34, 36–37, 43, 45–46, 49–50, 56–58, 62–68, 71–74, 76–77, 86–88, 90–93, 102, 108, 110, 115–116, 121–122, 180–183, 185–188, 192–195, 200–202, 204, 206, 210, 212, 217–223, 225–230, 232, 234, 236, 240, 242, 248, 309, 347–348
Providence, 10–12, 25–26, 50, 105, 114, 123–124, 132, 141, 143, 170–171, 173–177, 179, 181, 201, 203
Pseudo-Dionysius, 65
Putnam, Hilary, 35, 187

Quinn, Philip, 173

Ramsey, Ian, 67
Rational agents, 108, 111, 150, 197, 223, 302
Reason, 1, 8, 11, 15, 20, 25, 28, 37, 51, 67, 74–75, 82, 90, 98, 104, 112, 115, 117–118, 121–123, 128, 131, 136, 138–139, 147, 152, 164, 196, 205, 223, 229, 246, 250, 254, 264, 270–271, 275–276, 278–281, 303, 327, 329, 338–340, 342–343, 348, 359–365
Regularity, 74, 128, 162, 191–192
Religious experience, 105, 129–130, 209, 271, 299, 335, 340
Responsibility, 10, 12, 19–20, 26–27, 39, 48–49, 51, 79–80, 82, 117, 124, 126,n 153, 155–156, 158–159, 164, 169, 171, 178–179, 181, 185–186, 198–201, 203–204, 209, 211–212, 226, 238–239, 245, 247–252, 255, 257–258, 261–262, 266, 268–272, 279, 299, 347
Resurrection, 9–10, 12, 20–21, 27, 50–51, 70, 127, 129, 236, 263, 273–277, 279, 281–285, 287, 289, 291–305, 318–319, 321–322, 328–329, 332, 339, 352, 354–355
Revelation, 11–12, 20, 26, 50–51, 168, 235–236, 281, 288, 299, 301, 303–304,

306–309, 311, 313, 315–319, 321–337, 348, 354, 356

Schellenberg, John L., 363

Simplicity, 5, 17, 19, 43, 105, 110–111, 113, 115–117, 131–134, 137–140, 149, 230, 300, 345, 355

Sin, 26, 148, 154, 156, 163–165, 170, 235, 245–247, 259–262, 268, 272, 275, 279, 281, 284, 301, 316

Soul, 9, 12, 19, 27, 50–51, 178–179, 181, 183, 185, 187, 189, 191, 193, 195, 197, 199–201, 203, 205, 207, 209, 211, 220, 222, 233, 237–238, 264

Sterba, James, 168

Stump, Eleonore, 85, 246, 270, 359

Sturch, Richard L., 135, 362

Substances, 29–34, 37, 43, 49, 58, 71, 73–74, 88, 109, 120–121, 127, 180–183, 185, 192–195, 200–202, 206–207, 210, 215, 217–223, 225–226, 243

Suffering, 160, 173

Supererogatory acts, 48, 146, 154, 249, 253, 258–259, 263, 266, 327

Synchronic justification, 39, 345

Teleological argument, 19, 121

Temporal, 19, 29, 31, 39, 76, 84–86, 92, 98, 119–121, 165, 218, 224–226

Testimony, 38–39, 43–44, 49, 128, 130, 184–185, 210, 276–277, 282, 284, 294–295, 298–299, 305, 353–354

Theism, 1–2, 5, 7, 9–10, 12–14, 17–19, 21, 24, 27–28, 50, 55–59, 61, 63, 65, 67, 69–71, 73–75, 77, 79, 81, 83, 85, 87, 89, 91, 93, 95, 97–107, 110, 113–124, 127, 130–135, 137–142, 179, 201–203, 212, 215, 217, 219, 221, 223, 225, 227, 229, 231, 233, 235, 237, 239, 241, 243, 273, 297, 304, 329, 339

Time, 1–4, 6–7, 9–11, 13, 15, 30–32, 36, 39, 47, 75–80, 84–87, 92, 99, 104, 112, 115, 118, 123, 156, 158–160, 180, 182–183, 193–195, 200–201, 209, 215–221, 223–226, 228–230, 243, 250, 261, 264, 284, 293, 309, 313, 317, 321, 323, 327, 343, 345, 347, 350, 357

Timelessness, 85–86

Trinity, 9, 11, 20, 26, 51, 215–218, 226, 230–233, 236–244, 290, 316, 318, 323, 352, 354

Tritheism, 242

Universal transworld depravity, 157

Universals, 74, 182–183, 191, 219

Univocal, 66–67, 96, 312

van Inwagen, Peter, 93

Vermes, Géza, 284

von Balthasar, Hans Urs, 307

Warrant, 25, 198–199, 345

Worship, 14, 83, 91–92, 143–144, 154–155, 163, 165, 169, 263, 280–281, 286, 288–289, 316, 320, 346–347, 350–353, 356–358

You may also be interested in:

Christian Theology and Religious Pluralism

A Critical Evaluation of John Hick

David S. Nah

The question of religious pluralism is the most significant yet thorniest of issues in theology today, and John Hick (1922-2012) has long been recognized as its most important scholar. However, while much has been written analysing the philosophical basis of Hick's pluralism, very little attention has been devoted to the theological aspects of his argument. Filling this gap, *Christian Theology and Religious Pluralism* examines Hick's theological attempts to systematically deconstruct the Church's traditional incarnational Christology.

David S. Nah presents Hick's formulation of a Christology for a pluralistic age, referring to the fundamental arguments affirming Christianity. This is followed by a critical evaluation which considers Hick's theological theories whilst defending the traditional Church's 'two-natures doctrine' of Christ. Special attention is given to evaluating Hick's foundational theses "that Jesus himself did not teach what was to become the orthodox Christian understanding of him" and "that the dogma of Jesus' two natures ... has proved to be incapable of being explicated in any satisfactory way". Through his analysis, Nah concludes that Hick was unwarranted in breaking away from the Church's incarnational Christology that has been at the core of Christianity for almost two thousand years.

David S. Nah is Associate Professor of Theology at Bethel Seminary in St. Paul, Minnesota. He obtained his PhD from the School of Religion at Claremont Graduate University, Claremont, California.

Published 2013
Paperback ISBN: 978 0 227 68015 5
PDF ISBN: 978 0 227 90166 3